D1256340

TRIALS OF THE MONKEY

TRIALS OF THE MONKEY

An Accidental Memoir

Matthew Chapman

Duck Editions

First published in 2000 by
Duckworth Literary Entertainments, Ltd.
61 Frith Street, London W1D 3JL
Tel: 020 7434 4242
Fax: 020 7434 4420
email: DuckEd@duckworth-publishers.co.uk
www.ducknet.co.uk

To a Fat Lady Seen from a Train: reproduced from the
Selected Poems of Frances Cornford (1997) reproduced
by kind permission of Enitharmon Press.

Every effort has been made to trace and acknowledge all
copyright holders. We would like to apologise in advance should
there have been any errors or omissions.

A CIP catalogue record for this book is available
from the British Library

ISBN 0 7156 3002 4

Typeset by Ray Davies
Printed and bound in Great Britain by
Redwood Books Ltd, Trowbridge

Dedication

This book is dedicated to my mother, Clare,
who dropped off the perch a few years back.

Contents

CONTENTS

Prologue

In the spring of 1998, Tom Hedley, publisher of Duckworth, invited me to write a book. He had read a screenplay of mine and felt I could handle something larger. I decided I'd like to write about the 1925 Scopes 'Monkey' Trial, the trial of a schoolteacher accused of teaching evolution in defiance of Tennessee law. This was not an arbitrary choice. My great-great-grandfather was Charles Darwin, something I had given little thought to as an adult until I came to America and discovered his theories were still rabidly contested. A Gallup poll taken last year found that 40% of those surveyed favoured teaching creationism instead of evolution in public schools. That same year the Kansas Board of Education voted to delete virtually every mention of evolution from the state's science curriculum.

I suggested to Tom that I should take a Greyhound bus from New York, where I live, down to Dayton, Tennessee, the small town where the trial took place. Apart from doing historical research, I would also find out what had changed in the town in the past seventy-five years, if anything. I had heard that once a year the town staged a re-enactment of the trial. I would cover the event, the largest in the town's calendar, and this would become the hub from which I'd throw out the other spokes of the intended work. We could even call the book *The Voyage of The Greyhound*.

What I hadn't taken into account was that I was on the verge of my own crisis, spiritual and otherwise. I'd been writing screenplays for ten years, two or three a year, each one overlapping the next, and had taken only one vacation during that time where my computer had not accompanied me. Some years I made close to a million dollars but I was never more than a month or two away from bankruptcy. I was married to a beautiful and interesting woman, had a stepson I liked and admired, and a daughter I adored; but when I left New York in June, I was in a rage at my excessive life and all the obligations and stresses of middle age.

And then I was on the bus. At first I thought about the trial, then about my own connection to it. By an accident of birth, I was the descendant of one of the most influential men of the last two millennia, a man whose research and theories challenged not only Christianity but most other religions as well. How much of my sense of failure and panic, I wondered, could be traced to my freakish antecedents?

Now, when I looked out the window, what came to mind were scenes from my past, waves of them, too many to ignore. In particular, I thought about my mother, great-granddaughter of Darwin, a woman of enormous intelligence and promise whose decline into alcoholism was one of the great puzzles of my childhood. I started writing some of these memories into a second notebook. Another book, a book within a book, began to form, an accidental memoir, fragments of an overshadowed childhood. I could have suppressed this, but I began to see that what initially seemed a diversion from my main purpose might in fact be entirely part of it. The fundamentalists who tried to banish the theory of evolution from the schools did so because they feared it would destroy faith in God and leave only a vacuum in its place, and here was I, up to now a more or less cheerful and defiant atheist, suddenly overwhelmed by an inexplicable sense of spiritual emptiness.

I had fallen off the rails. Perhaps this other book would help me climb back on.

The End

It's a Sunday in June and I'm at the Greyhound Bus Station in New York, waiting to get on a bus. You buy the ticket but it does not guarantee a seat. For that you have to take an escalator down into the vast, clinical basement and stand in line at the appropriate gate. Two African-American women are ahead of me. One of them says, 'I wouldn't do that wit' my own flesh and blood.' The other replies, 'She did that, she did that, she did that wit' me.'

The gate opens and we all shuffle forward, deposit our bags in a cavity beneath the bus, and climb in. The seats are tall and narrow, the windows don't open, but the air is cool. The engine gurgles in a dull, self-satisfied way and the vehicle jolts forward and climbs a ramp into daylight. As the bus heads toward the Holland Tunnel, I look out the window and see a middle-aged man in a well-pressed beige suit, white shirt and tie, piss copiously through a chain-link fence, shake himself, and walk back toward a clean Honda with a brisk stride and a smile of accomplishment.

There are twenty-two passengers on the bus. Fifteen are African-American, four are white, two are Sudanese, and one is Hispanic. In front of me sits one of the African-Americans. It's eighty-five degrees and humid. He wears a wool hat with the hood of a sweatsuit top pulled over it. His eyes are hidden behind menacing shades and a thick beard conceals what's left. A wire goes in under the hood and I can hear the music from his headphones three seats back. This is not someone who wants to intersect with reality too much, perhaps even less with his own thoughts.

We enter the Holland Tunnel and a couple of minutes later are spat out of Manhattan into New Jersey. For the next five hours we grind down the Eastern Seaboard toward Washington, DC, through a suburban and industrial landscape so featureless, it's forgotten as it enters the eye.

I'm heading south to Dayton, Tennessee, the small town where in 1925 a schoolteacher, John Scopes, was prosecuted for teaching Darwin's theory of evolution. The first trial ever to be broadcast live – by radio – not only to America but also to Europe and Australia, it was given the title 'The Trial Of The Century', and for my money it remains so. A philosophical skirmish between religion and reason, between the most famous fundamentalist of his day, William Jennings Bryan, and the most famous humanist, Clarence Darrow, it was played out in an atmosphere of hucksterism and commerce uniquely and hilariously American.

Inherit The Wind, a play by Jerome Lawrence and Robert E. Lee, was a fictionalised account of the trial which then became a movie starring Spencer Tracy, Fredric March, and Gene Kelly. Not a bad piece of work, it cannot compare with reality, which is far funnier and more poignant.

Seventy-five years after the trial I'm going to see what has changed in the town, if anything. I want to find out if they still believe the world was made in six days and is only 6,000 years old. It seems incredible that they might, but word has it they do. Every year the town stages what they call a 're-enactment' of the trial. As the trial lasted for several days, and as the outcome was not favourable to the fundamentalists who still dominate the region, I'm intrigued to see what gets lost in the editing. I'm going down now, a month in advance of the show, to do some research, and will then return for the play in July. My idea, although it's not fully formed yet, is to spin the whole book out from the play. Revisionist religious history as theatre.

In my bag, I have two books, one a guidebook called *The Old South*, the other a biography of Darwin. I pull out the guidebook and find an essay by Tim Jacobson about the origins of the region. He says that while the North was colonised for ideological reasons, the South was always about business. Sir Walter Raleigh first tried to settle Virginia in 1584, but the settlers couldn't take the loneliness and hardship and came home to England without having turned a profit. In 1587, Raleigh sent out another 150 who made camp on Roanoke Island, now in North Carolina. Three years later he sent a crew out to check on them. All they found was a tree with the word 'Croatoan' carved on it, that being the name of the local Indian tribe.

In 1606, 120 men were dispatched by the London Company, also for commercial reasons. Sixteen died on the voyage. The rest sailed up the James River and settled. Within six months, all but thirty-eight of them were dead from malaria. In 1609, some women were sent out to breed with the survivors. Talk about Natural Selection.

Here on the bus I'm pondering a different but related matter: Survival of The Fattest. A black woman weighing at least 250lbs sits across the aisle from me. She is dressed in a large, colourful dress and, were it not for her obesity, she'd be beautiful. Her face is so large it almost engulfs her humorous eyes, and her chest and stomach have merged to become a monumental, rippling hillside. She feeds constantly on potato chips and Teddy Grahams. The hand she's not eating with holds a book. It's held high so she can read it over her cheeks. The door to the Greyhound shitter is very narrow. Even I have to turn sideways to pass through. So far she has made no attempt to enter. If she does, I'm convinced it will end in failure or worse and I'm getting curious. Next to her is an amiable, uncomplaining child. Everyone is amiable. You leave New York – or maybe any big city – and suddenly the neurosis level drops.

Much to my disappointment, the woman doesn't hit the WC until DC, when she scrambles off the bus, child dangling from her arm, and plunges into the crowd, the eyes above her cheeks seeking the symbol of the skirted woman.

I have to change buses and I've got some time to kill, so I get my bag out from under the bus and walk outside to the parking lot behind the bus station.

A white Southern woman in tight white jeans and a tank top is trying to compact ten boxes and suitcases into six or less. It's a comedy about futility, and it has drawn a good crowd. She and her African-American boyfriend are relocating to West Virginia, where she was born. They were going to get a train from New Jersey, where they met, but *he* – she casts an admonishing look at the man, who, in stark contrast to her, is extremely handsome and muscular – woke up late and so they had to change their plans. On the train you can take as much luggage as you want. On the bus, there's a limit and they're well over it. She must be around thirty, he a few years younger, and it's one of those pairings which is endearing if only because it seems so improbable.

She keeps saying, 'My Lord!' and 'I swear!' as she wrenches and pushes and tugs. Now she straightens up and brings her hands to the side of her head. 'Oh, my Lord,' she exclaims before leaning in again with all the heft of her upper body.

He stands back, shaking his head pessimistically. 'It's going to be an odyssey,' he declares, as if commenting on someone else's life.

'It's going to be shitty, that's what it's gonna be,' she responds.

I could take one of their bags – I only have one of my own – and I should offer to do so, but I don't. I'm not quite sure why. Maybe it's because I've been locked in a room writing for ten years. Or maybe it's because I've always felt myself to be exactly what the US Immigration and Naturalization Service describes me as: a Resident Alien. I am here but I am not here and I like it that way.

By paying an extra few dollars, they manage to get what has now become eight dense, misshapen bags onto the bus and we're all headed for Roanoke, West Virginia. It's a new gang on a new bus with a new driver. Every time you get a new driver he gives you the rules. Each driver has his own style. This one welcomes us aboard and then lists every single stop along the way to Roanoke. Finally, he concludes with:

'These are the rules: no smoking, no drinking, no sex in your seats, no sex in the bathroom, and no boomboxes. If you have a Walkman don't have it so loud it disturbs anyone. With that in mind, just lean back, close your eyes and dream about tomorrow. Or yesterday ...'

I'm finding it hard to concentrate on anything for any length of time. I pick up the other book, *Charles Darwin: A New Biography*, by John Bowlby and start to read it. The big question in the early pages is whether Darwin, an invalid for most of his life, was the victim of some tropical disease or was in fact a hypochondriac. His list of maladies is awe inspiring. One of them is eczema. As a child, I too had eczema. The eczema and the eczematous forefather have made me who I am.

People generally believe they are part of an evolutionary process, either physical, spiritual or both. At an absolute minimum they note with smug satisfaction how much taller and smarter and richer they are than their forefathers. This suggests that life is, if not meaningful, at least progressive. Your average Joe goes beyond this, of course, and convinces himself that not only does life have meaning, but so too does death: God awaits him on the other side to reward him with eternal life for pushing the species along. But how could any of these assumptions work for me? In early childhood I was told how Darwin's theory of evolution had demolished the biblical story of creation: God slapping it together in six days, Adam's rib, and all that. And if the very first chapter of the good book was nonsensical and untrue, why would the rest be any more credible or useful? My parents made an attempt to raise me Christian but ultimately lacked the conviction to boost me over the numerous improbabilities. I went through one highly religious phase, but, wonderful as it was, it didn't last. As for simple, earthly evolution, here too I got the short end of the stick. What was the likelihood of my evolving beyond grandpa? Even physically, I turned out to be a lesser man. Born in 1809, he grew to be six feet tall. Born in 1950, I barely made five-ten. I not only *got* the short end of the stick, I *was* the short end.

When Darwin called his second book *The Descent of Man* instead of *The Ascent of Man* he was thinking of his progeny. One only has to study the chronology to see the truth of this.

First there was Charles Darwin, two yards long and nobody's fool. Then there was his son, my great-grandfather, Sir Francis Darwin, an eminent botanist. Then came my grandmother Frances, a modest poet who spent a considerable amount of time in rest-homes for depression. From her issued my beloved mother, Clare, who was extremely short, failed to complete medical school, and eventually became an alcoholic.

Then we get down to me. I'm in the movie business.

At prep school in Cambridge, where I was brought up, I could not figure out what rung I was supposed to occupy on the social ladder. It was hard to believe I was beneath the brutish offspring of titled pig farmers and Tory MPs, but they clearly thought so. When I asked my father for help in the matter, he informed me I was 'a member of the intellectual aristocracy'. He said it with a laugh but he was right, and like most aristocracies it is in decline. I went to a Darwin reunion a few years back and it seemed to me that the whole family tree was hopping with regression, every smile verging on the imbecilic, every suit stuffed with the same sorry cargo of morphological deterioration.

By some genetic fluke, I retained enough of Darwin's powers of observation to be able to see clearly which way I was heading. My boyhood hero was Zozo the monkey, and when I was taken to the zoo at the age of six and saw live monkeys picking and scratching exactly as I did, and trying to have sex in public, I was convinced: evolution was a yo-yo and in my case the yo-yo had just about reached the end of the string. All I had to do was push it down another inch or two and it would rise again. If Charles was the top, I would be the bottom. If he was the beginning, I would be the end.

Simple academic mediocrity would not suffice. I had to do worse than that. I had to fight education with everything I had. As stubborn and diligent as Charles was in collecting facts, so I would be in holding them at bay. If this was my defence against the crushing weight of family history, and if the strategy ultimately failed, you certainly couldn't fault me for its execution on the ground: I emerged from school with an outstanding lack of knowledge.

I only took two significant exams and failed both. The first was the eleven-plus, which should have been called the eleven-plus/minus because if you passed it – at the age of eleven – you entered grammar school and had a shot at university, while if you failed you were subtracted from opportunity and condemned (unless you had money) to the purgatory of secondary modern, and life on the production line. The second exam was an O level. Most kids passed five to ten of these. I failed my solitary one and my parents and the system conceded defeat.

Thirty years later, here I am on a Greyhound bus, a screenwriter. I used to direct but now I get paid so much to write I can no longer afford to. I write for the studios in Los Angeles. They pay, I deliver, they own. Nothing I create belongs to me. The scripts I write rarely become films and a screenplay, however well written, is only a blueprint. I'm an architect whose only buildings lie in the past, each made by uncomprehending builders. Worse still, the scripts which have been made are not my best, and the rest, the unmade ones, the ones I love, have now accrued so much interest that I cannot afford to buy them back. This year I sold an idea for a million and a half dollars. It won't get made and before you know it I'll need two million to get it back.

And of course I won't get it back and it will be consigned to the great necropolis of dead scripts, a massive tomb under a mountain in Utah where the air is dry and cool. A friend of mine was sent down into this awful legacy of failure to root around and see if anything was worth bringing back to light. He found a script by F. Scott Fitzgerald and for a while, the studio was looking for someone to rewrite the great man; but I've heard no more about it and presume it's gone back into the darkness.

In my struggle for survival I have dragged my simian arse as far from its origins as I could – from the lawns of Cambridge to the Mercedes-littered lots of Hollywood, then to New York's Upper East Side – and all I've achieved, 'spiritually' is that: survival. I have a life which requires me to earn at least half a million dollars a year. I am always either in debt or on the verge of it. I have no money saved. I could be wiped out by a few months of studio indifference. I feel drained. What is the purpose of all this?

If I believed in God, I could comfort myself with the thought that once in heaven the bills would at least stop coming. Instead the only relief in sight is complete extinction. Circumstances change and in response, I simply become more anxious. It's as if my whole character has become vestigial to this constant fear. Somewhere in my mind there still swaggers the fine young, atheistic monkey waving his insolent hard-on at the world, but suddenly it's no longer amusing or effective and soon it will become embarrassing. I am not afraid of death, I'm afraid of a moment when, immobilised by something fatal, and unable to distract myself with work or sex or illusions of progress, I reflect on my life and see a rich and fascinating landscape, and me off to one side of it, a rat inside a wheel of darkness.

It's time to become wise and happy. But how? I am an adolescent lobbed into middle age without the necessary equipment. Sitting in the bus, cut loose from obligation and decency, I start to wander inward. When I look out the bus window now, what I see are scenes from my childhood, and I find myself compelled to write them down. Another book, an unasked for book, takes shape in my mind, *The Monkey And His Education*.

There's a sudden random swath of wild flowers on the meridian. It passes by like a brush stroke and jolts me back to the external journey. The country has become more hilly with tree-covered mountains in the distance. The highway is less crowded.

To my left a Hispanic woman sniffs constantly, every fourth or fifth breath. It's really incredible. If the seats reclined, she could lie back and the fluid would drain down her throat, but they don't. You get a two inch tilt that's barely noticeable and she doesn't have a tissue.

A sign on a mountainside says 'Endless Caves' but nothing can compete with the endless sniffing. Many hours have passed and many more are yet to come. Since the book I was reading on Darwin brought on a crisis of memory and self-loathing, I decide to go back to my book on the South.

Tobacco, it tells me, introduced to the whites by the Indians (some small revenge, I suppose for the theft of their land), soon became the major crop in the South. Tobacco was labour intensive. The first people to work in the fields were indentured servants from England who worked off their passage and were then set free, at which point they became expensive to hire.

Enter the slave. You could lease an Englishman for a year or two, but a black man you could buy for a lifetime. The outlay was higher but once purchased you could literally work him to death. I remember when a movie of mine was being shot in Atlanta, arriving late to my hotel and being ushered to my room by a young, gay African-American man. When I asked him where I could buy cigarettes, he told me it was too late and offered me one of his. I thanked him effusively. 'No, no,' he said, waving my gratitude aside with a complicit smile, 'I too am a slave to nicotine.' How ironic, I now think, seeing a larger meaning, that African-Americans who continue to smoke in America are in fact continuing a 400-year tradition of slavery to the deceptively beautiful plant.

The bus stops and about half the occupants leap out to smoke. It's quite comic this. Sometimes the bus stops for only thirty seconds. The true addict gets out none the less, lights up, sucks feverishly on his cigarette, then re-enters the bus, coughing. This, however, is a longer stop. I haven't smoked in a long while, but suddenly, I have the urge to have just one. I go to the mixed-race couple and bum a cigarette. We sit in the sun, our backs to a dilapidated convenience store. She is a Certified Nursing Assistant and he's in the building trade, bricklaying, concrete. I ask him how he feels about moving to the South.

'Well,' he says, 'as a man of colour ...'

He takes a drag on his cigarette, looks off into the distance, exhales, and lets the smoke drift off with the rest of his sentence.

An Alligator Up My Arse
In Roanoke, Virginia

About twelve hours after I get on the bus in New York, I arrive in Roanoke, West Virginia, and my buttocks are numb. I have decided to travel only during the day and to stay in the best possible hotels at night. Roanoke, known as the Capital of the Blue Ridge, is a small town on the Norfolk and Western Railway. It advertises itself as a centre for 'transportation, distribution, trade, manufacturing, health care, entertainment, recreation, attractions and conventions'. As I take a three-minute cab ride across town, I don't see much evidence of any of these. The place seems a little beaten.

The best hotel in Roanoke, The Patrick Henry, is a grand, faded downtown hotel not far from the railway station which, having spawned the place, now seems curiously irrelevant. A large lobby with antique tables and Fifties sofas is only slightly marred by modern signage. Behind the desk is a woman in her early twenties with five earrings in each ear. She is short and slight and has reddish brown hair pulled back into a ponytail. She wears a white shirt with the sleeves rolled up and has a rueful, mischievous look, as if she's acting a role and is slightly embarrassed by it. Her name is Tasha.

I ask her which room in the hotel is the most luxurious. It's the Governor's Suite at $250 a night. The next best is the Honeymoon Suite, which she'll let me have at a special rate of $99. She gives me both keys and I go upstairs. I prefer the Honeymoon Suite and go downstairs to return the other key to Tasha.

'If you have any questions,' she says, taking my credit card, 'don't hesitate to ask.'

'What's the meaning of life?'

'Love, Happiness, and Art,' she replies without hesitation.

'But if you have love, aren't you already happy?' I suggest.

'Oh, no, love is painful,' she says with a pained smile. It turns out she is a local artist, as is her boyfriend.

I go up in an old elevator, along some narrow corridors where no attempt has been made at 'decor' and let myself into the Honeymoon Suite. It's a big-piped, disjointed corner. It smells of old cigarettes, the curtains are tattered, but the antiques are real. There's a living room, about twenty-five feet by fifteen. In the kitchen there's a massive refrigerator which has the fat, rounded, confident lines of forty years ago. If you tipped it over and put fins on it, you could drive it. The bedroom has a king-size bed and off it a bathroom that was once grand but now has a chipped birthmark-coloured bath with one of those shower heads where the water comes at you like ten different squints. Such a room in New York would cost $500. It's a room where drugs are done, a room for provincial whores with a tendency to fall on their tits after a few drinks. It's perfect and I'm happy.

I wander along the street looking for a restaurant. I'm in the downtown area of a typical small town. Once the centre of commerce, it has been abandoned for the suburbs, for strip malls and modern office buildings with convenient parking. Too late, the community has realised the value of having a heart. Although parts of it have been recklessly knocked down, this remains the most beautiful part of town, with old red brick factories and warehouses waiting to become lofts and boutiques. At the moment, though, it's still in transition. The shops that have survived, a stationer's, a small department store, are dusty and understocked. Here and there you see a tall, pointless wall, a survivor of demolition, painted with a large fading advertisement in lettering from the Thirties, 'Virginia Carriage Factory' or 'Pepsi-Cola 5 cents, Fountains and In Bottles.'

A few blocks away, I find The Street, the one where development has taken hold. There are shops for tourists and several bars. I look in the window of one and see a short but fat conga-line thudding around between cramped tables. Few sights are more pitiful and depressing than fat middle-aged drunks dancing like teenagers, but I am immune and walk away smiling. I go by some antique shops, a health-food peddler, a pawn shop, and a restaurant called Awful Arthur's. Now I'm at the end of the street.

11

I turn around and go eat at Awful Arthur's, crayfish and melted butter served by a waitress who went into the Navy to study medicine but didn't like it.

'Now I'm thinking of animal training,' she tells me. 'You know, like Shamu at Seaworld, and dogs and so on, too.'

My guide book tells me there were several Civil War battles in the Roanoke Valley. In one of them Union General David Hunter was forced to retreat up nearby Potts Mountain and 700 of his horses died of exhaustion. It took the local people a week to bury them. On the top of Mill Mountain, just outside of town, is a 100-foot-tall illuminated concrete-and-steel star which can be seen from sixty miles away on a clear night. It symbolises 'the friendliness, industry and civic progress' of the town. Because of this Roanoke is sometimes known as Star City. I don't know about the industry or civic progress, but, as far as I can tell from the cab driver, Tasha, and the would-be whale trainer, it certainly is friendly.

A squad of students – they look like students anyhow, in fact they look like students of the late Sixties – hang around outside. One of them, a white guy with frizzy, colourless dreads, has an African drum which they all take turns beating incompetently and with obvious self-consciousness. One girl is really pretty and seems appropriately embarrassed. She doesn't beat the drum. One of the boys has a meagre moustache and wears a bike helmet which makes him look like an insect.

Having proudly pursued a life first of determined ignorance and then of almost compulsive solitary study, I've resisted the temptation to envy the more structured academic life. Lately, however, I have found it impossible to resist entirely. I have a stepson who goes to college and have seen the thing up close for the first time.

Diogo is a rare young man, completely his own person, eccentric, original, and a good poet. He attends Bard, a college a couple of hours north of New York. It's an amazing place. A typical semester consists of Russian Humour, Computer Science, and The Irish Bardic Tradition. You could fall backward into a second-hand bookshop and get the same effect without having to shell out $30,000 a year, but America has become addicted to the college degree and everyone is terrorised into attendance. You can't even get a job in the mail room of a Hollywood talent agency without a degree from Harvard and where previously an enterprising kid would drop out and leave for Paris or Haight Ashbury, he or she now dutifully stays and receives the scroll and hat or whatever token it is you receive for your $120,000.

Youth, as the saying goes, is wasted on the young. So, I would argue, to a large extent, is higher education. It's like force-feeding caviar to a baby. An incredibly rich experience is offered – access to a billion eggs of knowledge – but youth has no idea how rare and exotic this is. Their virgin palates are immune. Caviar? Knowledge? So what?

In my late forties, I've now worked up a discriminating appetite and taking even as little as a year off to fill in some gaps which the autodidactic method leaves in its wake is tempting in the extreme. My God, you could wake up in the morning with a question about philosophy or art or religion or quantum mechanics or history and before breakfast locate a man who knows the answer! Exams and degrees pollute the whole experience, but looking at the workload of the average student, I figure – if they'd let me – I could probably pick up two to three degrees a year.

'I have an essay to write,' a friend of Diogo's tells me. 'It's got to be at least five pages long. I should have it finished in a couple of weeks.'

Five pages?! I write five pages before *lunch*.

But the scholastic element is only a part of what I've come to envy. There's the *social* aspect. As Diogo writes:

> She saw me as we crossed.
> Across the bridge I saw her wink.
> It was the kind of thing you feel
> Before there's time to think:
> Love, it's batting lashes,
> Burning simple dreams to ashes.

You get the impression there's a lot of lash-batting and burning dreams and smouldering ashes, all occurring at an exquisitely leisurely pace. *Time*, this is what I never had, this extensive, carefree *time*, days passing in a slow miasma of cigarette smoke and anticipation. I started work at fifteen and haven't stopped since. No, I stopped once. When I was twenty I inherited some money from my paternal grandfather and took off for North Africa in a van with a Belgian dancer I met while working a spotlight in a nightclub. That lasted six months, and even then I was trying to write a play, actually two plays side by side on the same stage, which meant I had to lug around a typewriter designed for accountants, with a carriage twenty inches long. The rest of the time I was either writing or directing my way in and out of debt. And still am. My so-called youth was never like this, where you sit around for several hours at a time patting a drum and nodding your head.

So I'm watching these kids and envying them their idleness and irresponsibility, and then I leave Awful Arthur's and walk back up the street to the hotel, and along the way I look inside one of those metal vending machines and read the headline of the *Roanoke Times* which is: Cow Proves She's Not Part Of Herd – She Leaps Pick-Up With Single Bound.

And suddenly I'm not so envious of these particular students any more. There might be more exciting places to slap a drum.

Back in my hotel room I call my ten-year-old daughter, Anna Bella Charles Darwin Teixeira Chapman, who has inherited from me, along with the Darwin name squeezed in there for possible use during seduction of academic snobs (it worked for me a couple of times), a tendency to riff on a theme. She warns me to shake my shoes in the morning.

'They've got spiders down there, you know … and tarantulas and scorpions.'

'And alligators and crocodiles,' I add, untruthfully, trying to impress her.

'Don't be stupid, they won't get in your shoes, they're too big, but be careful of the toilets, the young alligators might come up the pipes.'

'Bite me in the arse?'

'Might go right *up* there, then you'd have to buy a pair of pants with a hole in the back. People would say, "Gee, what a beautiful, green scaly tail you've got," and you'd have to say, "No, that's an alligator up my ass." '

I got her mother, Denise, a Brazilian actress, pregnant almost on the first date. Denise is the daughter of Humberto Teixeira, a lawyer, composer, and lyricist, who wrote the musical copyright laws in Brazil. The author of 'Asa Branca,' one of the most loved of Brazilian songs – in a recent poll it came in just behind 'Brazil' and 'The Girl From

Ipanema' – he was a stubborn romantic originally from the harsh north-east of the country. Her mother, Margarida Jatoba, was an exceptionally beautiful concert pianist with pale skin, red hair and green eyes. When Denise was only five, Margarida left Humberto for a journalist who lived upstairs from their apartment overlooking the sea in Rio de Janeiro. An ugly divorce followed, during much of which Denise was not allowed to see her mother and was raised by her heartbroken father and his mother.

Humberto never remarried. He devoted much of his time and money to building and rebuilding a mansion on the hills just outside the city, as if in preparation for an ideal marriage, or the return of his red-haired wife.

Denise grew up between her grandmother's house in Ipanema, overlooking Rio's lake Rodrigo de Freitas, and the ever expanding mansion, a place of waterfalls and secret doors. Soon she became as beautiful as her mother. She was a good student, the youngest in her class by two years but always at the top. She wanted to be a children's doctor until she was sixteen, when, against the wishes of her father, she started acting, first in theatre and then on TV. By the time she was seventeen she was a star, recognised, as she is today, on the streets of any city in Brazil. When she was eighteen, she came to New York to study at NYU under Stella Adler, but dropped out two years later because of the pressures of her career in Brazil. Soon after returning, she married Claudio Marzo, father of the aforementioned Diogo.

The dictatorship was still in power and artists of all kinds were frequently jailed and tortured. Claudio, then and now one of Brazil's best known actors, was part of the left wing opposing the dictatorship. He was ten years older than Denise and very attractive. They married when she was twenty and separated a couple of years later.

Denise and I met for the first time in Los Angeles about ten years after this. She was very striking with the exceptionally white skin of her mother and long, dark red hair. She had moved to New York after the release of *Kiss Of The Spiderwoman* with Sonia Braga, William Hurt and Raul Julia, in which she played Michelle, the cigarette-girl. Though this was not the lead, she had attracted some attention. We were introduced by a mutual friend, a woman. Over dinner Denise produced some bent coins which she claimed had been telekinetically twisted by a friend of hers in Brazil, a guru named Thomas Green Morton. He also bent forks. I knew these were common magicians' tricks, and as I find credulity the most irritating of all vices, I put her out of my mind.

A year later, she moved to Los Angeles and the same friend, the actress, Dana Delaney, brought her along to a screening. Again, the three of us had dinner, and now I saw in Denise qualities which overwhelmed my irritation. Putting aside her lack of scepticism about the coin-bending guru in Brazil, she was intelligent, funny, informed, well read, and sexy. Capable and determined, she used words like 'fuck' and 'shit' and did not use words like 'commitment' or 'nurturing'. She was radiant with honesty and goodness and lacking in pretence, artifice, or guile. She drank and she smoked and she laughed. Diogo was turning eleven the next day. She invited me to come to his birthday party. I accepted.

Outside the restaurant, I gave her a hug. Her belly quivered. I was intrigued.

The next day I drove down from Laurel Canyon, where I lived, and soon arrived outside a Spanish-style apartment building in Beverly Hills, south of Charleyville. The door to the building was open so I entered and soon located her apartment on the ground floor facing the street. The door to this was also open, but I rang the bell anyway.

'Come on,' I heard her call out, 'I'm in the phone.'

Her English was excellent, but often peppered with prepositional mistakes like these. 'So, if you don't like it, throw it by the window,' she would say, or 'Matthew, you're driving me off the wall.' She was very well read and loved books and language and sometimes her mistakes seemed to improve conventional words and phrases. When something moved her, she'd say, 'I have a knot in my throat.' 'Bob's my ankle' and 'I'm out of the hoop,' were common mistakes. When someone offended her, she stared at him 'in appallment.' Later, when I knew her better and suggested we do something she wasn't too sure about, she said, 'It sounds interesting as a fantasy, but in reality, I'm a little squirmish about that.'

Then there were the Brazilian expressions. In a men's clothes shop, once she saw an old queen watching me. 'Look at him,' she whispered, 'his teeth are getting bigger by the minute.' Perhaps my favourite of her expressions is, 'Each monkey on his branch.' If I wanted to go out drinking with Diogo when he was older, she might say, 'Let him go with his friends, Matthew. Each monkey on his branch.'

Three weeks after I came to visit, she and I drove north up the California coast to stay in a little hotel named Deetjuns in Big Sur. In spite of her whiteness, Denise had, like many Brazilian women, the high, round buttocks of an African.

Two weeks later, she called me from Brazil where she had returned to shoot a film and told me she was pregnant.

I was thirty-six and I'd been drinking a lot. I had recently written an entire script drunk, starting each day with a shot of Mexican brandy flushed into the gullet with beer. It was a money gig and I was trying to stir up some enthusiasm. Tears of self-pity and minor car accidents were stirred up too, and I was thinking I might not make forty let alone have a child, so I said, 'Let me think about that.'

AIDS was just taking hold, in Brazil as virulently as in America. Denise pointed out that we both knew people who had received death sentences as a consequence of sex and here were we, rewarded by life. And then she said, 'A child born out of love cannot go wrong,' and I was so touched by the simple faith of the statement that I said, 'Okay, let's have it.'

This faith is the source of everything I love in her and everything about which we argue. Denise calls herself a Catholic, and yet believes in a woman's right to choose, contraception, and homosexual rights. Our daughter's Brazilian godmother is a lesbian. As well as being a Catholic, Denise believes – as casually and naturally as you or I believe in the weather forecast – in Candomble, the most African of all the Macumba sects. Brought over by slaves, Candomble has syncretistically combined with Catholicism to such an extent that the lucky African ribbons Denise wears around her wrists come from a church in Bahia where they've been blessed by a Catholic priest. Among many deities in the Candomble religion are Iemanja, the goddess – or saint – of the sea, to whom we throw offerings of flowers on New Year's Eve; Oxala, the father of all saints; and Oxum, the goddess of fresh water, who is Denise's saint. Everyone has at least two saints, determined by the high priests, or Pai de Santos, by throwing shells on the sand.

In Brazil, no one is thought primitive, insane, or eccentric for believing in all this. One night I had dinner with the Head of Protocol for the President of Brazil. She spoke perfect English and French and had a degree in political science from a European university. The next night, walking on the beach, I saw her dancing around a fire, while a white robed priestess from Bahia sang incantations to the sound of twenty drums. Intellectuals, CEOs, politicians, doctors, any one of these will visit a Pai de Santo and make animal sacrifices to bring on good luck or ward off evil and then go to a Catholic church to light a candle. A friend of mine, who is one of the most powerful men in Brazilian TV, was told if he folded his money a certain way, it would ensure his continued prosperity. He folds it that way. Denise believes if she lights candles in front of photographs of my dead mama and her dead papa, it will stimulate them to work on our behalf and bring us good fortune. Superstitious faith is the *sine qua non* of Brazilian life at all levels.

Denise's faith is so powerful, not just in God(s), but in herself, that she is often incapable of a balanced view. She is a partisan, a warrior. Right is right and wrong is wrong, and when she is wholly right, which is nine times out of ten, she has no doubt that the other person is wholly wrong. She will then fight with a ferocity which I, in this respect very much an Englishman, find at once impressive and terrifying. I look at her in 'appallment', which makes her even angrier.

Both she and I were neglected, in our own ways – I because of my mother's alcoholism, she because of her mother's literal abandonment – and both of us have a compensatory devotion to our daughter which verges on the obsessive. Since Anna Bella was two years old, Denise has read to her every single night, usually for an hour, sometimes more. We take her with us wherever we can because she gives us so much pleasure, and lavish everything we can on her because she at least deserves it. We live in the best building in the best neighbourhood nearest to the best school, so that Anna can walk there every morning, accompanied, of course, by both her doting parents. She must go to all the right parties in clothes she can be proud of. She must have piano lessons and tennis lessons and go to camp each year. She must not feel deprived in any way.

We live in a world of enormous wealth. Her friends are the sons and daughters of investment bankers and stockbrokers. As I often say to Denise, 'We're providing her with everything she needs to end up despising us.' I earn what in almost any other section of society would be considered a fortune, and feel like a wretched pauper.

Denise is an optimist. As much as she has faith in God and in herself, so she has faith in me. She is convinced that I will always do better each year, always be in demand, always pull down the necessary cash to finance our life. And herein lies a problem. I am a pessimist like my mother. Tomorrow I'll fall and break my wrist, or the studios will realise I'm no good, and then what? I have no other skills.

This is what cranks me up in bed at three in the morning, gasping with anxiety. In fact, Denise has been right so far, and I wrong. What a waste of energy, all this fear! But how long can it hold? What about *tomorrow*?

My pathetic contribution is this: because I love my daughter with an absurd and passionate commitment, I work ceaselessly and endure a life I would not choose for myself. The great relief of having a child is that it gives you the certain knowledge that you have the courage to die. I would die for Anna Bella in a second. Perhaps I am dying for her already, but slowly, wringing my heart into submission so she can live on the Upper East Side and go to Harvard.

If, as my dictionary states, being a liberal means being 'favourable to progress and reform in political or religious affairs; favourable to concepts of maximum individual freedom ... free from prejudice or bigotry; open minded, tolerant,' then I am certainly a liberal. But in the case of abortion, I wonder if it's as simple as liberals would have it or if it only seems simple because those who argue against it do so with such illogical fanaticism, linking themselves not to pure reverence for life, an easy and honourable position to defend, but to a drearily literal interpretation of the entire Bible which is, as everyone knows, full of vile instructions which no one in their right mind would obey. Out of intellectual good taste, one instinctively recoils and takes whatever position is as far from theirs as possible; but in truth, an element of what they say has virtue: abortion is more than just a minor surgical procedure. Contraception is different – one only has to whack off into a handkerchief and look at the stuff to know one isn't killing anyone – but when the sperm meets the egg a human life does begin, and deciding if it should continue or not *is* profoundly complicated and gets more so with every hour.

If I think about my mysterious daughter, this creature who I saw drawn from Denise's stomach looking rubbery and artificial and yet wholly miraculous, this baby who had a sense of humour even before she could focus her eyes, this child who dropped fearlessly off high walls into my arms, this willed, opinionated, exceptional girl, this beautiful young *woman*, this human I love beyond all things on earth; when I think of her and then think about abortion, which might have seemed the wiser choice given all the circumstances of her conception, a vacuum forms in my chest and something infinitely cold rushes in.

The Menace Of Darwinism

I sleep well in my large, uneven bed, high in the corner of the hotel in Star City, and wake up refreshed, ready to plunge further down below the Bible Belt. The bus that will take me to Chattanooga, only fifty miles from my destination, does not leave until late morning, so I get up slowly and take my time showering and getting dressed. I enjoy the silence of the room and the sight of small-town America beyond the windows. Where I live in Manhattan, on the East River, there is a constant vibration, even at night, out of which other unpleasant noises struggle to emerge. Here, at the height of rush hour, individual sounds clang out like church bells on Sunday.

After breakfast in the lobby, the hotel van-driver takes me to the Roanoke bus station. There's a Bible on the floor between the seats so I ask him which brand of Christianity he favours. He tells me he attends a Pentecostal church where they speak in tongues and fall over backwards.

As if offering incontrovertible proof of the existence of God he says, 'I've seen people fall over benches and ev'thing, ain't never seen one git hurt. It's amazin'. I ain't never done it myself but my mama would git to hollerin' and shoutin'.'

It requires so little proof on the one hand and so much on the other. People will inform you that Jesus was born of an angel-impregnated virgin and walked on water 'because it's in the Bible,' but think nothing of telling you with a sniff of contempt that evolution is 'just a theory, ain't no proof.' The inherent unfairness of this double standard is one of the things which attracts me to the Scopes Trial. The other is the characters who were involved. William Jennings Bryan, three-times Democratic Presidential Candidate, one-time Secretary of State, and at the end of his career, an evangelical fundamentalist is one of them.

Bryan began puffing around the South in the early Twenties trying to get laws on the books to prevent the teaching of evolution in the state schools. His initial intent had been to prevent the teaching of evolution as *fact* as opposed to *theory* and to balance it with the teaching of creationism. Soon, however, the crusade became more virulent and sought to banish the teaching of evolution completely. From my point of view, Bryan is the antagonist in the story of the Scopes Trial, but he is a tragic antagonist and an interesting one. He was not, at least in most areas of his life, the kind of bigoted conservative you'd expect to find behind a campaign such as this.

Born in 1860, in Salem, Illinois, he was the son of Silas Bryan, a judge and gentleman farmer. Silas was a deacon of the Baptist church, opened court with prayer, and prayed three times a day. William worked on the farm when not in school and grew up strong and healthy. At the age of fourteen, he attended a revival held by the Cumberland Presbyterians and converted. He remained a Presbyterian until he died, although he was at ease in any church.

When William graduated from Union Law School in Chicago, he married Mary Baird and returned to Jacksonville, where he practised law, without much success. He wanted to run for elected office as a Democrat, but Jacksonville was solidly Republican, so in 1887, he moved his family, now consisting of one child and two parents-in-law (Mary's parents would live with them for the rest of their lives) to Lincoln, Nebraska. Here he got involved in the Democratic Party. Throughout school and college he had honed his speaking skills in various debating societies and now put them to use campaigning for various candidates.

In his biography of Bryan, *A Righteous Cause*, Robert W. Cherny writes that Bryan came home one night, after a speaking engagement, woke Mary up and told her, 'I have had a strange experience. Last night I found that I had power over the audience. I could move them as I chose. I have more than usual power as a speaker.'

At that time, the farmers were suffering because of the way in which grain was bought and distributed. The grain buyers held one monopoly and the railroads held the other. This issue of the exploitation of the 'producer', the working man, by the bankers, distributors, merchants, and lawyers was central to Bryan's campaign when he ran for Congress in 1890. One of the other big issues of the time was Prohibition. In the

First Congressional district, where Bryan was running, the electorate hated the idea. Bryan, a teetotaller all his life, who not only disapproved of alcohol socially but also considered it a sin, took a deep breath, spoke against prohibition, and won.

He entered Congress at the age of thirty in 1890. Mary, who, like Bryan, was at first considered 'a hayseed', or country bumpkin, would help him write his speeches and then watch him from the gallery, giving him directions with a nod or a shake of her head. He became famous as an orator while fighting to overturn unfair Republican taxes on the dirt farmers of his adopted state. Without seeming to raise his voice, he could make himself heard to even the largest crowds. His speeches were beautifully written and delivered with passion. Before long he was known as 'The Boy Orator of the Platte,' then as 'The Great Commoner.'

His best speech – in my opinion, not his – was given at the Democratic National Convention in 1896 when he advocated changing a gold-based currency to a silver-based one, believing it would benefit the working man. I don't understand the economic principles behind the speech and probably it was hogwash, but if so, hogwash was rarely more dazzling. Known as his 'Cross Of Gold' speech, the most noted line of it is, 'You shall not press down upon the brow of labor this crown of thorns, you shall not crucify mankind upon a cross of gold.' His talent – to mix the language of progressive politics with that of old time religion – was a great talent and in the early days he used it well. Listen to his defence of the working man in the 'Cross Of Gold' as he talks to the gold delegates:

'When you come before us and tell us that we are about to disturb your business interests, we reply that you have disturbed our business interests by your course.

'We say to you that you have made the definition of a business man too limited in its application. The man who is employed for wages is as much a business man as his employer ... the merchant at the cross-roads store is as much a business man as the merchants of New York; the farmer who goes forth in the morning and toils all day – who begins in the spring and toils all summer – and who by the application of brain and muscle to the natural resources of the country creates wealth, is as much a business man as the man who goes upon the board of trade and bets upon the price of grain; the miners who go down a thousand feet into the earth, or climb two thousand feet upon the cliffs, and bring forth from their hiding places the precious metals to be poured into the channels of trade are as much business men as the few financial magnates who, in a back room, corner the money of the world.'

At the age of thirty-six he was nominated Democratic Presidential Candidate. He got 47% of the vote and won in more states than his opponent. Voter fraud, however, stole six states from him and he lost this election and then two more.

In his thirty years in politics, he fought for minority rights, women's suffrage, workmen's compensation, the minimum wage, the eight hour workday, and the expansion of education. The first presidential candidate to promote himself using movies with sound (in his 1908 campaign), he was incredibly popular and drew vast crowds wherever he went. He could be funny too. Once, when he was about to give a speech in a rural area, he realised he was standing on the back of a manure spreader and remarked, 'This is the first time I have ever spoken from a Republican platform.'

But only those who have mainlined the powerful narcotic of applause can know its transcendently addictive and corrupting effect. To keep it flowing into the ego's main vein, a great actor becomes a ham and an orator of conviction becomes a pompous windbag. Nor can one calculate the effects on an already religious man of the seemingly unjust defeats which Bryan suffered when he ran for President. And as battered wives and hostages will often feel gratitude to their persecutors for at least not killing them, so believers will suffer the most outrageous and undeserved bashings from God (including in Bryan's case, diabetes) and in some weird paradoxical way find in them increased evidence of His goodness.

So, if you read Bryan's speeches you see that as time goes by the political conviction and humane passion start to be subsumed by tedious religious dogma. He becomes a rampant Prohibitionist. The preacher overwhelms the reformer. Now what you get are the leaden, inane pronouncements of the typical Christian. In his 1904 speech, 'The Prince Of Peace,' he tells us that 'The mind is greater than the body and the soul is greater than the mind,' and 'A belief in immortality not only consoles the individual, but it exerts a powerful influence on bringing peace between individuals.' (How come I never heard of an atheist kamikaze pilot and how easy a sell would Jihad be without the promise of eternal life?) You get questions such as: 'Can God Perform A Miracle?' or 'Is the Bible True?' (yes to both, according to Bryan) and suddenly, and sickeningly, you've sunk to the level of the religious tract.

When he ran for President for the third and last time in 1908, the reporter, H.L. Mencken called him 'a charlatan, a mountebank, a zany without shame or dignity, the Fundamentalist Pope,' and many people, including Clarence Darrow, his eventual foe in the Scopes Trial, now came to believe his presence on the ticket was what kept the presidency Republican. In the elections of 1912, Bryan, perhaps exhausted by so much defeat, supported presidential candidate Woodrow Wilson who, when elected, rewarded him by making him Secretary of State. Three years later, Bryan resigned in protest over America's decision to enter the First World War. He was in his mid-fifties and his political career was over.

Partly because of Mary's ill health, he moved to Miami where he quickly made a fortune in the Florida land boom; but the craving for applause is not satisfied by money, nor, more charitably, is the craving for a cause. The only fix he could now get was from his fellow Christians, and so, like a plant seeking the light (if I may use a biological metaphor in this context), he headed in that direction. He told his son, William Jennings Bryan, Jr, 'It's time to move from the politics of the ballot boxes to the politics of saving souls.' As Mencken put it, 'Since his earliest days ... his chief strength has been among the folk of remote hills and forlorn and lonely farms. Now with his political aspirations all gone to pot, he turns to them for religious consolation. They understand his peculiar imbecilities. His nonsense is their ideal of sense. When he deluges them with his theological bilge they rejoice like pilgrims disporting in the river Jordan.'

Being one of the most famous orators of his time, Bryan had no trouble getting speaking engagements. Meanwhile, his syndicated newspaper column, the 'Weekly Bible Talks' reached an estimated fifteen million people.

And slowly the focus narrowed toward the trial that would kill him. By the early 1920s it was over sixty years since *The Origin of*

Species had come out and forty since Darwin had died. Evolution had been taught in American schools for decades. Since the turn of the century, Bryan had occasionally spoken on the subject, but generally in an 'I'll believe what I believe, you believe what you believe' fashion.

In *Summer For The Gods*, by Edward J. Larson, which is probably the most comprehensive and intelligent book written about the trial, Larson describes how, as a man who loved peace, Bryan was not only appalled but puzzled by the brutality of the First World War. Eventually, he came upon the theory that the war was a consequence of Darwinian theories fed to German intellectuals via Nietzsche. Darwin's concept of Natural Selection, the idea that nature destroys that which is weak and favours whatever minute adaptions strengthen the species, was rephrased by others into the more brutal-sounding Survival of The Fittest. This was then used as moral justification for violent struggle. And of course there may be some truth in this: after all, if religion can be so used, why not biology and philosophy? Further aroused by a report that students in higher education, particularly the sciences, were moving away from God, Bryan decided he had to act.

In 1921, he hit the road with a new speech, 'The Menace Of Darwinism,' and added 'The Bible And Its Enemies' soon after; but still he had no concrete political objective. In 1922 he heard that Kentucky's Baptist State Board of Missions had called for a law forbidding the teaching of evolution in public schools. He wrote the next day to offer his services on the anti-evolution bandwagon and was enthusiastically accepted. And that was it. Here was a real campaign, one that joined his two interests, religion and politics. Here was a campaign to bring him back onto centre stage.

He had fallen from the glory of 'The Cross of Gold' into the tawdry mud of an attempt to limit knowledge. When it was over everything he had ever done would be overshadowed by its absurdity.

The law failed in Kentucky by a single vote, but largely because of Bryan the movement rapidly gained momentum. Church leaders accused biology teachers of being atheists, anarchists and socialists who were poisoning America with their ideas. The Ku Klux Klan agreed. Six states soon considered anti-evolution laws, with William Jennings

Bryan involved in most, one way or another; but only two, Oklahoma and Florida, actually succeeded in getting anything on the books. In both cases, the language of the legislation was mild and without punitive bite. Partly because of the slow nature of politics in the South of that time, it was not until 1925 that the cause was able to claim its first real victory and it was in Tennessee that it occurred.

The law that brought about the Scopes trial was proposed by a Tennessee Democratic congressman and lay preacher named John Butler. It stated 'that it shall be unlawful for any teacher in any of the Universities, Normals, and all other public schools of the State, which are supported in whole or in any part by the public school funds of the State, to teach any theory that denies the story of the Divine Creation of man as taught in the Bible, and to teach instead that man has descended from a lower order of animal.' And the bill had some sting in it too, a real penalty, a fine of between $100 and $500 for anyone convicted of breaking the law.

To the credit of the state, the law didn't come into existence without debate. Many modernist clerics vigorously opposed it. So did several newspapers. A congressman suggested legislation should be passed to forbid the teaching of 'the round earth theory.' But no amount of ridicule could overturn the forces of primitivism. The bill passed in the House, seventy-one to five, and in the Senate, twenty-four to six, and the Governor, a Baptist, signed it into law on 21st March 1925.

The recently formed American Civil Liberties Union (ACLU), which had been watching developments in the South, heard of the anti-evolutionists' victory. In early May, it bought space in some Tennessee newspapers, the *Chattanooga Times* among them, and announced 'We are looking for a Tennessee teacher who is willing to accept our services in testing this law in the courts. Our lawyers think a friendly test can be arranged without costing a teacher his or her job.'

The ensuing trial could have taken place anywhere in the state, the somewhat liberal Nashville being the more likely venue, had it not been for the vision of a strange and interesting man who had washed up in Dayton. One of those characters in history who provoke a great event and then disappear, his name was George Washington Rappleyea.

27

On the evening of 4th May, he read the *Chattanooga Times*. In the morning he hurried from his home and drove toward Robinson's Drug Store on Main Street.

What Goes On

At the Roanoke bus station, a teenage girl and her father huddle together on a bench. She is in tears and protests continually. He holds and comforts her. Eventually, she boards. I watch him sitting on a barrier. His exhausted eyes are focused on some distant hour beyond this sorrow and awkwardness. The girl sits behind me and continues to cry as the bus pulls away.

The man waves fatalistically to his daughter. I turn in my seat and watch her wave back. Then I look out of the window as the town thins out and eventually releases us into the country.

I wonder what the crying girl is crying about. I imagine paedophile stepfathers, implacable court decisions, cokehead mothers, baby brothers with cancer, shotgun suicides, bankruptcy and other dramas too numerous and depressing to mention; but before I can get up the courage to dredge her for this material and then offer comfort in return, she falls into a deep sleep from which she does not wake for a hundred miles.

I've picked up a copy of the *Roanoke Times* and start to read it. Only two marching bands played in the Vinton Dogwood Festival this year. These days, the bands aren't interested in parades, which are boring and traditional, so much as in the big competitions at Disneyland. 'Another Small Town To Drop Charter,' reads another headline. Clover Town Council has voted to accept an agreement with Halifax County to dissolve the town. Clover, which has 200 residents is basically broke and has eliminated most services except for its twenty-three street lights. This is depressing stuff. I flip quickly to the obituaries for lighter fare.

'McGee, Frederick. 76. After retirement he was a very important partner with his wife and daughter at their Macbeth Kennels in

Troutville. Mr McGee will be greatly missed by his many dog and cat friends and his bird, Buck.'

That's better.

The bus turns off Route 81, the main highway, and onto US 11, an old, winding road through plump, wooded hills – broken by meadows. I assume when this was the only road – it forced people through the small and now forgotten town of Pulaski, a sign on the outskirts of which reads: 'Take Heed. The Lord Is Coming. The End Of Time Is Near.'

He's coming *here*? He's going to take a detour off Route 81 which leads to all the sinners in Nashville and Memphis (or better still, Atlanta with its huge gay population), just to stop off in *Pulaski*? Even putting aside its no doubt world-class reputation for incest, why would he? But even before we get to the sad centre of the dying town, I have a strange feeling I've read the name Pulaski in some interesting context … I flip through my book on the South and quickly locate the reference. A town named Pulaski was the birthplace of the Ku Klux Klan in 1865, but that Pulaski was in Tennessee and we're still in Virginia. We are, however, right on the border. Could the border have moved? How many towns can there be called Pulaski? Could this really be it? And if it is, maybe Jesus *would* consider a detour.

As the bus leaves town, and we finally escape the malignant little place, I see a sign which says, 'Sword Of Jesus – Revival Meeting. Preaching The Book, The Blood, and The Blessed Hope.'

The *blood*? My *God*.

The crying girl wakes up and rubs her eyes. Five minutes later, I've got my spoon in her head and I'm scooping out segments of her life to chew on as the journey continues: she's sixteen years old, her father is a doctor, her mother lives in Las Vegas with her new stepfather, she goes to school in Roanoke and prefers it to Vegas.

'There's nothing to do in Las Vegas for a teenager,' she tells me.

Without tears, she is quite pretty and answers my questions politely but with suspicion. She is going to visit her mother for a month. The trip is going to take almost three days with no stopping in hotels to sleep. She was crying at the bus station because originally she was going to go out to Vegas by plane but her mother insisted she come by bus. It would be good for her. Crying for a plane? After all I'd imagined for her?

'So, what do you want to be when you grow up?' I ask.

'I want to be a teacher,' she says 'I love school, I just love it.'

I turn away, vaguely disappointed.

The first school I went to was Dartington Hall in Devon, where my father was the head of the adult education centre. I was in nursery school and can remember almost nothing of it.

When I was four and my sister, Sarah, five, my father went into business with a man who invented and manufactured scientific instruments just outside Cambridge. As this was where Clare, my mother, was brought up and where her mother still lived, she was happy to move back there.

At first, we all lived with my father's partner in the Old Vicarage in Grantchester, where the poet Rupert Brooke once lived. Life in the village was still pretty much like that, at least on the surface, quiet and leafy with punts on the slow river nearby. (Now the Vicarage is lived in by that paragon of Conservative values, Jeffrey Archer.)

In 1954, my parents bought their own house about seven miles from the centre of Cambridge. It was a large mill house, actually two houses crudely stitched together. The back part, a cottage, was built in 1600; the front, a more imposing, red brick Queen Anne building, was added on in 1750 when the miller got rich. The mill next door was a very large off-white brick structure more reminiscent of an eighteenth-century factory than a typically quaint mill, a large cube, four floors tall if you included the one under the sloping roof. The top floor was the most exciting because at the front was a gantry used for hoisting things up from the bridge below. It jutted out dangerously and as children we'd go up there and scare ourselves by looking down through the cracks in the trapdoor.

Across the gravel yard was a large thatched barn. To one side was a wooden shed. My father bought it all, along with several acres of land, for £5,750. He and his partner now moved their business into the shed. At first it was just the two of them, then there were three, then four. Eventually, the company would colonise the entire mill and employ a hundred men.

The river ran down toward the back of the house, the cottage, through lush green fields, past the living-room windows, and under the mill, which straddled the river. In the millrace the water was channelled over a weir, rushed past the place where the mill-wheel once was, and finally emerged from under an arched bridge into a large, oval millpond. Here the current slowed, meandering and swirling, until it reached the second broad weir at the end of the pond, where, depending on the season, it either trickled over the thick weeds or sat upon the lip, fat and lethal, before descending into the shallow river below.

Many dramas occurred on the weir. Once a dead cow got stuck on it and had to be hauled out by tractor. Everyone said we should stand back as sometimes a carcass would explode if it had been in the water a long time. A short time later, however, a man upriver lost his pet donkey to the river and it too got stuck. The man came down and tried to pull it out by hand. When that didn't work, he fetched a large saw and sawed the donkey in half. It did not explode. Another time, some debris got caught here and my father went out to clear it off with a rake. The river was high and dangerous. I watched him balancing in the middle of the weir and when he nearly toppled over I laughed at his panic-struck face and waving arms. He was furious, thinking, I'm sure, that I was being callous, was showing how little I cared for him; but it was not this. It just never occurred to me that he would not survive all accidents. He was my father and invincible.

Sarah and I did not go to the local school because our parents had found another, better one, a state primary school in a village about five miles away, and somehow managed to persuade someone to let us go there.

Kingston Village School had only one teacher. The tiny schoolhouse was on the village green behind a white picket fence with a playground to one side. There were usually fewer than twenty children here, most of them the sons and daughters of farmers or farm labourers, ranging in age from four to eleven. Each day began with a hymn or two, 'All Things Bright and Beautiful' and 'Jerusalem' come to mind. Then we'd say the Lord's Prayer and get down to work.

Our teacher, Mrs Marshall, was a round woman; not fat because that suggests indulgence and this woman was not indulgent, she was simply intended by nature to be spherical. She had shining brown eyes and her long dark hair done up in a large, lustrous bun. A farmer's daughter from the Fens, her accent was broad East Anglian and her laugh, which was frequent, was a roiling chuckle flung without censure from her plump throat.

I was her student from the age of four to seven. She was the first and only teacher from whom I learned anything.

When she was a girl, Mrs Marshall wanted to go to university. She was a good enough student to achieve this, but in her last year of school there was an agricultural slump. Potatoes rotted across the Fens, the expense of shipping them to London being more than the profit that would be returned. Her father, a small farmer, nearly went broke and everyone had to help. To her immense disappointment, she was forced to go to work immediately as an 'uncertificated' teacher.

Lacking the government's seal of approval, she always felt she had more to learn and so, as she was still learning, learning was not something static or complete which she imposed upon you, but a process of discovery which you shared with her. Her curiosity was so obviously genuine it provoked your own. There was nothing patronising about her, nothing complacent, nothing fake. She was so bad at Maths (and so uninterested in it) that to teach my sister, Sarah, who was eighteen months older than I and ten times brighter, she was forced to bone up on the lessons the night before.

What she really loved to teach was Art. Each year we would enter the *Daily Mail* Art Contest, a nationwide competition to find the best work produced by any school in the country. In the single classroom with its vaulted ceiling, Mrs Marshall moved peaceably from group to group, sharpening pencils for the four-year-olds, discussing essays or poems, or helping the older ones to learn italic. But always, a few students would be at work on our entry, and Mrs Marshall would inevitably drift back to them, to give advice, to praise, to encourage. Usually, our entry into the contest was a mosaic made of coloured squares cut from magazines and pasted on a piece of paper about the size of a single bed-sheet. One year it was a jungle with a vivid tiger prowling among the trees. Although we were up against schools that had hundreds of students and well-financed art departments, we won twice. This made Mrs Marshall locally famous and eventually she wrote *An Experiment In Education*, a book about the school and teaching art in which can be found my first published work:

What Goes On

Outdoors On Water:
Ducks bob up and down,
And boats pass by with people chattering.
Indoors On Land:
Telephones ring and mothers rush,
Babies cry, children scream,
Only fathers work.

I was four years old, it was the Fifties, and indeed my mother didn't work. In the morning she would drive us to school and in the afternoon around three she would pick us up. I remember her most clearly in the summer, leaning against the car, smoking. She was a striking woman, not beautiful but attractive, with dark, melancholy eyes and a proud, almost defiant bearing. Her brown hair was held back by tortoiseshell combs, and in the summer she wore cotton dresses with large bold designs. These dresses were always cinched tight below her impressive breasts.

Her drinking, which in later life would shape and deform us all, was, in those days, only wild and sporadic. Around the time my younger brother Francis was born however our previously peaceful existence was shaken by a long series of violent arguments. Sarah and I would creep halfway down the stairs and listen as our parents shouted at each other. One night we heard my mother yell 'Why don't you go and jump in the river and drown?' and then my father replying reasonably, but as if deeply depressed, 'Because I can swim, it wouldn't work.'

We suspected something catastrophic had happened, and it had, a betrayal which would mark their marriage forever. Sarah and I felt something shift, but were too young to guess why and would not learn what had happened for decades. Thinking we would get a choice, we discussed who we would go with if they divorced. I thought I'd probably go with my mother, Sarah was more inclined toward her father. But after a while, the fighting became less frequent and when they came to the Nativity Play or the Harvest Festival together they were a good-looking couple and we were proud of them. They seemed younger and lighter on their feet than other parents.

I know people who remember a period in their childhood when they had no interest in the opposite sex. I was *always* interested in girls. If I wasn't in love, which was rare, I was always curious about someone's body. What would she look like naked? How would she smell? What would she feel like? How would it be to stroke her here … or there … or in between? Would she be warm and soft or would she have goose bumps?

From infancy to beyond puberty, some part of my body was always experiencing the itch of eczema. There was never a time when an outpost of the disease was not established somewhere, and every month or so, as if creeping from a grating, the disease would emerge and blossom forth. Usually, it would take possession of my hands first, around the knuckles and between the fingers and then spread to my elbows, the backs of my knees, and my ankles. The hands were the worst because they could not be hidden. The itch seemed to be only a millimetre below the surface, taunting me, demanding to be extinguished and then, when I tried to reach it, retreating deeper and deeper. More and larger scabs would then erupt, and vanity and curiosity required them to be picked off. Now when they re-formed, there would be dark, bloody gullies in their midst. The itch became so intense on my right ankle once that, using only my nails, I scratched away the flesh until I could see bone. Frequently, I would put my hands under a tap, turn the water on, and let it get hotter and hotter until, as I rubbed the fingers together vigorously, the water scalded the itch away. There was something erotic in this. As the pain of the itch became the pain of burning, there was a moment of intense relief, of delicious self-punishment. But, appropriately, this moment was followed almost immediately by sensations of shame and despair, because, having done this, I would usually bring on septicaemia. When I was twelve, I read Shakespeare's sonnet about lust. For me, however, the poem did not evoke images of carnal lust, about which I was always shameless, but of this itch and my scrabbling around in my own flesh, abandoned to this futile and costly moment of relief.

35

The expense of spirit in a waste of shame
Is lust in action; and until action, lust
Is perjured, murderous, bloody, full of blame
Savage, rude, cruel, not to trust,
Enjoyed no sooner, but despised straight,
Past reason hunted; and no sooner had,
Past reason hated, as a swallowed bait.

My mother took me to an allergist. When we went back for the results, he shrugged and shook his head and said, 'I'm sorry, but this boy is allergic to life.'

Skin pain and skin ugliness made me eager to experience skin pleasure and skin beauty. Until I was four, I often had scabs on my face. People smiled down at me in disgust. I fell in love the first time when I was three, with a girl whose name was Cherry. I remember sitting with her on a window sill at Dartington, discussing the nearby woods. I remember there was almost no distinction between the woods as I saw them and the woods of fairy tales. I wanted to take Cherry to a woodcutter's cottage, and live with her there forever in the glades. Whatever glades were. Our cots were next to each other in nursery school and when it was time to take a nap after lunch, I would climb the side of mine and drop down into hers. I wanted to touch her, to hold her, to feel her hot, soft skin. Once, when I found another boy there, I was furious and punched him on the nose. At this age the disease was so ferocious that at night my mother sometimes had to tie my hands to the bed or I would dig holes in myself while sleeping. When I could not sleep I would beg my mother to fetch Cherry so she could sleep with me.

At the age of five, and with my mother pregnant with Francis, my passion for girls became more intense. I was not only romantic but deeply sexual. My physical desire had no idea how to satisfy itself, but knew the secret lay in the flesh of girls. There were three girls of my age whom I desired. One was called Nicola, a pretty, respectable girl whose father was a successful farmer. I went to visit once, and was shown a plethora of hogs and cows and horses and dogs. The horses and the dogs were kissed repeatedly by Nicola, but when I suggested it was now my turn, all I got was a smack in the chops. The other two girls were village girls, cross-eyed, adenoidal, and willing.

I'd ask Mrs Marshall to be excused and then signal one of these girls to follow. The designated girl would then make a similar request. To get to the outdoor toilets you had to pass through a kitchen where a crone named Lucy – who wore black lace-up boots and had a circulatory disorder which swelled her fingers shiny blue – recooked the already overcooked lunches brought in by van. Once past this gorgon, a door admitted you to a small courtyard and the toilets off it. I would wait out there and soon one of the girls would step shyly out. On the first of these occasions, both girls saw my signal and both followed me outside. Undaunted, I stood them next to each other in the chilly courtyard and asked them to drop their underpants and lift their skirts; then, pulling down my own grubby little shorts, I suggested we all touch our bottoms together.

A gong rang inside my body, and this was my first religious experience. To this day I remember the luminous twinge of concord rising in my lower abdomen.

In the absence of breasts, my primary focus was buttocks. I would ask the girls to lie down on their stomachs on the large cold step and then stared in wonder at their smooth, plump, *different* bottoms. A little stroke, a little slap. What beauty. How soft the skin, how sweet the motion.

The other object of my desire was Mrs Marshall's daughter, Pru, who was probably fifteen or so, an erotic colossus whose naked body I imagined daily. When I was six, there was a snowstorm that blew in so fast my mother couldn't fetch us before the roads were blocked. Mrs Marshall (there was no Mr Marshall, nor was he ever mentioned) lived with her old mother and the aforementioned Pru in a small ivy-covered cottage adjoining the school. This is where Sarah and I would now have to sleep.

Sometimes in life, things just fall into your lap and sometimes in life you just fall into someone else's lap. This latter was now the case. To my astonishment and joy, I was told I'd be sleeping with Pru.

When we got into bed, I lay as close to her as I could without actually touching and allowed myself to be swamped by the rich pungency of her smell. She was lying on her back, her arms above her head. She already had breasts. I loved her with all my heart. After a while, she said good night, turned away, and soon fell asleep. The thick snow silenced the already quiet land. Feigning sleep – a light snore tossed in among regular breaths – I moved closer and pressed myself 'inadvertently' against her back. If the ratio between she and I remained the same and she were lying beside me today, she'd be eleven feet tall and weigh 400 pounds and her buttocks would be ... well, they'd be fantastic.

They *were* fantastic. Beneath the slippery material of her nightdress I could feel the vast, hot swell of them, the resilience and the sloping cleft. I moved lower in the bed and sealed myself under the sheets so I could inhale pure, unadulterated Pru. And, oh, the smell of her! Why did I have to be only six? *Why?* What a cruel accident of chronology! If only I could grow up *now* and marry her and have this every night.

I was in a swoon of longing and despair and halfway down the bed when she turned over. A thigh swept across me and settled on my chest, squeezing the air out of my lungs. It lay across me like a hot tuna, submerging me deep in the mattress. Her stomach was in my face and her breasts rested on the top of my head. I was physically and emotionally overwhelmed. I could not move and could hardly draw breath. This limb of implausible but delicious corpulence and weight was going to kill me. Because the blankets were over my head, what little air I could gasp into my lungs was soon devoid of oxygen. I was suffocating. I decided I'd rather die than wake her up and have her move away. One more breath ... Another ... As I was about to faint, she threw off the covers. Now at least I had access to some new oxygen.

I didn't sleep at all, just lay there under the marvellous thigh, feebly puffing in air until dawn. The next day I walked around in an awed stupor.

This was my second religious experience.

My third religious experience occurred a year later and was more conventional, having in fact to do with God. My sister and I were raised in the Church of England until we were about ten, at which time both parents sheepishly admitted they didn't really believe. Going to church was just the decent thing to do, putting it on offer until we were old enough to decide for ourselves. Needless to say, we decided against it.

At the age of seven, however, a year of so after my brother Francis was born, I started to read the Bible avidly and pray every night. This began because our house was tall and dark and if I told my parents I wanted to pray, they'd come up with me when I went to bed. Once they were there, the longer I prayed, the longer they stayed.

Perhaps there was another reason too, of which I was not then aware. Christianity is perfectly designed to provide a replacement family – God, the father; Mary, the mother; Jesus, the older brother – and at this time I feared my own family was about to self-destruct.

Although my mother and father had their doubts about this sudden religiosity, I was such a wicked boy they wanted to encourage any urge toward goodness even if it might not be genuine, and so they dutifully climbed the stairs to pray with me. Dredging about in newspapers and magazines, I located an endless and astonishing vein of human misery from which to mine the elements for my nightly pleas. I then became so moved by my descriptions of these sorrows that before long I began to think I'd like to offer my life in service to the poor wretches of whom I spoke. What had started out as fakery became authentic.

I had always thought of becoming either a naturalist, a gigolo, or a sailor. Now I began to think I'd take a shot at sainthood. I dreamed constantly of being a missionary, not in an evangelical way but in the sense of being where I was needed, as a worker in a leper colony, say, or among the maimed and dying. Usually I was in Africa, sometimes India. I had no wife or children. God's love (I saw it almost as a friendship) and the adoration of those for whom I'd given up my life, was more than enough. It was a glorious dream.

To qualify for sainthood, I assumed it was necessary to read the Bible from Genesis to Revelation, and so I began. Although some of the stories were inspiring and comforting, a lot of it was incomprehensible and boring. Soon the arcane rules and the obvious contradictions began to irritate me and after a while I was driven off. I had no idea there were other religions to choose from, nor could I conceive of any way to achieve a state of grace without religious faith.

The phase passed, I sank quickly into delinquency. But if I close my eyes, I can still remember the sensation of purity, the profound reward that a life of such devotion promised: the transcendent relief of waking up each morning knowing that where you are is exactly where you should be, and that what you are doing is unquestionably right.

A policy of bussing children to larger schools closed Mrs Marshall down. I think she fought this development hard and won certain concessions. No new students would be allowed to attend but those who were there could stay. Before long there were only ten children left. And then they closed the place. Approaching fifty, Mrs Marshall applied for a place at New Hall, Cambridge. Thirty years later than she intended, she became an undergraduate.

My sister stayed almost to the end, but I, thinking I was ready to start my war on education, demanded at the age of seven to leave the kind, inspiring Mrs Marshall and go to a school I'll call St Anne's, an all-boys prep school in Cambridge, where you were forced to wear uniforms and got thrashed if you misbehaved. Here was a worthy adversary, I thought. And so it was.

From Mrs Marshall I took with me the only weapon I had. The brutality of the new place would be escaped through dreams, by the aforementioned fantasies of heroism and sacrifice, and later of marrying an heiress or joining the Merchant Marine. Most frequently I dreamed of furtive erotic encounters with one of the few misshapen females who taught there, this latter orgy of the inner screen being consummated several times a day in the wooden stalls of the putrid bathrooms.

This dreaming of all kinds became a way of life, compulsion, and finally a source of income.

'The Trail Of Tears'

At 2.30 p.m., we cross into Tennessee at Bristol in the north-eastern corner of the state. The first sign I see is on a pawn shop. 'Guitars, Guns, Knives, and Jewelry.'

Tennessee, my guidebook tells me, is famous for Elvis Presley, the Scopes Trial, the Ku Klux Klan, and Oak Ridge, the once-secret city which helped develop the first nuclear bomb. It's also known for moonshine, which in turn gave birth to stock-car racing. Moonshiners built special cars to outpace the cops on back roads and tracks and in their spare time raced against each other. Along with moonshiners, there are now 'sang diggers who dig for ginseng in the mountains and sell it to Asia for as much as $500 a pound.

As we leave Bristol, I look down out the window of the bus. A car drifts up from behind. A bumper sticker on the front reads, 'Got Jesus?' As the car goes by, another on the back says, 'Yes, Lord, I will ride with you.' In between sits an overweight woman with a sullen face and a set mouth. The more I see of it, the more convinced I become that there's something sexual about this adoration of Jesus. Every slogan confirms it. 'Oh, Lord, Hold Me In Your Arms, For I Am Thine.' 'I Give Myself To Thee, Sweet Jesus.'

I see a woman married to some blundering, be-gutted, half-bankrupt Bubba who's been trying to beat her down for years and hasn't quite pulled it off. They rarely have sex because it's become a weapon of denial for both. It's war. One day the wife finds Jesus. Now she has a secret and profound relationship with another man and what's more the guy is often depicted half naked (he's got nails through his hands, but his stomach is *flat*) and he's like a young, great looking hippie (which pisses the husband off right there), but he's also extremely well connected (unlike the husband), universally loved, and *highly* dominant – 'Thou shalt do this, Thou shalt not do that' – and Mrs Bubba rolls over and gives herself to him as flagrantly as any 'sub' – *right there in front of the husband!* – floundering around and 'hollerin'' like … well, you've seen it on TV. You tell me when you last heard a woman make that kind of noise.

And all the husband can do is stand there and watch.

Victory for the wife? I'd say so.

Except you don't feel it's working. The philosophical question this woman asks herself is universal and interesting, but the answer, aptly reduced to a bumper sticker, is narrow and trite. She states that she is convinced, but everything about her says otherwise. Even when you see the wild demonstrations of belief, the hollering and falling down, you feel you are watching not someone who has been saved, but someone who has merely found another outlet for their hysteria.

The racial composition of the bus has changed. When I got on in New York there were almost four times as many African-Americans as whites. Now the ratio has been inverted. There are eighteen white people, five African-Americans, two Hispanics, and unless I'm much mistaken, a Redskin just got on board. Oh, no, I'm sorry, *Native American*. Oh, no, sorry *again*, I just heard it ought to be *First Nation Person*.

How I despise this Index Expurgatorius of 'inappropriate' words. I understand what it is attempting to do, but as a writer it feels like someone's putting their hand in my toolbox. The whole concept seems Orwellian to me, a way of changing appearance without changing substance, a hypocritical ploy designed to varnish brutal reality, a means by which self-satisfied closet racists and bigots can safely hide behind a set of linguistic rules and so feel immunised from either criticism or the need for action.

My paternal grandmother was a kike, my sister is married to a nigger, my favourite uncle is a fag, and my wife is a beaver. Is the world changed by that sentence? Of course not. Crime against language is committed every day in America, but it has nothing to do with the use of 'bad' words. No, the real crime is the theft of *good* words by corporations: brutal oil and timber companies crooning reassuringly about how much they 'love' and 'cherish' the great outdoors, Insurance companies who'd rip your liver out and stomp on it for a buck, sentimentalising about how they want to 'nurture' you, 'care' for you, and be your 'lifelong friend'. Younger, smarter black people see this linguistic fraud for what it is and mock it with their own inversions: 'bad' means good, 'down' means up. And when did you last hear one black man say to another, 'Whassup, African-American?' Consciously or not, they give the finger to it all.

Moronic racial epithets flourish on the Internet, empowered by denunciation, while the National Association for the Advancement of *Colored* People is made to blush. This double attack upon the vocabulary is akin to Necrotising Fasciitis, that flesh-eating bacteria which greedily consumes a leg in an afternoon.

We arrive in Knoxville and I have to wait an hour and then change buses to get one to Chattanooga. A woman sits in the bus station holding a large bed-pillow complete with pillowcase. A man comes up to her and says, 'Came prepared with a pillow?'

The bus is late and I soon find out why. The driver is incredibly slow and verbose. As we finally leave the station, he starts his routine: 'Smoking is prohibited. If you don't know what prohibited means, it means, don't ask for it, don't do it, don't even want it. No boomboxes and no sex in the bathroom. If you get the desire, I'll pull over at a motel, but I won't wait.' He then goes on to explain where we're going, how, and at what speed. He's like one of those airline pilots who just as you get to sleep insists on telling you his name, the kind of plane you're on, how fast you're going, at what height, 'and if you look out the left of the plane, you may just be able to see Las Vegas ...' But this driver is worse. It seems like he's never going to shut up. A woman across the aisle from me says, 'What's he goin' on about? I can't understand a word he says, it's like he talks with his mouth shut or somepin.'

In front of me, a one-legged man discusses the pros and cons of city life versus country life. 'I just can't believe people spend $200,000 on a house that's so close to another one that you could spit on it, an' it's like everyone's flinging around attitude an' he's gonna hit you before you hit him 'cause maybe you've got a hidden gun. I was in auto-repair – expect you to do work for nothing, don't even want you to earn a living wage. And the cops have gotten pretty bad too – think they're God or something. The only drawback to living in the country is you get less opportunity.'

I refer to my book on the South which gives definitions of Southern types. A Southern Belle seems to be a kind of aristocrat who has a coming-out party. The cognoscenti don't call her a belle, referring to her instead as 'a real cute girl'. Adult Belles are known as 'ladies'. 'Women' are workers and whores.

A 'Bubba' is a Southern man who's not too bright but not necessarily low class. A 'Redneck' drives a pick-up truck. He's rural, profoundly conservative, enjoys guns, Country and Western music, fighting, fishing, and camping. A 'Good Ol' Boy', though he may come from either end of the social scale, seems to be in better shape financially. He's into guns (everyone is), fishing, football, and women, all of which provide grist for the many anecdotes he tells his buddies with whom he may have bought land for a hunting club. The 'Good Ol' Boy', unlike the other two categories, takes expensive foreign vacations.

Late in the afternoon, after two days of more or less constant travel, I arrive in Chattanooga. It's a pretty town with a gracious, civilised air. It has an opera and a symphony orchestra and private schools and there seem to be a lot of trees and wide streets. Site of one of the most decisive battles of the Civil War, it became, after the war, a place where veterans from both sides settled together amicably. To me it still seems amiable and relaxed, like a resort or a spa town.

I check into the best hotel, The Reade House, another big downtown hotel that's seen better days, but this is more typically Southern somehow, grander, less to do with industry and farming and more to do with pleasure and politics. There's even a black shoeshine man in the lobby. He's in his mid-twenties and he smiles at me every time I go by, so after a couple of passes I figure I'll get my shoes shined and chat with him a while. I climb up onto a beautiful stand with brass footplates and he starts working on my shoes. He tells me this used to be his father's spot.

'Now he's up the street. I also do the airport, but I come in here coupla times a week 'cause I'm also a bellman.'

I ask him how long he's been doing it.

'Been doin' it since I was twelve. Used to be a good business, but, man, it's slowed down. Different people these days. Businessmen. I shoulda done somepin' else, but there it is, I stuck a fork in it.'

' "Stuck a fork in it"?'

'It's off the grill. Stick a fork in it. It's done.'

He gets back to work on the shoes. He's brushed in the sweet-smelling polish and now reaches for a long piece of lambskin.

'Okay,' he says, 'now it's time to take these shoes to ultra-space, where they ain't never been before.'

In the evening, I walk down wide, empty downtown streets to Sticky Fingers, a rib joint a few blocks from the hotel. I'm tired and contented. It's still early but the restaurant has already slowed down. I sit outside on a terrace and munch away at some stringy but tender beef drenched in barbecue sauce. A couple of middle-aged women sit nearby, talking and drinking. A group of young people, good-looking, ill-matched but expectant, finish their dinner and stroll away. You see people enjoying themselves in New York, but there's usually something frantic about it, squeezing in pleasure between important matters of ambition or survival. Here, this evening at least, pleasure seems to be an end in itself.

I finish the food and then go into the empty bar to have a drink. The bar itself is an oblong with a barman in the middle. The place has more the atmosphere of a college-town bar than anything redneck. A pretty blonde girl comes in to meet a friend working in the restaurant. They order two shots of something and then stand around on the short end of the oblong, glancing at me now and then and adjusting themselves. The one who works here, a tall, slender girl with a long, flat face, casually lights her cigarette by bending back a match on a book of matches and striking it with her thumb. It's a stylish, deliberate move. Having lit her cigarette, she tosses the matches onto the bar, but, to her surprise, the match keeps burning and now she has to make a decision: admit defeat and retrieve it, or wait for the whole thing to explode. She laughs and lets it burn. The barman stubs it amiably. The young, who I find interesting because they're so uncluttered, find themselves uninteresting for the same reason. Their mannerisms and affectations, the lighting of the match, the way they dress, the belly-button rings, which I love, all these are there to take the place of scars earned in the process of life.

The blonde girl moves a shoulder bag so the strap bisects her breasts diagonally, and glances at me again. She's wearing a white shirt and she's not yet twenty. After a while, they leave. I go in search of a 'Duelling Piano Bar' I've been told about where two blues pianists face off on opposite pianos, but I cannot find it so I return to the hotel and go to bed. In the morning I rent a car and set off for Dayton to do my bit for history.

Through my internet server, American Online (more commonly known as AOL), I've made contact with a woman who runs a bed and breakfast in Dayton called The Magnolia House. Her name is Gloria and her AOL profile reads:

Marital Status: not married, not good at it. Hobbies: horses, field trials, bird hunting, antiques, cooking, fun, skeet shooting, shopping, people, life. Personal Quote: most people are about as happy as they make up their minds to be. not knowing when the dawn will come, i open every door. i am a sweet thing. i do not like to be teased ...

On the phone, she had a smoky, flirtatious voice and one of those laughs that comes hacking out in sudden nervous bursts. Later, she e-mails me some pictures of herself. She's blonde and appears to be in her late thirties. Some of the photographs show her with horses. Another group of four show her wearing a tight leather dress – and she looks good – but then there's a picture of her standing on a bridge and she does not look quite so good.

The second time I call, closer to my arrival, she tells me she's selling up. Things haven't worked out somehow and she's leaving town. I'm to be the last guest at The Magnolia House.

After about forty-five minutes driving along a highway littered with yet more warnings of Christ's imminent return (it really is astonishing how obsessed they are by this) I arrive outside Dayton. The road around which the town grew has been atrophied by Highway 27 which, like a big artery, bypasses Dayton along the eastern edge. The cholesterol of modern life, Arby's, McDonalds, Kentucky Fried Chicken, clusters around the new highway. I fork left off the highway and take the old varicose vein into town.

Dayton lies in Eastern Tennessee alongside the Tennessee River. Before the whites arrrived, Tennessee and the Carolinas were home to 40,000 Cherokee Indians. The Cherokee Nation consisted of about 200 red and white towns. The red towns were war towns, the white, peace towns. The chiefs of each town answered to a supreme chief of either war or peace who lived in the headquarters of the tribe. The white towns were sanctuaries, and the similarity of these to Hebrew 'cities of refuge' is why some people believe American Indians are descended from one of the Ten Lost Tribes Of Israel.

I wonder what would happen if it turned out to be the other way around, that the Jews were in fact descended from American Indians? The true spiritual home of the Jews would then become Nashville instead of Jerusalem, and a Holocaust Museum would have to be erected there to commemorate another genocidal episode in their history, an episode which, during an epidemic of memorial building, is conveniently overlooked.

According to the *History Of Rhea County, Tennessee*, compiled by Bettye J. Broyles – a massive tome which can be purchased at the Chamber Of Commerce in modern Dayton – the Cherokee and the settlers lived together peacefully in the early days of white incursion into the area, even marrying each other and raising children. As in all things, however, the Indians soon got the shitty end of the stick. In 1650, a smallpox epidemic cut the Cherokee Nation in half and soon land grants were being freely given – 20,000 acres here, 40,000 there – although the land still legally belonged to the Indians. Later, the government itself would grab 7,000 square miles of territory in a single day.

A complaint of the time, and an excellent excuse for genocide, was that Indians were difficult to 'civilise'. Whatever that means, it was not true of the Cherokee. Having come in contact with the white man's alphabet, they created their own and, having done so, wrote several books about their culture. They adopted a written national constitution, built houses and paved roads. In 1828, the tribe even started its own newspaper, the *Cherokee Phoenix*. When parts of the tribe were forced west, they tried to hold their nation together, in spirit if not in place, by writing back and forth. They were, in short, considerably more civilised than the rapacious Christians who pushed them further and further back into their mountainous lands in north-western Georgia. One Profitable Nation Under A White God was what these God-fearing men were after, and if the Indians had to be cheated out of their lands or killed, so be it. God Bless Genocide! Pass the turkey!

There had been rumours of gold in Cherokee country from the very start. John G. Burnett, a soldier who participated in the goldrush which followed and later wrote a memoir about it, says an Indian boy living

47

on Ward Creek in Tennessee discovered a gold nugget in 1828 and sold it to a trader. The Cherokee were doomed.

Through bribery, corruption, and violence, the last of the Cherokee's land was taken. In 1835, the Treaty of New Echota was achieved by a five-million-dollar bribe to a portion of the tribe. The treaty demanded that the Cherokee now move west of the Mississippi. When some of the tribe refused to leave, the government decided to 'remove' them.

Chief Junaluska, who had fought alongside President Andrew Jackson in a battle against the Cree, and indeed saved his life, was sent to Washington to plead with him. Junaluska explained that the majority of the tribe were not in favour of the treaty, which was internally unconstitutional. Jackson was cool to him and said there was nothing he could do. Davy Crockett and Ralph Waldo Emerson, among others, expressed their outrage at what was about to happen, but to no effect.

In the summer of 1838, 7,000 US troops arrived. They rounded up all but a few hundred Indians and put them in stockades. Many Indians died here either of disease or what is now known as *bungungot*. A Filipino word, *bungungot* describes a spiritual homesickness, a sorrow so profound it kills. It occurs among people who believe their land is imbued with spirits, including the spirits of their ancestors. To be torn from this land is to be torn from your soul.

By the time the tribe had been captured and imprisoned, it was already November. Undeterred, the soldiers loaded the Cherokee into 645 wagons and set off for Oklahoma. They travelled through the winter and did not arrive in Oklahoma until March. Four thousand Cherokee died of exposure and disease and the route they took became known as 'The Trail Of Tears.'

The 'Trail Of Tears' passes right through Dayton. In the early 1880s an English company under the direction of Titus Salt Jr came to town and formed The Dayton Coal and Iron Company. Dayton was almost unique in its natural resources and means of transportation. In the nearby hills were both coal and iron, as well as timber for props and clay for making bricks. Chickamauga Lake, which came right to the edge of town, was actually an offshoot of the huge Tennessee River only two miles away and so, with the coming railroad, the city would have two ways to send its heavy goods to market.

Within five years of the company's formation, the population of the town shot up from 250 to 5,000. The price of real estate jumped by 300%. By 1890, the population was over 6,000 and Dayton was a bona fide boom town. Soon there were several elegant hotels, and a year-round resort known as Dayton Springs.

What no one in Dayton knew was that the parent company in Britain was in financial trouble from the start and that the boom was founded on debt and chaos. As far back as 1884, Titus Salt had been forced by lack of capital to sell much of his stock to James Watson and Co, Iron Merchants, of Scotland.

In December 1895 an explosion in one of the mines killed twenty-nine miners, including two boys, one aged fourteen, the other aged fifteen. The company, now entirely controlled by Watson, reorganised again, seeking to protect itself from possible law suits from the families of the victims. They need not have worried. The naïve Daytonians settled for between $125 to $400 per dead miner. In the next few years there were two more explosions, which killed another fifty miners. From the turn of the century, the company operated at a loss.

In June 1913, Peter Donaldson, President of both the Watson company and Dayton Coal and Iron, drove down to the Thames in London, chained himself into his car, and took the plunge. As the car took the man, so the British company took the American company. Dayton Coal and Iron was declared bankrupt in 1915 and the boom was over.

In 1924, with the population of Dayton shrunk from 6,000 to a mere 1,800, one last attempt was made to revive the mine. A company named The Cumberland Coal and Iron Company was formed and an engineer was employed to explore the mine's potential.

His name was George W. Rappleyea.

George, described variously as a chemical engineer and a metallurgical engineer, was from New York. He had married a local woman, Ova, a nurse he met in a Chattanooga hospital after he hurt himself playing touch football. In 1925, he was thirty-one years old. He had a grey-streaked mop of black hair which seemed to shoot directly up from his scalp. A short man, he always dressed well, favouring snappy suits, bow ties, and a straw boater. Fast-talking and jumpy, his eyes were dark brown behind round horn-rim glasses. He was not good-looking, but clearly his intelligence and energy made him attractive.

Always in motion, always busy, he danced and played tennis and drove his car too fast along the country roads as if he might miss something.

In 1925, prohibition was in full swing, along with heavy drinking, flappers, the Charleston, and art deco. The first issue of the *New Yorker* magazine was on sale. Scott Fitzgerald published *The Great Gatsby*, Theodore Dreiser, *An American Tragedy*, and an obscure Adolf Hitler, volume one of *Mein Kampf.* And on 4th May, before dinner, George read the ACLU announcement in the *Chattanooga Times*.

George, who had fully accepted the idea of evolution while in college, was outraged by the law. He saw immediately – and this is where his genius came in – that this was a big issue and could become a big trial which, apart from being important and fascinating, might also attract investors to the ailing town. The whole state had read the ad somewhere or other. Only George saw what it could mean. The next morning, he drove through town to F.E. Robinson's drugstore. Although there was some industry in the town, a lumber company, two canning factories, a hosiery mill, and Morgan Furniture manufacturing, all but one of the hotels, The Aqua, had closed down and the place had an empty, defeated quality. Robinson's drugstore, which had a soda fountain, was a thirty-second walk from the large three-storey courthouse, and was the social centre for the town's business elite. Fred Robinson, known as either the 'hustling druggist' or 'Doc', was also chairman of the school board. In typical Southern fashion, where politics and business so often commingle, his shelves were stocked with school books.

George told him his idea. If the trial was staged here, it would attract publicity to the town and then perhaps investment. Perhaps the mine could be brought back to life. George was convinced that no matter where the trial happened, it was going to be a historic event. Why not Dayton?

The Christians down in Dayton say the 'hustling druggist' was no more than that, that the entire appeal of the thing was in the hustle; but his family and people who knew him well, say Fred Robinson was a genuine believer in evolution. He was, after all, chairman of the school board. George and he called in some other civic leaders and the idea gained momentum. The group phoned the principal of the high school, who was also the biology teacher, and asked him if he'd care to be arrested, but he refused the honour. He was a family man. Attention soon focused on football coach, and young bachelor, John T. Scopes.

CHAPTER SIX

The Last Guest At The Magnolia House

Set in a half acre of unfenced garden dripping with rain, The Magnolia House is a big wooden ante-bellum Greek Revival house with a porch facing the street. There are two white rockers sitting on the porch, shaded by a vast magnolia tree which grows between the house and the sidewalk. Four tall and slender columns support an overhanging roof. A small balcony juts out above the front door. Before I've even rung the door I hear the clatter of boots and look up.

A large blonde woman, somewhat older and considerably heavier than the one in the photographs, appears on the balcony with a cigarette in her hand.

'Hold on,' she says, 'I'm on AOL talkin' with a guy in Atlanta. He has a boat.'

I wait outside, listening to the splatter of rain falling down the tree. Now I hear her boots again as she comes thumping downstairs and opens the door. She has slightly downturned eyes and a strong pointed nose. A faint air of suspicion lurks beneath her forthright manner. She has broad shoulders and narrow hips in tight pressed jeans over riding boots, all of which accentuate her confident strut. She's very much a woman, and yet she is a tomboy too, a sportswoman. A loose T-shirt veils her midsection. Two dachshunds scurry around her, barking.

Having greeted me warmly, ('How y'all doing?'), she leads me down a windowless corridor toward the back of the house. The day is a black-and-white photograph that wasn't left in the developer long enough, and in here it's even worse. What little light the day has to spare cannot penetrate the lace curtain on the front door nor creep in from the two large front rooms on either side. 75 watt bulbs excrete a dim yellow glow which is instantly consumed by the heavy wallpaper and the many dark antiques.

My room is on the left at the back. A huge wooden bed juts out diagonally from the far corner. More lace curtains prevent light from entering, but as far as I can see the place is tastefully done with more antiques and some historical pictures of Dayton. On a table just inside the door are some home-made cookies and a jug of water.

Even on this trip, the peasant brings his hoe, a laptop, so he can keep on toiling for the Squire. I've been writing a screenplay for MGM/UA. Set in Manhattan during the Christmas season, it's about a highly educated woman who uses chemical and biological warfare agents to intimidate the city into giving her millions of dollars.

I took the project because I needed the money and liked the studio people and the producer. I've done one draft, which is as scary as any thriller I've ever seen (too much so, as it will eventually turn out), but no one really likes it. It's too complicated here and not complicated enough there. I'm interested in the psychology of it, they're disappointed by the lack of action. It's doomed to fail and if I had any balls I'd walk away. The trouble is I need the money a rewrite would bring and, even more embarrassing, I've fallen in love with my characters. Like a sentimental nun at an orphanage, I can't bear to let them go into foster care. What if some hack comes along and stuffs a cigar and clichés in my hero's mouth, gives him a big pistol, and writes BLAM!!! KERCHUNK!!! every time he fires it? And what if my wonderfully intelligent, shamelessly erotic woman becomes coy and simpering? No, it's unthinkable.

So … I ask Gloria for a desk and set myself up for a couple of hours of work, a long, grovelling letter to the Lords Of The Manor: I failed with the tomatoes, please, *please* let me try tobacco.

My pathetic letter soon sickens me and I go in search of Gloria. She's upstairs in her den. The place is stuffed with antiques and dachshunds and ashtrays. The curtains are partially drawn and most of the light comes from a bulb mounted above a ceiling fan. This means the light flickers incessantly. The fan does not appear to cleanse the room of nicotine. She's taking pennies from a brass bowl stocked over many years and inserting them in cardboard tubes to take down to the bank. Her computer is in a corner, connected to AOL, and she glances at it hopefully, as a fisherman checks his float; but for the moment the e-males lurk elsewhere.

I ask her why she's selling the Magnolia House. She tells me she bought it after many years of saving and then married a man who should have been an ideal partner – he was a chef – but the marriage failed and he left her in debt.

'Now I gotta go back into retail. I've got a job up in Pennsylvania. Amish country. Imagine what the men are gonna be like up there.'

Her hoarse smoker's laugh hacks out. She ain't gonna whine, hell no, she's a survivor, tough as nails, donchoo worry. That being so, she jumps up and says she has a few errands to run and would I like to come with her and she'll show me some of the town along the way? I grab my notebook and join her outside. She has a Ford Explorer which she climbs into with a cigarette in one hand and a beaker of fluid in the other.

'Yep, when I leave here I'm off to Hershey, Pennsylvania,' she tells me as we set off. 'It's where they make the chocolate. They say they got street lamps in the shape of chocolate kisses.' In the melancholy process of closing down one dream, she's already reaching for another. Chocolate kisses, roses, and champagne: the heart is a lonely hunter but there's a Hallmark card at the end of every highway.

As we turn onto the main street a car goes by. Gloria raises four fingers of one hand while keeping its heel on the wheel.

'That's the steering wheel wave,' she says. 'If you like someone, it's like that. If it's just an acquaintance, it's this:' A single finger rises in polite acknowledgement. 'And on the subject of greetings, when you actually come face to face with someone? "Hey," never "Hi" or "Hello." Like this: "Hey, how ya doin'?" '

How *am* I doing? I'm doing fine. But I'm looking at the town and it's not how I imagined it. Dayton's population is now just over 6,000, about what it was a hundred years ago at the height of the boom. I had imagined a quaint Southern town done up for the tourists, but the place seems small and run-down and not very historic at all. I mention this to Gloria, who tells me a lot of old houses have been knocked down recently to make room for parking lots. A sign goes up saying, 'Another Parking Lot Brought To You By The Town Of Dayton.' These parking lots are for the tourists, who will of course stop coming if there aren't any old buildings left to see, and it's not until much later I realise this perfectly symbolises how Dayton feels about itself. It's proud such a historic event as the Scopes Trial took place here and happy to take the tourists' money; but it's also embarrassed because what H.L. Mencken ridiculed it for being in 1925 (a hick town full of 'yokels' and 'Neanderthal' fundamentalists) remains unchanged. In fact, even before the trial began, Dayton had qualms about how they might be viewed.

'Today, with the curtain barely rung up and the worst buffooneries to come,' wrote Mencken in a dispatch to the *Baltimore Evening Sun* in 1925, 'it is obvious to even the town boomers that getting upon the map, like patriotism, is not enough ... Two months ago the town was obscure and happy. Today it is a universal joke.'

Modern Daytonians prefer to talk about the economic promise of the highway or about the biggest La-Z-Boy plant in the US, which lies just outside of town and provides employment for around 2,000 men and women. As good Baptists, they must stick with Bryan; as men and women on the verge of the twenty-first century, they blush.

We drive along Main Street, a pretty but unkempt street with several vacant storefronts, past the place where Robinson's drugstore used to be – it's a furniture store now – and come to the Courthouse where the trial took place. Set back in the middle of a grass square, it's a tall, red brick building surrounded by old shade trees. It's beautiful in a way and unchanged since before the 20s. We park off to one side and enter.

Gloria struts in, toes turned out, good ol' boy tummy thrust forward, and engages all she meets with gregarious élan. 'Hey, how ya doin?' 'Yep, that's right. I'm closin' out, I'm on my way.' Everyone seems to like her ... but they also seem a little nervous of her too. Her mother's family is from here and she still has relatives, but she grew up in Los Angeles, only coming here for a year of school and during summer vacations. She must have been a real beauty in those days and if she doesn't have the circumspection of the small-town dweller now, in middle age, you can be sure she didn't then.

I wander outside and then down into the basement where the Scopes Museum is. It's open Monday to Friday from eight to four, but not on weekends when people might actually come to see it.

There are old photographs of Clarence Darrow, William Jennings Bryan and all the other characters. Darrow looks rumpled and exhausted but amiably pugnacious, Bryan prim and foolish with his palm fan and his pith helmet, confirming my impression of an aging actor still desperate for an audience. From the photographs, you see no sign of ill-health in Bryan, who would die a few days after the pictures were taken and the trial ended. Rappleyea is wiry and alert, with his huge brush of greying hair. John Scopes is young and handsome and shy. There are shots of Mencken and crowds of other press and radio reporters, and of 'Mendi the Monkey,' actually a trained chimpanzee, cranking the handle of a movie camera. It's a carnival, a vaudeville show on the subject of God. It must have been the most fun Dayton ever had.

I don't have time to read everything so I walk upstairs to the courtroom which is on the second floor. No one's there. It's a spacious court with large windows on three sides and it's quiet and impressive in its simplicity and I can imagine how it must have been during the trial, Darrow standing there, Bryan there, the jury – who in fact were almost never in court – over there and the judge issuing his rulings from the bench.

I go downstairs and find Gloria, who has registered whatever bureaucratic admission of failure is required and is ready to go. We drive over to City Hall, or some modern section of it over by the equally modern library, and while she clatters off in her boots, I read old framed news clippings on the wall. One of them tells of a local resident, W.C. Gardenhire, who returned from Fiji in 1871 bringing four Fijians whom he 'exhibited in Woodward Gardens in San Francisco, sometimes for $150, before selling them to P.T. Barnham for $20,000.' Gloria returns and we get back in the car and drive to the One Hour Photo out on the highway. I sit in the car. A weather-beaten woman parks her pick-up next to me, gets out, spits on the ground, and then enters the shop. Gloria comes out. The photographs she wanted aren't ready. 'As we say in the South,' she explains, ' "We're fixing to start thinking about getting ready to do it." '

We start driving around town.

There are two big events in Dayton these days. One is the Strawberry Festival. Strawberry farming has always been a large part of the local economy and this is its celebration. There are strawberry pie contests and all that kind of thing and a carnival comes to town. This latter draws all the rednecks out of the surrounding hills. Gloria says you can't imagine how they've been up there all year long and you haven't seen them, a scary crew, inbred retards, illiterates, and nuts. I'm devastated to have missed this, but I was busy poisoning New York when it happened and couldn't get away.

Still, I've got the *other* big event, which will take place in about a month. In fact I'm only down here as a prelude to that, to pick up local colour.

The other event is the 'Re-enactment of The Scopes Trial'. In most people's opinion the trial was a blow to the cause of fundamentalism. That the town would re-enact this humiliation each year – presumably to pull down some cash – strikes me as hilarious and I can't wait to see it. Gloria tells me that the real sheriff, Leon Sneed, actually plays the sheriff in the show. It is at this point that I decide for certain to make the play the centrepiece of my book.

As we continue driving around, I now see that Dayton is defined by two straight lines, the highway on one side and the railroad track on the other. The railroad goes from Atlanta to Chicago and carries only freight. Beyond the highway are some nice suburban houses scattered on the hillside. Beyond the tracks are the projects where most of Dayton's black people live. No black families live in the hills. One tried a few years back and the rednecks burned the house down.

We cross the track, which has barriers but no gates. According to Gloria – and it's confirmed later – more people have been killed on this section of track than on any other section *in the entire United States*.

No one seems to know exactly how many have been killed in the last decade, but it's approaching twenty. The railroad that brought Dayton to life and made it the number one city in Rhea County is now knocking off its citizens at an alarming rate. Six people were killed between March '96 and August '97. The train drivers call Dayton 'The Big Blow' because when they get to the edge of town they put their hand on the horn and keep it there until they make it out the other side. Why so many people have allowed themselves to be killed in this gruesome fashion is a mystery to everyone. And soon there's going to be another mystery.

The projects are not like city projects. Cheap but not egregiously ugly two-storey houses are dotted around a loop. There's not the same atmosphere of overcrowding and fear that you find up in Harlem or in Watts. Kids play amiably on the streets and sidewalks and residents stroll around gunless. I notice there are many kids of mixed race and remark on this to Gloria.

'Oh, yeah,' says Gloria, casually, 'there's a lot of that round here. A lot of the white girls think it's sexy.'

I ask her how she feels about this.

'I don't care who has sex with who,' she replies, driving with her knee and drawing on her cigarette between sips of the unspecified fluid, 'so long as they love each other, but I was always attracted to Caucasians.'

'And lots of them, I would imagine,' I say, flatteringly.

It doesn't get the laugh I expected. Instead she glances at me flatly and then looks forward again before saying with just a hint of weariness:

'Yep, I always liked men. Even when I was a kid my mommy says I'd go up to a guy and cling to his leg and call him "daddy". I guess that tells you something about how much my daddy was around.'

When we get back to the Magnolia House, Gloria proudly shows me around her garden. 'These are my Elephant Ear, these are my hollyhocks, these are my gladioli.' She stares down sadly. 'I ain't even gonna be around when my gladioli bloom.'

We walk around the side of the house.

'These are Cantors, gettin' ready to bloom. This is a Dinner Plate ... shit I forget the name of it, anyway, it was real hard to come by, I had to order it, and this is its second year and it'll bloom this year for the first time. It blooms these flowers that are just awesome.' She stares down at the plant and then moves on. 'These are getting ready to bloom. And these are getting ready to bloom,' she says, her voice sadder each time.

We move to the front of the house where the magnolia tree stands. It's an old, extensive tree which grows high above the house and all around the front and is much of the reason why the house is so dark inside. There's something exquisitely Southern about the magnolia. It's a beautiful, overloaded tree with large, exotic white flowers that smell sweet and languorous, but at the same time it's nothing but trouble.

'Damn thing never stops,' says Gloria, 'sheds all the time, all year round: leaves, acorns, fuzzballs, the blossoms, then the leaves again, then the fuzzballs ... Drives you nuts.' She grabs hold of a branch with a flower on it and poses as I take a photograph.

That evening, Gloria has to have dinner with some neighbours. Rhea County, in which Dayton lies, is as dry today as it was in 1925, but it's unclear quite what this means and it certainly doesn't seem to stop anyone drinking. You can cross the county line, get drunk, and drive back. You can open a hunting or fishing club and serve liquor there, and for some reason no one seems to understand, the restaurant where I'll eat tonight, Ayola's Mexican Restaurant, is allowed to serve beer. However, in the house where Gloria is going, they don't drink, so she reaches into the refrigerator (we're hanging out in the kitchen, smoking) and takes out a square cardboard flagon of white wine which she purchased in Chattanooga. She hefts the thing up under her arm and expertly squirts herself a substantial drink. Then she asks me, would I like a glass?

Since I was fourteen, I have always drunk too much. Drinking too much is the way you drink in England. It's the point. I have friends there who consume eight pints of beer every single night. Eight *pints*. An aborigine can live for a month on eight pints of liquid, and wash himself off with what's left at the end of it. In my twenties, I was arrested, thrown in jail, and banned from driving for a year for drunk-driving. (I was also, to my surprise and the amusement of the court, charged with 'attempting to bribe a Metropolitan Policeman with a sausage.' I'd stopped outside an all-night sausage vending outfit in Notting Hill in a futile attempt to sober up and when the cop arrived, I offered to buy him one too.) Because of alcohol I drove away my first wife and lost several friends. I've made career-killing, weirdly coherent but utterly sinister remarks to studio executives who remember what I said fifteen years later and back away as I approach on toes curling with shame. I've seduced women of all ages, both beautiful and ugly (and one who was beautiful but weighed 300 pounds), and even woke up one morning with a perky young woman I'd never seen before, who asked if I really did want to marry her because she had always wanted to marry an English film director, which I then was. Worse still, I've damaged my memory, lost hours to blackouts, and wasted years of life on hangovers and alcohol-related despair.

Of course, I'd love a glass.

I walk a line. I've been to Alcoholics Anonymous once or twice, once with my mother, whom I tricked into coming to an unfortunately glamorous meeting at Cedars-Sinai in Los Angeles, where she promptly fell into a rebellious sleep, dressed in her Marks and Spencer slacks, snoring, while I, mortified, watched one gorgeous, vulnerable, sexually exploitable, corn-fed, would-be model/actress take the stand and 'fess up to crimes of abandon, each one more arousing than the next. And the point is, in spite of the voyeuristic fascination of it all, AA is not for me. Not if it's *me* who eventually has to go up there and tell the awful truth, and certainly not if I have to prostrate my ego before 'A Higher Power.'

So what I do is this: every now and then I stop drinking for a year. I swim a mile a day (which I do in under thirty minutes, on the wagon or off) and when I come back – back to the thousand gloriously depraved memories conjured by the lush sensation of red wine flooding my sinuses, one of which is the curious phenomenon that no matter where I am, all I can smell is cheap scent and nicotine-saturated nightclub banquettes – I return with a store of other memories, of a year of clarity devoid of guilt, and I find that the next year I drink in moderation. This see-saw behaviour is the essence of who I am: a stable individual if you take the long view.

I'm about due for some abstinence. Shortly before I came down here to Dayton I was arrested for drunk-driving in Upstate New York. I was merely speeding. I was not very much over the limit. But it is embarrassing. I'm married now. I have a daughter. A twenty-year-old drunk can be amusing. A 47-year-old drunk is merely forlorn. I'm not a drunk, you understand, not since I had my daughter, but I have the *fear* of it. To make matters worse, I'm applying for American citizenship and this doesn't look good. A second offence while awaiting trial, even down here in Tennessee, would be disastrous.

Another glass?

Of course.

Clarence Darrow

When Gloria goes off to dinner, I drive cautiously to Ayola's which is just outside of town, towards the La-Z-Boy factory. The low-slung restaurant stands alone on the left side of the road and I've already pulled into the middle lane to make the turn when I see the place is surrounded by cop cars. If I drive on now it will look suspicious. I cross oncoming traffic and park. Now, obviously, I have to go in. Where else would I be going?

Six cops feed at a large table facing the door. They watch me as I enter. I take a table as far away as possible without looking as if I'm taking a table as far away as possible, and order some burritos from a Mexican waiter with one dead eye. When I look up again, the cops are still watching me. I nod. They don't nod back. After a while, three of them leave and stand outside. The oldest of them, a tough little cracker with an enviable head of dark, slicked-back hair, takes out some chewing tobacco, thrusts a wad inside his cheek, chews once or twice, spits on the ground, and meets my eye.

A consequence of my battle with education is a deep and real fear of authority. No amount of defiant contempt can quell a surge of adrenalin during moments such as these. My entire childhood was one protracted sin against the system. I have sinned so much it's still spilling out of the pockets of my psyche, metaphorical condoms and burning cigarettes visible to anyone who's looking. Even to visit my daughter's school, an Upper East Side girl's school where most of the fathers are bankers in suits, and where I used to get stopped from entering – 'Where do you think you're going?' 'I'm a father. I have a daughter here' – even here, where I've come to realise I'm now almost *liked*, I start to sweat with fear as soon as I enter, and once I'm in I'll always find a way to make some inappropriate crack to someone, just to show I'm not afraid, this habit making every trip to school sheer torture for Denise, who, though outspoken and with her own fund of illicit peccadilloes, was always a good girl in school and remains a woman who would rather fit in than not.

The other cops now lumber to their feet, pay laboriously, and leave the restaurant. But then they too hang around outside, laughing and glancing at me. I order another glass of iced tea from the one-eyed waiter to kill more time. Somebody must commit a crime in Dayton sooner or later. Some hick must crash his pick-up, prostrate himself upon the tracks, or detonate his shack while brewing moonshine. *Something* has to happen to distract these cops from their endless spitting and strutting. And finally it does. Their radios crackle and they all jump into their vee-hickles and rush off.

Confident that adrenalin must by now have flushed my system of alcohol, I leave the restaurant and drive into town. In the humid evening, its quiet, tree-lined streets allow one to imagine a more peaceful era, the small-town America of myth, a pre-delinquent time when – so long as you weren't black – you had a better chance of dying of typhoid than from a bullet. I stop outside the Courthouse and listen to summer sounds not unlike those of my village childhood in England, lawnmowers, a distant shout, the crack of a ball against a bat. I drive across Main Street and find the high school where John Scopes taught. It's still light, so I park the car, get out, and stroll around. The school is two storeys high, a squat, long building, municipal and uninteresting. I know, however, that it has been considerably rebuilt in the last seventy-five years. I wonder how it looked on the afternoon of 5th May 1925 when the 24-year-old John Scopes was playing tennis on one of the courts behind the main building.

School term had ended four days earlier, but Scopes, who came from Kentucky, had stuck around because of a girl. Having never seen her around town before, he asked flirtatiously if this was because she spent her whole life in church, singing hymns and praying. She replied that indeed her family was involved in the church and if he wanted to see her again he'd have to attend a church social which would take place a few days after school let out.

John stayed and became, in the curious and sometimes painful way of these things, famous. His autobiography's title, *Center Of The Storm*, accurately describes his role in the affair, but only if you think

62

of a storm as having an eye. His name became known all over the world, but in the trial itself he never took the stand and anything he said was overshadowed by the grand figures who paraded around him. None the less, he was perfectly cast for the role. His father, a machinist on the railroads and an important member of the recently formed Machinists Union, was an agnostic and freethinker. A self-educated working-class man, he often read to John at night. Together, they had even read some of Darwin's work.

John had already had one memorable encounter with William Jennings Bryan when he delivered the commencement address at Scopes' high school graduation. The Sunday before, John and some friends had been preached to by a Minister whose loose false teeth caused him to whistle his sibilants. This had caused an outbreak of giggles, and when Bryan began his speech a week later and whistled his first "s", John and three others laughed. So unused was Bryan to being laughed at that when he met Scopes in 1925, six years later, he recognised him and reminded him of the occasion.

Between high school and college, John worked on the railroads and spent a while as a hobo before finally enrolling at the University of Kentucky. He had been teaching at Dayton High School only a year and was not a biology teacher but a general science teacher and football coach. Good-looking, charming, funny, free-spirited, and athletic, he was well liked by his students. The daily assemblies so bored him he found a way to take a group of students down into the science lab where he let them discuss whatever they liked while he smoked cigarettes and listened. On Saturday nights he went to the dance up at Morgan Springs, a resort in the hills above town. Amusingly, in light of current attitudes, he says in his autobiography, without a trace of shame, that his dates were usually high school seniors.

About halfway through the match, as Scopes was about to serve, he noticed a small boy arrive and sit quietly beside the court to watch the game. When it was time to change sides, he came over to Scopes and told him Fred Robinson would like to see him down at the drugstore as soon as it was convenient. John finished the set and then, still sweating, strolled through town toward the drugstore.

When he arrived, he found a group of men gathered around one of the tables. Apart from Rappleyea and Robinson there was now Sue

Hicks, city attorney (and subject of the song, 'A Boy Named Sue'), Wallace Haggard, known as 'Mr Dayton,' banker and lawyer, and a Mr Brady, who owned the town's other drugstore. Several more people would claim to have been there, but these are the ones Scopes remembers.

Rappleyea asked if it was possible to teach biology without teaching evolution. Scopes said no and took down a textbook from one of Robinson's shelves, *Hunter's Civic Biology*. This had been used in Tennessee schools since 1909 and Scopes showed the men the book's explanation of evolution. Robinson asked him if he'd ever used the book and Scopes said he had, although he wasn't sure if he'd taught evolution from it, even when he was subbing for the biology teacher toward the end of the year.

This did not seem to bother anyone. This would do for the moment. Robinson asked Scopes if he'd be willing to let his "name be used" in a test of the constitutionality of the Butler Act forbidding such teaching? Scopes said okay. He could not possibly have imagined how profoundly his life would be changed by this casual decision.

Sue Hicks and his brother, Herbert Hicks, also an attorney for the city, were dubious about the teaching of evolution, but were equally dubious about the law's constitutionality. However, they agreed to prosecute the case and a warrant was sworn out charging Scopes with violating the law. The "Hustling Druggist," wanting to get the publicity going immediately, called the *Chattanooga Times* and told them Dayton had "arrested" one of its teachers for teaching evolution. Rappleyea wired the ACLU.

John Scopes walked back to the high school and continued playing tennis. Within a few years, an academic life would become impossible for him.

On 13th May 1925, William Jennings Bryan offered his services to the prosecution. He hadn't practised law for forty years, but he was a big draw and Dayton was not about to turn him down. The town was already puffing itself up for the big event. A Scopes Trial Entertainment Committee had been formed to find housing for the expected visitors and press, and the merchants were already rubbing their hands together in glee.

At this point, the most famous lawyer in America, Clarence Darrow, entered the picture. Darrow is one of my heroes, a compassionate humanist with a sense of humour. Enraged by injustice and wary of superstition, he loathed pomposity, cruelty, and hypocrisy and carried a linguistic sword capable of puncturing them all.

Darrow was born in 1857 and raised in Kinsman, Ohio. His father, rather like Scope's father, was an agnostic freethinker, an outsider in a rural religious community. Clarence, though clearly bright, did not do particularly well in school. In his late teens, he was, however, sufficiently qualified to teach young children in his home town. In his biography of him, *Clarence Darrow For The Defense*, Irving Stone describes how Darrow was much loved by his students for abolishing all corporal punishment. On Saturday nights there was a debate in town, followed by a dance. Darrow, alone in his agnostic views, relished being an absolute minority in these debates, some of which were staged in front of as many as five hundred people. Again like Scopes, he loved to dance. It was at one of the dances which followed these debates that he met his first wife, Jessie.

After three years of teaching, he decided he might be interested in law and with financial help from two of his six siblings went to law college at Ann Arbor, Michigan. He found his teachers boring and preferred to work alone and formulate his own opinions. After less than a year, he came home. He took a menial job in an attorney's office in a nearby town, and began teaching himself the law. At twenty-one he went before a committee of local lawyers who pronounced him qualified.

He married Jessie and for a few years was an ordinary country lawyer. One day, someone he didn't like asked him in a patronising tone how he was doing. He told them he was doing so well he was moving to Chicago. Having said this, he felt compelled to follow through.

During his first year in Chicago, he had almost no work. Partly as a way of looking for cases and partly out of genuine interest, he got involved in Democratic politics and social issues. A local judge named John P. Altgeld had written a book which greatly impressed him. *Our Penal Machinery And Its Victims* made the case that social injustice in the form of poverty and lack of opportunity was what caused crime and that harsh punishment not only compounded the injury but created further resentment leading to further crime. Darrow eventually met with Altgeld and the two became friends. With Altgeld's help, Darrow got a job as special-assessment attorney for the city. Four years later, he was offered a job with the Chicago and North Western Railway, which he took for the money.

He bought a house, repaid the brother and sister from whom he'd borrowed money, and kept the job until 1894 when the American Railway Union went on strike in sympathy with workers of the Pullman Palace Car Company. When Darrow heard about the strike, he went out to where George Pullman had built a town for his workers.

Named eponymously by its creator, the town of Pullman was advertised as 'a perfectly equipped town of twelve thousand inhabitants ... bordered by bright beds of flowers and green velvety stretches of lawn ... the homes, even to the most modest, are bright and wholesome and filled with pure air and light.' What Darrow found was a fiefdom. The workers were forced to rent the substandard houses at 25% above the going rate; all savings had to be deposited in the company bank; and anyone trying to join or form a union was fired and his name put on a blacklist which was then distributed to every railroad in the country.

Since the panic of 1893, the same one that speeded the decline of Dayton Coal and Iron, a Pullman worker's set wages of $3.20 a day had dropped to a maximum piecework rate of $1.20 a day. Hungry and exhausted men fainted on the production line. When Pullman was asked to lower rents on the houses, he refused in spite of the fact that the Pullman Company was doing good business and was valued at $36 million. In desperation, with their children on the verge of starvation, the Pullman employees organised. Extracting a promise from Pullman that he would not fire them, they sent a delegation of forty-three men to petition him in person. After they had spoken to the vice-president, Pullman stormed into the room and told them he had nothing to say to them and the next day they were all fired.

The workers struck and shortly thereafter the American Railway Union, led by Eugene Debs, joined the strike, refusing to move any train with a Pullman car on it.

Having visited the town of Pullman, Darrow went down to the stockyards and watched the strikers. They had been portrayed in the press as lawless, violent anarchists and socialists. Darrow found them determined but peaceful. When, in clear violation of law, Federal troops became strike-breakers and started moving trains out of the yard, fighting broke out and shots were fired. Three men died immediately and many others, women included, were beaten and bayoneted.

Darrow, who was now thirty-seven, resigned his railroad job. When Eugene Debs was arrested on charges of criminal conspiracy, Darrow took on his defence. The strike continued until, out of money and with the church and the press against them, the men finally gave in and went back to work for the same wages.

In a Senate Hearing to investigate the cause of the riot, Pullman was forced to admit that during the year in which he had slashed wages below subsistence level his company had declared a profit dividend of $2,800,000. 'My duty is to my stockholders and to my company,' he stated. 'There was no reason to give those working men a gift of money.' This was the climate in which both Clarence Darrow and William Jennings Bryan were formed.

Darrow lost the case and Debs was sentenced to six months in jail. Debs became a hero and Darrow found the kind of law he wanted to practise. Over the next two decades, he represented poor criminals, underdogs of all kinds, unions, and working men. He established the legal right of workers to strike in the Woodworkers' Conspiracy Trial. Through his work with the United Mine Workers, he revealed the use of child labour in the mines and the terrible conditions under which all miners worked.

Although his views were 'radical' his style was folksy and conversational. Scruffy, rumpled, snapping at his suspenders, slouching against the rail, he came across like a country lawyer, a man you could trust, a simple man bemused at how 'cleverer folk' couldn't see obvious human truth at the heart of things. As an agnostic, he despised the hypocritical cruelty and rigidity of organised religion. More interested in compassion than condemnation, in understanding than vengeance, he was passionately opposed to the death penalty.

In 1924, he undertook the defence of Leopold and Loeb, two Chicago rich kids who had kidnapped and murdered another boy just to see if they could get away with it. They had been caught, eventually confessed, and now faced the death penalty. Darrow by this time was sixty-seven and had been involved in 102 death penalty cases.

Guilt or innocence was not in question. The best Darrow could do was stop the boys from being hanged and instead get them life in prison. This was all their families asked for and they begged him to help, promising him any amount of money for his services. Darrow, champion of the poor, knew he'd be attacked on all sides as a sell-out if he took the case. On the other hand, it was an opportunity not only to save the lives of the boys, but to widely publicise the issue of capital punishment. He suggested his fee should be left to the Bar Association to decide after the event and signed on, taking only a $10,000 retainer.

If ever two people deserved execution, Leopold and Loeb would seem to be they. The crime was premeditated and perverse. Both boys were rich and highly intelligent. Richard Loeb, an athletic, handsome boy of seventeen was the youngest ever graduate of the University of Michigan. Since the age of fourteen, he had been obsessed with crime and had conceived the murder/kidnapping as a way of proving he was capable of 'the perfect crime.' During the investigation, he hung around with the police, offering advice. Nathan Leopold, who was eighteen, was the youngest graduate of the University of Chicago. He was as ugly as Richard was handsome, but according to Darrow had 'the most brilliant intellect' he had ever encountered in a boy. He spoke nine languages, was an advanced botanist, and had read all of Nietzsche's books. He believed himself to be a Nietzschean superman, a man so superior to others that moral codes did not apply to him.

Unfortunately, he fell in love with Richard who consented to a homosexual relationship so long as Nathan became his sidekick in petty crime and finally murder. Neither boy showed any remorse.

In his argument for the defense, Darrow sought to show that his theory of criminal behaviour being the result of a unique combination of genetic and environmental forces beyond the criminal's control applied as much to the rich as to the poor, and that compassion was in order even for these two. He believed both boys were abnormal if not mad. A psychiatrist for the state, however, declared them sane. Dr Krohn always declared everyone sane, and in so doing had condemned many men to death. Here Darrow compared the motives of Richard Loeb with those of Dr Krohn:

'As I think of the story of Dick trailing that little boy around, there comes to my mind a picture of Dr Krohn – for sixteen years going in and out of the courtrooms of this building and other buildings, trailing victims without regard to their name or sex or age or surroundings. But he had a motive, and his motive was cash ... One was the mad act of a child; the other the cold, deliberate act of a man getting his living by dealing in blood.'

In answering the proposition that the killers deserved the same fate as their victim, he declared that if the state was not kinder and more humane than these two mad children then he was sorry he had lived so long. He described in detail what a hanging entailed, the months of waiting, the useless hope of relatives and condemned man alike, the final day, being woken at dawn, the long walk to the scaffold, the feet being tied and stood upon the trapdoor, the black cap drawn over the head, the hangman pressing back the spring ... He was aware, he went on, that this would bring 'immense satisfaction' to some people. He spoke with pity and contempt of the cruelty of righteous indignation, and disparaged the easy assurance with which men speak of justice.

Who really knows what justice is? No man, he argued, can suffi- ciently understand another, know the billions of biological and genetic forces and the millions of incidents in his life, the humiliations and cruelties that formed him. No man can grasp the enormity of these influences and say, 'Had all these forces acted on me, *I* could have resisted them.' And no mere mortal has the omniscience required to assess these elements, judge them, and then extinguish a life because of them.

Many bizarre and painful facts came out about the boys. Nathan Leopold had all kinds of physical problems, including an adrenal deficiency and a diseased thyroid that was thought to have led to far too early a sexual development. Some other malady had given him round shoulders, an abdomen which stuck out weirdly, and extremely coarse hair. Because he was shy around girls, his parents had, to his great embarrassment, sent him to an all-girls school. Later on, when he was fourteen, a governess forced him to perform oral sex on her.

Richard Loeb's problems were less apparent but can be inferred from the behaviour of his parents. Before the murder he was given a car, an allowance of $250 a month, and access to whatever other money he required from his father's secretary. After the murder, his father never once came to visit him, did not attend the trial, and refused to hear his name mentioned from then on.

Everything, Darrow argued, has a cause, including crime. To attempt to terrorise people out of criminal activity is futile. The only cure for the problem is to understand it, as doctors do with disease. To execute the boys would not only be morally wrong and cruel, but pointless. Far better to keep them alive and study them.

Toward the end of his two-day speech, the exhausted Darrow said:

'I am pleading for the future; I am pleading for a time when hatred and cruelty will not control the hearts of men, when we can learn by reason and judgement and understanding and faith that all life is worth saving, and that mercy is the highest attribute of man.'

Leopold and Loeb were given life in prison.

As if proving Darrow's theories, at least on the 'nurture' front, the parents of the boys neglected to pay him. When he finally sent a note requesting that they at least talk about the bill, they wrote back saying the suggested arbitration by the Bar Association was unfair to them because Darrow was a lawyer himself and therefore at an advantage. Would he suggest a figure? He and his firm had spent months on the case. He suggested $200,000. The families came back at $75,000. Disgusted, Darrow agreed and told them to send a cheque. The next day it arrived.

It was for $70,000. Darrow banked it.

Because of the Leopold and Loeb case, the ACLU were against Darrow getting involved in the trial. It had made him too famous and they feared he'd turn the Scopes Trial into even more of a circus than it already was. Worse still, he'd focused attention on Nathan Leopold's fascination with Nietzsche. He had even suggested it was partly his interest in the idea of the Superman, of the survival of the fittest, which had inched him closer to the crime, and this seemed like an obvious gift to the prosecution. Hadn't Darrow already proved their case for them? Wasn't this precisely the danger of teaching evolution? Darrow himself had thought of this problem and decided not to get involved, but when he heard that Bryan was in, he could not resist the challenge.

He offered his services in so public a manner that the ACLU was forced to accept, particularly when Scopes himself – he was, after all, the defendant – turned out to be a huge admirer of Darrow and said he liked the idea of being represented by him.

And so the play was cast and the stage set.

I walk back to the car and drive slowly through town toward the Magnolia House, thinking how sad it is that three-quarters of a century ago, Darrow was in despair at the judicial system's barbarity and defeatism, and nothing has changed. When you contemplate the blind refusal of even sophisticated Americans to acknowledge that crime must have a cause which, if understood, would undoubtedly lead to a remedy far more effective than the slammed door of harsh punishment, you cannot help but wonder if this is because the cause is so *hard* to find or because it might be so *easy*? Are they afraid that to probe beneath the surface of this land of Christian promise would instantly expose a rebuke to their very existence, a starving shadow-race which has for generations been denied either spiritual or material opportunity? And if this were so, what, as decent Americans, would they be forced to do?

It is almost heretical to say, but obvious none the less, that so long as 95 per cent of the wealth is held by 5 per cent of the population, those whose snouts are excluded from the golden trough are liable to express their discontent in crime. Like everyone else, however, Americans love their illusions and would far rather suffer the consequences of crime than face the ramifications of its cure: with Communism dead, is it time to take a critical look at capitalism?

Beyond this disturbing question lies an even less appealing one: why is America, a country where 98 per cent of the people believe in God and over 50 per cent believe in the literal existence of angels, why is this so holy place *infested* with serial killers, rapists, paedophiles – often men of the cloth – drug addicts, gangs, cults, and madmen? Why, in short, isn't Christianity having the advertised effect?

CHAPTER EIGHT

Gloria In Excelsis Deo

I find Gloria up in her den, smoking and drinking and somehow finding limbs free to peck out messages on AOL, ('u r 2 Sweet,') and stuff clothes into suitcases, among them a hot pink one, the last of a set given her when she was a child.

She offers me some wine and I take it. The light flickers gloomily as we talk. Freight trains, hooting their horns to avoid killing more Daytonians, pass by every now and then, making the house vibrate even though the track is a quarter of a mile away. At one point Gloria gets up and goes into the next room, her bedroom. I can see her reflection in the glass front of a cabinet. She's undressing! She seems to be getting into some light blue medical scrubs such as surgeons wear when they're about to cut you up!

Have I fallen into a Roald Dahl story? Is she going to skin me and take my epidermis with her up to Hershey to see the street lamps in the shape of kisses? She returns in the scrubs and I see that the legs have been cut off about six inches above the knee. I make no comment and she falls back onto the sofa. I'm not sure if my being here cheers her up and distracts her, or if I'm just another irritating bump on the road out. Either way, she's friendly and open, and before long she tells me her story.

Her maternal grandmother owned a farm in Dayton but was forced to sell it by the Tennessee Valley Authority. The TVA administered a huge endeavour involving dams and reservoirs and hydroelectric plants. Intended to bring prosperity to one of the poorest regions of America, it succeeded to a large extent. Gloria's Aunt Ruth and several other family members stayed in Dayton, but her grandmother and mother moved to Los Angeles where they ran a boarding house. Gloria's mother married a mysterious Filipino war hero who had worked for the US fighting the Japanese and had been caught and tortured. Later, it was rumoured he went crazy and shot a lot of people in Manila. There was a price on his head so the Americans allowed him to immigrate and change his name. He became an alcoholic hairdresser in Hollywood. When Gloria was young, he'd sit her on his knee and say, 'Your daddy's gonna die young.' When she was four, he left, and when she was seven he fulfilled his prediction, dying, I believe, of cirrhosis of the liver at the age of thirty-four. He was buried in Long Beach military cemetery with full honours and Gloria and her sister received $15,000 each from the government.

Her mother then married a rich but mean-spirited man who Gloria remembers with great distaste. The marriage didn't last.

Third time out, her mother found true love in the form of Steve Brodie whom she met at a singles gathering at the Hilton in Beverly Hills. Brodie was an actor who played bad guys in Westerns. In life he was the reverse. Kind and gentle, he treated Gloria and her sister as if they were his own and Gloria adored him.

Gloria often spent summer vacations in Dayton, but when she was fourteen she came for a year, staying with her Aunt Ruth who ran a flower shop out of the Aqua Hotel. She was a cheerleader at the high school. She was beautiful and from out of town and God knows what the local boys made of her. Her best friend was named Bobby-Sue.

At fifteen she returned to California and promptly ran away, became a flower child, and hitched around the state. She returned a year later and graduated from Encino High and then did two years of college at Long Beach. But, still in her late teens, before she even went to college, she married the first of three husbands, a 36-year-old guitar player and professional hunter. Being so much older, the husband knew everything and was right about everything, which irritated Gloria. One Christmas while listening to the hymn, 'Gloria In Excelsis Deo,' Gloria said, 'Oh, listen, they're singing about me.' The husband said the word was not 'Gloria' but some other word. Gloria said, 'No, it's Gloria.' He said, 'No, it's not.' Gloria said, 'Listen, I can't be wrong all the time. Sometimes I have to be right.'

They argued. Gloria left. The marriage was over.

She was twenty-one and didn't get married again for another ten years, during which time she got some kind of degree out of Arizona State, and entered 'retail'. When she was thirty-one she married a guy who owned the oldest bar in Long Beach. He was her age, but a spoiled rich kid and smoked a lot of pot. The marriage lasted until she was about thirty-eight. Her retail career, which had begun at Contempo Casuals, ended with her being the District Manager of Target Stores in Los Angeles, and later in Atlanta.

One day, shortly after her second marriage ended, she saw a lump of chewing gum on the floor of her store in Torrance. She bent over to scrape it off and an avalanche of toys fell on her back, injuring her. She took some time off and was then transferred to Atlanta. She had already bought the Magnolia House, having seen it on one of her periodic visits. For twelve years, she had worked on it whenever she could, restoring it in vacations, paying others to work on it whenever she had money. It would be the only first-class bed and breakfast in Dayton and it would provide her with a constant flow of interesting guests to satisfy her gregarious nature. Now in Atlanta and only a couple of hours drive away, she soon had the the place almost finished. All she needed to make her dream a reality was someone to help her run it.

Her third husband was a chef and restaurant manager. A good-looking thirty-five to her ... well, at this point her age starts to disobey the usual laws of mathematics (she's 38, four years go by, and she's still not 40, and even I can tell there's something off) ... But anyway, he was younger than her, and perfect. He would do all the cooking, she would run the business.

And so it was for a year, and the place did well and they were happy. Then he started getting jealous and abusive. She could not even look at another man without his screaming at her when they got home. He was even jealous of her girlfriends. After a while, he refused to answer the phone, even if Gloria was out. It became her job to buy the food. She'd go to the store, leaving him to greet incoming guests and return to be told they'd not arrived. Later they would call from the Best Western outside of town, saying no one answered the door. The husband would swear they never showed and then, when she remonstrated with him, he'd yell, 'Fuck them! They're lying. Who are you going to believe, them or me?'

Unable to count on him for anything, and wanting at all costs to avoid arguments which were becoming increasingly frightening ('We got through eight mobile phones, him throwin' them at me'), she began to do everything herself. As business began to go down, his spending rose. He bought eight guns and hid them in the garage.

Then it got even worse.

He'd go to the hardware store and not come back for two days.

'He always came in, the door *slammed*. Then he'd say, "So what the fuck's your problem? Go on, tell me!" I'd go, "I don't have a problem." "Wanna know what I did?" he'd yell. "Okay, I went out, met somebody at the store, played poker, what else the fuck is there to do in this town?"'

When Gloria simply said she wanted to go back to sleep, he'd say 'You don't talk. How are we gonna resolve anything if we don't talk?' She'd point out that every time they talked he would end up yelling at her. 'Well,' he'd then say, 'our marriage is going down the tubes and it's never going to be resolved if you can't talk ...'

In other words, it was all her fault. Sociable and lively Gloria sank into a prolonged silence. He began doing coke. He'd get $500 cash advances out of her account using a card. If that didn't work, he'd buy things with a credit card and sell them for cash. Clearly he was screwing around too, perhaps he had been from the start. A tough, capable woman, Gloria could not understand how she was allowing herself to be treated like this. Her friends, equally perplexed, and finding the tension unbearable, drifted away.

One day, she drove to a bookshop in Chattanooga and scanned the self-help shelves for advice. She found a book on verbal abuse and bought it. It described her husband perfectly and stated that the next step would be physical abuse. It told her not to engage. If he lost his temper she was to look at him and in a calm voice state, 'I will not allow you to disrespect me that way and until you can talk to me cordially, I have nothing to say,' and walk out of the house. Of course, it was hard to run a hotel under these conditions and soon the Magnolia House was deeply in the red.

Gloria became convinced he was trying to sabotage the business so they'd be forced to sell the house and he could then take off with 'his' half of the money. She found a secret box of his with credit cards she didn't know about and a camcorder he'd bought recently and hidden. Using the cash card, he began to drain the bank account and build up a stash. Still she continued with her strategy of non-engagement. It infuriated him, but what could he do? He wanted to fight her but she wasn't there. She had a friend with a farm above town and would go up and do yardwork or ride one of the horses through the hills.

'I did that for three months,' she tells me, 'by the fourth month he was ready to go.' When the credit cards hit their limits, he left.

For a while, she tried to run the place alone, but the interest on the cards was too high: the debt he had caused could not be paid through the enterprise they had created. It got worse with every week, growing exponentially as these things do. It became clear that the only way she could escape the debt was to sell.

Soon after she'd made this decision, the husband phoned. He was in bad shape and begged to come back. In spite of everything, Gloria still loved him in a way, but she knew it was hopeless and told him so. He started crying and saying how much he loved her. He'd come back and help her 'catch up on the bills.'

'Look,' she said, 'I don't have no money. You've ruined me. I'm done.'

And then she hung up.

Now she's on her way to a chilly town in Pennsylvania, back into retail on the wrong side of forty. Undaunted.

CHAPTER NINE

My Mother

Downstairs, my bed is huge and comfortable, but when I turn over it creaks loudly. I hear the hoot of an approaching train and then the house starts to tremble. The train is so long that when the last car beats by and the engine hoots again it's already a distant sound far off in the night.

I try to go to sleep, but can't. My mind plunges inexplicably from one disturbing image to another and I cannot stop it. I feel certain that my mother, from whom I inherited the Darwin gene, suffered similarly, as did her mother, whose episodes of anxiety and manic depression were so severe they put her in the asylum. Clare's superficial, almost humorous pessimism – no picnic could take place without rain, all dinners were doomed to failure – was something we laughed at; but we knew her gloom was real and profound and her imagination uncontrollably tortured. Eventually she sought relief in alcohol and died from it.

I choose to vent my imagination through writing, by grinding and reshaping life. It has enabled me to survive, both financially and psychologically, but it has also been a curse. In a letter to his wife, quoted in the John Bowlby biography, Darwin, who worked seven days a week as I do, says, 'how fortunate I am to have plenty of employment … for being employed alone makes me forget myself.' I think it was Flaubert who said the same thing in a different way. 'We don't write to live, we write in order *not* to live.' I stay in my room, in my invented world, absorbed in play. No one looks at me in disgust except myself, and if I can trick myself into a productive trance, even that diminishes. I am only really comfortable when 'I' am lost.

But, as with all addictions, there are side effects. Every day, you stimulate a kind of mental infection. The brain's septicaemia is released, oozes up toward the surface, and makes itself accessible to your nib. The transfer of this substance from brain to paper is the transmogrification of chaos into order, and so long as the brain is narrowly engaged in this activity, all is well: the illusion of meaning, of release, of cure even, is maintained and apprehension is held at bay. But when the day is over, sometimes it is impossible to stem the flow provoked in the morning. The infection continues to produce pus, but no nib is there to draw it off. At best, I feel removed. At worst, apprehension blossoms into anxiety, paranoia even. Perhaps this is why so many writers become alcoholics. They attempt through drinking to experience life directly, as others do, as it *is,* not as it might be, and discover, over and over again that reality cannot compare to the fermented emotion of their imagined worlds. For me the use of alcohol, at least in sufficient quantities to make me feel part of the community of man, carries too great a price. A hangover renders me incapable of taking to the streets. Cornices and air conditioners will fall on me, terrorists have poisoned the air, and everyone I love is dying. Should all this somehow be miraculously prevented, it is only so I can die alone and mediocre, back in the slug-infested basements of my early twenties.

When it's time to sleep, I lie on my back, a book suspended above me on locked arms. When I can no longer hold my arms up, when I've read the same sentence ten times, when I feel oblivion close enough to fall into, I dump the book off the side of the bed and try to turn the light off before the visions begin. Since my daughter was born eleven years ago, the most awful of these centre on her. Abduction, pain, disease, death, loneliness and sorrows of all kinds ...

I have read by the dim light beside the noisy bed and I am exhausted and still cannot sleep. I lie in the darkness, trying to find my way out of an adrenal tube echoing with regret and grief.

On nights like this I try to calm myself by going back to a time in my life when I was happy and at peace. Often I find myself returned to the mill house where I spent most of my childhood. Usually I start by remembering my bedroom, an attic room on the second floor where, on quiet nights like this, I could hear the trains which ran between London and the north. They were further off than the ones here in Dayton, but had the same quality of loneliness, yellow-lit boxes hurtling through blackness.

I try to recall in detail my narrow bed under the low vaulted ceiling and the sound of the weir. I remember the hours spent tramping across the fields with my two cousins and the day when, passing by an old tapped-out quarry by the tracks, we heard someone working below, picking away at the chalk. Having crawled like commandos to the edge, we looked down and saw, a hundred feet below and to one side, a solitary man working steadily with a pick. As we watched, he stopped and walked over to a rock where he'd placed his bag. He opened it, took out a Thermos flask and a china cup and poured himself some tea. Having taken a sip, he put the cup down on the rock and went back to work. My cousin, Dan, who was older than me, said, 'I'll have that,' and picked up a stone.

It was an impossible shot, the cup a speck below us, but the idea of it was too sweet to resist. No matter what happened, the man could not possibly climb out of the quarry before we had fled back across the fields and disappeared.

Dan stood cautiously so he could see the cup of tea but not be seen by the man who was now back at the face. Without even seeming to take aim, he unleashed the stone. The mug evaporated. With a light pop, it simply ceased to exist. The man turned and stared at the damp patch, steaming on the rock. And we were off across the fields, laughing so hard we could hardly run, heads down, arms across our aching stomachs.

I remember the winters when we would skate on the millpond, or the summers when we would swim in it, or the time when the River Board came to dredge it, sandbagging the millrace to divert the river through a side stream and then pumping out all the water. This process took a day or two and each afternoon I ran down the lane from the bus which delivered me from prep school to see how small the pond had become. For years, we existed on the surface. Now the mysterious depths would be revealed. Before long, the half-acre pond was reduced to a rich-smelling, slippery brown oval crater and, down in the bottom, ten square feet of muddy water thrashing with fish. The first time the pool was dredged, the digger dug up a bomb. The man saw the bomb in his bucket and ran for it. The RAF was called. To my disappointment, it turned out to be an English practice bomb, not a live German one. The sight of all the unlucky fish, however, was some compensation. There were minnows and trout and pike and eels. Here was revenge for the hours spent gazing at floats which remained placidly on the surface, for the tangles, for the grotesquerie of digging and impaling worms. Even now, however, the fish were victorious. My mother tried to cook one but it had ingested so much mud it was inedible.

When the pond was full again, I put out night lines, lengths of ordinary string with a rock tied on one end and a large hook, baited with bacon on the other. In the morning I'd wake up early and hurry into the cold dawn to see what I'd caught. Usually I'd pull out at least one eel. Eels were fantastic beasts, prehistoric, mythical, and hard to kill. They could survive out of water, travelling through damp meadows like snakes, and, or so it was said, their heart was in the tail. In the evening when my mother finished the washing up, she would take the plastic rinsing bowl and lie it upside down in the kitchen sink to dry. One morning, I got a two-foot-long eel, black, shiny and alive, and hid it under the bowl. When she came down for breakfast, she lifted up the bowl as usual and after that night-lining for eels was frowned upon as cruel.

I bring to mind my father's small engineering company, which I watched grow each year, from just my father and his partner, Peter, in the wooden shed, until the enterprise filled every floor of the mill. I remember the early days, when there were ten men or fewer, ping-pong at lunch-time, fishing, and most of all, the practical jokes: the day some workers lifted a car-enthusiast's old Austin Seven onto the parapet of the bridge while he was out, and balanced it there, or the time they put stones in someone's hubcaps; or the man who didn't mind electric shocks and how he'd electrify the factory door-handle and then, holding it with his left hand, greet unwanted salesmen with a handshake. Or being in the shed with Peter and my father, listening to the radio, 'Music While You Work,' and 'Before Time Began,' the latter being dramatised accounts for schools of prehistoric times. 'I'm looking down on a *vast* plain dotted here and there with *huge* trees and among the huge trees, I can see *enormous* dinosaurs feeding on the lush vegetation …' All this and the smell of oil and metal and the low, powerful grinding sound of a lathe.

I remember strange things, days you'd think would be forgotten. I remember with extraordinary vividness an hour – perhaps it was only half an hour – spent with my father when I was four. It was just after the mill house was bought and we had not yet moved in. The two of us drove over there, I don't know why, and kicked a soccer ball up and down the sloping gravel drive alongside the house, I above, he below. It was summer and I was covered in scabs from the eczema, which itched incessantly in the heat and which I scratched at without control; but all I remember was the intense joy of being alone with my father, entirely in his focus. (When I was born I was so ugly, he said, 'Oh, dear, we're going to have to be very kind to this one,' and as a child I was convinced, correctly I'm sure, that he preferred my sister.)

And then I remember the birth of my two brothers, first Francis, when I was five, and then Ludovic, when I was ten. I never went through a phase where I thought it unmanly to enjoy babies and adored them both. Francis was the most beautiful of children with long, curly blond hair and an amiable disposition. Ludovic, a more aggressive child, was born at home. Each day, as I had waited for the pond to empty, so now I would race down the lane to see if the baby had arrived. One day, I rushed into my mother's room and there he was, only minutes old. 'Look at him,' my mother said, 'he has balls down to his knees.' It must just have been his scrotum, I suppose, but anyhow the two of us laughed in amazement.

All these and other memories I call to mind during the hour of the wolf, that sleepless hour plagued with the sorrow of wrong choices and impending death. All this and more I run on my inner screen, trying to trick myself back to a period when I was, if not happy, at least at peace.

But when I remember these times, my other mother, my dark, intoxicated mother intrudes and a burst of something more powerful than sadness flowers in my torso. Sometimes I try to remove her from the picture, but it's impossible; she was, after all, my *mother*. I try and cloak her in memories of happiness. I try to remember her when she was young, the striking woman in the bold floral summer dress cinched tight at the waist, her hair gathered back by two large combs. I try to remember her humour, which was savage and mordantly perceptive, or her kindness when at night my itching became intolerable and I scratched my flesh through to the bone and she would sit with me. I'll remember her retelling with rueful pride the story of the allergist saying, 'I'm sorry, but this boy is allergic to life.'

I try to remember happiness, but I cannot. I can remember almost no *incidents* of joy. I hear her singing in the car on the endless journeys of childhood, 'Greensleeves,' 'My Bonnie Lies Over The Ocean' and 'Early One Morning.' I remember her cooking breakfast, the smell of bacon and coffee. But if I try to flip back through the pages of the internal album of my life, I can bring to mind no picture of a woman dancing out of sheer delight at being alive, no memories of interrupted sex or furtive parental kisses. I remember, instead, returning home from Prep School to find the mother of the morning, the kind, oddly childlike mother, transformed into a bitingly cruel wreck, and the same feeling, decades later, bringing back girlfriends and wives and finding the same tragic figure in the kitchen.

There must, I tell myself, have been *some* happiness for her, some tranquillity at least. I try to think of what she loved: the swans on the river, the rare flash of a kingfisher, the changing seasons. Yes, she enjoyed nature. She would see a flower out of the window of the car, frequently on a dangerous bend, and say 'If you wouldn't terribly mind, I wonder if ...' We'd pull over and watch her step gingerly into a nearby field to gather a plant which she would then identify later. She was only interested in wild flowers. Our back garden, the one that ran down to the river, contained no 'kept' flowers, which she considered distastefully suburban. She did, however, have a herb garden under her kitchen window and, behind the barn, a large vegetable garden.

She came from a class of women who had been raised in households with cooks, most of whose culinary skills were basic at best. Now, when no one in the middle class was rich enough to afford a cook, this duty fell to them. As they often spent their holidays in France and Italy and therefore knew what good food was, they began a revolution in English cooking. Clare had a bookcase full of mostly French cookbooks and cooked as well as anyone I've ever met, beautifully, almost obsessively. Two thoughtfully prepared meals were served every day, lunch and dinner, at least part of each coming from the kitchen garden. This large garden behind the barn was a source of delicious suspense for us all: the arrival of asparagus, digging up the first new potatoes, watching the sweetcorn ripen.

In Norfolk, she and my father owned a cottage less than a mile from a converted windmill which her parents owned when she was a child. She would drag us along the mile-long dyke at Thornham to a beach where the sea often receded yet another mile, and where the wind was so strong the blown sand stung your legs. Although she had no interest in gems or jewellery, she loved pebbles which she collected at the shoreline, her favourites being cornelians. She had a bowl of these on the kitchen window sill, kept in water to make them shine.

A moment: once, when I was grown up and already writing, we were walking out along the dyke, the wind as usual ripping at our clothes, when she saw a plant and rubbed her hands together. She had the habit of stretching monosyllabic words or pausing in the middle of longer ones and then stretching out the following syllable for emphasis.

'I think you're going to like this one, Matthew. I can't imagine who on eaaaarth would come up with such an extra—oooordinarily unpleasant name for such a harmless plant but that is *shrubby sea-blite*! Isn't that abso—*loootely* marvellous?'

These forays into the fresh air were when she was happiest and when my father clearly loved her most. There was an innocence to her, something invigoratingly fresh and pre-war English about her. 'Crumbling jumbos,' she'd declare as we tramped back from the beach, leaning against the wind and shivering, 'it's not *that* cold. Pull your socks up!'

Yes, this she loved, the bleak, chilly, windswept beauty of Norfolk. And she loved us, her children.

But nothing works, least of all this last assumption, because now my mind lurches, as always, back to the great mystery. How could she be so melancholy when she had us, her four children, to love? How, if she loved us, could she inflict so much pain? How could she be so miserable that nothing would induce her to seek help *if only for our sakes*? What incredible depths of sorrow could so contort a woman that she'd lay waste to all she loved with this ravaging despair?

I want to believe that my mother's life was worth living, that the sum of happiness was greater than that of sorrow. I want to believe this, but cannot. I think she was fundamentally and profoundly unhappy most of her life.

Born in 1924, she grew up among the most interesting and artistic people in Cambridge. Her mother, Frances Darwin, daughter of Sir Francis Darwin, had married another Francis, Francis Cornford, Greek scholar and Professor of Ancient Philosophy at Trinity College, Cambridge. Both Frances' parents, Francis and Ellen, were prone to depression. Frances was far worse, suffering, during her life, three long and severe depressions, the shortest lasting two years, the longest six. Hugh, my uncle who was a doctor, described the condition as 'depressive psychosis'.

My grandmother is most famous for a poem she did not much like, 'To a Fat Lady Seen from a Train.'

> O why do you walk through the field in gloves,
>   Missing so much and so much?
> O fat white woman whom nobody loves,
>   Why do you walk through the field in gloves,
> When the grass is soft as the breast of doves
>   And shivering-sweet to the touch?
> O why do you walk though the field in gloves,
>   Missing so much and so much?

Her husband, Francis, was a brilliant but introverted scholar, whose translation of Plato's *Republic* is still used in universities. He also wrote *The Origins of Attic Comedy*, *Thucydides Mythistoricus*, and *Before and After Socrates*, all of which examined Greek philosophy from a modern psychological perspective.

Clare was the youngest of five children, three boys and two girls. Until she was ten, her life was that of a fairly normal upper middle class girl. The family lived in a large house a mile outside Cambridge. Named Conduit Head, it had been given to Frances and Francis by her father as a wedding present. Frances did not like being a grown-up and had no interest in taking care of domestic matters, but this was not a problem because there was a cook and two or three other domestic servants, including a gardener who maintained the large garden with its tall hedges, beds of roses and snapdragons, and at the end, most important to us children, a rotating wooden sun-house which could be spun like a roundabout.

When she was not depressed, Frances was lively and engaged. For the first decade of her childhood, Clare was close to her. Summer holidays were spent in Norfolk, in the converted windmill overlooking the sea. Before the Second World War, the servants were sent ahead by train while the family went by car, a Bean. The eighty-mile journey took all day. Later on, after Francis died, everyone would go by train to Hunstanton. On arrival Frances and the younger children would take a taxi while the rest of the family rode a collection of bikes brought up in the guard's van. My oldest cousin, James Cornford, described them as 'hair-raising contraptions' which sometimes collapsed while being ridden. They were provided by the gardener at Conduit Head and if there were not enough of them the family would play bicycle leapfrog. One person started out on a bike and after half a mile or so got off it, left it in a hedge, and started walking. Whoever had started out walking, now picked up the bike, rode past the first rider, and left the bike for him another half mile along the road. Once they were settled in, there were rides on these bikes to the vast beaches of that coast. In the evenings they'd play games and talk. It was a large, happy, intelligent, gregarious family.

In the middle of the summer of 1934, however, when my mother was ten, life suddenly changed. Frances sank into her longest and most severe depression and was sent to a nursing home. Two and a half years later she was still there when Clare's eldest brother, John, father of James, a strikingly good-looking poet and Communist, went off to fight with the International Brigade in the Spanish Civil War. In January 1937, he was killed in battle, shot through the head by the Fascists on his twenty-first birthday. His body was never recovered.

Clare was then twelve. If you look at photographs of her as a child, there is, long before any of these tragedies, a withdrawn, melancholy expression on her face. Afterward it is more marked. I see the same expression in my own face and sometimes in the face of my daughter.

Clare was sent to St. Christopher's, a co-educational, vegetarian boarding school in Hertfordshire, where I would later go myself. One of her two remaining brothers, Hugh, the closest in age to her, was also there. He fell in love with a girl from the school, Jean, and later married her. They adored each other until she died. Clare's older sister, Helena, a dancer, went off to America and married Joe Henderson, a psycho-analyst and former patient of Carl Gustav Jung, who later wrote one of the chapters of Jung's final book, *Man And His Symbols*. They also loved each other deeply, even after she collapsed into mental illness and, like my grandmother, had to be hospitalised. Her other brother,

Christopher, became Dean of the Royal College of Art. He married a beautiful older woman and they too loved each other.

Clare was not so lucky.

After school, Hugh decided to study medicine. A year later, Clare chose to do the same, although her nature, which was often sardonic and intolerant of human frailty, seemed ill-suited to such a profession. In her first year at Newnham College, Cambridge, she met a fellow medical student, Katherine Priestman – always known as K – who would become her lifelong friend.

K introduced her to my father.

Half-French, half-English, K was, and remains, a lively, highly intelligent woman. As capable as my mother of unleashing the biting *bon mot*, she did so less frequently, perhaps because she was happier. (Though I have watched them together, 'stitching' as the Brazilians say, discussing their friends, and sat mesmerised and laughing, while at the same time praying the bright beam of their wit would not pan in my direction.) One of those women who seem to grow old without losing any of their beauty, K is small and slender and has a laugh so natural and affectionate it seems like a reward. When I asked her what my mother was like when she was a student, and if she displayed any signs of the despair and alcoholism which would plague her later life, K thought for a while and then said: 'No, she was a very happy, scathing woman.' And laughed, remembering her.

She was bold, advanced, and witty. She smoked and drank, but neither to excess, and was considered somewhat 'rakish'. Her confidence, so notable then, so absent later, came, K believes, from having a large, interesting family in which all the members took pleasure in each other's company even as adults. When Frances threw tea parties at Conduit Head for academics and fellow poets, the children were always invited.

When they were finished with their studies, Clare took K out with Hugh and Jean to go pub-crawling. Because of the war, it was often hard to find a pub which had beer and they would wander around the city in search of one, and, having found it, drink and talk until closing time. During this period, Clare and her mother started to attend a small church in Cambridge, Little St Mary's. It was K's impression that this began because of a monk Frances had met who was both charismatic and intellectual. Clare enjoyed the ritual, the songs and the incense.

Throughout the war, K received occasional letters from an officer in the Navy, a childhood friend named Cecil who wrote from Australia and the Far East. Clare, who had no such glamorous friends, pretended not to believe in his existence and insisted on meeting him when he came back on leave. By the time he did, the war was almost over and Clare was studying at St George's Hospital in London. The three of them had lunch in a Chinese restaurant in Soho. My mother, already in her twenties, arrived with a yo-yo which she played with constantly. My father was handsome and intelligent and had a girlfriend in Australia, which made him all the more desirable.

A short while later, with France liberated, K decided to go and visit relatives in Paris. When Clare heard Cecil would also be there, she insisted on going too.

As a Naval officer, my father had access to the Officers' Club, which was in the former Rothschild mansion not far from the British Embassy. The cook at the club was French and the food was not only excellent but plentiful. Coming from rationed England, this was the greatest of treats, and the three of them ate and drank there constantly. By the end of the week my mother and father were in love. Not long afterwards, they were engaged.

Cecil was the son of a professor at Oxford, Sidney Chapman, a theoretical physicist who discovered a magnetic layer around the earth, now known as 'The Chapman Layer.' Cecil already had a degree in physics from London University and after the war would pick up a second, in history, at Trinity College, Cambridge, where his father and grandfather had been Fellows. When I was a child his mind seemed as different from mine as an athlete's body is from a paraplegic's. He could do calculations with numbers that were absolutely baffling in their complexity, feats of mental agility for which I was simply not equipped. He also had an extraordinary memory and allowed no factual question to go unanswered, rushing always to the nearest encyclopedia to extract the truth. He was kind, decent, honest, ethical, rational, objective, and fair.

He was the wrong man for my mother.

Perhaps there could never have been a right man. As a teenager my mother climbed into the attic at Conduit Head and found boxes and boxes of love letters her parents had written to each other, hundreds of them, mostly from her father to her mother, most written after they were married. K, who was taken up into the attic a few years later to be shown some of them, says the letters expressed a love of such depth and power it was almost shocking. It was as if Francis and Frances were as close to each other in spirit as they were in name, as if each had found in the other the absolute ideal.

This rare state of romantic and intellectual passion is, I think, what Clare expected in her own marriage. Maybe it was the war – kamikaze pilots crashing into the decks of the ships on which my father served, the scent of foreign ports, or simply his good looks – which convinced her Cecil could provide the grand romance which her father had provided for her mother. If she was thinking at all, perhaps she also concluded that whatever their differences, the similarity of their academic backgrounds would sustain them.

They got married in 1947. By now she was in her final two years of training. Soon she was pregnant with my older sister. And if you are looking for a determining moment, a moment where life could have provided her with sufficient pride or structure to overcome her instinct toward self-destruction – or not – this is where you might find it. Taking the final exams that would qualify her as a doctor she failed one paper. As I remember the story, it had something to do with the anatomy of a cat, although why someone who was almost a doctor would be studying that I do not know. In any event, she abandoned medicine for motherhood and, compounding the sense of failure that descendants of great men tend to have, she never went back. From then on, it often seemed that if she could not immediately do something perfectly, she had no interest in it and gave up.

Though I believe they were genuinely fond of each other, right through to the end, in spite of her alcoholism, theirs was not a happy marriage. At least for the last thirty to forty years it was not a happy marriage. In the beginning, for about nine years, my father thought they were happy, and probably they were by normal standards. And then one day, my father found out she was having an affair and had been for at least a year.

Cecil's partner, Peter, was a graceful man, slender and quick. Educated at Stowe and Cambridge, his mother was a German aristocrat, his father a correspondent for the Manchester *Guardian* in Berlin until the First World War. His paternal grandfather, however, had been the ticket clerk at Rugby railway station. A long distance runner for Britain in the 1936 Olympics, Peter had been expected to win in 1940, but the games were not held because of the war. His bearing was upright and athletic but diffident rather than haughty. He spoke with an upper-class accent and voted Conservative, but was a man who didn't seem to quite fit in anywhere and to me this was his charm, a kind of awkwardness, a shyness handled with rueful dignity.

After the war, he started making mechanical wooden toys and musical boxes in London, but one night the place burned down and he lost everything. He was married to a woman who had money and he liked solitude. They bought the Vicarage in Grantchester and he decided to apply his engineer's mind to scientific instruments, which he began to do in a folly at the end of the garden. As a hobby he continued to restore and collect musical boxes and mechanical singing birds, these latter being clockwork devices of great complexity and delicacy, birds the size of your fingernail with plumage of real feathers. They would spring out of the silver surface of the box and chirp and turn from side to side and move their beaks and wings. I still remember visiting him, sitting at his workbench in the folly, surrounded by tiny cogs and gears and brightly coloured feathers.

When my mother introduced him to my father, he had just started the scientific instrument business. The two couples had dinner in the Vicarage. Afterwards, Peter showed my father a device which at that time was still novel, a dishwasher. The two men opened it up and studied it and my father commented on a way in which the design could be improved. Although my father had no qualifications as an engineer, Peter saw how intelligent the comment was and offered him a partnership, thereby doubling the size of the company. Because of my father's inexperience, the terms were not particularly favourable to him. Peter's instincts, both human and financial, were correct. My father quickly became an excellent engineer and more than doubled production within a year. The first devices they made were temperature control units, small baths in which test tubes could be stood and retained at an exact and constant heat. Later on they would make refrigeration units for the same purpose, then shaker baths to keep fluids agitated for long periods, and finally computerised temperature measurement devices, one of which was used to monitor the heat of the skin of American space rockets.

Peter and my mother had met in 1936 when she was only thirteen years old and he in his late teens or very early twenties. Their families knew each other and he had been invited to a party at Conduit Head. He was at his most glamorous, having just run in the ominous, Hitler-dominated Olympics. Innocently or not, he kissed her and she never forgot it.

Eighteen years after that first kiss, they started an affair.

A day or two after the birth of my younger brother, Francis, my father noticed a letter in Clare's hand-writing, addressed to Peter. As he saw both of them every day and could easily have passed on whatever my mother might have wanted to say, he was at first puzzled and then suspicious.

He opened the letter.

It said she was glad to be having Peter's baby even if they could not be together. 'He took to the breast very quickly,' she wrote, 'just like his dad.'

My father was furious, confused, and then depressed. Everything was so entangled. The business, which had expanded out of the folly, was now in the mill and literally attached to our house. He already had two children and, in spite of everything, he still loved Clare. When he sought an explanation, Clare told him of that first kiss and how, even now, whenever Peter came into the room, her stomach 'turned over'. Peter was married and had a child and could not, or would not, leave his wife. Cecil decided that as far as he could, he would forgive Clare, and accept the situation without further recrimination. Francis was an exceptionally likeable child, gentle and funny, with a sweet smile. His paternity was kept secret and he was brought up as one of us, loved by all. He *was* one of us and remains so to this day, no less a brother than my other brother.

Not long after Francis was born, Peter's *au pair* came to see my mother. 'I'm sleeping with Peter,' she wept, 'and I just don't know what to do.' My mother did. She went around to his house and threw a brick through his window. In her early thirties, she now became wilfully promiscuous. Whether this was her way of exacting revenge on Peter for this humiliation, or whether it was simply an attempt to drown her depression in sensation, who can know? She began to drink more heavily.

This was the period when my sister and I began to discuss divorce.

Until Francis was about four years old, Peter came to lunch at the house every day and would feed him and play with him. After that – after my father and he split the business because Peter did not want to run a company which had grown so large – he would come only once a week. Eventually, he sold all his shares in the company to my father. They remain friends.

What can you know of anyone's marriage, even the marriage of your parents, but I suspect that in my father's decency in forgiving my mother lay the death of this one. There is an element of unintended cruelty in such forgiveness. It gives you a possession no one should have. As she slid into alcoholism, perhaps he felt, albeit unconsciously, that like a character in Greek tragedy, her self-destruction was inevitable and deserved.

My father was an attractive and capable man. He could have left the family and had a better life, but didn't largely for the sake of us, his children. A friend of mine once said, 'If only my parents had divorced I'm sure I'd be happily married by now.' But how was Cecil to know in 1956 that the wound Clare had hacked into the marriage would never heal, that after Peter would come others, and that she would not stop drinking until she entered hospital to die in 1992? Four years after Francis they had one more child, my youngest brother, Ludovic, and so by the time I was ten, we were a family of six.

For the first fifteen years or so, we did not acknowledge she was an alcoholic, though to any modern family it would have been as obvious as a confession. Living with her was to live with two women, the woman of the morning, bright and funny and loving, and the woman of the evening, cruel and despairing. So different were these two that to speak to the woman of the morning about the woman of the night before seemed somehow indecent and unfair. And so we didn't.

When she started to fall down stairs, however; when the ambulance had to come in the night, when she lied to the doctors at the hospital and told them my father had hit her, then we began to discuss it and tried to get her to do something; but to her AA was shameful, for toothless boozers in the gutter. When we suggested it, she wouldn't take part in the discussion. She was an intellectual, albeit one who often mocked intellectualism, and she was the great-granddaughter of Charles Darwin. AA was not for women like her. Whatever the complicated causes – genetic depression, shame, or the weight of history – the solution she chose was brutally simple. She wanted oblivion and alcohol would do the job.

Had she been from a family with less money, she would have hit a wall. Instead she hit stoicism and denial, and so, with every year, her drinking got worse. Sometimes she would drink wine, sometimes whisky, sometimes gin, and in the summer, cider. She would drink out of a mug instead of a glass and hide bottles all over the larder. Once or twice it seemed as if she tried to stop. My father tried drinking with her, refusing to drink with her, speaking to her about it, and ignoring the whole thing. Nothing worked. Sometimes there would be a period of days where she would not drink, or an even longer period where she seemed to drink in moderation. When she was not drinking, her eyes often wandered away, their expression so intensely melancholy it almost resembled fear. And then she'd have a drink, and in those first moments I would see a look of relief pass across her face which reminded me of how I felt when I scalded my hands to quell the itch; release from endless tension, the voluptuous rewards of failure.

Ludovic, who remained stranded in the worst of her decline after the rest of the children had departed, swears that when he opened the front door – long before he saw her – he could tell if she was drunk or not. I left home as soon as I could, but when I came to visit at weekends from London, I had the same sensation as I drove down the lane and hit the gravel yard. Her unhappiness seemed to cause even the bricks and mortar to exude despair. And when one's worst fears were confirmed, such a weight of sorrow, such a feeling of being let down: the beautiful house, the wind and the trees, the sound and smell of the river, all extinguished by this pervasive gloom.

The children scattered away from her. Sarah took to the road, off to India and Nepal. I went to live in London and then Los Angeles. Francis moved to London a few years later. Ludovic, unable to stand any more of her corrosive tongue and overwhelming misery, was sent to school in America. Eventually, Sarah and Ludovic returned to live not far away in Cambridge, but none of us ever went to the house without our guard raised, and none of us could help her escape her misery. Her incisive comments, her scathing wit, were seen less and less often. Now she would sit at the table, eyes frequently closing, and simply groan with despair at any comment she did not agree with. Sarah, who got on least well with her as a child, came to be closest to her in the last years of her life.

In her late fifties, ill health and overweight brought on by decades of drinking and smoking slowly began to take from her the few things she did enjoy. The vast Norfolk beach, the one where she had shown me shrubby sea-blite (for which I rewarded her by giving it to her as a nickname), was now too far away for her to reach. Walks in search of elusive flowers and birds became rarer. Before long, she could only stand at the kitchen window, staring through the bottom of her glass at the river flowing toward her. One day she lost all interest in making the meals around which the family had united in praise. Cooking, she now claimed, had never given her pleasure and she had simply decided to stop. The kitchen garden was abandoned. Perhaps she knew already what my father was doing and felt too fundamentally betrayed to continue these last fundamental acts of nourishment.

Cecil, who for thirty years lived under the suspense of what each evening would bring, fell in love with someone else, an old family friend. One night he was speaking to her when on the phone he felt Clare's presence behind him and turned.

Now the final agony began.

I must have gone to sleep at some point because I wake up and find myself exhausted and hungover. Gloria cooks me breakfast, a slab of ham, fried tomatoes with herbs, and biscuit with gravy. How anyone stays under 300lbs. in this place is a miracle that can only be attributed to heavy smoking. Eventually, I will go to almost every eating establishment along the highway and in none of them find anything that would remotely fit the Surgeon General's definition of a healthy meal.

Wheezing and bilious, I stumble outside and sit on the porch. It's still raining. The magnolia tree sheds. Gloria comes out and smokes in the other rocking-chair. She looks bleary and ragged, but seems remarkably calm for someone who is about to relinquish a dream and enter what could so easily be a nightmare.

I ask her to tell me about the house. She says it was built by W.F. Thomison, MD, who was the chief physician for the Dayton Coal and Iron Company and also the attending physician at William Jennings Bryan's death. The house used to sit where the street now is, but was put on rollers and dragged by mule to it's present position in the late 1890s, to make way for boom-time traffic. It was easier to move a house in those days because there was no plumbing or wiring to deal with. In fact, according to Gloria, a man would sometimes, at the request of his wife, move his house several times 'until the light came through the kitchen window just so.'

When she returns inside, I go and look at a plaque by the front door. To my astonishment it tells me that the house was indeed built by W.F. Thomison, but adds an almost spooky detail. He built it for his wife, Ella *Darwin*.

The word 'wow' comes to mind and I waste the rest of the day trying to track down some relatives. Eventually I find a Darwin down in the local library. Her name is Henrietta and she's married to local historian, Seth Tallent. Both are in their seventies and are funny and charming. Henrietta trots off home and returns with a family tree.

Seth says, 'I'll bet you didn't expect to find some country clodhopper on the family chart, did you?'

The chart, however, proves inconclusive. It all begins with a William Darwin coming over from England a couple of hundred years ago, but it's impossible to see if he was related to my branch before he left.

Later, back in New York, I put in some more work on this, encountering, among others, a Darwin popcorn farmer down in Alabama, but in the end conclude, alas, that the connection cannot be proved, much to my sorrow and even more, I suspect, to the sorrow of the popcorn farmer.

Heyall Is A Lake Of Fah

When I return from my fruitless genealogical quest, I find that Gloria has another dinner date. After her husband left, her friendship with the man who owned the ranch on the hill, deepened. Lester, a doctor, was also going through a divorce and they comforted each other. It was he who gave her the cut-off scrubs. He has also given her two horses. After a while Lester, a doctor, met a woman named Ruth-Anne and they all became friends. Tonight they're going out for their last dinner. Ruth-Anne arrives in a red Jaguar. She's a pretty woman with short hair and a pleasant shy quality. Gloria squirts out two generous beakers of wine and they get in the car to drive the forty-five minutes to Chattanooga to meet Lester, whose surgery is there.

I head back out to Ayola's. An incredibly sad song is playing. A man sings and a little girl interjects with questions like, 'Que pasa, Papa?' Eventually it ends with the father saying 'Adios, chiquita.' I look out the window and see that the cops are feeding across the highway at Long John Silver's tonight. Leaving the restaurant I encounter a large woman. On her neck is a hickey that got infected. It's not a pretty sight and the two burritos and the iced tea ($7.95) lunge into my throat. I manage to contain them and start cruising around town, killing time until Gloria returns. There's a defeated looking strip mall right behind the restaurant so I tool over there and give it the once over.

Two porky ten-year-old girls throw a little bouncing ball around the parking lot. Behind them is a shop entitled Get-It-N-Go: Video & Tanning. I remember that when this contraction of 'and' into 'n' first began in England my father, disapproving pedant that he is, would walk into a 'Fish 'N' Chip' shop to demand 'two orders of fish *ENNNN* chips, please.' Not far away is Kwik Kash Title Pawn. Then there's Mountain Air Natural Foods, which contains no food whatsoever, only a sparse scattering of vitamins on shelves. Discount Outlet can be discounted: it's gone. *Godzilla* plays at a tiny, shabby modern theatre, the name of which has dropped off, leaving only the word 'inema'. Next door is The Gem Shop – Diamonds, Gold, Engravin (no g). In the window is another sign, 'Pearls in June. Sale 30% off. Remember Dad's Day, Sunday JUN   E21.' How or why the E got moved fifteen inches to the right to join 21 is a mystery. Then there's Dollar General Store, Ekerd Drugs, and Shop-Rite.

I enter Shop-Rite. Actually, it's not a bad shop. Amazingly, the shelves have little signs listing the content of the fruit above. It's a lost cause, but you have to admire the plucky optimism of the gesture. I buy some apples from under a sign that states, 'An apple a day keeps the doctor away.' Very lofty. All I'm looking for is some fibre to help shunt the burritos through before they shape up into something nasty and hurt me on the way out.

In the check-out line ahead of me is a stringy 30-year-old redneck in clean overalls, no shirt, a baseball hat and worn-down work boots. I check his neck and it is indeed red, a ruddy, brick red. He's carrying a jumbo-size bottle of Coke and orders a tin of Skoal chewing tobacco. Now he dumps about a hundred pennies, nickels and dimes (no quarters) onto the counter.

'Should be a few dollars thar,' he says, grinning in embarrassment.

The checkout girl politely picks up the coins one by one, counting them as the rest of us wait patiently in line. I notice that the redneck's hands are shaking violently. I wear a pouch around my waist in which I'm carrying $500 in cash, a camera that cost me $1500, and a wallet containing two credit cards good for $30,000 apiece.

I look away almost in shame and study some tabloids on a nearby stand. 'Bible Predicts 2nd Great Depression,' says one of them.

The redneck's trembling hands picks up some change and he departs with his nutrition. I pay for my apples and follow him out. He gets into a rusting pick-up and drives away.

Suddenly I feel depressed. I came down here in part, I must confess, to poke fun at just such hillbillies as this, but I didn't take into account the reality of rural poverty. I remember the man on the bus. 'The only drawback to living in the country is you get less opportunity.' Yes, and there's something claustrophobic and scary about this. Where do you go out here in the boonies when the well runs dry? Furthermore, compounding the problem of maintaining a snide, superior tone, everyone's been so damned *nice* to me. For seventy-five years people have been coming down here to mock, from Mencken to me, and all day long I've been running around asking questions and everyone's been 'just as nice as all get out,' which means as open and friendly as you could wish.

I must locate a cliché soon or I'm in trouble.

I drive alongside the railroad track, along a street of shabby one-storey wooden houses with cluttered porches. At the end of the road, where the town is starting to thin out, I see, to my amazement, a sign.

'Tent Revival 7.00'

Around the bend, a marquee with a blue-striped roof is pitched on the grass beside a small, plain brick church. Parked alongside the church is an ancient bus painted mauve. It's evening but the rain has stopped and the air is thick and humid. The sides of the tent are open to let what little breeze there is blow through, so I blow in with it.

A preacher in his early fifties, dressed in narrow black pants, a white shirt and black tie is up on a small raised platform at the front. There's a pair of guitars up there and an electric piano to one side, but no one's at them. The preacher's shouting at twenty or thirty po' white folk. He yells and jumps on and off the little stage and pumps his arms, and then he quietens down and speaks soothingly, temptingly, stretching out the words. He can switch from one style to the other in a second and it's a fine performance.

'God wants to give you a new life, new way, new worrrrld. Old Devil say, well you don't know, you might wanna come back, I'll take you. But if you ever git in the King's Highway, if you ever git set free ...'

'Tha's right.'

'Set free, set free ...'

'Yeah, Preacher.'

'Set free! Set free!' He reaches a pitch and now lowers his voice to a croon. 'Set freeee, set free ...' He wipes his sweating brow and takes a breath. 'They got a lot of po' black people around here, there's a lot of po' black folks in this nation, jes like there's a lot of po' white folks. Well, I'll tell ya, I betcha tonight we could go to every black folk, every black person in Rhea County, say, "You're po', ya up against it, ya havin' a hard time, ain'tcha friend? How about being my slaaaave? How about going back in under slavery? How about goin' back, let me ruuuule over you and make your decisions. You jes give up your freedom and be my slave." You won't find a one that'ud say, "Oh, that'ud be good, take me back." No, no, *no*! You know why? Ooooh, that taste of freedom! That taste of freedom!'

'Amen!'

'That's right, yessir, brother.'

'God wants to set you free tonight, set you freeee. Been saved twenty-three years ain't never tasted another drop of alcohol.'

'How long is that, brother?'

'Been saved twennnnty-three years, ain't never smoked a joint of dope.'

'Amen.'

'Been saved twenty-three years, ain't been out with no other woman.'

'Praise the Lord.'

'Been saved twennnnty-three years, ain't never been in another dive or honky-tonk. Been saved twenty-three years, ain't robbed and stolen or cheated. I made a lot of mistakes. I been misled, I've got stubborn, I've tripped up, I've disobeyed, but I ain't never liked it.'

'That's right, brother.'

'Oh, no, what I like is, I like bein' saaaaved, bein' a chiiiild of God, bein' borned again. That new worrrrld, that new life ... Oh, tonight I feel so happy, can't explain it.'

But he tries. He tries to explain it in terms of what it would be like trying to describe the world to a blind man. While he's doing that (because I know where that's leading) I look around. There are no black people here. In the row across from me are three fat women draped in long dresses, a trio of featureless profiles, heads dumped in a tutu of fat; hard, depressed eyes and set mouths but neither jaws nor necks. The men are thinner, thinned out by labour perhaps, and wear jeans and plaid shirts. They are of all ages and, to my surprise, are more vocal than the women. There are some kids too, eyes exhausted in the heat, pensive, a little wary, as if they know that pretty soon the preacher's going to do a one eighty on the King's Highway and start screaming about the terrors of hell.

Looking over my shoulder, I see a man at the back with a Bible clutched against his chest like a child clutches a teddy-bear. He's a clean-cut, unimpressive little fellow with round rim glasses and a moustache. Thirty years old, sandy red receding hair, white shirt, tie. He projects none of the raw growl of the preacher but has a sanctimonious, proprietary air to him, so I go over and ask him if he thinks it would be okay for me to take some photos. The answer is no, but I discover he's the pastor of the church, one Leland Frazier. Turns out the preacher up on stage is a jail preacher. Leland asks me where I come from and I tell him England. I ask what a jail preacher is doing here. He's about to reply when the preacher starts shouting and sobbing so loud we can't hear each other.

'And Jesus says, "Except you be born again, you cannot *seeeeeee!!!*"' he yells. 'I was blind but now I *see!* I see the hand of God in ever'thing!'

A young woman walks in from the rear of the tent and starts to play the electric piano which now accompanies the preacher as he hollers on. As if obeying a signal, a number of men walk down to the front of the stage and prostrate themselves. It's funny because they're all wearing sneakers and the soles stand up behind them bright and geometric like toy ducks at worship behind their masters.

'He's doin' a revival for us,' Leland says.

'Ah,' I say, trying not to smile at the sneakers.

The preacher's yells swoop down into a tone of soothing seduction, a voice one might use while stroking a child's head at bedtime. 'They're comin' to the Lord Jesus tonight. Tha's enough. He'll take care ... He'll take care of it. "I need a new life, Preacher, pray for me." That's enough, come to God, he'll take care of it. "Help me, Preacher, I got so backslidden in my heart, ain't nothin' there but coldness and indifference." So down, so out, so discouraged, so defeated, so doomed and down! Amazing Grace, how sweet the sound, salvation is at hand! Come to Jesus, he'll take care of it ...'

And now the electric pianist begins to bang out the tune for 'Amazing Grace,' and everyone starts to sing. It's a song I happen to like, a sweet sound from my own past in the little schoolhouse in the English countryside, and I'm almost getting teary-eyed when Leland comes in from the side with a sly, knowing expression on his face.

'So, it's no coincidence that you happened to stop by here tonight I don't think, do you?'

'Maybe not,' I say, thinking of how in need I was of a good solid cliché for the book. And Leland drops right into the scheme, still looking up at me sideways like a salesman sniffing out a weakness to slink in on.

'Are you saved? Do you know what that means?'

'Er, saved?'

'Yeah. Goin' to heaven instead of heyall.'

'I don't know, like I say, I'm from England, we think about things a little differently.'

'I understand that, I understand that, but God thinks the same way. He thinks the same over here as he does over thar, do you know that? Old-time preachers used to preach the same way over thar as we do over here. I read after 'em, they's from England, used to be some great preachers, but they're slidden away, farther and farther from God, over in England.'

'In England?' I ask, the patriotic nerve (more or less dead) brought to life for a second as I think of the comparative crime statistics, particularly those for murder.

'We are over here too. America's goin' farther and farther away from God.'

'I don't know,' I say, 'seems like everybody's religious.'

'Not saved.'

'How do you get saved then?'

'Through the Lord Jesus Christ. See the Bible here tells us that it's not by good works that we've done ... See a lot of people says, "I've been pretty good. You know, I ain't never killed nobody," (interesting definition of 'good') "you know, I ain't never been a really bad thief," but God says, "For by grace are ye saved through faith and that not of yourselves: it is the gift of God: not of works lest any man should boast." See it's not in works, it's not in how good that you are.'

'So what does "by grace" mean?'

'Grace ... Grace is this. God sayeth "For God so loved the world that whosoever believeth in him should not perish." He don't want nobody to go to heyall. It's a gift, see, it's something He'll give to you that you don't deserve, you don't earn it. "For all have sinned and come short of the glory of God." That means you. You've sinned.'

Me? My *God*, yes. If he only knew. I cannot confess the worst of it, not even here. I've stolen, cheated, lied, fornicated, and written scripts for Hollywood, and that's not the half of it. I am to sin what the LL. Bean catalogue is to rugged outerwear.

'Me?' I ask. 'How do you know?'

'You've sinned,' he assures me.

Not wishing to get into a discussion on this, I try to change the focus.

'So, do you believe in a literal hell?'

'Yes I do, it's right in this Bible. Let me read to you about a man that went thar. Would you like to hear a story about a man that actually went thar?'

Oh, dear.

'Look, it's in red letters,' he says, pointing to a passage in the much-clutched book which is indeed in red. 'That means the Lord Jesus actually spoke these words out of his mouth' (where else would he speak them from, his arse?) 'and they penned it down as he spoke it.'

There follows a story about a rich tightwad in purple and a beggar named Lazarus who gets his sores licked by dogs but doesn't get much joy from the rich guy. One goes up, the other down. Lazarus appears to get Abraham's bosom, but for the tightwad it's strictly behemoths and flames.

'If you go to hell, you never get out again?' I ask.

'Out of heyall?' he asks, not understanding my odd pronunciation of the word.

'Yeah.'

'There'll be a day and that's called the Great White Throne Jerdgement Day. What happens is God's going to take those that were put into heyall. They're gonna be brought out of heyall and jerdged according to what they've done and then they're going to be cast back into heyall. Let me show you this ...' He's at the Bible again. I try to head him off from another endless and incomprehensible story.

'Wait just a second!' I protest. 'You mean you get thrown in, then you get taken out, and then you get *thrown back in again!?*'

'Into a lake of fah. Let's step right over here, mebbe you can hear a little bit better. Okay, now listen to this. Just ...'

'No, you listen to me,' I insist, willing to debate on any level if it's not going to come back to endless quotes from a 2,000-year old self-contradictory book of dubious origin translated into an archaic language I barely understand and stuffed with statements like, "And the beast that was, and is not, even he is the eighth, and is of the seven, and goeth into perdition." 'Let me tell you where I have a hard time with Christianity. It's this whole idea of hell. It's so cruel, it's so final, I can't imagine a God who had a big heart,' (let's keep it simple) 'condemning anyone to that forever.'

This doesn't stop him for a second; he has another parable at hand, Folksy Parable No. 7, fit for a retard and ready to go:

'Okay, now listen to this. Have you got a son?'

'I've got a stepson and a daughter, yeah.'

'Okay. Let me asked you this.' What if your son was with you here? Let's say that jes all of a sudden here come a car come down through here, jes slidin' sideways an' layin' over in that ditch over thar and turned over an' ...' To cut a long story short, after much crawling around and heroics, my son, who has been reduced to the age of six, gets burned to death and the driver of the car lives.

'Now that man, the driver, he jes turn aroun' and laughs and says, "Hey, so what?" an' walks off. Now wouldn't you want that man to go to heyall? Wouldn't you want that man to die an' go to heyall?'

By now, although the blessing up the front is still continuing, a gang of Christians has left the tent to watch this debate.

'I might,' I say, 'but I'd try to find some forgiveness, and I'm not even God. You'd think if God was in control of all this, he'd know what made that man that way. In fact he would have *made* him that way, and so he'd be able to understand him and forgive him.'

'Well, but thar, that's my point. If that man, before he die, if that man gets saved, if he accepts the Lord Jesus Christ as his saviour, he can go to heaven.'

'I see, but a guy who did good things all his life, never got involved in any of this car crash and murder stuff, that man won't go to heaven unless he asks?'

'That's right. You see the Lord, he puts out his hand to all of us. It's like a drowning man. All we gotta do is ask and he'll reach out and he'll admit us to the Kingdom of Heaven.'

'But if we don't ask, we're damned to eternal hell?'

'That's right.'

'Even if we've been good all our lives?'

Out comes the Bible again and it's back to the original passage, but this time I'm not taking it. I've got a little parable of my own.

'Okay, so try this,' I say. 'I'm on the bank of a river and this guy comes struggling up and he's drowning and he reaches out for me and says, "Help me out! I'm drowning!" and I say to him, "Only if you ask nicely." You don't think maybe that's a little childish at best? I mean what kind of behaviour is *that*?'

Well, now everyone's weighing in and pretty soon I'm swamped in Bible quotes and tales of personal redemption, guys who drank but don't any more, guys who beat their wives with pool cues and quit – 'The power of the Lord' – and then there's Leland, a tiny figure among these converted ex-brutes, and soon I'm into capital punishment with 'So how can you be into capital punishment when you've got the "Thou Shalt Not Kill?" thing in there?' which gets a "Ours is a warlike God," and I'm dodging this way and that to avoid biblical passages flung at me from all angles and I'm trying to parry them with irrelevant questions to Leland like, 'So did you go to the Baptist college up there?' 'No, sir, he went to Knee School,' says one of the burly men who used to beat his wife or drink, I can't remember which, and someone else says, 'Don't you realise Amerca's goin' heathen?' and pretty soon everyone's squawking about the fact that I'm from England and I'm not saved and it becomes clear if I don't beat a hasty retreat they're going to save my soul by sheer force of numbers and so I start photographing them and edging back toward the tent, determined to at least get one shot of the Jail Preacher before I run to my car and flee, so I manage to get up near to him and he's still preaching and saving souls so I shout over to him, 'Will it bother you if I take a photo?' and he grins at me and yells back, 'Listen, son, I had Bibles thrown at me in jail an' they

flush the toilets all the time so I don't think one itty-bitty camra's gonna
bother me at all!' and he grins and keeps on preaching and I snap a few
and he waves and now I'm ready for a drink but the only way I'm going
to get out of here without actually saying, 'Willyouleavemethe-
fuckalone?' is to promise to come back the next day and let Leland
take another crack at me, which I do, and, Praise The Lord, I'm
finally at my car door which I open – and bong, bong, bong goes
some signal from within, like a bugle sounding the retreat – and now
I shut it and I'm inside in blessed silence, and with a grin of defeat,
I departeth and headeth off for the relief of the squishy flagon of
wine in Gloria's refrigerator, which, verily I say unto ye, I intend to
drink deeply therefrom (or should I say 'tharfrom'?) just as soon as
I can.

And do.

Gloria is not in good shape. As I aim wine into a glass, she tells me
Lester's gone home and Ruth-Anne has followed. For the last
month, whenever the subject of her leaving has come up, Lester 'just
bawls.' This evening, he spent the whole dinner cracking jokes and
then when they all got back to the Magnolia House, he took a glass
of wine and went and sat out in his pick-up. After a while, he roared
off home without even saying goodbye. It's like he *can't* say goodbye.

'I'm gonna put on my scrubs,' declares Gloria, now in tears, 'and go
on up there and make him hug me goodbye.' After a while, however,
he calls and everything is smoothed out. She's coming back for their
wedding in a month. They will bring up her two horses in August when
she's settled.

Gloria sniffles. 'I was driving back home tonight and I was crying
and I was thinking, three months ago I went up to my church and
prayed. I needed a new job, I wanted Lester to find happiness, and I
wanted to get along with his new love. Well, I got what I prayed for and
now the Lord must think I'm ungrateful, but I'm not, I must be the most
fortunate person in the world. It's just that I got what I wanted and now
I have to leave.'

A firefly comes into the kitchen. 'Did you know if you squish off his butt and rub it on your nose, your nose'll glow in the dark? Used to do that a lot when we were kids ...'

She wipes her nose and smiles. Two more days and she's out of here, but she won't give in to despair. She got what she prayed for.

John Thomas In Exile

The pressure of academic expectation helped make my mother who she was and was passed on to me, to make me who I am. I responded to this pressure with resistance. Some schools tried to seduce me, some ridiculed me, some ignored me, and some brutalised me.

St Anne's Prep School for Boys would have to be placed decisively in the 'brutalising' category. The school was all about violence, the strong inflicting suffering on the weak, the master bullying the boy, the boy bulling the smaller boy. Brute force, power through the threat of physical pain; it coloured everything, or, more accurately, removed colour from everything. Masters might smile and crack a joke or cajole, but such amity was pure hypocrisy. In the end, if they didn't get what they wanted, out came the stick – or sticks if it was one of the old homos – and down came the grubby white underpants.

In later life, I endured many vicious places, one of which brought me in contact with some of the most violent criminals in London, but St Anne's was the most vicious of them all, a vile *institution* infested with tweed-clad homosexuals, sadistic, dictatorial inadequates who voted Conservative and pulled you against their erections as they were about to beat you, all this ruled over by a cold, bullying, power-mad headmaster so dry and heartless that many years later when I had an opportunity to run him down while taking my driving test I was instantly inclined to do so, although he was now an old man with a stick and it would have meant my not getting a licence which I desperately wanted. But he moved too fast and the moment, regrettably, passed.

The school was a series of ugly red-brick buildings set back from a broad but quiet road on the outskirts of Cambridge. I was a day boy and started there at the age of seven in 1957. I would get there each morning by catching the 108, a double-decker bus which I scaled in my village and descended from eight miles later, about a hundred yards from the school. On my first day, my mother drove me there in her small red Mini Minor and was about to leave me at the main entrance when both of us lost our nerve. So many boys, so many caps covering so many bullet-like heads, such intimations of abuse …

She drove on and parked around the corner.

'It's going to be all right,' she told me.

'I know,' I lied, 'but if I don't like it, can I go back to Mrs Marshall's?'

'We'd have to think about that,' she replied, an answer which I knew meant no.

She took out a handkerchief, licked a corner of it, and wiped some dirt off my face. I carried the smell of her sweet, nicotinic spittle throughout the rest of the day and carry it still in my memory.

'We're early,' she said. 'I'm going to have a cigarette.'

I sat next to her in the smoke-filled car, scratching anxiously at my scabs and watching the cigarette burn down. She took one last drag and threw it out the window.

'Okay, let's try again.'

She turned the car around and five minutes later I was striding bravely in through the gates while she waved bravely from the smoky confines of her miniscule car.

The absence of girls was shocking. Why had I not thought of this? Wherever I looked there were armies of fierce boys or skulking loners as terrified as me. I'd gone from pink round bottoms and 'All Things Bright And Beautiful,' to the stench of grey socks and 'How would you like a kick in the balls?' The conformists were happy in their sadism. The rest plodded along miserably. I was afraid all the time. I did not want to learn and pretty soon I could not learn. Even drawing and painting, which I'd always loved – even language – ceased to be interesting. Art and artists were despised. This was boot camp for future colonels, estate agents, pig farmers, and Tories.

I missed girls so much that when a master began to speak, my head would turn involuntarily toward the window to stare at the swaying oaks, and I could feel myself in the arms of a warm, soft, soap-scented imaginary sweetheart who loved and admired me. When I was *forced* to study, particularly mathematics or Latin, another reaction set in: the consequences of failure were so disagreeable my mind skipped over the possibility of comprehension and fixed directly on the violence which incomprehension would bring, and then it went completely blank. The sensation was similar to that of the first drag of a cigarette after a long period of abstinence: tension overwhelmed by the bitter, masochistic joy of defeat. A despairing miasma folded around me, temporarily shielding me from reality. I might as well have been blind and deaf.

Because my sister was the only female around, she became the object of my frustrated desires from the age of seven to ten. We both slept in rooms up in the attic. As I have said, it was a tall, three-storey house, so when I crawled out of my window onto the pitched roof, I was at least forty feet up. I would do this in any weather. Hands and feet spread for maximum traction, I edged my way across, old tiles cracking and shifting under me, until I reached her window. Clinging by my fingers to the wooden ledge, I would try to catch a glimpse of her as she undressed.

Had I fallen, I would have died. There was absolutely no question about this. I knew it then and didn't care. The power of my sexual fascination was so overwhelming I was willing to take that risk. If you offered me a million pounds to do the same now, I wouldn't put so much as half a leg outside the window. Eventually, she caught me during a rain storm and asked me what I was doing. I told her I was plucking moss off the tiles and throwing it onto the roof of my mother's car, which was parked below, because I liked the sound it made.

Unsurprisingly, she didn't buy it. From then on, her curtains were tightly drawn.

I drilled a hole in the bathroom door, right up in one corner where the panel met the frame. It was a discreet, perfectly-aimed little hole focused on the tub. Now whenever she took a bath, I would find an excuse to rush upstairs and spy on her. One day I brought my eye to the hole and saw a gigantic mouth hurtling toward me. There was a vehement hawking sound and, next thing I knew, my eye was shot with spittle and little bits of sawdust. After which the hole was filled. Now I would go out in the coldest winter night and lurk on the other side of the river in the hopes of a distant shimmer of breast seen through a steamed-up, lace curtain-covered window.

I still cannot pass a lit window without stopping, and if the person or people within don't know they're being watched, I find even scenes of mundane domesticity mesmerising. I once lived in the top half of a beach house in Venice, California. Directly below lived a somewhat attractive young woman. Whoever had lived in the house before had poked a hole in the wooden floorboards. If you looked though it you saw her bed, or to be more accurate, *some* of her bed, because she'd built the bed up onto a platform and so it was too close. If you pressed your eye to the hole when she was having sex with her boyfriend, which I must confess I did once or twice, what you saw was completely incomprehensible. Was one becoming aroused by her thigh or a section of his upper arm? Which portion of whose left buttock was that, if indeed it was a buttock?

This curiosity remains, intellectualised to some extent, used in the pursuit of my career – and not. If one must use the word 'Art', is this where it comes from? In my case, unquestionably. I am a voyeur in search of respect through the fetishistic organisation of glimpsed details.

In the early part of my sentence to St Anne's, someone made a prediction that the earth was going to end on a particular day and the newspapers, as gullible then as they are now, printed the story. The world was about to fall out of orbit. Gravity would cease to exist and we'd all scatter into space like breadcrumbs. With the Cold War in full swing and marches against the nuclear bomb under way, the idea of a natural conclusion to the world seemed almost quaint. None of us quite believed it, but no one was entirely unafraid either. I and another boy sat on a bench at the appointed hour, wanting something to cling onto should we be cast drift. The hour came and went and we immediately returned to our petty cruelties, unenlightened by our brush with death.

I did so badly at school, I was held back a year. I managed to retain some of my alliances with the few reprobates and misfits I'd encountered in the first year, but could only keep their respect by becoming increasingly rebellious and violent. By the end of that year of repetition, my brain was numb and my emotions dulled.

My only friends were my cousins, sons of my mother's brother, Hugh, a doctor, who also lived in Cambridge. Dan and Ste would come over to play sometimes, Hide and Seek and Kick the Can and throwing stones at things. English boys of my generation had a passion for throwing, probably because of cricket, and if you lived in the country, what you usually threw was stones. You threw them at birds, at bottles, at the water, into the sky, and if you could find some windows to smash, there was no greater pleasure – none, that is, short of going to the newsagents and stealing a copy of *Health and Efficiency*, the official magazine of the English nudists, and masturbating yourself into a daze while imagining what lay beneath the airbrushed bits. *Health and Efficiency*! Who but the English would give that title to pornography?

Dan was a couple of years older than me, Ste about the same age. When my grandmother, Frances Cornford, died, we were left alone while the grown-ups went to the funeral. We were lurking around the grounds when we heard some village boys shouting downriver. I did not go to the local school so never become friendly with these boys and, for reasons I have now forgotten, but probably stemming from a mixture of snobbery and fear, considered them the enemy and was so considered by them. We stalked down to the bank of the river and peeked through a tall hedge. The boys were lounging on a footbridge about a hundred and fifty feet away. We backed up into the apple orchard to formulate a plan. From where we now were, the boys were obscured by the hedge. We could not see them and they could not see us. We, however, had ammunition. We took down a load of apples from one of the fifteen trees and then I went back down to the end of the hedge. Looking through a hole in the foliage, I could see the boys. Aiming from memory, Dan lobbed up some apples, handed to him in rapid succession by his brother. They fell in the water just short of the bridge. From my vantage point, I signalled to Dan to throw a little longer. Soon a lethal fusillade rained down upon the boys, who ran this way and that in utter confusion as apples smacked into the bridge and exploded. Of course, they soon worked out where this unprovoked and invisible attack was coming from and moved into sight. Now we threw apples directly at them and they picked them up and threw them back. The battle lasted for hours.

By the time my parents returned from the funeral not a single apple remained in the orchard. It was midsummer and the trees were as bare as winter.

Around this time I invented a new method of inflicting pain at school. There was a boarder, an unfortunate, obnoxious fat boy so lacking in either physical strength or humour that he decided, wrongly, that his only chance of survival was to completely align himself with the teachers. He was, or had become, an arse-licking toady and sneak and everyone hated him, particularly those like myself who were inclined toward insurrection and destruction. I cannot remember what enabled him to get me in trouble, but he had seized the opportunity and I had been punished.

In class, I sat on the outside line of desks almost against the wall. Directly in front of me sat another boy I did not like and then came the fat rat. One day, as the teacher droned on, I removed my right shoe and pushed a drawing pin through the toe from the inside so the point stuck out about an eighth of an inch. I then cautiously stretched my leg past the intervening desk, jabbed the pin through the sneak's little grey trousers, stretched tight over his endomorphic frame, and with an adroit flick of the ankle, gave his plump backside a good scratch. By the time everyone turned to stare at the screaming boy, my foot was back under my desk and a frown of surprise and curiosity was on my brow. I was not discovered and the boy in front of me was punished. I kept a pin in the toe of each shoe from then on and used them whenever the mood took me until, inevitably, I was caught.

Three years went by, during which I never stopped pining for girls. Long before it became a general symbol of defiance in England, I had started to grow my hair long. As early as 1958, this was an issue. My parents were called in to discuss the matter with the ghastly Mr White and, though irritated by the whole thing, largely supported my point of view. What effect, they argued, did the hair on my head have on the brain which lay below? The school, in partial concession, said that in that case if it was to be this long I'd have to wear bows in it. I cut an inch or two off.

But the long hair was not at first grown to piss anyone off. It was simply plumage, one weapon in a magical array of magnets. I never came in contact with girls and so I thought 'If they can see this fine hair, perhaps they'll look at my face, and if I arrange my features like this and hold my shoulders like that – if I can just make myself a *fraction* more attractive – I will become irresistible. She – whoever she is destined to be – she will see me and be forced by an uncontrollable urge to approach me on the bus, to write me a note, to break into the house at midnight and slide into my bed and say, "I love you, I can't help myself." '

In this magical effort, my vanity became demented. I spent hours staring at myself in the mirror, practising expressions. One time, I decided in the middle of a school day to adopt one of the younger master's smiles. He was a lean man with a long sharp jaw that hooked out beyond his nose. When he smiled his cold blue eyes disappeared into an array of radiant crinkles and his mouth widened and turned down at the corners. It was a roguish smile, wickedly flirtatious, and the female teachers giggled and looked away whenever he applied it.

I borrowed it and used it all day. I said hello with it and I said goodbye. I used it on the bus home and on a woman coming up the lane. Charm? Devilish! It was the new me. I presented it to my mother and then I took it upstairs to the mirror.

I stood there, staring at myself. Then I raised an eyebrow and began to crinkle up the eyes at the corners.

'Hi,' I said, and smiled.

To my horror, I saw a leering, retarded trout-like boy grimacing back at me. It wasn't even a smile. It was an absurdity, grotesque and bizarre. Why had no one said anything? Had they all thought I was unwell, that I had some facial tic, a nerve problem? From that time on, all new personalities had a test run in the mirror before release.

As for my hair, I was obsessed with the parting. I moved it half an inch up, half an inch down, I combed it straight, then slightly crooked. I had it go all the way to the back of the head and then stopped it three-quarters of the way there and swept it around the curve. I angled it up at the front and down at the back, and down at the front and up at the back. I combed it, combed it again, and then recombed it. I combed it so relentlessly I eventually tore out a half-inch gully. It was like a fire-break in a forest and looked so bad, I had to move the parting to the other side of my head and comb the hair over to cover it until it grew back.

And, for all this effort, not a single girl came forward.

My charms, however, were not *entirely* overlooked.

There are teachers who have gone from school to college and then right back to school again and, knowing nothing else, remain essentially schoolchildren. 'Bunter' was one of these. A rotund and gentle bachelor with a nose like the tip of an overcooked sausage, he often wore khaki shorts and knee-high socks. In these, he looked like the mischievous comic-book character, Billy Bunter, grown perversely old. Bunter was the only teacher who was ever kind to me at this school and I remember him with affection; but his motives, though undoubtedly benevolent, were not entirely pure.

One weekend, having got permission from my parents, he took me and a friend to stay with his mother at the seaside. I don't know how old I was but I couldn't have been more than ten because I left the school by eleven. Bunter drove an old, very solid, very round British car and he drove it very slowly. When we asked him to drive faster, he said, 'Better to arrive too late in this world than too early in the next,' a phrase I still sometimes say to myself while hurtling across town to avoid being late. (I had a job once where if you didn't arrive on time you got punched in the stomach, and since then I've always been obsessively punctual.)

It was winter at the seashore, but Bunter took us down to the sea to go fishing. The beach had no sand, only large, round pebbles which rolled around beneath your feet as you walked. Bunter, knot expert and general all-round outdoorsman, was also an accomplished fisherman. With much hands-on instruction, he taught us how to cast the line far out by turning your back on the sea, then whipping up the rod to fling the lead weighted line over your head. *Zzzzzzzzzzzz* went the reel and you could turn and see the weights splash into the water what seemed to be *hundreds* of feet out. Pretty symbolic, all this rod stuff, now I come to think of it.

His mother's home reeked: a pungent, respectable odour of polish, gas of all kinds, and the damp fifty-year-memoir of English cooking which had sunk into the carpets and the old green armchairs with their lace doilies, this fusty stench wired through at the top with lavender-scented widowhood and just below that, with the faint medicinal bouquet of old age itself, all this trapped inside a red-brick Victorian semi-detached house with its windows closed against the endless cold grey wind off the cold North Sea.

When we had had our 'high tea' (an early dinner which usually consisted of some combination of eggs, baked beans, sausages and bacon dumped on a slice of white bread and washed down with hot tea and milk) it was time for bed. Bunter lurked helpfully nearby. My friend and I scrambled into our pyjamas, brushed our teeth, and hurried beneath the sheets and blankets.

Bunter settled himself into a chair next to the bed.

'Would you like me to read for you?' he asked.

'Oh, yes please, sir,' we replied.

'Would you like me to read this adventure story here about a boy scout named Nigel or ...' he smiled roguishly. '... *or* would you rather I read a chapter of *Lady Chatterley's Lover* by D.H. Lawrence?'

'I think we'd rather have the D.H. Lawrence book, sir, if that's all right with you,' I replied swiftly, in case my friend opted for reef knots and tents and marlinspikes.

The book was very much in the news at the time. It was still against the law to sell it in England and America, and two highly publicised legal cases were under way to change this, one in New York and one in London. The book's scandalous details were being euphemistically discussed by everyone. Not only, therefore, was the book sexual, it was also fabulously illicit. How brave was Bunter?

Bunter settled his glasses on the end of his misshapen snoz and started to read. He had obviously been through the book before because we only got those passages which dealt with the lusty comings and goings of 'John Thomas,' the name given the hero's penis. This was an excellent book, I remember thinking, well written, a fantastic glimpse into adulthood which made it seem extremely desirable.

After about ten minutes, Bunter closed the book.

'Well, there you are. Did you find that exciting?' he asked.

'Yes,' I replied.

'Somewhat,' said my friend.

'Are you touching your John Thomases down there?' he smiled.

'Yes,' I replied. My friend was silent.

'Would you like some help?' asked Bunter, looking at me.

'No, thank you, sir,' I replied. 'I can manage, but thanks all the same.'

'Are you sure?'

'Oh, yes, I've done it before. I'll be fine, thank you.'

'All right,' said Bunter in a tone which suggested I was missing something pretty special. And left.

The next morning, my friend woke up with a huge lump in his cheek and my ears hurt. We had mumps. Bunter took us home.

Alfred Kinsey, the first scientist to study human sexual behaviour in the twentieth century, believed the incidence of paedophilia and incest remain fairly constant. What changes is the amount of *attention* they get. This goes in cycles, often provoked by a single gruesome event, or simply because a religion or a newspaper needs a campaign or story. The more intense the interest and the more hysterical the condemnation, the worse it is for the victim. Responding as much to the outrage as the incident, they feel outrageously violated, and suffer accordingly. During periods when these things are viewed as pathetic rather than monstrous, the abused suffer less and recover faster.

In my youth, the world was full of 'dirty old men' and 'flashers,' old geezers lurking in the public toilets, men in raincoats, and types like Bunter. To me Bunter was just a dirty old man – a rather sweet dirty old man – and I was neither shocked nor damaged by his masturbation-proffer. In fact, had I been alone, curious as I always was to experience a new sensation, I would probably have accepted it, and I'm sure that would not have done me much harm either.

I didn't tell my parents about the incident for a while, only because I figured it was meant to be secret. I was not afraid. When I did tell them, they looked slightly appalled and asked if I thought they should do something about it. I said no. Bunter went on being my teacher and remained my favourite. Perhaps if the other teachers had not been so implacably cold and cruel, I might have seen him in a more malevolent light. Believing as I do in original innocence not sin, I think any violation of the sanctity of childhood is the worst of all crimes and an instant addition to the future miseries of human relations; however, the salacious obsession with sexual crime draws so much light to one particular and obvious area of abuse that the far more damaging institutional offences against children sneak by unnoticed and arouse almost no outrage at all. In America, the most callous and brutal violation of youth is collectively tolerated by the whole nation. Visit an inner city school – if you dare – and you'll know what I'm talking about.

It is, I suppose, an amusing comment on the English prep school, that by far the nicest teacher was a predatory homosexual, but that was the case. Bunter's suggestion of digital assistance had at least the virtue of intending pleasure. 'Scratchy', who was by some weird ethical quirk, only allowed to beat boys with a sneaker – the honour of the cane was the sole privilege of the headmaster – intended both pain and pleasure: you got one, he got the other. He was a vast man whose bald pate was compensated for by wildly hairy ears and nostrils and eyebrows. Everything about him was fibrous and scratchy. Before administering the punishment, he'd pull me against his tweed jacket in a fatherly embrace. (When I took my first beating from him, my face was only inches above his prominent erection, which I could feel against my chin. As I grew older it was against my sternum, then finally at my lungs. Before it could turn into a dick-to-dick situation, I was gone.) Having impressed himself upon me with his embrace, he'd now lean down, stroke my buttocks with one of his massive hands and, with deep emotion, growl the time-honoured chestnut (and I swear this is true): 'This is going to hurt me more than it's going to hurt you.'

Perhaps it was already a joke, this line, among the masters, something they tittered about in the staff room, but, pathetically, I believed him, and in the beginning, felt sorry for him and was moved by his affection. Here at least was someone other than my mother who would take my scabby little body and hold it. Having tenderised my flesh with his gentle hands, he'd reach for the famous flail, a long, stained tennis shoe without laces whose springy rubber sole he'd now whip expertly against my buttocks three to six times, rarely more. This over, he'd minister once more to my stinging cheeks, sometimes slipping a cool, dry hand down inside the back of my pants to ease the pain, and then, with tears in his eyes, he'd let me waddle out, sobbing with a mixture of pain and – how droll – *gratitude* for it not having been worse.

I hated the masters who sent me to be punished by this man more than I hated the man himself. At least there was a certain intimacy in being beaten, while he who *sent* you simply expressed hatred. Beneath the artificial, fear-engendered politeness, the antipathy which existed between the boys and the teachers was intense and pervasive. When a master cut off his finger in the carpentry shop and left it on the floor as he stumbled off to call an ambulance, a boy kicked it into some sawdust beneath a cabinet so if he returned in hopes of getting it sewn back on, he'd be out of luck. I would have done the same.

I was good at nothing except sport and drawing. My drawings were not appreciated and, though I would win in solitary sports such as the high jump and the hundred yards, team sports brought out the worst in me. I made no effort in 'Crafts' where other educationally subnormal kids would often excel, and when the year ended and all the other losers presented their mothers with teapots or bird-feeders made of plywood, I had nothing to offer. My mother would walk around with me on the last day of term and look at all the silver cups I had not won and at all the clay and wood that other boys had fashioned into gifts for their mothers, and she was visibly saddened. One year, her disappointment was so palpable, I took pity on her. As we passed a carpentry display, she admired a small wooden tugboat, painted grey and red.

'Well, I'm glad you like that,' I said, 'because I made it for you.'

'You did?'

'Yes. Here it is,' I told her, snatching it from the display and handing it to her. 'Now put it in your bag and let's go.'

She kept the boat on her dresser almost to the end of her life, a modest and solitary symbol of her son's artistic potential and filial love. When I eventually told her it was stolen, she still kept it. Touchingly, I would later find out, she had kept other mementoes of my wickedness.

As I endured my third unhappy and confused year there, I began to run out of excuses for why I was not doing my homework or randomly beating up other boys and was forced to tell ever more extraordinary lies. One excuse for not doing homework began with the statement that my mother was never home in the evenings.

'I'm so worried about her I can't concentrate.'

'She's not home. Where is she then? Does she work?'

I shook my head.

'Is someone in the family ill? Is she looking after someone?'

'No.'

'Well, what is it then?'

'I'd rather not say, sir.'

'I'm afraid you have to.'

'My father works all the time and my mother goes out dancing in jazz clubs and gets drunk,' I finally admitted with a trembling lower lip.

I don't know if there were such things as jazz clubs in Cambridge then. If there were, she certainly didn't go to them. Whatever she was up to at the time – and this must have been during the promiscuous phase which followed Francis' birth – I never consciously doubted that she loved me and never stopped loving her. Furthermore, the mechanics of motherhood continued. No matter how drunk she was, dinner was always on the table at the same time each night – and not just dinner, but a rich, inventive, fresh dinner such as one might be served in a first-rate provincial restaurant in France; and the next morning, no matter how hungover she was, she was always first up, down in the kitchen, smoking a cigarette with her coffee as she cooked breakfast and made a packed lunch for whichever child still required it. Even these lunches seemed to me to convey her love. They were better than anyone else's packed lunches, a Penguin biscuit, or fat cherries accompanying the sandwich with its crust carefully cut off.

This is what was so tragic and so English about the whole thing. Everything continued normally. She never gave up, never collapsed as her mother had, never cried out, 'Help me! For God's sake, someone help me!' even though, somewhere, she must have wanted to. Perhaps seeing her mother in asylums when she was ten or eleven had terrified her. Perhaps she thought if she confessed her symptoms that's where she'd end up. Or perhaps her concern was for us: if she collapsed, we would be abandoned as she had been.

Whatever her motives for not seeking help, I believe my motive for inventing the story about her wild nightlife was a hope that it would force her to take action of some kind. I remember a feeling of gratification at the scandal, as if I had struck a blow.

Clare and Cecil were called in by the headmaster and my story was repeated. They managed to laugh it off. That Matthew, strange boy, what a character! But I'm also sure that behind my lie lay enough truth – my mother's drinking undoubtedly expressed her *desire* to be out of the house – to make the encounter with the humourless Mr White both distressing and humiliating. The idea of moving me to another school became increasingly attractive.

A boarding school perhaps …

If I had gone to St Anne's still vulnerable to educational seduction, by the time I left I was impenetrable. In my last year, I sent two boys to the hospital. One got his leg snapped during a football game when I deliberately kicked his shin against a goal post. I was naturally strong and agile and was good at sport but not considered sportsmanlike. It was hard, however, in this instance, to prove malicious intent. It could, conceivably, have been, as I claimed, an accident.

The incident with the other boy was not so easy to explain. I hit him over the head with a cactus during a nature study class, and everyone saw me do it. I picked the thing up – and brought it down. I was sent to Mr White for a beating. I lied with all the conviction fear could muster. I didn't do it. Whoever said I did was lying and if it was the whole class then they were *all* lying. Mr White hesitated. First of all, the crime was so bizarre. Secondly, he couldn't quite believe a young gentleman would lie so blatantly. He toyed with me a while, relishing my apprehension. He draped me over the cracked leather arm of his big armchair. I heard the ping as he removed one of his canes, arrayed in clips of varying sizes depending on the stick's girth, but eventually let me go without satisfying his disiplinary urges. A week or so later, however, he concluded that in fact I was guilty. The evidence was overwhelming. A cactusing had occurred, I was the culprit, and I had lied. My time was up.

I had served three years there, the only girl in my life being my sister whom I hated and longed for simultaneously. Nothing in my life would ever be as bad again. I spent a night in jail once and was immediately reminded of that school, the atmosphere of fear and helplessness, the relentless tension of impending violence. The difference was that while some of the men in jail were larger than me, none were twice my size and none had the legal right to beat me.

I went to tutors to complete the year and was then sent to the same school my mother went to when she was a child, St Christopher's. It was a boarding school and it was co-educational.

I was eleven, the sixties had begun, and the exile of John Thomas was over.

God Takes A Shot

Gloria has got up early and taken twenty croissants out of the freezer, enough to feed all the ghosts of the Magnolia House. It's raining. It's been raining off and on ever since I got here. It's either raining or so humid it might as well be. As you walk around, your clothes chafe damply against your skin. Last night the thunder competed with the trains to keep me awake.

I shuffle into the kitchen. A cigarette burns in an ashtray but Gloria is nowhere to be seen. On the table is a magazine called *Discount Store News* ('Wal-Mart – Back To The Customer,' and 'Employee crunch leads to creative recruitment.') Fate is pulling her away. Under the magazines I find a copy of yesterday's *Dayton Herald-News*. Gloria appears from the garden and starts heating up the croissants. I go to the dining-room which adjoins and drink coffee and read the newspaper.

In some places the local paper publishes a list of men caught visiting prostitutes. Here the *Dayton Herald* prints a list of people who have not returned their library books. On the front page, the big news is a fatal crash on Route 27. At the back, mobile homes are offered for sale. A brand new one goes for $11,995 and that includes 'Blown ceilings, (not buttons); 2 by 4 sidewalls; appliances; dead bolt locks and FREE SATELLITE!' A used one can be had for well under $3000. There's a syndicated column by the conservative John Whitehead of the Rutherford Institute, warning us to watch our 'values' as the millennium approaches. F.R. Duplantier of America's Future Inc, talks about students putting on hip-hop records for 'their rutting peers' who will then 'writhe on the ground like toxic cockroaches.'

There's a local Religion Page with several tract-like articles by various preachers surrounded by paid advertisements taken out by rival men of God seeking to poach some business. There are forty-five churches in Dayton, despite it having a population of only 6,000. This means, according to someone I know who can do long division, that if every single Daytonian, man, woman, and child, went to church every Sunday, there'd only be about 133 people in each church. In other words, competition is fierce and the Scopes Trial was a waste of time.

The personals are wholly innocent. The women, many of whom are divorced, enjoy church, country dancing, the great outdoors, and 'cuddling by the fire'. They are looking for an LTR (long-term relationship) with an honest, sincere Christian man who enjoys old-fashioned values. The men enjoy hunting, fishing, camping, racing, movies, and fun! They're looking for the type of woman the women claim to be. Many of the men insist almost coyly that 'friendship must come first'.

Of course there's crime news too, everything from alcohol abuse to vehicular manslaughter: an alphabet of sins. Five students make a home-made bomb, put it in someone's mailbox and detonate it. Drunks crash with unnerving frequency, and dope is imported, grown, bought, sold, and used.

There's a Sports section which includes, along with articles on local football, basketball and baseball teams, others on fishing contests and hunting achievements. Participants in these two latter sports can be viewed proudly holding up their victims. The Chamber of Commerce figures prominently in many articles, and everyone recognises photographs of Sam Swafford, the banker-mayor and Leon Sneed, the farmer-sheriff, both of whom have lived here all their lives.

At one end of the town is a big Walmart supermarket, at the other end the La-Z-Boy factory. In between are some cut-and-sew operations, a couple of small agricultural businesses near the railroad track, and, at the Courthouse and City Hall, the business of local government. It's a typical small Southern town except for the Scopes Trial and one other thing.

Up on a hill at the northern edge of town is a Christian college founded in honour of the Great Commoner himself, after his comical and humiliating visit to Dayton. Comical and humiliating in my view, not theirs. It's proudly called Bryan College and today I intend to pay a visit.

I finish my croissant and depart. It isn't raining. I drive past the Courthouse and then make a right and get onto the highway, heading north. Toward the edge of town at the side of the highway, a sign reads,

'Christ Above All – Bryan College – Founded 1930' and an arrow points up a winding residential street. Two fat drops of rain smack the windscreen ominously, but no more are forthcoming. After a while the street opens out into a small campus. The first building I see is a modern church on my left.

Is it a coincidence that since Nietzsche said 'God is dead,' churches, once the most beautiful of buildings, have become the most ugly? The entire world is littered with these concrete and/or red brick malevolencies, deformed pyramids, hunched and angular, with jabbing spires and blundering stained glass windows. You can see them in India, you can see them in Europe, and you sure as hell can see them in America. Is it a kit you buy? 'Erecta-church ~ Designed by the Devil to test the devout.' If so, this is the mid-size version and, aesthetically speaking, is pretty standard; in other words a tad less inspiring than your average bunker.

I'm thinking these thoughts and smiling to myself when suddenly, as I drive past the Main Building and a sign saying 'Thou Shalt Not Park Here,' a gigantic bolt of lightning shoots out of a modest grey sky and hits the driveway about thirty yards from my front fender. It's followed instantly by an equally huge explosion of thunder which is so violent the antenna vibrates and the raindrops on the windshield tremble.

He's going to take me here! He's going to strike me down only yards from the 'Thou Shalt Not Park Here' sign! Hilarious! A great-aunt of mine snuffed herself, leaving a note saying, 'Hey diddle, diddle, here goes,' but I reckon if I get struck by lightning on the campus of a conservative Christian college, my death will provide even more laughter than that.

About five seconds later, as I'm parking, God takes another shot. I see the lightning hit the hill across the valley. Not even close, pal.

But then I think: with these Christians it's all about threes – the cock crowed thrice, the Trinity, et cetera – so I park quickly and jump out. Give Him a moving target. I'm plunging up the steps toward the main entrance when – Bang! – and this one nearly *hits the church!* I slow down and walk calmly to the front doors, laughing. There was a time He could demolish whole armies with a single smite; now He can't even hit an overweight atheist.

I have an appointment with Tom Davis, a teacher at the college, who has been organising the Scopes Re-enactment Show for the last few years. I find him in an office off the large, quiet corridor on the ground floor. He is short man with unruly hair and a gentle smile. He gives the impression of someone who has a lot to do but whose good manners will not permit him to dodge his social obligations, in this case me.

He tells me this year he has turned over the direction of the Re-enactment to a woman named Gale Johnson, wife of a local preacher, who has some theatrical training. She rewrote the script and came to him with it. Now she's already preparing the play.

'It's a slightly different slant,' he says. 'Are you coming back for it?'

'Oh, yes,' I assure him. 'It's going to be the centrepiece of my book.'

He offers to give me a tour of the college. The four-year course, he tells me, as we start walking around, costs about $14,000 a year, but most of the 500 students get financial aid or scholarships. When they graduate, they tend to go into teaching, business, or accounting. Some become missionaries.

In the basement of the Main Building is a library sparsely stocked with religious books, and homilies for sale. Everyone in the library is very nice. One of the ladies behind the counter asks Tom if I've been up to see Professor Wise yet. Tom smiles to himself and says, no, Wise is busy this morning, and we leave.

We go up to the second floor. The lights are on, but as we emerge from the stairwell there's instantly a change in atmosphere and I realise why.

Dead things. Lots of them.

The broad corridor is lined with specimen cases from one end to the other, large, glass cases with deep shelves. Some are stocked with stuffed animals and birds, others with skeletons and bone fragments (Prehistoric Elephant, Mammoth), and fossils (Ammonites and Trilobites). There are snakes from Africa and India. There are lizards and fish, international insects of all sizes, and rocks of all ages, (Geothite, Petrified Wood). To an uneducated eye, it seems like comprehensive proof of the great antiquity of earth and the slow development of species. Tom tells me the specimens have been sent in from all over the world from ex-students, many of them missionaries.

'Who to?' I ask.

'Well, to Professor Wise,' he says with another smile. 'You should talk to Kurt if you get a chance, he's a brilliant man.'

'Who is this Kurt Wise?' I ask.

'He's our science teacher. He's busy this morning, teaching a class in Origins, but he'll be around this afternoon. He's one of the leading creationists in the country. Studied under Stephen Jay Gould at Harvard.'

This is someone I want to meet. Stephen Jay Gould is one of the most eminent evolutionary biologists and palaeontologists in the world. A professor at Harvard, he is a great admirer of Darwin. Like most modern biologists, he disagrees with Darwin's adherence to an entirely gradualist theory of evolution, believing evolution can also occur in rapid bursts over periods as short as a thousand years; however, he vigorously defends his essential ideas, particularly when they are under attack from creationists.

And here is one of his students out in the sticks, a creationist.

I tell Tom I'll come back in the afternoon.

I want to interview Sheriff Leon Sneed, who plays the sheriff in the re-enactment, so I drive back into town and find the police station. It's a small one-storey bulding next to an even lower-slung brick jail such as you might find in Soweto.

Sneed has been variously described to me as 'coy as a catfish' and 'tough and effective'. He's facing re-election and his opponent and predecessor, Paul Smith, has already started a vigorous campaign. It's a nasty race and it's going to get a whole lot nastier.

Leon takes me into his office and sits down. He's a compact man in his fifties with grey hair and smiling eyes, an amiable good ol' boy and nobody's fool. He wears tan pants, cowboy boots, and a plaid shirt. As I talk to him, the sun moves around so it shines right in his face and his eyes get narrower and narrower until eventually I can only see the faintest glimmer of eyeball in one eye, and the image of a catfish lurking back there watching me seems increasingly apt.

He tells me about the county and its crime. He's very down on drunk-driving, for which he's not popular with a lot of people. They have some drug problems, a lot of domestic abuse, a small amount of cock- and dog-fighting, and some moonshine production. The mari-juana growers, he tells me, now use global positioning systems. In the spring they go up into the woods and sow their crop. Each plant stands alone, deep in the woods. A note is made of each plant's exact location on the GPS. The growers then return on dark nights, using the GPS to guide them in, and harvest the plants one by one. This makes it extremely hard for the cops. Even in the unlikely event they catch someone, they've only got a small portion of his crop. Sneed says he enjoys playing the sheriff in the re-enactment but this is his last year. He doesn't say as much, but I get the sense that he isn't enjoying this year's preparations as much as usual.

After a while, he tells me he has to go off somewhere, but next time I'm down, would I like to ride with a cop for a night or two?

I tell him I most definitely would and shake his hand gratefully. It's one of those big clamping wads of muscle and dense flesh.

He grins at my discomfort and says, 'Okay, old chap, awfully nice to have met you,' in an English accent to which I instantly reply, 'Okay, ol' buddy, thank ya'll for lettin' me visit with y'all,' and he laughs and leaves me in the company of a couple of his detectives, who show me the property room at the back. It's full of dozens of sawn-off shotguns and jam jars of moonshine and marijuana seeds.

I ask one of the deputies how things are with the Ku Klux Klan.

'Well, you don't git a lot of that now. I tell ya, the Klan used to be okay till all the nerts started comin' in.'

'Nerts?'

'Yeah, the nertcases spoiled it. In the old days the Klan 'ud take care of people: guy didn't work, take care of his family; fella beat his wife, they'd go in there and whurp the piss out of him.'

I go to meet Gloria and her Aunt Ruth for lunch at the Dayton Diner.

The diner is about three blocks from the Courthouse and is the social and business hub of the town, but only at lunch-time. In the evening the place is closed, beaten no doubt by the flashier fast-food temptations of the highway. An oblong room with booths down one side, it's packed. We find a table at the front and sit down. Aunt Ruth is about to hit ninety and is a small, alert woman with neat, permed hair and bright eyes. She and Gloria look around and comment on a few people.

Bobby-Sue, Gloria's girlhood friend, and her new husband, Jimmy McKenzie, grandson of Ben McKenzie of Scopes Trial fame, occupy one of the booths. About seven hundred hamburgers ago, Bobby-Sue, like Gloria, must have been quite a girl. Jimmy is a local attorney running for judge in the upcoming elections. He's a short, anxious looking man with darting eyes. Gloria waves desultorily at Bobby-Sue who responds in kind.

For forty-two years Aunt Ruth owned the Highway Gardens, a flower shop in the old Aqua Hotel. When Gloria was in school here, Aunt Ruth would wake her up at 5.30 in the morning by playing 'Amazing Grace' on the big pump organ downstairs in her house on the hill above Dayton; then they'd drive down to the flower shop and Gloria would go to sleep again in a storeroom upstairs until it was time for school. One night, I think in the Seventies, Aunt Ruth received a call. The Aqua Hotel was on fire. She had laryngitis, but drove quickly to the place to save what she could. She got lost in the smoke and when she tried to call out for help her voice wouldn't work and no one heard her. Finally, she escaped with whatever she could carry, but both the hotel and her shop were destroyed. She sighs and then, apropos of nothing in particular, she says, 'People don't care about the finer things, they just want to gratify their own wishes.'

We lapse into an uncomfortable silence. Since Gloria came back to live here, she has been taking care of Aunt Ruth, driving her to the doctor in Chattanooga and taking her to lunch every week, and I can see the old lady is dreading her departure.

After a while, Bobby-Sue and Jimmy McKenzie get up and start walking out.

'That Bobby-Sue's put on some weight since she got together with Jimmy,' Aunt Ruth observes.

'Yeah, an' Jimmy's lost some since he got shot,' says Gloria.

McKenzie, it turns out, was representing a woman in a divorce case. One day he was crossing the Courthouse lawn from his office on the corner when the woman's husband came out from behind a pick-up truck and shot him six times with a semi-automatic, mainly in the gut and legs. The seventh bullet, which would have been the finisher, jammed. McKenzie managed to stagger over to the bank and survived.

After lunch, I drive over to see Leland Frazier as I had promised. Before I get to the church doorway, I encounter one of the big brutes from last night and he turns out to be a jail preacher too. He tells me that 90% of the crimes that put people in jail are 'drug or akyhol related, but child molestation's a lot too, big, big number now.'

'Why's that, d'you think?'

'Well, they just miss order for their lives, they left God out of their lives and they's just hooked on sin. This whole world's gone wild and crazy just like God said it would in the last days.'

At this point, Leland, a moustachioed bloodhound in search of lost souls, scampers out of his church and takes me back inside to show me around. Behind the altar is a baptismal jacuzzi where one may be born again under a painting of Mount Hermon (I think) rendered in Italian restaurant style. Next door to this mystic trough is a little room with a curtain.

'This here's the dressing room,' Leland tells me.

'So they strip off in here and then ...?'

'No, no' he interrupts, 'they go in in their clothes but they bring some spare to change into afterwards. Mebbe one day you'll end up in thar,' he says, nodding into the pit, his round little eyes glistening with the desire to plunge me in and get me all wet and sobbing and going 'Boo-hoo, Lord save me,' but today I've come prepared and as soon as he starts in on any of that, I shut him down.

'So, what else have you got in here? Any tracts? Any tapes?'

'I got plenty of tracts, but I don't want to give you no tapes unless you's comin' back tonight.'

I tell him I'll do my best and we head to the rear of the church and into a back room where he has a tape duplication machine. He can duplicate a whole tape, both sides, in a minute and a half. While he duplicates a tape of the jail preacher, he starts dispensing the tracts.

Where Will You Spend Eternity? The Choice Is Yours contains such lay questions as, 'Now that I realise I'm guilty of sin, deserving hell, and hopeless on my own; where do I turn for help?' *The Bible Believer And Heretics* gives you ten tips on how to deal with people like me: 'Try them. Mark them. Rebuke them. Have no fellowship. Withdraw thyself. Turn away from them. Receive them not. Have no company with them. Reject them. Be ye separate.' Is it just me or do the last seven seem to make the same point? *Mary's Command For Catholics* ends with the question, 'What is Your Decision?' under which are two boxes to be filled in, presumably with a cross. The first option is: 'I choose to believe what Jesus says.' The second option is, 'I feel this tract is anti-Catholic,' under which is written, 'Friend, the reason we gave you this tract is because we love you and do not want to see you go to hell when you die. If you feel this tract is anti-Catholic, you had better re-examine your beliefs. Anyone who rejects what Jesus Christ says is Anti-Christ.'

This interdenominational squabbling reminds me of the South American writer's comment on the Falklands War: 'It's like watching two old bald men fighting over a comb ...'

When I finally get back outside, clutching my tracts and the tape, the jail preacher's children are jamming on the stage. It's *One Step Of Faith*, and you can hear honky-tonk and the blues in there. They're good-looking kids, but there's something wary and worn down about them, particularly a twelve-year-old boy, draped over a too-big guitar, watching me through narrowed eyes.

Now the jail preacher comes rolling up. He's rough and wild, a thick-skinned, laughing old boy and whatever his purpose – and jail work can hardly be profitable, so I don't doubt his sincerity – the rogue lives on behind his eyes. He slaps me on the back and I slap him on the back and he laughs and winks at me. He knows I'm not saved but he's ministering to a fourteen-year-old right now who knocked off an entire family just for the fun of it, so one dissolute Englishman is small beer. The difference between him and Leland is that he has a sense of humour and I can forgive almost anyone almost anything if they're funny. There has never been a monster of the Hitlerian type who has had a sense of humour. Humour, celebrating not only the imperfection of human life but also its *imperfectability*, is a kind of objectivity and so the antithesis of fanaticism.

After a while, I take a bone-crushing from his big calloused hand and bid him goodbye.

Monkeyville

It's still too early to go visit Kurt Wise, so I hurry down to the Courthouse to see if I can find Jim McKenzie. Shot six times! I've never met a man so comprehensively riddled. I catch him scurrying around taking care of business, but manage to get him to sit down in the hallway and talk for a minute. He's a small grey-haired man and a little twitchy. His eyes dart this way and that, checking the hallway as we talk.

When I ask him what it was like getting shot, he tells me, 'Well, it's not fun, let's put it that way. You know the only reason I'm here today is that the Lord decided it wadn't my time 'cause the man had more bullets in there and the seventh one jammed, so I only got six of them.'

'But what does it feel like?' I ask. 'Is it like a burning sensation or what?'

'Oh, yeah, it's burning, I still burn today if I start perspiring.'

'And all the bullets, they got 'em out?'

'No, they just dug one of 'em out. The rest of 'em all went through.'

I notice that he's beginning to perspire, but I'm still fascinated by the whole thing. I mean getting *shot*, Jesus ...

'So you were walking across the courthouse lawn and this total stranger just ...'

'Oh, no, I'd seen him before. I knew who it was right when he came out from behind the pick-up. I didn't know he had a gun because he had it behind his right leg and when he got close to me, just a little bit further than between you and me, he pulled it out and started shooting.'

He's looking increasingly uneasy and the beads of sweat on his forehead are beginning to trickle down toward his eyes and I'm thinking he probably isn't enjoying reliving this thing, which opinion is confirmed when he shifts uncomfortably in his chair and asks in a businesslike fashion, 'What else can I do for you?'

I'm too embarrassed to ask for a viewing of the bullet holes, which is what's on my mind, so I thank him for sharing his experiences with me and go into the basement to check out the Scopes Trial Museum in more detail. It's dark down here, and dank. Towards the back is a boiler room and sitting in it an old man, a very pretty girl, and what looks to be an imbecile. They are all smoking and when I ask them how they're doing, they don't reply, just stare at me with the blank resentment of the profoundly bored. I turn around and examine some of the pictures of the trial and their accompanying texts.

The trial of John Scopes was set to begin on Friday, 10th July 1925 and by mid-June, you can see that Dayton was pumping with promotional zeal. There is a photograph of J.R. Darwin's Everything To Wear Store, above which a newly-painted sign states 'Darwin is right – Inside,' while F.E. Robinson has one above his drugstore saying 'Where it Started.' Inside the store, another photograph shows him selling a Simian Soda. The town's motorcycle cop smiles at the camera from astride his steed upon which he has painted 'Monkeyville Police.' And a pin sold at the time states 'Your Old Man's A Monkey.'

Within a week of creating this carnival, Rappleyea had wired H.G. Wells inviting him to attend, but Wells declined. H.L. Mencken, however, one of the funniest and most biting of reporters, announced he was on his way to cover the trial for the Baltimore *Evening Sun*. An argument about evolution broke out in the town's barber shop, the alternative meeting place to the drugstore, and a man ran out into the street followed by his adversary shooting at him with a pistol. Scopes believed it was a stunt organised by the enterprising Rappleyea and called him to suggest he stop.

A vacant lot was designated as a campground for tourists. An airstrip was created. The state sent a mobile chlorination unit and the railways scheduled extra trains from Chattanooga. Rappleyea took over a large, abandoned house and started making it fit for the defence experts. Judge John Tate Raulston, the Baptist judge who would hear the case, got so over excited he suggested constructing a vast temporary court so an estimated 20,000 spectators could observe his judicial brilliance. (Darrow described Raulston as 'an affable man ... who had been elected on a fluke due to some political mix-up.') The existing Courthouse got a fresh coat of paint and 500 extra seats were installed, along with a platform for movie cameras.

Before long, the hucksters and the crazies began to arrive: John The Baptist the Third came, along with Lewis Levi Johnson Marshall, 'Absolute Ruler of the Entire World without Military, Naval, or other Physical Force.' Next up were Joe Mendi, the trained chimp and his handler and a man who called himself 'The Champion Bible Demonstrator.' Wilbur Glenn Voliva, of the flat-earth school of geology and The Anti-Evolution League came, the latter hawking pamphlets like *Hell and the High Schools*, and *Jocko-Homo Heaven-Bound*. All these and more were joined by a horde of Bible-thumpers from out of the hills and way beyond, along with purveyors of hotdogs and sandwiches, ice cream, lemonade and popcorn.

Nor was the excitement confined to Dayton. Debate raged across the nation. The *New York Times* gave over most of its front page to letters expressing conflicting views. Modernist Christians distanced themselves from Bryan and the fundamentalists, saying you could accept the moral and religious precepts of the Bible without having to accept its opinions on nature. During a debate in London, George Bernard Shaw said: 'The great American statesman, William Jennings Bryan, the sort of man only America can produce, has suddenly taken the lead in the movement against evolution and called himself a Fundamentalist … What he calls Fundamentalism, I call Infantilism.' Even Hollywood got in on the act, offering Scopes $2000 a week to appear in Tarzan movies.

As the trial date came closer, telegraph wires were run into the Courthouse and three microphones were installed and connected to loudspeakers outside so people on the lawn could hear what was going on inside. Using these microphones, WGN, a radio station in Chicago, planned to send the first live coverage of a trial to the nation, then on to Europe and Australia. Sixty-five telegraph operators were employed and eventually would transmit more words on the subject than had ever been sent about any other American event.

Two hundred reporters, all needing accommodation, soon chuffed into town with their secret stashes of whisky, chief among them the mischievous Mencken. Mencken brought with him 1,000 handbills advertising a fictitious evangelist named the Rev. Elmer Chubb, LL D, DD who would perform miracles, such as speaking Coptic, and swallowing poison without harm. At the designated time and place – the Courthouse lawn one evening – only a very few people turned up for the non-existent event. Discreet enquiry revealed this was because there was nothing unusual about such claims in Tennessee.

Now, in came Bryan three days before the trial, arriving on a train from Miami which usually shot through Dayton without stopping. Most of the inhabitants were at the station to meet him, along with various reporters. He soon emerged in a pith helmet and waved regally at his adoring rural fans. That night there was a banquet for him where he said, 'If evolution wins, Christianity goes. Not suddenly, of course, but gradually, for the two cannot stand together. They are as antagonistic as light and darkness; as antagonistic as good and evil.'

Scopes, who was seated next to him for dinner, was amazed to discover that Bryan recognised and remembered him from the commencement address he had given over five years earlier at Scopes' high school in Salem. He lightly reprimanded Scopes and his friends for having laughed at him. Having told Scopes he was a diabetic and could eat neither starch nor sugar, Scopes watched in alarm as Bryan quickly scarfed down all his food, refusing only bread, then glanced at Scopes' plate and asked if he could finish his uneaten mashed potatoes and corn, not knowing, or so it seemed, that both contained far more starch than the bread he had refused. As Scopes says in his book, 'The incident was a good tip-off to Bryan's scientific knowledge.' Bryan had a ferocious appetite and reportedly carried a large bag of radishes with him wherever he went so he need never go hungry.

The next day, Bryan, ever the good American, joined in the spirit of commercial enterprise by having a loudspeaker truck, a thing never before seen in Dayton, driven around town advertising Florida real estate!

For two days, Bryan had Dayton to himself and made the most of it, giving speeches all over the place and wandering the town, shirtsleeves rolled up, pith helmet on bald pate, a palm fan waving in his hand. As Mencken put it, 'Bryan has been oozing around the country ... presenting the indubitable word of God in his caressing, ingratiating way, and so making unanimity doubly unanimous.' Everything Bryan said was widely reported and went unanswered until Scopes' attorneys arrived on the day before the trial.

Darrow and Bryan would not be facing each other alone in court.

On Darrow's side were two Tennessee lawyers, the notoriously scruffy chief counsel John Neal, a radical, committed law professor from Knoxville who pledged himself to the case from the day it began, and F.B. McElwee an ex-student of his. From New York came Arthur Garfield Hays and his law partner, Dudley Field Malone.

Dudley Malone, who would figure prominently in the trial, had worked for Bryan for a while at the State Department. Now he spent much of the year in Paris handling the European end of his and Hays' international divorce business. Malone was an elegant, convivial man, rarely seen without his jacket and tie, even in the overwhelming summer heat of Dayton. A divorced Irish Catholic, he was married to suffragette Doris Stevens, who, much to the titillation of the town, checked into his room at the Aqua under her own name.

Hays, in his early forties, was a good looking man resembling the young Spencer Tracy. Hayes, who was Jewish, was the most respected lawyer on the ACLU executive committee and was their official representative at the trial. Made rich by his successful New York practice, he got his real pleasure from the passionate defence of civil liberties. He was agnostic.

On Bryan's side, A.T. ('General') Stewart, Attorney General for the Eighteenth Judicial Circuit in Tennessee, was in charge of the prosecution team. Assisting him was Bryan himself; his son, William Jennings Bryan Jr, an attorney in Los Angeles; and from Dayton, Ben McKenzie; his son, J. Gordon McKenzie; Sue K. Hicks, Herbert Hicks, and Wallace C. Haggard.

Malone and Hays arrived in Chattanooga on a train loaded with reporters. They were met by George Rappleyea and driven to Dayton. Darrow meanwhile took off from Chicago but not before lashing out at the 'narrow, mean, intolerable and brainless prejudice of soulless religio-maniacs.' By the time Darrow arrived in Dayton that afternoon, the population of the town had swollen from 1,800 to 5,000, almost its size in the boom days of Dayton Coal and Iron. Whatever else his faults, Rappleyea had delivered an event.

Although there had been a well-planned banquet for Bryan, no such affair had been arranged for the atheistic Darrow. A small dinner was quickly organised at which Darrow spoke, charming all who listened with a folksy speech about coming from a town just like this and 'falling into the law.' As no one on the defence side was getting paid (nor was Bryan on the prosecution side) and as Darrow was not a rich man, he and his second wife, Ruby, roomed with the Morgan family, whose son, Howard, attended the high school and was one of the witnesses against Scopes.

The next day, Friday, 10th July, everyone set off for the centre of town and the tall red-brick building in the shaded square. As each of the participants entered the Courthouse, they stopped to pose for the numerous photographers and newsreel cameramen. The show was about to begin in earnest.

The court transcript, which was first published in 1925 and is now reprinted by Bryan College, can be purchased in Dayton. Its title is, *The World's Most Famous Court Trial*, and under that it says, 'A word for word report of the famous court test of the Tennessee anti-evolution act, at Dayton, July 10 to 21, 1925, including speeches and arguments of attorneys, testimony of noted scientists, and Bryan's last speech.'

It is a fantastic document which can be read for sheer enjoyment.

As soon as the court was stuffed beyond capacity, the record tells us that Judge Raulston called upon a Reverend Cartwright to open court with a prayer. Which suggested to Darrow that he didn't have one.

'Help us to remember that Thou art on Thy throne and that Thou knowest the secrets of our hearts, and that Thou are acquainted with the motive back of every act and thought; and may we also be conscious of the fact, our Heavenly Father, that there is coming a day in which all of the nations of the earth shall stand before Thy judgement bar and render an account for the deeds done in the body ...'

Added to this sly spiritual threat was Judge Raulston's reading of the charges to the grand jury convened to re-indict Scopes. Since the law which had been broken stated it was unlawful to teach any theory denying the divine creation of man as taught in the Bible, he felt it proper to read into the record the entire first chapter of Genesis. He then went on to say: 'In making this declaration I make no reference to the policy or constitutionality of the statute, but to the evil example of the teacher disregarding constituted authority in the presence of the undeveloped mind whose thought and morals he directs and guides ... Now, gentlemen of the jury, it is your duty to investigate this alleged offence without prejudice or bias and with open minds.'

As my daughter would say: 'Yeah, right.'

Darrow insisted that if the lead prosecution lawyer, ex-Attorney General A.T. Stewart, was going to be referred to as 'General', when in fact he was not a general, then he, Darrow, should also be given some equally meaningless title. 'Colonel' was agreed on and, much to his amusement, Darrow was referred to as such whenever anyone remembered.

The grand jury returned the new indictment and the rest of the morning was taken up with discussion on the admissibility of scientific testimony. Stewart said he would object to it; Darrow wanted to know immediately if it would be allowed so that he could bring in his witnesses, or not. The prosecution agreed to a quick disposal of the matter on Monday and the court adjourned for lunch.

Outside on the Courthouse lawn, preachers preached and vendors vended, and tracts were offered, all to the accompaniment of various musicians, including a black string quartet and a blind man with a guitar and a mouth organ. Four steers were roasting over a barbecue pit and two planes, commissioned to take newsreel footage to the cinemas in the North, buzzed the town.

In the afternoon, the jury was selected. Darrow, who would sometimes spend months on jury selection, now spent a few hours at most. Only white males were eligible and none were impartial. All he could hope for was a modicum of honesty from the wholly religious pool. One man was asked if he'd ever read anything by Bryan on the subject of evolution.

'No, sir, I can't read.'

'Well, you are fortunate,' said Darrow and then asked him why he couldn't read.

The man replied frankly, 'Because I'm uneducated.'

Darrow picked him right away. Another, a preacher, was asked if he preached for or against evolution. 'Well, I preach against it, of course!' He got a lot of applause but no seat in the jury box. Only one juror, a part-time teacher, seemed to have any real understanding of, let alone sympathy for, the concept of evolution. 'Such a jury, in the legal sense,' wrote Mencken, 'may be fair. That is, it may be willing to hear the evidence against Scopes before bumping him off. But it would certainly be spitting into the eye of reason to call it impartial.'

The court adjourned until Monday. Bryan had not spoken the entire day. He was saving himself for closing arguments and would, for the moment, content himself with sermons and speeches made outside the courtroom.

On Sunday morning Bryan preached at a Methodist Church. Judge Raulston and his family sat among the cheering crowd as Bryan reiterated his position on the irrelevance of Darrow's so-called 'expert witnesses.' In the afternoon, he gave another speech to an estimated 3,000 listeners on the Courthouse lawn where, on Saturday, a freethinker had been arrested for giving a speech critical of the church. By all accounts, Bryan's speech delivered him the required tonic of applause.

Mencken went up to the mountains to watch a revival. He thought he would be amused, but instead returned to town depressed. He found the clashing theologians monotonous and expressed a longing for 'a merry laugh, a burst of happy music, the gurgle of a decent jug.'

On Monday, the 13th, after the obligatory prayer, the defence made a motion to quash the indictment on the grounds that the law violated numerous articles of the constitution of Tennessee, fourteen of them to be precise. A typical example was Section 12, Article 11 of the Tennessee constitution which, in reference to education, states, 'it shall be the duty of the general assembly ... to cherish literature and science.' The defence also believed the law violated the part of the constitution guaranteeing the right to 'worship Almighty God according to the dictates of his own conscience.' In banning the teaching of evolution because of something said in the Bible, the law favoured one form of religion over another. Neal laid out the legal details, Hays then followed with a more impassioned plea. He argued that if the law was against not evolution, but the Copernican 'theory' that the earth moved around the sun it would be clearly unconstitutional. 'The only distinction you can draw between this statute and the [hypothetical] one we are discussing is that evolution is as much a scientific fact as the Copernican theory, but the Copernican theory has been fully accepted.'

In fact the Copernican theory had *not* been fully accepted in 1925, at least not in some quarters. For supporting Copernican theory in the mid-1600s, Galileo was tried by the Roman Catholic church and put under house arrest for the last eight years of his life. He was not 'pardoned' until 1988 when Pope John Paul II finally conceded that the church had made a 'mistake'. *1988!* Over three centuries to concede a scientific point that every man of reason had accepted two hundred years before.

Darrow closed the day with a long speech. He started out by thanking the court for its courtesy, in particular for giving him the title of Colonel which 'I hope will stick to me when I get back north.'

He then went on to sum up the major issues. When you read the transcript of the trial, you can understand most of the complex legal issues expressed by Darrow's fellow lawyers – *if you concentrate*. However, when you get to Darrow, he rambles, he makes jokes, he repeats himself, but by the end of it, everything is not only clear but obvious.

'There are in America at least five hundred different sects or churches, all of which quarrel with each other over the importance and non importance of certain things or the construction of certain passages … There is such disagreement that my client, who is a school-teacher, not only must know the subject he is teaching, but he must know everything about the Bible in reference to evolution. And he must be sure that he expresses it right or else some fellow will come along here, more ignorant perhaps than he, and say, "You made a bad guess and I think you have committed a crime." No criminal statute can rest that way … Every criminal statute must be clear and simple. If Mr Scopes is to be indicted and prosecuted because he taught a wrong theory of the origin of life, why not tell him what he must teach? Why not say that he must teach that man was made of the dust; and still stranger, that Eve was made out of Adam's rib.'

In other words, it was not only a bad law but badly written. Darrow went on for over two hours. As he walked around the courtroom, he played constantly with his suspenders, even at times putting his arms right through them and then pulling them out again. He would pause and stop to think, and then renew his argument with increased vigour.

He concluded by saying, 'There is an old saying that nits make lice … It is a good idea to clear the nits, safer and easier … Ignorance and fanaticism is ever busy and needs feeding. Always it is feeding and gloating for more. Today it is the public school teachers, tomorrow the private. The next day the preachers and the lecturers, the magazines, the books, the newspapers. After a while, your honor, it is the setting of man against man, and creed against creed, until with flying banners and beating drums we are marching backward to the glorious ages of the sixteenth century when bigots burned men who dared to bring any intelligence or enlightenment and culture to the human mind.'

Although some of the audience hissed at the end of the speech, most said it was one of Darrow's best. 'It was not designed for reading but for hearing,' wrote Mencken. 'The clangorousness of it was as important as the logic. It rose like a wind and ended like a flourish of bugles.' Bryan sat through it, tight-lipped and unmoved. He looked 'mangy and flea-bitten' according to Mencken. 'His eyes fascinated me: I watched them all day long. They were blazing points of hatred. They glittered like occult and sinister gems. Now and then they wandered to me, and I got my share. It was like coming under fire ...'

The Judge adjourned court so he could work on his decision about the motion to quash. That night there was a storm. Some townspeople suggested it was an expression of God's anger with Darrow. In any case, the electricity failed.

As usual, a preacher was called to give a morning prayer before court began on Tuesday. Before he could start, Darrow objected. As this was a case involving a conflict between science and religion he argued that to have prayers at the opening of every day was clearly prejudicial.

Stewart and Malone got into a brief but nasty argument over this. The Judge intervened, overruling Darrow's objection and asking for the prayer to be said. When it was over, he explained that because of last night's power outage, he had been unable to complete his ruling on the motion to quash and needed to adjourn court until the afternoon.

'If you want to make any pictures,' he told the photographers, 'make them now. I will give you fifteen minutes.' Having struck several judicial poses, he left the court for the rest of the morning.

That afternoon was one of the comic high points of the trial.

Yesterday, Raulston, told the court when it reconvened, he had dictated most of his ruling on the motion to quash and had given it to the court stenographer, a reputable woman, with instructions that no one should see it. Today, however, several newspapers in the larger cities were stating which way he had ruled. He was furious. He ordered the members of the press to stay while he dismissed the jury and the public and read a wire from St Louis saying the St Louis *Star* was carrying a story that the motion to quash had been denied. How could they possibly know? No one except he and his stenographer knew. The motion was not yet even completed!

He appointed a committee of pressmen to get to the bottom of the matter and report back to him as soon as possible. The five pressmen spent the night playing cards and getting drunk on bootleg liquor. They knew exactly who was responsible for the leak and had from the start.

The next morning, Wednesday, Raulston called on the chairman of the press committee, Richard Beamish, to make his report. Beamish was an outlandish character who wore extraordinarily loud shirts, each of which, according to Mencken, was given a name, 'Garden of Allah,' 'Who is Sylvia?' 'I'm Called Little Buttercup,' and so on.

In fine judicial style, Beamish stated that the reporter who had leaked the story had believed it to be correct and true and did not obtain it in any unethical manner. Beamish was prepared to leave it at that. End of story. Of course, he teased, if the court *insisted*, he'd be willing to give more details …

Raulston took the bait. 'I think the court is entitled to know how this information was had,' he declared pompously.

'Upon investigation,' Beamish told him, 'we find that the information came from you.'

'Well …' said Raulston, gaping at the courtroom in shock.

Beamish immediately went on to tell the story. A young reporter named Hutchinson had seen the judge leaving court after Monday's adjournment. Noticing he had a lot of papers under his arm, he asked if this was his decision. The judge had replied, no, the decision was being copied by the stenographer. Hutchinson then asked whether the judge was going to read his decision that afternoon. The judge replied that that was his intention. Hutchinson then asked if, having given his decision, the judge would adjourn until the following day? The judge had said yes, that was his plan. Now, of course, if the motion to quash were granted, there would be no next day. The trial would be over. Hutchinson deduced therefore that the judge was denying the motion to quash and sent the information to his paper.

The judge was mortified but soon recovered himself and got ready to take center stage. 'I shall expect absolute order in the courtroom because people are entitled to hear this opinion,' he declared and turned again to the photographers. 'If you gentlemen want to make my picture, make it now.' And once again, he posed for them. Quash the indictment and miss this? Not a chance. It took him several hours to over-rule all the defence's objections and when he was done, the poor man was worn out.

It was unbearably hot and during lunch Scopes and Bryan Jr went up in the hills to swim in a waterhole in the mountains. Scopes liked Jr but thought he had been crushed by his famous father. They were late getting back to court, which began without them. Hays was furious with Scopes. No one else seemed to have noticed his absence.

At last the jury was sworn in. The Judge asked the attorneys to make their opening statements.

Stewart spoke for about a minute, stating their side's theory of the case. There was a law. Scopes had broken it. It was that simple.

Malone then got up, dressed as always in an elegant suit and necktie. There was, he stated, more than one theory of creation in the Bible and, through expert witnesses, both scientists and theologians, the defence would show that many people found no conflict between the Bible's stories and the theory of evolution.

Malone then glanced at his old boss, Bryan.

'There may be a conflict between evolution and the peculiar ideas of Christianity which are held by Mr Bryan as the evangelical leader of the prosecution, but we deny that the evangelical leader of the prosecution is an authorized spokesman for the Christians of the United States.'

He then told the court he was going to read from the writings of 'a great political leader' commenting twenty years earlier on Jefferson's 'Statute of Religious Freedom.'

' "Jefferson said, in the first place, that to attempt to compel people to accept a religious doctrine by act of law was not to make Christians but hypocrites ... that the regulation of the opinions of men on religious questions by law is contrary to the laws of God ... that God had it in His power to control man's mind and body, but did not see fit to coerce the mind or the body into obedience to even the Divine Will; and that if God Himself was not willing to use coercion to force man to accept certain religious views, man, uninspired and liable to error, ought not to use the means that Jehovah would not employ ..." ' Malone turned to Bryan. 'These words,' he said, 'were written by William Jennings Bryan and the defense appeals from the fundamentalist Bryan of today to the modernist Bryan of yesterday.'

Bryan sat tight-lipped, fanning himself with his palm-leaf fan and did not respond.

Stewart objected to Malone using Bryan's name and personal views in the case. Malone asked Bryan if he minded. Bryan primly stated, 'Not a bit. The court can do as it pleases ... I ask no protection from the court.'

Superintendent White was brought on as a witness for the state and testified that Scopes had admitted to him that he'd taught evolution. He was followed by two boys from the high school who confirmed it. When asked by Darrow if this had stopped them going to church or done them any other harm, they replied that it had not. Doc Robinson was called to testify that he'd sold Hunter's *Biology*. Darrow read the offending passage from the textbook and then asked Robinson, if, having sold the book to many children, he'd ever 'noticed any mental or moral deterioration' as a result.

Stewart's objection to the question was sustained and the prosecution rested.

Darrow now brought up the first of his expert witnesses, Metcalf, an eminent zoologist, graduate of Johns Hopkins, and member of many scientific associations. He was also a member of the Congregationalist Church and had taught Bible class to college students when he was at Oberlin in Ohio.

Because he had not yet made up his mind on the admissibility of scientific testimony, the judge excluded the jury, who would in fact stay out for the rest of the week. Having chosen to be jurors so they could get front row seats, they in fact saw far less of the trial than the average Daytonian.

Darrow guided Metcalf through an explanation of evolution. Metcalf explained that there was a difference between the *theories* of evolution and the *fact* of evolution. That organisms have evolved 'is a thing that is perfectly and absolutely clear.' However, there are dozens of *theories* of evolution, some of which are absurd, some of which may be largely wrong, and some of which are probably largely right.

At the close of the day, Judge Raulston told the lawyers to prepare their arguments about expert testimony which would be argued the next day, Thursday.

My Favourite Creationist

Most modern scientists – perhaps 99% – believe the world is about 4,000,000,000 years old. Professor Kurt Wise of Bryan College puts it somewhere around 6,000. The gap between these two figures is so huge it's almost impossible to grasp. It's the same difference as exists between six and four million.

Six years ago I moved to New York. Four million years ago I ...

When I emerged from the Museum, the sun was out and the humidity was down to 90%. Without further lightning bolts, I drove to Bryan College, and now find my way up to Kurt's office, off the corridor of dead and ancient things.

Kurt is a tall man with brown hair, a moustache, and large wire-rimmed glasses. He is probably in his mid to late thirties, but it is hard to say because he is so boyish. You might almost think the moustache was grown to make him look older. A white T-shirt saying, 'Ho-Ho, The University Of Chicago Is Funnier Than You Think' is tucked into his corduroy jeans.

I tell him I'm writing a book about the Scopes Trial and Dayton, and would like to talk to him about creationism. He ushers me in.

His official title is Associate Professor of Science and Director of Origins Research at Bryan College. On his desk is a Bible.

Born and raised in Rochelle, Illinois, a small agricultural town, he was the first student from his high school ever to go on to the University of Chicago, even though it was only eighty miles away. To earn money for college, he worked at the Del Monte canning factory, canning factories being one of the mainstays of the town's economy. His father was general manager of the local newspaper. You can imagine Kurt as a child, collecting and hoarding things with enthusiasm and then defending his hobby with the resolution of the lonely but determined nerd. Little has changed. He is polite and willing to discuss whatever subject arises (to an extraordinary degree as will become evident), but the defensiveness remains, a prickly arrogance which rears up at the slightest provocation. He expects to be ridiculed, but also knows that nine times out of ten, whoever ridicules him will be less intelligent and less informed than he. He sits down in a squeaky metal chair behind his desk. The afternoon sun cuts into the room illuminating a row of photographs, some of his wife and his two young daughters, some of a graduation ceremony, perhaps from Harvard: a younger, paler Kurt in a pink robe with three black flashes on the arm.

Kurt teaches his Origins course in two parts, the first from the perspective of theistic evolution, that is the idea the God used evolution over long periods of time to create the universe. The second half of the course is where he teaches what he really believes.

He believes the 'six days of creation,' which some creationists see as metaphorical days, were in fact regular 'earth rotation days' because the same word for 'day' is used in the Ten Commandments when we are instructed to work six days and rest on the seventh.

He rocks back in his squeaking chair and laughs. 'So if the first word for day actually means "several million years," then that means we're going to have to work for several million years before we ever get to rest!' He does this a lot, laughing as he talks, a high laugh, almost a series of yelps, but it's not always clear if it's from embarrassment or genuine amusement.

He also confirms that he believes the world is 6,000 years old – 'on the order and magnitude of that' – and suggests that the fossil record was 'formed catastrophically, possibly the third day of creation, the rising of the continents, and in events such as the flood in the days of Noah, and in the post-flood period as well.'

To further bolster the idea of a young-age earth, he cites an early Egyptologist from the University of Chicago who put together a chronology based on ancient Egyptian records of solar eclipses and other planetary events, and Bishop Ussher (1581-1656), who worked his way back through the Bible from the birth of Christ to arrive at a date for the creation of the earth of 4004 BC. Ussher's chronology was so widely accepted it appeared in the introduction to the King James Bible, the official Bible of record in the Scopes Trial.

But Ussher did not just look back, he also looked *forward*. By taking literally the Old Testament quotation from Psalm 84, verse 10, 'A day with the Lord is as a thousand years and a thousand years is as a day,' and figuring human history as a week, he somehow concluded that Jesus would return in 1997.

Kurt does not seem to take this seriously. Why, I do not know.

When I ask him what he is doing to try and prove his theory of a young earth, he throws himself forward in his chair so vehemently I think he's going to smack the desk with his hand.

'Science doesn't prove a thing!' he declares. 'All I'm doing is searching around for a theory that best fits the data of the universe *and* the data of scripture. Science doesn't arrive at truth except by accident, and you don't even know you've got it when you get there. Look at the history of science: a hundred years ago, what they believed is largely rejected now. A hundred years from now, most likely any theories that I come up with are going to be rejected. Let's not be chauvinistic about our time period.'

I point out this is not always so. For example, our understanding of the human body has been largely progressive and is unquestionably closer to the truth than it was a hundred years ago. He concedes the point, but says that with the historical sciences, where we're displaced from the events and have only relics to interpret, it's another matter.

His position is unusual, though, I suggest, in that most scientists are looking at information and then forming theories based on that, whereas he arrives with a theory in place – that of the Bible – and tries to fit the information into it. Again he disagrees vehemently. He is no different from any other scientist, he states. They all enter the field with preconceptions. What about Darwin, I ask, a fairly traditional Christian with no particular view before he set off on the Beagle, and yet by ...

Before I can finish, he has come tilting forward in his chair again.

'That's bunk! That's bunk! By the time he got done with his five-year voyage on the Beagle, he hated Christianity with a passion, because of Fitzroy's fanaticism.' (Fitzroy was the Captain of the Beagle and a devout Christian.) 'I mean if you know anything about Fitzroy or if you've read anything about it ... He committed suicide! He was a fanatical individual. Darwin left the boat many times just to get away from Fitzroy. Collected specimens for that reason.'

I look at him in amazement. 'You think he gathered all that information and then threw together the theory of evolution just to *irritate Fitzroy*?'

'No, no, but my point is he wasn't a traditional Christian; he was not a Christian. He was not a believer in God. There is no way you could make that argument. He is not a believer in the God of Scripture.'

In that case, I ask, would he have gone to hell?

'If he did not believe in Jesus Christ as his personal saviour, he went to hell, he is *in* hell. That's the entrance requirement.'

This seems so harsh and forlorn that instead of feeling sorry for Darwin I feel sorry for Kurt. I suggest that the tension between the two sides of his life, the scientific and the religious, must be very painful. Does he get lonely at times? He nods. Like everyone else, scientists crave the recognition of their peers. When Kurt goes to a scientific meeting, his fellow scientists often clamber across chairs to avoid walking down the same aisle as him. He often wishes he was not a young-age creationist. Life would be so much better. But he cannot. 'The Bible makes it clear where I must stand – and there I must stand. Like Martin Luther, here I stand. I have no choice.'

He tells me this with real regret, the last statement about Martin Luther lying at the end like something dead, almost as if he knows that no matter how courageous his stand, no matter how brilliant his work, ultimately his is a Quixotic journey which will consume his life. I am both touched and fascinated by him. He is so clearly intelligent and so completely without guile. I ask a question and he answers it like a scientist, on its merits. He does not say – you don't get the impression it even occurs to him to say – 'What business is it of yours?' or 'Who do you think you are?' He simply looks at the question as he might at any question about the natural world, and then replies as truthfully as he can.

When I ask him when he became interested in science and at what point he realised it would come in conflict with the Bible, his answer is so strange and so highly personal I find myself in a state of almost trance-like fascination.

'I would say the two paths converged very early on,' he tells me. 'At age nine, I was struggling with issues of reality, of what exists and what does not, I was going through – I didn't know it then, but what I now understand to be – deconstructionist philosophy. I was asking myself, what do I know for sure ... I had this thing I called my imp which was inside of me, and this imp was controlling my emotions, my sensory perceptions and making me believe things existed when they didn't really exist.'

Perhaps this imp, which began to look increasingly evil, had created Kurt himself, as an illusion, and then fooled him into thinking other things existed which did not, in order to distract him from his own non-existence. He might, in fact, be nothing more than the imp itself.

'I concluded I didn't know that anything in the universe existed for sure. All I really knew was that evil existed ... If I rejected the existence of everything else, if I went back to the *only* thing I knew ... the only thing I knew was that evil existed.' As an example of the kind of evil he is talking about, he describes watching his dog find a 'rabbit's nest' and how it ate one baby rabbit after another. This was 'evil' because he knew the dog was well fed and didn't need to kill. He also saw tornadoes and the destruction they caused. This was the evil which haunted him, not moral evil, but what modern philosophers call 'natural evil'.

He sits back in his chair and puts his hands behind his head and says: 'And that drove me to ... actually to suicide.'

I remain very still. He is talking about himself when he was nine.

'I decided I should destroy myself, because either I was the incarnation of evil or I was the imagination of evil. Either way if I committed suicide, I'd either destroy evil, which was good, or I wouldn't do anything because I didn't exist. I was in my tree-house at the time – I said, "One week from today" that was a Wednesday – "I'm going to come back up here, and I'm going to figure out the most efficient way of killing myself." I had my day chosen and everything and I would have done it *without telling anyone*. People say that people who are going to commit suicide will warn people and leave a note, but that's stupid because not in all cases. I wouldn't have left a note because *no one else existed!*'

Again, a big laugh.

However, that Sunday at the independent Baptist church where his family worshipped, his life was saved. The pastor read from Romans 5.8, 'But God commendeth his love toward us, in that, while we're yet sinners Christ died for us.' He realised that if Christ had given his life for our sins, and if he, Kurt, also wanted to destroy evil, even if it was his own evil, then evil couldn't be all there was.

He goes on to talk about his relationship with God, how powerful it was at that moment and how, over the years, it has become like an old friendship. The way he describes it reminds me of the relationship I imagined having with God when I was a child.

His love of science continued without coming into conflict with his love of God until his sophomore year in high school. Suddenly he knew too much about both to be able to ignore their contradictions. He had to decide whether or not the Bible and science, specifically Darwin's theory of evolution, could co-exist in his life and he came up with a bizarre physical test which he hoped would resolve the problem.

He went out and bought another Bible and took it home secretly. Each night, underneath the covers with a flashlight, he systematically read through it from Genesis to Revelation. The idea was to see how much would have to be thrown out if evolution were true. Whenever he came to a verse that made no sense in the light of evolutionary theory, he cut it out. Actually, to be fair, he cut out every *other* verse, because when you cut out one side of a page, you also cut out the other. He poked around the verse with the tip of his scissors, leaving the margins intact, and then extracted the verse, leaving a rectangular hole in the page. It took him a year and a half.

The last verse which had to be excised was from Revelation. It is the third from last verse in the entire Bible, and an ominous one: 'If any man shall take away from the words of the book of this prophecy God shall take away his part out of the book of life and out of the holy city.' The book of life is a list of all the names of the people who end up in heaven. As heaven would not exist under the mechanistic theory of evolution, he cut the verse out with trembling hands.

'The question now was, could I physically pick the Bible up? Would it hold itself together? This was the purpose of it all. It was a physical test of how important the concept of evolution was in undermining Scripture. I knew what the answer was going to be, and I'd known it for months, but I didn't want to come to this point because if the Bible didn't hold together I was going to have to reject evolution – and that meant to me rejecting science, which was everything I loved.'

He takes hold of the Bible on his desk, lays back the covers, and holds the outer margin of all the pages between finger and thumb. 'I tried very hard to pick it up, but each time it would start to tear. I'd put it back down and try a different spot. I was trying to find a place – I was *desperately* trying to find a place – where it would hold together. But it wouldn't.'

He lets the pages fall, leans back in his chair, and looks out of the window for a while before going on. 'My encounter with Jesus Christ had saved my life spiritually and physically, so I couldn't reject him and I came to know about him through that Bible so the words of that Bible had to have a higher priority than the claims of science. So I rejected evolution.'

Nothing could be more tragic. He sank into a long depression. There was a part missing in his life. After a few weeks, however, and quite by chance, he heard about creationism. Here was a way out of his dilemma. At first he swallowed all the material uncritically, but soon realised that most of the creationists were mediocre scientists and most of their theories untenable. There followed a period of disillusionment out of which he emerged with the basis for his life's work: he would start over, go back to the beginning, *rebuild* science from the ground up – and in the process exclude evolution.

'You still include evolution,' he amends, 'you know, it's just certain types of evolution that are excluded.'

He was accepted at the University of Chicago, where he studied astrophysics. He was trying to stay away from his first love, palaeontology, but after a year, he could resist it no longer and changed his major. He graduated with a Bachelor of Arts in Geophysical Sciences and applied to five different graduate programmes, one of which was Steven Jay Gould's at Harvard. No one mentioned on any of the applications that Kurt was a creationist. Gould accepted him without knowing and didn't find out until it was too late. On the day – or rather night – when they met, Kurt had driven his sister down to her college in South Carolina and then driven another fifteen hours up to Harvard. By the time he arrived it was one thirty in the morning and he was exhausted.

'I didn't know where to go, I didn't even know where my dorm was. I stepped out of my car. Went twenty feet. Ran into Steve Gould. One-thirty in the morning!' he laughs. 'He's going to his office!'

According to Wise, Gould wakes up at seven in the morning and goes to work. After a normal workday, he returns home to spend the evening with his family, goes to sleep with his wife at a regular hour, then wakes up around one a.m., and returns to work. After a few hours, he then goes home again, hops into bed for an hour, and wakes up to have breakfast with the family.

'I just ran right into him and he chewed me out right there. It's like, "Oh, my word." I mean I was completely out of it and I'm going, "I'm sorry, I didn't mean it. It really wasn't my intention. I didn't know they hadn't told you. I thought they would." '

The issue of creation didn't come up for another two years. One day Gould stopped and asked him, 'Do you still believe the same way?' 'Well, I'm still a creationist, if that's what you mean.' 'Oh, okay,' replied Gould. Another couple of years later, it came up again when Kurt was sitting in his office chatting. Again Kurt reaffirmed his position. Since then they have spoken of it calmly and seemingly without tension. Unfortunately, it was not this easy with everyone. One graduate student declared war on Kurt. 'I'm going to do everything in my power,' he told him, 'to make your life hell while you're at Harvard.'

'And he tried,' Kurt laughs, but you can see, beneath the laughter, memories of considerable pain.

Because he had to stop and work – as a landscape gardener – to be able to afford to stay at Harvard, Kurt was twenty-nine when he finally got his Ph.D. Since seventh grade, he had dreamed of teaching at one of the more prestigious secular universities, but when the moment came to look for work, he no longer wanted to and applied only to Christian colleges.

He had never heard of Bryan College until he applied for the job he now holds. It is, he states, the ideal situation. In a secular university he would never be able to conduct creationist research. His wife, whom he met in church and is not an academic, home-schools his children and runs a daycare centre in their home.

'And so you're happy here?' I ask.

He nods.

'It must be a big relief to be at a place like this after all these years.'

'Yes,' he says and nods again, 'to be released of that pressure ...'

'Do you find, if I may be candid here,' I say, lowering my voice, 'do you find that you don't encounter people here who are as intellectually stimulating as you might like?'

'That's been my universal observation, no matter where,' he answers, and then yelps with laughter before catching himself. 'Here at Bryan College,' he says more judiciously, 'there are students and fellow professors who are challenging for me and that's good.'

Still bewildered by the idea of a nine-year-old contemplating suicide for ostensibly philosophical reasons, I ask him if he can remember anything else that could have made him so unhappy. He thinks for a long while, wondering, it seems to me, how best to express what follows.

'There was a recurrent dream,' he says after a while, 'that I had just about every night. I would lie down in bed and whatever the attitude of the window – you know, you're looking at it kind of weird, it's kind of a weird shaped thing – when I closed my eyes the window's still there, still that light … that shape of lightness, and the whole dream was just that window, getting smaller and smaller and smaller and smaller, very, very slowly, and I would wake up screaming. And this for years. I knew precisely what it meant, it was the greatest fear I had as a child: I realised as soon as I began to talk to people that they knew instantly – they labelled me instantly – as a brain, and they rejected me instantly in like manner. I tried to speak differently, unintelligently. I did everything I could to thwart my intelligence. I was afraid that my intelligence was distancing me from people, from relationships. It was a terrible, terrible fear, and I did a lot – and I think successfully – to reduce the intellectual potential I had at that time, trying desperately to hold onto relationships …'

We sit in silence for a moment. I'm exhausted, physically, intellectually and emotionally. I can think of nothing more to ask him.

'It's been very interesting talking to you,' I tell him truthfully.

'Well, it's weird, I know,' he says, and laughs his high, boyish laugh.

Out in the corridor, I photograph him leaning against a specimen case containing fossils which would to 99% of all the scientists in the world provide incontrovertible proof that the world is thousands of millions of years old, and then we shake hands.

'Lord be with you,' he says and next thing I know, I hear myself saying:

'And Lord be with you too.'

All my adult life I've despised religion, in particular its resistance to scientific progress. Galileo is a greater hero to me than any saint. Yet here is Professor Wise, one of the most influential creationists in the world – and a religious nut by all previous standards – and I like him and feel sympathy for him. I didn't tell him I was a descendant of that hell-dweller, Darwin, but from my questions he must have known I was neither a believer in the young-age creation theory nor a fellow Christian, and yet he generously revealed himself to me. My intellectual views remain the same, but in some significant way, my *feelings* have changed. Faith in God or any of the fairy tales that surround Him may be absurd, but the *need* for faith is anything but. When you encounter someone like Kurt, you realise that faith is sometimes an absolute necessity.

CHAPTER FIFTEEN

How To Get Along Sensibly With Girls

St. Christopher's was a school for the semi-delinquent children of the relatively rich. It was vegetarian, the idea being, I think, that avoiding meat would reduce the violent or sexual urges in these sorry offspring. After a year, I opened an account at a local grocery store and ordered in thirty cans of corned beef. I had eaten about four of them when I read in the paper that several people had died of food poisoning from just such cans as these – I think it was typhoid – and so I had to go back to subsisting on nut-meat rissoles and banana cakes. My violence subsided to some extent, not through lack of meat, but through the sudden, wonderfully civilising presence of the opposite sex.

At last I was among girls again! Oh, the bliss of their little bodies and their shy glances, the smell of them, the way they giggled, the movement of them, the tenderness and malice, the promise in their blushes, the taste of their soft lips, the flick and whip of their skirts, and the marvellous hot, different *swell* of them. So many characters, so many different shapes, so many romances to be had, peeks to be taken, and feels to be felt.

Resurrection! Praise the Lord!

I was coming in at an unusual time and so my arrival was closely noted by the girls. A fresh boy. A good-looking boy. By now, mercifully, eczema no longer came to my face, and only flared up periodically – usually between my fingers, more rarely now in my elbows, at the back of my knees and on my ankles. If I remained dressed and kept my fingers pressed together, I could pass as normal. I arrived with my flowing locks and three years of pent-up desire pumping in my athletic body – and the girls, the girls *wanted* me! I did not select, I simply allowed myself to be carried off by the most insistent of them. I'd been in an all-boys school for over three years; anyone was welcome.

No sooner had I acquiesced to whichever girl it was, than the others turned against me. Spurned hormonal girls formed into a lethal pack and loving lips became blowpipes from which, instead of murmurs of encouragement and flattery, came barbs of sarcasm and spite. One girl dubbed me Mr X, a reference to my eczema which had been discovered. The boys, resenting my romantic success, also hated me. I had several fights, most of which I won. Finally, when I was dumped by the first girl, I was forgiven by the boys. William, one of those who'd beaten me in a fight, became my friend and remained so, even after I was expelled three years later.

The school was in a town called Letchworth in Hertfordshire about twenty miles from my family's home. Letchworth was a 'garden city', an experiment in idealistic urban planning intended to do away with tenements and inner-city squalor. It had succeeded: it was an utterly boring suburb. The main part of the school, which was on the edge of town, was a large red brick house with lots of additions – an assembly room, classrooms, extra dormitories scattered around it with little or no thought to aesthetics. On the other side of the playing fields were two more 'houses' which functioned as dormitories for the younger children.

Once the girls turned against me, I was often lonely and miserable. My mother sent me carefully-wrapped packages with food inside and letters about life at home, news of my brothers, Francis and Ludovic. My sister, Sarah, was at another boarding school, Bedales, where she excelled. The letters were written in a neat hand which often got less neat as the letter progressed. They were witty and descriptive and always filled with her obvious affection for me. The anticipation of these letters and packages, and then their arrival, bringing as they did the reassurance that somewhere out in the cold and unexplored world was at least one woman who loved me constantly, enabled me to survive the gloom and anguish caused by girls my own age whose love was as jagged and uncertain as broken bottles.

My first housemaster was a small, bearded man in a tweed sports coat whose larger and more vibrant wife performed the role of house-mother. Both drearily vegetarian, they were also ardent devotees of homeopathy and I remember arsenic being freely dispensed for certain ailments. The house was divided in two, one side being for the girls, the other for boys. My dormitory contained six boys in three two-tier bunk beds.

Masturbation was endemic but because the bunks were old and made of metal, they squeaked noisily. As a result, just as you were about to achieve orgasm, someone would always make a joke or complain they couldn't sleep and you'd have to start all over again. As all the boys except one were dedicated wankers, I suggested we drop the furtive aspects of the sport and adopt a more communal approach: mass-masturbation, timed to commence as soon as the lights went out. The suggestion was accepted and so the next night we all set out together, each in our own bunks, squeaking and groaning, all our little hands feverishly at work, the beds shaking and rattling, until the last boy finally came and we all went to sleep. Only one boy remained uninterested in the activity. He had a great love of lederhosen and racing bikes, but absolutely no interest in sex. After a few nights, he began to be a problem.

'I just don't get it,' he'd suddenly say at some crucial point in the endeavour.

'Shut up!'

'No, but what's the big deal? I just don't get it.'

'Please! If you don't like it, just be quiet, we're begging you.'

When that didn't work, when he continued to complain and interrupt, we tried to tempt and provoke him.

'Just close your eyes, put your hand on your willy, and imagine … Imagine your hand inside Sally's shirt … Or imagine Cora's legs … her buttocks … imagine long thighs … big tits … Imagine you're under the stairs and Jane goes by and you look up and you can see *right up her skirt!!!*'

'So what?'

It was shocking how sexless he was. We even tried to tailor fantasies for him which would integrate his own obsessions.

'Okay, lie back and dream … Pink nipples, drop handlebars, soft thighs, ten speed gears, your hand in her knickers, racing wheels, *pudendahhhh!!!!*'

'Uuugh!'

It was hopeless. Perhaps we should have crammed Jane or Sally into lederhosen and beat them with bike chains, but we were young; our limited imaginations could think of nothing sufficiently exotic to arouse this doughty little cyclist. Eventually, the chummy community of spermy boys disbanded and each of us slunk back into the frustration of muffling the once-again solitary vice. Several of us experimented with a new erotic technique in the hopes of bringing about orgasm more quickly. You would lie on one of your hands until it went numb and then take hold of it, wrap its insensible fingers around your penis, and jerk it up and down with the other hand, the idea being that as the hand felt nothing, you could imagine it belonged to someone else.

In the morning, we'd be woken by the bearded housemaster who would herd us into the boys' bathroom. Here, in summer or winter, a cold bath awaited us before the morning walk. You had to get into the bath and then lie down in the icy water until it covered every inch of you, including your head. Then, and only then, could you surge out and dry yourself. The bearded one would sit on the edge of the bath, fully dressed, grinning his sanctimonious grin, to make sure you complied with the total immersion rule and if you did not, just as you rose into the relative warmth of the room, he'd push you back down. He was a harmless enough man, but I didn't like him. There was no beating at the school, but there were other ways to make your life miserable. In retrospect, some rules verged on reasonable, like the prohibition against smoking, but some still seem manifestly goofy, like forcing you to cut your hair a certain length or this cold bath routine.

One day, after I'd been there about a year, I entered the bathroom and saw his nimble, tweedish figure perched on the edge of the bath. I had developed young and, at the age of twelve, was strong and quick. Suddenly – and it came out of nowhere, no plan, not a moment of decision – I felt inspired to give the little man a dose of his own medicine. I gave him no warning. He was completely unprepared as I lunged at him and with a single shove, sent him floundering backward into the bathtub. He flailed around, scrabbling to extricate his scrawny arse from the freezing water.

He didn't like it.

He punished me in some irrelevant way, but no serious trouble came of it. I suspect he was so embarrassed at his loss of dignity he didn't want to advertise it further. I was a hero for a week until my tendency to revel too cockily in my successes undercut my admirable achievement.

My longing for sexual contact of any kind increased with every day. Shortly after my dunking of the master, a boy whose claim to fame was that he could dangle a massive flashlight (including large square battery) from the tip of his erect penis, discovered that if you climbed along a thick branch of a nearby tree you could get an unimpeded view into one of the girl's dormitories. As I was always lurking about at night in search of romance, I was the first to catch him crouched up in his masturbatorial roost and quickly joined him. The clarity and closeness of the view was exquisite beyond words. There they all were in their fluffy sweaters and skirts and jeans, moving around and chatting like in a silent movie, except this movie was in glorious colour. Before long, the sweaters started to come off and down dropped the lower garments and there they were in their snappy little brassieres and pretty knickers. Then *they* came off revealing all the beautiful pinks and whites and little fuzzy bits, and up went the arms and on went the nighties – and oh!

Well worth my allergic reaction to the tree bark.

To the boy's considerable irritation, I told William about the carnal pleasures of the bough and the next night the three of us were up there, perched in a row, studying the mysteries of female development. Here was the girl from India with hair so long it reached her slender buttocks, a princess it was rumoured, who on the first day of school crashed to the floor after grace because no servant had pushed her chair in for her. How svelte and elegant she was with her tiny breasts and her beautiful light brown skin. Here was the one from Egypt with breasts so large they swayed from side to side as she moved. Standing awkwardly to one side was Sally, a sweet, chubby girl fumbling to release her Playtex pantygirdle. Here was pretty Lucy with her firm, protuberant breasts and long, athletic legs. On a bed sat Gaby, rolling down her stockings, a pretty, soft-fleshed girl, up whose skirt my hand would be a year later when the news of JFK's assassination came on TV (God forgive me, but I still remember my annoyance at the interruption). And finally, here was lissom Jane, a slightly older girl who could (and would, if asked nicely) make farting noises by sucking air in and out of her vagina.

This voyeuristic gold mine was more than any boy could ask for. It was heaven. It was too good to keep secret. Soon there were four of us up there, then five, then six. When an army marches across a bridge they break step because if they march in unison the bridge cannot endure the stress. We did not know this and one night our little fists must have fallen into synch because suddenly there was a loud *crack!* and the sturdy branch – which had not so much as groaned before – snapped and crashed to the ground. Six scratched boys, clutching six shrivelling penises, limped and scurried off into the darkness, pulling up zips and cursing.

Those girls ... Having seen them, how I missed them. How I longed for those bodies. Just to *glimpse* them even for a second, the indescribable perfection of them ... It was beyond lust, it was love. I *loved* the sight of them. Had I been old enough I would have married any one of them on a simple promise they'd stand naked on a plinth and let me walk around them. I was in awe. It was a welling up of the deepest feeling, an abdominal surge of transcendent adoration and insatiable curiosity.

Study? How could I? How could anyone with all this magnificence prowling around or sitting at the next desk, plump bottoms flared on chairs, breasts resting on desks, and the whole thing veiled by a mere *wisp* of cloth?

What would they look like naked? How would they feel? How would they behave if we were alone? How would they smell? How would they taste? If I listed all the memories I have, memories that are as clear today as they were thirty-five years ago, of all the kisses and caresses, the furtive glances, the tastes and smells, of matches struck in dark places to illuminate an unleashed breast, of tight hugs and creeping fingers, of ears and necks, of cheeks and slippery tongues, this book would be a thousand pages long. If I listed all the *fantasies* I had of all of the above, it would be a million. Knowledge? Facts?! What *for*? Who needed them? I was an explorer waiting for a journey to begin. I wanted love and flesh and sensual and romantic oblivion. I wanted intercourse. I was *twelve* for Christ's sake! I was in my prime.

And no one would accommodate me.

It was agony, double agony. If I could have separated lust from love, it would have been far easier, but at that time if anyone let me touch

158

them anywhere in any way, my gratitude was so profound it *became* love.

Eventually, I could resist temptation no longer and scaled the fire escape outside the girl's dorm. As soon as my eager face appeared in the window, a girl saw me and called the others over. To my astonishment, I was invited in. For one marvellous minute the sheer novelty of having a boy in their room so confused them that no one ran for help. I sank into the saturating, voluptuous scent of the place, my eyes feasted orgiastically on the teddy bears on the pillows, a bra hanging from a hook, photographs of mums and dads, the slippers and the slips, the pad of naked feet, calves and knees, thighs disappearing at the swaying hem, the swell of hips and buttocks, the narrow waists, the round bounce of satin covered breasts, the giggles of the bolder ones, the brush of long hair against my face, the smiles and the blushes … And then a little Puritan snuck out, a vegetarian was tipped off, and here came outraged wholesomeness personified.

When my mother died, the following letter from the headmaster was found among the few mementoes she'd kept of my childhood.

Dear Mr and Mrs Chapman,

I think I should just report that Matthew is spending a week as my 'guest' at Arunfield because he has been rather a lot of nuisance at Arunwood, particularly with regard to night time visits to the girls' dormitory. As you probably know this is one of the rules we do insist on being kept, even as young as Arunwood, and as Matthew is still very much in the process of finding out how to get along sensibly with the girls, I think it is as well to take a firm line with him about this from now on …

I do not remember my parents being particularly upset. In fact, I don't think they did anything to hide their amusement. Get along sensibly with the girls!

We were allowed home every few weekends and I would usually go. My mother's drinking was less of a problem for me now than at almost any other time. I was too old to be a victim and not old enough to be attacked as an adult. I was a teenager, egotistical and cruel, and far more interested in developing into a man than worrying about her. When I brought a friend home, she was welcoming and warm. As soon as we entered the room, she came toward us with her arms open and embraced, first my friend, 'Ah, my dear William. How *are* you?' and then me. As my friends tended to be delinquent boys from dysfunctional middle-class families where physical contact was rare and expressions of affection muted, she was adored. When she got drunk around them, it upset me, but didn't seem to bother them. She was a heavy drinker. She closed her eyes when talking. So what? And, no matter how bad things got, I loved her.

When I returned to the dorm after my stay with the headmaster, the fire escapes were painted with purple dye and every morning before breakfast my hands were inspected. I suppose you couldn't blame them for trying, but like all prohibitions on personal desire, this one was doomed to failure. There were other things in my life apart from sex, but all were coloured with desire. I would play sport and play it well, but refused to do it on weekends because that would cut into my romancing hours. I had some bikes, including a tandem, and loved to ride around on them, but on every trip out into the country, I hoped I'd meet a girl or catch a peek of illicit lovers in the back seat of a car.

My friendship with William was the only security I had. A far better scholar than me, he had a bitter, nihilistic air about him and read Sartre and Camus and despised convention. One time he read something – something Buddhist I suspect – about the nature of experience and for a while insisted on eating his food in silence, with his eyes closed. As girls tempted and withdrew, fell in love with me and then fell out, often leaving me in such anguish I'd sob myself to sleep while masturbating, the eccentric William remained my good and constant companion. Sometimes he'd even spend the holidays with me. His mother was dead and his father lived alone in the New Forest and I sensed it was a gloomy place, although I never visited.

Not all the boys came from rich homes. I remember two boys who didn't, both of whom were friends of mine from time to time. Nigel was a short, wiry boy, a great footballer and an exceptional pisser. We once put him on the jumping-off mark of the long-jump pit and found he could piss an incredible eighteen feet, a phenomenal arc of urine. (Bet he can't do that any more.) Throughout the three years I was there, he and I were at times rivals for the affection of a girl named Nina. He did better than me, until I did better than anyone – and got expelled for it.

Then there was Andrew. Andrew was also a good footballer. He was handsome, or would have been had his face not been a galaxy of leaking pimples from which his narrow, aggressive eyes stared out. Like William, he was a good student but unpredictable and savage. He'd punch you without a second thought and then finish the job swiftly and without flourish, like he'd done it many times before. He, William, and I were probably the toughest kids of our age and, apart from the nerds, the brightest.

The Sixties were beginning and black, elastic sided boots with Cuban heels were in fashion. I desired a pair with almost fetishistic passion, convinced, as one can be at that age, that if I had them, everyone would look at me differently, and life would change completely and forever. I biked to a nearby town where rumour had it you could get these boots. I found a pair with three-inch heels and was biking back when I got a puncture and had to walk the rest of the way. My feet hurt for a week, but I continued to wear the magic boots which were not magic. Soon after this, William, Andrew, and I managed to convince the school we were spending the day with my parents and jumped a train to London to go visit Carnaby Street. Carnaby Street was *the* street, *the* place to be in all of England, in all the world. I was wearing my boots under jeans with inverted Vs sewn into the sides below the knee so they flapped rakishly around my calves as I walked. William was similarly dressed. But when I looked down at Andrew's feet, I saw he was wearing a pair of *tartan bedroom slippers*. I was appalled. He didn't care. Some years later, having taken a lot of acid, he jumped off a bridge and killed himself.

After a year, we all moved on to another house. We returned to Arunwood only when we learned the bearded one was departing. On his last night, William and I went over there and urinated extensively into the petrol tank of his van. The next day we were told he only got to the bottom of the drive before the vehicle spluttered and died.

I can't remember much about the next house, except for the night President Kennedy was killed. It was in the evening and we were all watching TV. Gaby was wearing stockings with a suspender belt and her flesh bulged softly from the tops of them. I had my hand between these legs. When the news came on, the hand was ejected and was never invited back.

Two new girls came to the school. One of them was Rebecca. She had dark hair, big eyes, a long nose and a wide mouth. There was something exotic and gypsy-like about her. She was by far the coolest girl of our age, slender, sophisticated, and beautiful. I fell in love with her instantly, but she was from London, Hampstead, I think, and although I went out with her for a short while during term-time, I could not compete with the big city boys, older boys mostly, who were already smoking dope and screwing. We had a brief romance and kissed a lot. She let me touch her here and there, but I was too possessive and insecure and we broke up. There was one time, *one time* when I could, I'm *sure* I could, have made love to her.

We had broken up, but I never stopped wanting her. By now we had moved to the dormitories of the main school building. There was a dance in the assembly hall and I persuaded her to leave it and come and smoke a cigarette with me in a loft above the pottery classroom. We had a cigarette and then lay down and started kissing in the darkness. She was adept and willing. Her lips were huge and lazy and hot. Suddenly, her long-wristed, long-fingered hand scurried down inside my trousers and felt me. I put my hand up her skirt and felt her. She opened her legs. She was wet. I was wet.

My *nose* was wet.

'What's wrong with your nose?'

'Nothing,' I panted, 'just a cold.' I wiped it across her blouse as if pursuing a nipple, sniffed hard, then brought up my sticky-fingered hand and tried to staunch the snout with a sleeve before plunging the hand back down her stomach.

'No, what is it? It tastes like blood!'

'No, no, it isn't, I promise. It's not blood, it's not.'

But it was. In my excitement, my blood pressure had risen to an intolerable level, my nose had started to bleed, and I'd covered her in blood. She hurried off to change her clothes and I never got another chance. I was depressed for weeks. After all these years, I had had one real, genuine, delicious opportunity – and my nose had failed me. My *nose*, for God's sake … It was intolerable.

I was thirteen when eventually, the great day of penetration came –

and I was prepared. The geography master, a cold, falsely enthusiastic young man, had recently got married. Someone had found out, I can't remember who or how, that he'd bought, in bulk, a year or two's supply of what we then called 'rubber johnnies', condoms, rubbers. I suppose in this at least, his enthusiasm was genuine.

I was in the habit of burglary. I was always hungry and honed my burglatorial skills by repeatedly breaking into the kitchens at night using a semicircle of Perspex to spring the locks and catches. Then, with another boy, I robbed the clubhouse of the local golf course. I don't know if the place had a secret alarm or if someone saw us, but suddenly we heard a siren and saw blue flashing lights approach. To make my escape, I had to scale a tall gate with spikes at the top and jump down the other side. As I jumped, the back of my sweater caught on one of the spikes and I hung ten feet up, suspended by my armpits. Luckily, the police went in through another gate and I was able to extricate myself before they got to me.

The contraceptives were liberated. Imagine the man's embarrassment: how could he launch an investigation without admitting that he'd been robbed of not one, but *hundreds* of condoms? He stalked around glowering for a few days, but the theft was never mentioned. I kept a johnnie in my pocket at all times, a talisman of hope.

Because smoking was banned, it provided the perfect excuse for furtive encounters which often led to sex. 'Want to come for a cigarette?' enabled everyone to pretend that all they wanted to suck on was a cigarette. By this time, I carried a silver hip flask which I kept filled with whisky stolen from my mother, so I had two lures in my armoury of seductive tools. My favourite place for this consensual bait and switch was the groundsman's shed, a wooden hut with a couple of fixed benches along the sides. The floor was littered with cigarette ends and it had a damp, sour smell. To me it was the most wonderfully dark and erotic place.

It was here that I invited sweet Sally.

We had been here before a couple of times, fumbling and kissing and negotiating. She was a short, swelling girl with long hair and plump lips and I think she was in love with me. She wanted to do it, she told me, but was afraid if we did I would not respect her.

On the great night, we didn't even bother to smoke, but started to kiss

163

and touch each other right away. She allowed me to undress her item by item ('Just the sweater, Sally, please.' 'Take your bra off, just for a second, just one second, *please*.') until, finally, she was completely naked, white and shivering in the chill of winter. There was enough light to make out her chubby figure and her pale, upturned face with its expression of embarrassed arousal. I embraced her. How warm she felt, how round and resiliently female. I took off my shirt and my trousers and embraced her again and kissed her. After so many years of rejection, a naked body was pressed against my naked body. After so many years, a girl wanted me as I wanted her. Because it was cold and my desire was so urgent, I kept my socks on, but Sally draped all our other clothes over a bench as I clumsily rolled the geography master's condom down onto my penis.

Now she arranged herself on the bench and I got on top of her. She was afraid and asked me not to hurt her.

'No, no, it won't hurt. This is lovely,' I said.

I put it in (actually, I think it put itself in) and then stayed still for a second, shocked by the hot, enveloping sensation.

And then I came.

I don't even know if it was in there long enough to have taken her virginity, if it had not been taken already, but as far as I was concerned this counted. If she hadn't lost hers, I'd certainly lost mine. I had been inside a woman. I was a man.

I got up and we stood and kissed some more, me still in my socks, and then I pulled off the condom and we hurried back into our clothes before other smokers and fornicators came visiting. I kept the rubber in my hand and when I was fully dressed, surreptitiously pocketed it. We walked back towards the school. She held my left hand. The sticky rubber lay cradled in my right. I'm sure I made promises along the way. I'm sure that one of them was never to speak of what had happened.

As soon as we parted, I started to run. When I got to the dormitory all the other boys were there, doing their homework, getting ready for bed, lounging around in their childish pyjamas and reading *Guns and Ammo* and *Exchange & Mart*. I burst in the door, pulled the loaded condom from my pocket, and held it dangling above my head.

'There!' I yelled. 'I did it! I did it!'

Sex had been my main preoccupation since I was five years old, vague at first, just a strong, indefinable urge, but defining rapidly toward this, this intercourse, this putting yourself inside someone – and what a thing it was when finally achieved. The perfection of it and the relief! It was not only possible, but just as good as advertised. My bragging was a crude betrayal, but I couldn't help it. I had been kept waiting so long and I was so happy; and when I lay in bed that night and thought of Sally, it was with tenderness and gratitude. She had allowed me inside her. I had been *inside* her! *Inside!*

This pathetically brief moment of connection stretched out and became a permanent repudiation of my sense of alienation, of ugliness and difference. It was as if we'd left earth and floated in space, rolling in the darkness, indivisible in our desire. It was a moment of such intense and complete involvement I could never again think of myself as being entirely alone.

Soon after this, my eczema began to fade, retreating first to my hands, then to a final colony between my fingers before, within a year or so, disappearing completely, never to return.

My report for that term read, 'Matthew has developed a very superior attitude toward his work and his classmates. He can be pleasant when he wants to but is more often inclined to be "cocky and difficult."' I had lost my faith in God before the age of ten, now here I was, not yet fifteen and already risen to communion of another kind. Of course I was cocky. Yes, it was a grand thing, this fucking, communion, no question about it.

Unfortunately, my next attempt at such communion would get me thrown out.

Ever since I arrived at the school three years before, I'd had my eye on Nina. With an upturned nose and light brown hair, she was pretty and coquettish. The word 'pert' comes to mind. Nina and I had gone out once or twice for walks, but there had been no romance. In fact, I always felt she didn't like me. She was a teacher's daughter; my anti-authoritarianism compounded the awkwardness of her position. Tonight, however, was the last night of the summer term and I was fourteen.

She approached me with a couple of her friends and started to flirt, sweetly, but with an odd determination. She made a joking challenge. I responded in kind. It was as if she'd made up her mind to dispense with her virginity and had chosen me to take it. Perhaps she had been teased for being a good girl and had decided her survival depended on doing something bad with someone bad.

We started walking. I was amazed, in shock but not unprepared: one of the geography master's aging condoms nestled optimistically in my pocket.

It was a warm evening, still light. We went past the tennis courts, past the hut where I had lost my virginity with Sally almost a year before, and found a place among some bushes on the other side. We lay down and I kissed her. Soon clothes bunched at her ankles and rode up around her narrow waist. I touched her and she touched me. I was hard and she was wet. I rolled on the condom, put the tip of my penis just inside her – and came.

We got dressed and walked back together. I remember wondering if I'd ever learn not to come so quickly. I'd stolen a copy of the *Karma Sutra* from a local bookstore (in fact several copies, the rest of which I'd sold above market price) and studied it, but when push came to shove, I came. She was subdued but not unfriendly. We parted company. I didn't brag about this one. By now I knew more was expected of me and I felt ashamed. Sally was a sweet girl and wanted silence. Who knew what this girl would want?

Late that night there was a knock on the door of my dormitory. A girl named Ginny was calling for me. I went out into the corridor.

'You brute,' she said, her eyes slits of teenage indignation.

'What?'

'Nina's crying. How could you do that?'

'She wanted me to. It hardly ...'

'Pah!'

And she walked off. Another hour passed and then the same girl was at the door again.

'You're in big trouble. She's bleeding and she's going to see her mum and dad.'

'No!'

'Yes! You *rapist*.'

The next morning at assembly, the usual hymns were sung and announcements made. So and so was off to Oxford. The first eleven won the ... I glanced at Nina's father. His lips were tight, he did not look my way, and neither Nina nor her mother were in the hall. The headmaster, Harris, a radical vegetarian with a settlement of boils on his neck, droned on, then stopped. I looked up at him and it seemed as if his whole head was beginning to shake.

'... and lastly I'd like to see Matthew Chapman in my office right now.'

He stared at me and I at him and yes, his head *was* shaking.

The shaking continued in his office. He tried to act 'disappointed' and 'concerned' but in fact he was simply furious. The mother was down at the hospital having her daughter checked, but the father was here, the angriest pacifist you ever saw, unable even to look at me. I was certainly out of the school, Harris told me, but it could also be a matter for the police. I was to return with my mother or father in half an hour to hear the results of the examination.

I ran outside. My mother stood beside her red Mini Minor, the trunk already open to receive my luggage. She waved cheerily as I approached. My parents were never censorious in any conventional way ('Tory' was a far more offensive four letter word to them than 'fuck'), so I gave it to her immediately and without euphemism:

'Listen, I sort of fucked the housemaster's daughter and now she's saying it's rape and she's down the hospital being checked.'

Clare looked quickly around, saw a gap in a nearby hedge, plunged through it, and disappeared. When I caught up with her, she already had a cigarette in her mouth.

'Here, have one of these,' she said. 'Let's think about this.'

'It wasn't rape,' I promised her, as she lit my cigarette. 'It was barely ... I only just got the end in, I swear.'

'I went to school with that Harris,' she mused. 'An extr*eeeemely* priggish little chap even then. I think I'd better call your father.'

Cecil was duly called and before long the three of us were back in Harris's office. The atmosphere was sombre and threatening. The doctor had confirmed damage to the hymen.

'The question is, whether or not her parents want to call the police,' Harris said.

'How old is the girl?' asked my father.

The parents were consulted. She was a year older than I.

'It seems to me,' said my father, 'that it's a question of whether *we*

167

want to call the police or not. She's past the age of consent, Matthew isn't.'

I remember a long silence during which a smirk irresistibly took possession of my lips. I tried to resist because I liked Nina's father very much, a really good man, but the headmaster was another matter. He was a sanctimonious, overbearing, second-generation vegetarian. I looked up into his eyes. He turned away.

'Well,' he said, 'none the less, I think Matthew should leave the school.'

And so I did.

I got in the car with my father. Up to this point, I had not been close to him. I loved him because he was my father and admired him because he was so incredibly intelligent, but I didn't really know him. He was too abrupt, too distant, too busy. In thirty seconds this would change. We drove in silence. I waited for his rebuke. Finally, without looking at me, he spoke.

'Anything I might say to you, you will already have thought of.'

'Yes,' I said and we never spoke of it again.

He was right. It was very simple. This was one of the most liberal schools in the country. To get kicked out required some doing and no other school would now be eager to take me. Shocking though the whole incident had been, there was a certain victory in it. I had literally fucked myself out of an education.

Mth4U

When I get back to the Magnolia House from my visit with Kurt Wise up at Bryan College, Gloria is up in her den watching *Pippi Longstocking* on TV. A lethargy seems to have seeped into her, which even her indomitable optimism cannot fight off.

It's been hot and humid all day. Now it's evening, but still light. I drive down to the river where there's a boat ramp and a half-sunken dock and go for a swim. The water is streaked with hot and cold and there's a skin of broken leaves on the surface. I stroke lazily out into the wide bulge of the river and then lie on my back and stare at the sky before swimming back.

On the bank of the river is a pastor from Knoxville and his wife and two grandchildren aged maybe two and three. As I'm drying myself, the older of the two boys, who is soaked in his clothes from walking out on the sunken dock, falls to the ground and gets himself dirty. The pastor takes him by one hand, lifts him up, and dangles him in the water to clean him off. There's nothing intentionally brutal about it and the kid hangs there uncomplaining, but there's an ignorance in it, a kind of jovial ignorance.

He tells me he and his son-in-law, who is choir director in a local church ('He's so musical you put a piece of sheet music in front of him and he'll jes play it.') belong to a Pentecostal division of the church where people speak in tongues.

'It doesn't happen every time, but we like it when it does 'cause it means we've been visited by the Lord,' he tells me as I dry myself. The Pentecostal services, he says, are more 'uplifting' than the Baptist ones. 'We have singing and we stand up and wave our hands around.'

They ask me what I'm doing down here and I tell them I'm writing a book about Dayton and the Scopes Trial. When the pastor's wife asks me when my book will be in the libraries, I say, 'Well, in a year or so, God willing.'

The place is definitely getting to me.

When I arrived I was afraid because of my preconceptions about the rural South. As a neurotic city-dweller from the North, I feared the overt violence of the redneck with a banjo in one hand and a pistol in the other. The ceaseless friendliness has lulled me, but in another way, I'm more disturbed. The depth and pervasiveness of religious faith is overwhelming. Everyone believes absolutely, and seemingly without question, that God exists, that prayers work, and miracles happen.

I feel adrift. It makes me uneasy. What I find disturbing is not so much the belief in God, but the habit of credulity which it engenders. If they can believe in God – who never shows his face – simply because it makes them feel good, what else might they be persuaded to believe in? What is the difference between religious evangelism and political propaganda? Might one prepare you for the other? Was it not, after all, credulity as much as 'evil' (whatever that is) which made the attempted extermination of the Jews possible? To quote from *Diary of A Man In Despair*, the wartime recollections of German aristocrat, Friedrich Reck-Malleczewen, 'This people, only yesterday so intelligent and discriminating, seems to have been overcome by a disease of the mind. They now believe everything they are told, provided it is done with sufficient aplomb.'

But were they in fact so discriminating before the rise of Hitler, or did they merely confine their lack of discrimination to the more common absurdities of the Church? What if down here in the South, where babbling hysterics are instantly assumed to be speaking with the voice of God, someone stated 'with sufficient aplomb', that Englishmen with short hair are emissaries of the Devil and ought to be shot? Impossible to sell such an idea? Why? Because it's unreasonable? How would that get in the way of anything? As the New Agers say when you dispute one of their unfounded beliefs, 'Don't be so closeminded?'

I decide to have dinner with Gloria. She'll keep me safe no matter what. I find her in her den, still watching TV. The cut-off scrubs, however, have been replaced by a dark blue satin nightie from Victoria's Secret. I hesitate a moment, wondering after all about my safety, and then suggest Ayola's. She agrees. I go downstairs. She gets dressed.

At Ayola's she begins to cheer up. Tomorrow is Saturday and I say I'll spend the day with her and help in whatever way I can. Sunday she's leaving and so am I, although of course I'll be back in a few weeks for the great re-enactment. I've already bought my tickets and booked a room at the Best Western.

We return to the Magnolia House and go upstairs to the den. Gloria switches on her computer.

She has met about a dozen men through AOL. I get the impression that two of these encounters resulted in more than a handshake. Some of the men drove hundreds of miles to see her. One even flew his own light aircraft into Dayton to have lunch with her. Most are nice 'as all get out', but few are as they describe themselves. A man who said he was tall and cute with a full head of hair turned out to be, as Gloria puts it, 'a bald butterball of approximately five feet six'.

'But was he cute?' I ask.

'Cute? Sure, he was cute,' says Gloria, 'I'd put him in my pocket, I guess.'

The man with the plane was pleasant enough, but had made his fortune in the tattoo parlour business and was literally covered from head to toe in tattoos. Gloria knows what she wants now and has learned to extract truth from hyperbole. If a man talks about being 'equal partners' it means he's broke, and Gloria's had enough of that. She has developed a theory about sex too, which expands on the 'equal partners' theory. Women are at their prime at forty (roughly her age), while by the same age men are long past it. But this is not bad news after all: their lack of vigour forces them to be skilful and attentive, which is what she wants, so she asks, 'In bed, do you like to be equal partners, give pleasure, or receive it?'

Only the givers get.

I watch her talking to another man in Atlanta. He's in his forties but has never married. A Christian, he's looking for a wholesome woman with whom to settle down, maybe have a family. He sends a photograph. He is a clean-cut, handsome guy with a moustache. Over forty, never married, lives in Atlanta, *and* a moustache? To me, it's as clear as vodka: the guy's a guilt-ridden Christian fruit looking to jump ship. I share my thoughts with Gloria who doesn't see it that way at all and gets a little miffed at my pessimistic view. To her, the guy looks like a red blooded all-American, a pilot maybe.

I've cruised around on AOL. It's fascinating. Particularly the sexual side. You are admitted to a spruce suburban home and instantly find a dungeon in the basement. Take the American male, for example. You walk around in the world above ground and he's a cheery hetero man in a baseball hat chomping on a hotdog and talking endlessly about football statistics; he takes his family to church on Sunday and heartily slaps the backs of his fellow businessmen on Monday, but when you encounter him in the anonymity of the AOL chat room, he's a BiMM (bi married man). He's 'Wearing Hers' and 'Ready2Meat'. Your more ambivalent MM is 'Lking4Shemale' or wants to see his 'Wifewith-othermen.' The moustached 'BiCop' is having fun with 'SubM4Dom', after which he'll practice his headlock on 'MM4MWrestling'. As for 'VeryHairyBiMM', well, he has a shot with 'BigBellyBi', and everyone has a shot at 'Mth4U'.

I just got this off AOL. It's not yet ten on a weekday morning and that's not the half of it. There are guys who crave enemas from 'nurses' in thick black stockings and others who beg BBWs (big beautiful women) to sit on their faces until they faint from lack of oxygen.

Somewhat less graphic as a general rule, the women seek love and romance ... or not. A lot of them are looking to get tied up like a package from Guatemala and get whacked into submission by a sadistic DOM. Some like to dress up as ponies and canter around for their masters naked but for saddle, bridle, stirrups, and a butt-plug tail made of genuine horsehair. A large number of them are extremely interested in each other – and who can blame them once you've seen what the guys are up to?

Then there's the photos. You can get anything you like, from straight *Playboy* cheesecake to shots of women being screwed by mules. You can get pictures of females so hirsute they look like monkeys or gynaecological close-ups of hermaphrodite genitalia. There are 'peek' shots, blurry snaps through holes and vents, or interracial sex, or Shemales with floppy dicks and hard eyes. There are vast breasts, flat chests, 'puffy nipples,' and snatches stuffed with zucchini or trout or the more conventional vibrator.

But most amazing of all? 'Amateur'. A post-shower Mrs Foster by

Mr Foster, or the Sherrils and the Jankovitches having sex on the living-room couch. And you see the faces! There she is, smiling at you over her shoulder from the plaid divan, 'Hey, look at this, two dicks up my ass!' and there he is, off to one side in his favourite chair, studying the situation, 'Gee, two dicks up my wife's ass. How about that?' And these are not the faces of degenerate, drug-addicted sex-workers, these are the faces of your local bank manager and his wife. I disapprove of nothing – in fact a lot of it looks like fun – but how can they be so trusting? How can they reveal themselves like this? You look at the faces and you just absolutely know if they can take time off from ingesting dicks, they're going to vote Republican.

How can such flamboyant hedonism co-exist with such oppressive Puritanism? Or maybe the question is, How can it not? In England, isn't it always the conservative minister who, having just given a speech on traditional family values, goes home, dresses in a corset and a pair of stockings, and accidentally asphyxiates himself while hanging by his neck from a pulley? Nature seeks balance, I suppose: thwart the most primal instinct, the one without which none of the others can exist, and inevitably when it demands release, it bursts forth deformed and seeks the most extreme sin it can conceive of. In other words, every time Jerry Falwell or the Pope opens his mouth to preach, another pervert is created.

'Family Values.'

Boom! Mr Jones asks his wife to do it with the family dog and Mrs Towne gets fist-fucked by the Fedex man while hubby masturbates inside the closet. As Nietzsche put it, 'Christianity gave Eros poison to drink; he did not die of it but degenerated – into vice.'

Saturday is a beautiful day, sharp and bright, not even humid and Gloria and I drive out to Mom's Diner, 'The Cleanest Restaurant In Town,' which lies up the hill. Gloria has slept well and is in a good mood. She shows me the new newspaper in town, the *Mountain Morning News*, a right wing anti-government paper which objects to zoning and so on. It has the usual resentful, whining tone of such rags, thwarted self-interest masquerading as conviction. I like the *Herald-News* better, it's an honest paper which tells you about the town.

Stuffed with egg, biscuit, gravy, and grease, we return to the Magnolia House and Gloria starts to pack cheerfully. Fifty pairs of shoes are thrust into large garbage bags which I take downstairs. Twelve pairs of Levis ('I gotta get these pressed and starched'), six hats, and hundreds of assorted clothes are on the bed, waiting to be culled and suitcased. She's wearing a tie-dyed T-shirt, grey wool exercise shorts, and white sneakers. Thinking about tomorrow, she realises she has no shoes to wear with jeans. 'I gotta have platforms for jeans,' she tells me, so I go fetch the fifty pairs of shoes back up and a pair of platforms are extracted.

A couple come to pick up something they bought from Gloria in last weekend's yard sale. These are the people who will look after the Magnolia House until it's sold. Gloria says the handyman never came to fix the roof, kept promising, never came.

'Did you dawg-talk him?' the man asks.

'Sure,' says Gloria, 'but it don't seem to have no effect.'

After lunch, Gloria wants to go up to Lester and Ruth-Anne's farm to say goodbye to her horses. Lester and Ruth-Anne are away for the weekend. The requisite goblet is filled with fluid and ice and carried out to the Explorer, a cigarette is lit, and the knee steers us up the hill. Gloria tells me of the joys of riding. 'You take a ham sandwich, a Diet Coke, some water, a piece of leather and a hole-punch and you just go, all day, ridin' through the woods an' hills.'

We arrive up at the farm to be greeted by a one-eyed dog. It's a modern ranch house, surrounded by rolling pasture stocked with grazing horses. I stay very close to Gloria as she enters one of these beast-infested fields. It's terrifying. The horses, and there seem to be at least ten of them, are massive. Their heads are massive, their teeth are massive and their hooves are massive, and they have us surrounded. Gloria tramps confidently among them.

'You gotta be careful not to treat them like pets,' she says, reaching up and petting a huge, dribbling, log-like head, 'or they'll start to play with you.' *Play* with me?! 'See how they jump on each other? Well, they'll start doin' that to you, an' that can hurt.' As if I didn't believe her, she shows me some scars.

I suspect there's something sexual in this 'jumping on each other' business and I can't help wondering what would happen if inside one of these vast prehistoric heads the thought is forming, 'I think I'd like to make that little fella down thar my wife'? What would I do? Fight? Out of the question. Take it? Anatomically impossible.

As Gloria locates her two horses and fondles their snouts in tearful farewell, I leg it to the fence, leap over, and lock myself in the car. The one-eyed dog lopes miserably around. Gloria returns, wiping her nose, and we drive home.

An inexorable calm settles over the Magnolia House. As Gloria extracts her life from it, so she diminishes its power over her. The choice has been made and most of the work done; Gloria rests in a gap between her past and future, the one too poignant for reflection, the other too frightening to contemplate. I leave her upstairs in the den, wandering around picking at things, and go downstairs to type out some notes. When I return an hour later she's prone on the couch, the dim light flickering down on her through the fan. The TV is on and she's switching back and forth between two Westerns, in search of Brodie, the last decent man in her life.

The light starts to die and now it's time to go say goodbye to Aunt Ruth. We drive up the hill again on Route 30 which, I now find out, is in fact 'The Trail Of Tears'. It seems appropriate.

We drive past the farm and turn off onto a one-lane road. To one side is a Christian Camp. A sign reads, 'Pay at the office to ride the blob,' and the blob can in fact be seen, a large brightly coloured rubber float tethered in a small lake. Above the camp's entrance is a picture of an angry skull with a rifle. The man who runs the place describes himself as 'A black belt for Jesus.'

Aunt Ruth's house is a low slung California-style house with vertiginous views over the valleys of eastern Tennessee. Down below, the Tennessee River meanders among the hills, and in the distance there's a nuclear plant crouched in haze. Aunt Ruth shuffles slowly to the door and lets us in.

'I've prepared a soufflé, but it's going to take another hour.'

'I told you not to cook anything!' says Gloria, an edge of panic in her voice.

'I don't have to do what you tell me,' Aunt Ruth replies, keeping her head down and moving back toward the stove where she's stirring melted cheese.

Gloria, unable to face a long goodbye, had indeed told her not to

cook and now negotiates the old lady down to a sandwich. The bub-
bling cheese is abandoned as Aunt Ruth sets off toward the refrigerator.
I sit and watch as they talk. For the first time, I feel I might really be
performing a useful function, if only that of distraction. Gloria says
Aunt Ruth's birthday is coming up. She's going to be ninety, but she
doesn't want a party. 'What's the point ... all that fuss and bother,' says
Aunt Ruth. Gloria rolls her eyes and tells me in a loud voice that when
Aunt Ruth's husband died some time ago, the old lady had her own
gravestone put up next to his, already engraved with her name and date
of birth, leaving only the date of her demise to be filled in.

'Why did you do that?' I ask in astonishment.

'Well, I wanted it to age at the same rate as his,' Aunt Ruth tells me.
'I thought it would be neater that way.'

I'm silenced for a moment and so are they. Eventually, I ask Aunt
Ruth what Gloria was like as a kid and get a portrait of idyllic rural
youth – days running free in the hills, ticks and jiggers the only danger,
under-age driving with Ruth's complicity, the red light Gloria ran, and
the unbelievable coincidence of Uncle Wallace happening to be there,
right there at the light, can you believe that, right *there*? But at the
conclusion of each burst of memory lies silence, the drag of sorrow.

As we eat our sandwiches, Gloria applies artificial respiration to the
dying hour ('Oh, you still have those great old TV dinner trays!'), but
only artifice survives. Gloria wipes her lips and sets down her napkin.
Aunt Ruth's hands rise involuntarily to her mouth, first one, then the
other clamped on top of it, and she stares at the Formica counter.

'Well ...' says Gloria, standing.

Aunt Ruth looks up at her.

'We ain't gonna say goodbye,' she says, trembling, 'we're going to
say, "See you along the road." '

But they do say goodbye, Gloria tearfully, Aunt Ruth with resolutely
muted sorrow. She must not cry, must be maternal even now when
shrunk and Gloria, a woman, must be the adult or become the orphan;
but the effort compels the hands back to her mouth again and her eyes
glitter fearfully above their knotted veins. I turn away in shame at
watching from outside.

As we drive away, her frail figure hangs behind the screen door,
ghostlike.

This too is the consequence of failure and Gloria knows it and later, as we drink heavily up in her crepuscular den, she curses her ex-husband for battering her Magnolia dreams which will, officially and forever, die tomorrow.

Home Is Where The Heart Is

As so often happens, the drama of Gloria's departure from the Magnolia House is mercifully diminished by practical details. Garbage bags, the unplugging of TVs, packing the car. There are no tears. The last guest writes the last message in the guest book. 'The Magnolia House is beautiful but not as beautiful as your spirit', or words to that effect.

I help her settle the dogs in the back of the car and then give her a kiss on the cheek. She lights a cigarette, hoists the ubiquitous cup, and sets her knee for Pennsylvania.

I drive out of town to Evansville, some five miles north of Dayton where Darwins are rumoured to be buried. I find a graveyard on a hill above the high school. There is a plot of Darwins. I set my camera up and photograph myself sitting on one of the stones.

I need to take a piss and walk to a distant edge of the cemetery overhung by trees. When I've finished, I notice some red beads hanging in the branches. I look down and see an old unmarked grave, more red beads, and a small modern sign which I'd almost urinated on. I pick it up and turn it over.

It says, 'Eleanor Darwin.' Having not at this point concluded there's almost certainly no connection between me and this bunch of Darwins, I intone the obligatory 'Wow' and walk away.

I drive to Chattanooga airport and eat a sandwich filled with moist barbecue pork, which is the best food I've had since the start of the trip. On the flight back to New York I'm sitting next to a gastroenterologist. He tells me how frustrating it is when patients expect you to know everything and be able to cure anything, because you know enough to know you don't know much, while your competition, the New Age practitioners, who know almost nothing, happily give the impression they know everything, and as most diseases cure themselves and others

178

are psychosomatic, often seem to succeed in a way scientific doctors don't.

'Your chakras are out of alignment.'

'Gee, I feel better already.'

Soon I'm in the back of a cab, rising up out of Astoria on the approach to the Triboro Bridge.

Manhattan. The shock of the monumental city. It should be spelled *Man!?*hattan. You look at it and think: *man* did this? It seems more like a natural phenomenon, giant crystals thrust into the sky by a billion years of … thrusting. It's beyond belief. I've only ever met one New Yorker who doesn't, even after years, feel a surge of awe and affection at this sight and he used to be in charge of the bridges and tunnels and so maybe saw the sight too often and with collapse and dilapidation in mind.

Next morning I walk to my office and everything is angular, sharp, clean and solid. The old buildings in Tennessee tend to have a rickety quality and the new are merely shoddy.

I call my lawyer.

'How was the trip?' he asks.

'Fine,' I tell him, 'but I've got bad news. We're going to burn in hell.'

'I was afraid of that,' he says.

I've got a month before I return for the re-enactment of the trial. I am absolutely sure now that the comedy of the re-enactment will be the centrepiece of the book, the event around which everything revolves and out of which I can shoot whatever digressions I want.

I settle on the idea and explain it to my publisher, Tom Hedley, who loves it. I am about to get to work on the book when my rewrite of the New York script is approved.

When I write a script, I take no days off. I work seven days a week for as long as it takes. It's a question of momentum. If I stop for a day my memory of what a character was feeling thirty pages back fades. I used to have a problem working, now I have a problem not working. I wake up at six to be at my office by seven. I work all day and when the night comes I stop for dinner and then go back to work; the characters are in me and I want to return to them. I took an acting class at the Strasberg Institute once and The Method was explained to me. I've always been sympathetic to actors, admired their nerve, indulged them. Now I saw why. I had been doing this for years, looking for techniques by which I could trick myself into a mood and hold myself inside it.

But it's hard. I can feel myself running out of money. I get up even earlier. Soon, I'm drinking so much coffee, my liver twitches. My drunk-driving problem is looming closer. What am I going to do? If I don't have a licence, how am I going to get around when I go back to Tennessee?

I hire a researcher to try and find out what happened to Rappleyea after the trial. She turns out to be a Christian Scientist and I get some tracts, but she also turns out to be pretty effective. We find out he had some legal problems and got sent to jail somewhere in the South.

Sometimes I go out to dinner and talk about my trip; but as soon as I begin, the eyes lock on too fixedly. My friends pay attention, and then drift. It's all so alien, so preposterous, dismissable, a cartoon, not so much America as Americana. When I tell them about the jail preacher or about Leland with his baptismal jacuzzi, they laugh. They've seen it at the movies. When I tell them about Kurt Wise, they become irritated and wave their hands around in a brushing aside motion. What a fool, what a joke. Sometimes I find myself defending him, but it's impossible. Defence rests in who he is, in a sideways glance, the quality of his laugh, and I'm not a good enough raconteur to conjure up the poignancy of the whole man; I cannot seduce my friends into the humanity behind the cliché.

'You had to be there,' I say apologetically.

You had to be there at Leland's church, had to see the shacks along the road, smell the unleaded gasoline of the dispossessed, hear the train hooting and rumbling through. You had to look into Kurt's eyes. You had to feel the rough, gouging sweep of history through the valley, the thousands of miners who scrabbled beneath the ground to make clean-fingered men in London rich, or picture Rappleyea strutting down Main Street and knocking open the door of Robinson's Drug Store, or imagine the requisitioned houses beneath the waters of the TVA, or see the end result of it all, Aunt Ruth trembling behind the screen door, Gloria with her wayward, uprooted laugh.

I stop talking about it.

At one point, one of the studios flies me out to LA for two days to discuss another script I might do. On the way back, I'm sitting in First Class when Muhammad Ali steps gingerly in with his wife. He walks slowly and deliberately across the aisle and starts to sit down right in front of me. In spite of his uncertain walk and his shaking hands, in spite of a mask-like quality in his face, he is the most beautiful man I've ever seen. As he shuffles into his seat, he turns and looks at me. He puts out his hand and I reach to shake it, but he's merely trying to steady himself on the seat and I'm left touching the back of his hand, like a Catholic toadying up to the Pope. He smiles at me, twists, and drops out of sight.

We're stuck on the ground for a while and I can hear him talking to his wife. It is hard for him to talk, each word is pushed out against his body's will. At one point, she says, 'Don't be so anxious, Muhammad.' *Anxious?!* Muhammad Ali? How dare she!

I have never asked for an autograph but I want to get one for my daughter. The first time he goes to the bathroom, I ask his wife if it would be all right and she says, 'Sure, go ahead, do what you like.' He comes back. I'm too embarrassed to ask. Why shouldn't the guy get some peace? Then I hate myself. An hour later, he gets up to go to the bathroom again. The same laborious process, bend at the waist, ease up, grasp the backs of the seats – freeze. He stands there motionless for five seconds as if calculating the push and pull of all his muscles and then straightens up. He exits the row and stands. His shoulders are very broad, his hips narrow, and now he walks like an athlete, slow as he is, that stiff but rolling walk, the arrogance and implied menace.

When he comes back, I get up and ask him for the favour. With great effort, he dedicates a piece of newspaper to my daughter and signs it. I thank him effusively and sit down. I remember a friend of mine in LA, Paul Getty, who was kidnapped, had his ear cut off, and then, having survived that (and who he was to begin with), fell victim to a drug overdose. Now he cannot talk or move and is strapped into an electric wheelchair. All you can offer in this circumstance is to be as entertaining as possible. So, when Muhammad and his wife stand up again and are in the aisle, I get up and start talking to them. I tell them I've just come back from the South, how I'm a descendant of Charles Darwin, and how I'm writing a book about an old trial down there. Muhammad leans in, smiling faintly, nodding now and then, intrigued.

When I've spoken for a few minutes he asks, 'Where is this?'

'Dayton, Tennessee.'

A smile – a smile of mischief I've been watching since I was ten – spreads over his face and he looks at me sideways.

'Bible Belt,' he says, and shakes his head, laughing.

I'm so embarrassed about the drunk-driving thing, I'm taking no risks. I hire a lawyer whose last big case was defending one of the terrorists who blew up the World Trade Center. He has an office in the Woolworth Building, an old, ornate, peculiar building downtown near City Hall. He collects expensive antique watches. He has a hard time getting excited about my problem.

'Hey, I'll deal with it.'

And, for three grand, he does. I come out of court with a choice. Lose the licence for ninety days, which will complicate matters in Tennessee, or keep some provisional version of it and attend a series of alcohol education classes, which will complicate matters in New York, emotionally because I cannot stand to be talked down to and will become infuriated, and practically because it will cut deeply into my writing time. None the less, I decide on the latter, the classes. I go down to the DMV and a woman behind the counter spells it out for me. It's ten classes, one a week, and each one takes a couple of hours.

'Take the licence,' I say. 'See you in ninety days.'

Later that week, I remember I still have a British licence. I find it and look at it. It's valid for another twenty years! Ah ha …

In so far as I can drag myself out of the script, I begin to anticipate going back to Dayton with an almost furtive pleasure. I wonder about the re-enactment. How many people will come to the town? What kind of people will they be? How can they tell the story without making William Jennings Bryan – and thus everything they believe in – look ridiculous? How bad will it be? How amateur? How distorted?

As exhaustion sets in, there are more and more mornings where I wake up at three, sweating, convinced of my mediocrity. The hour of the wolf. During the daylight hours, I can ignore his scratchings on my psyche's door, but at night he creeps in and whispers how I made the wrong decisions; another life was mine, I let it go. He compares me unfavourably to other more successful men, gnawing with unerring subtlety at whatever confidence or hope is left. I wake up and stare at the black windows, try to flush him out, banish his scent, but only work can drive him away and seal back the door. I wait until four and then get up. By five I've walked the cold, deserted streets to my office, crossing sometimes with women stumbling out of cabs in evening dress or men with ties askew, and find myself back among friends whose sufferings, unlike my own, I can manipulate and control.

Another movie I've written based on a Donald Westlake book called *What's The Worst That Could Happen*, looks like it might get made, but now there's the problem of hooking a director, actors. I make calls, I take calls. I buy plane tickets back to Dayton in a thirty-minute gap prised out of the middle of a day.

I try to spend time with my daughter, but I'm distracted and she's too smart not to notice, and hates me for it. My million-and-a-half-dollar sale runs into problems. I'm not going to get all the money without a fight. I can see a lawsuit shambling down into my life, malicious and well funded. When my wife, Denise, calls and asks me to take care of some small domestic detail, I feel my scalp tighten around my head (Not more! Please not more!) and then an even tighter feeling as if I'm being zipped into a bodybag. I hyperventilate, I sigh, I gasp for air. I'm killing myself, I know it. The wolf has made his burrow in my brain and my heart is ready to blow.

Denise and I are not getting on well. It's nothing serious, she just hates me. She hates me for attacking and damaging her faith, for undermining her optimism, and for my tedious and pervasive whining about the fact that I have been forced by our excessive life to work day and night for years on end without rest. She has a quick temper. Sometimes it explodes in my self-pitying face and I walk around wounded for a week, unable to forgive, stepping aside when we cross in the corridor of our apartment.

But she is wounded in a more profound way.

When she first went to see Thomas Green Morton, her fork-bending guru, Denise's twenties had come to an end, concluded by the death of a child. Believing in Thomas, she recovered from this and found peace. When we first started living together, she had mantras and prayers and meditational techniques which he'd taught her and they seemed to work.

Uneducated though I was, I knew enough about science to know that if the 'miracles' Thomas performed – the 'phenomena' as they were pretentiously called – were genuine, then all the laws of science were meaningless. I also knew enough about human nature, having inhabited the margins of a criminal life, to recognise Thomas for what he was.

And I was jealous.

Here, after all, was a man who dictated what my girlfriend hummed after breakfast, whose bent coins she carried in her purse, a man to whom she believed she owed her happiness, even her life. Faith has a proven physiological effect on the body. It's called the placebo effect. Thomas was Denise's Grand Placebo. He had no 'powers' – obviously – but he worked for Denise *so long as she had faith in him*. Without asking myself if I had anything better to replace him with, I set out to destroy that faith.

We lived on the second floor of a two-apartment Spanish stucco building on La Peer Drive in the wrong part of Beverly Hills. Anna Bella was less than a year old and we were so broke we had recently taken an art deco lamp belonging to Denise from one antique shop to the next and finally, after considerable humiliation, sold it to help pay an electricity bill. In spite of this I went out one day and bought a four-head video machine. Denise had some tapes of Thomas performing some of his 'miracles' and I intended to study them in detail.

The tapes were at once amusing and alarming. Thomas was a funny little man, a simple country type who had some training as a pharmacist and had turned it into alchemy. He had a beard and a bump on his forehead which, so the story went, was caused by his getting struck by lightning. This was the source of his power, along with an encounter with aliens from a planet called Itibi-Ra. I found it all extraordinarily hokey, a lame amalgam of Uri Geller and a bunch of New Age bunco artists. In Denise's defence, however, there were eminent Brazilian doctors and scientists who were also taken in: you could see them on the tape, open-mouthed. How could Denise know that scientists, trained to deal with nature, which is not intentionally mischievous, are the least capable of exposing human fraud? A magician would have busted him in a second.

It took me about an hour.

Amid a lot of shouting and distraction, I watched as Thomas turned paper into aluminium and made childish patterns appear on its surface. He squeezed perfume out of his fingers. He put a coin in the palm of someone's hand and asked them to make a fist around it. When they opened their hand, the coin was bent. (Why one never actually saw a coin bending on a table was not explained.) When things were going well, he relished the presence of the camera. When he was unable to perform some sleight of hand without the camera catching him, he insisted it be turned off. The moment was too 'sacred'.

I ran the tapes at normal speed and then more slowly. When I got to the second tape, I caught him.

Denise and Diogo sat in a dark room. Two months had passed since the death of the child. The son of one of Denise's girlfriends, and Diogo's best friend, he had died of cancer after a long and appalling fight. Denise, a passionately loyal friend, had come to New York, where the boy and his mother were installed in Memorial Sloane Kettering Hospital, and she and Diogo had been there throughout the last weeks. Denise had actually been there at the moment of his death. It had been a gruesome and tragic ordeal.

Here now, or so I had been told, I could see Thomas contacting the dead boy's spirit. As usual, he yelled a lot. Soon lights started to flash in the room. The first one was almost in Denise and Diogo's face, the next couple further away. You could see the vague outline of Thomas moving about and waving his hands.

'Look, look, look!' he yelled. 'He's talking to you!'

They were bright flashes, like flashlights. I selected one in particular and slowed the tape down, moving the video forward a frame at a time.

Darkness. Darkness. Yelling. More yelling. Flash!

I reversed the video a frame. And there it was.

A clearly identifiable flash unit off a camera.

By its light, you could see Denise and Diogo's rapt faces. Off to the right, part of Thomas was visible, his arm, the side of his face, yelling, and the hand with the flashlight in it.

I called Denise in to look.

She stared at the frame in shock. It was brilliantly simple. The first flash going off in total darkness, with Denise and Diogo's pupils dilated, effectively blinded them. The yelling then covered the sound of

185

the flashlight recharging and popping again. The audacity of it was startling. If he was capable of this, what else might he be capable of?

I showed the tape to Diogo, who was then thirteen. He was furious.

A week or two passed. Denise seemed a little depressed. When she spoke to a friend of hers in Brazil, she told in amazement of what I had discovered, and admitted ruefully that she'd been conned. After a few weeks, however, she began to revise herself. Thomas was not a scam artist, after all; he just performed this *one* scam, perhaps a couple of others. It was hard to have these powers, sometimes he couldn't conjure up the real thing, so he faked it. That's how it is with gurus. They don't want to disappoint anyone.

Such reasoning is irrefutable. If a man claims he's bred a herd of pigs that can fly, but when you test them they all stay earthbound, you haven't proved they *cannot* fly, only that they *didn't* fly that day. On the other hand, having thrown his entire herd off a cliff and seen them all crash, you might rationally conclude that in *probability* the claim was false. And whatever Denise told me, or even herself, I believe that deep down she now knew her old friend was a charlatan. I thought she'd be outraged at him and grateful to me. Instead, she has never forgiven me. And why should she? I had taken from her something she valued.

As ridiculous and grotesque as it was for Thomas to pretend he was invoking the spirit of a dead child, he at least had the intention of comforting Denise and her son. What I had done, out of a genuine love of truth, certainly, but also out of petulance and jealousy, was to take away that comfort. What I had done benefited no one.

Within a year, I would be facing the death of my mother, and I would have only Denise to comfort me.

Flowers And The Promise
Of Moonshine

The day arrives for my departure back to Tennessee and, to my great disappointment, the script is still not finished. I pack the computer and kiss my wife goodbye. She and Anna Bella stand outside our apartment building with our little white dog, Gracie, and grin at me and wave. They are amused, you can tell, by my Quixotic journey.

I'm disappointed that I have to take the script with me, but soon I'm on a plane, out of my narrow railroad office into a tubular arrow, sprung from the ground, whistling south. The rubber rips, the body-bag unzips, light surges through the rounded window and life yawns and stretches and opens her arms.

Next to me on the plane is an irritable woman. She's in her mid-to late forties and well dressed. She is reading what appears to be a self-help book called, *Going To Pieces Without Falling Apart*. In front of me is a child. The child keeps throwing himself against the back of the seat and then peeking over the top at me. I eventually snake a hand around the edge of the seat and prod him in the ribs.

The woman next to me seethes as I relentlessly turn the key in the child's hysteria. She's a big, blonde voluptuous woman, magnificent in her way, and now she's throwing her big tanned legs around, one across the other and back again, twisting around on her big arse, and grunting softly each time the child's head appears over the seat.

She's going to pieces *and* falling apart.

I observe her out of the corner of my eye and make some guesses. Fifteen years ago she was a real beauty and married some guy with money in Atlanta, maybe in real estate or hotels. The guy dumped her, or even worse, didn't. Now she's a confirmed and bitter Republican who plays golf and drinks too much, and right now she's angry. She's angry at me, at the passage of time, at the kid, at the turbulence, and at the fact that she's not in First Class and the seat's too small. Furthermore, the plane is late taking off and the pilot won't stop talking, and this is really annoying her. Every time he comes on with his capable, piloty voice, she sighs massively and lunges from side to side on her big cheeks. In this area of her pissed-offness I'm in total accord. When the stewardess arrives to take our orders for food — against the pilot's continuing description of the geographical features below and exactly how high we are above them and exactly how late we're going to be — I grumble: 'Maybe if he'd stop talking and concentrate on his driving we could pick up a little time here.' And the irritable woman laughs wildly and introduces herself.

This is what I like about travel: it's such an antidote to your preconceptions. The woman and her husband live in Mexico where they own a large flower farm. She spends most of her day painting in a big white studio. Their life is a big adventure: big money, big risks. The book is by a Buddhist psychiatrist in New York and when I read it later it's fascinating and smart. She and her husband have been married for over twenty years, sticking by each other through poverty and wealth, and still adore each other. They have two children who are doing interesting things and from the way she talks about them, amused at their individuality, you can tell she loves them and they love her back. She's curious, lively, acerbic, and, the more you look at her, the more beautiful she becomes.

We spend the rest of the trip laughing.

When we get off the plane and she and her husband have hugged and kissed and grinned and laughed and patted each other with the delight of teenagers, she asks me if I have time to come smoke a joint with them in the car park before I catch my next plane. I don't, but thank them. They walk off, she with her big arm around his shoulder, he looking at her and smiling as they talk.

I imagine them waking up in Mexico in the middle of a billion swaying flowers, a light breeze carrying the scent of their crop into their white bedroom, a distant church bell, the husband on his side watching as she rolls toward him with her smile and her big tanned legs. And there was I putting her on a dry, shaved golf course with her bitterness and disappointment.

I've decided to fly all the way to Chattanooga and pick up a car there with my British licence. Now, however, it starts to rain and the next plane out is late and getting later and I have a very bad feeling about the whole thing so I decide to rent a car here and try to make the two hundred miles to Dayton before it gets dark.

When I was younger I broke the law without much thought, once seriously, a crime that could have put me away for several years. I figured then that if I ended up in jail I'd have time to write. But middle age in general, and fatherhood in particular, has made both a coward and a hero of me; a hero should it be necessary to protect my daughter, a coward should it result in separation from her. Trucks rear up behind me and slam on their brakes, impatiently waiting to pass. I'm so intent on keeping within the law my eyes are on the speedometer not on the road and once I almost crash into a car ahead. The rain gets heavier. The earth rotates the invisible sun away.

In spite of losing my way and having to cut across country through dark hills, sensed rather than seen, I arrive in Dayton and check into the Best Western. It's an ugly, sprawling hotel out near Ayola's, the Mexican restaurant. The woman behind the counter can't find my name in the reservations book, but it's not a problem. I ask for the best room in the hotel. It's available and it's the bridal suite. The best room in all these rural hotels seems to be the bridal suite.

A monumental light-green plastic Jacuzzi in Grecian style occupies at least a third of the room. It's right *in* the bedroom, one tortured edge, scarred with cigarette burns, almost touches the bed. I decide to go for a drink.

The Best Western bar is the only other place apart from Ayola's where you can get alcohol, beer only, and so I assume it'll be a festive place, brimming with Dayton's fun loving, mirthful set. Maybe there'll even be some fellow sceptics in the bar, down here to laugh with me at the re-enactment.

As I round the corner of the hotel in the drizzling, damp, enveloping hotness of the night, I encounter a sodden behemoth standing at the rear of his rusting car. He's in the act of pulling a vast, sweat-stained T-shirt up over his head, revealing a pallid stomach as big as a VW Beetle but covered in matted hair. I nod at him as I go by and enter the bar.

It's a corridor drenched in a dull, gloomy yellow light. There's a jukebox at one end. Two or three tables and chairs are crushed up against the wall opposite the long bar. There are five inebriates here, two women and three men. A young pregnant girl stands behind the bar, smoking voraciously. I take a stool down the far end and order a beer. Conversation starts up again. The behemoth enters in a clean shirt and engulfs a bar stool which you feel is his and his alone.

The men are obviously manual labourers, tough and stringy, hands ingrained with dirt. Everyone's exhausted, surfing on the sugar of alcohol, waiting for the wave to beach them. The barmaid is a pretty, dark-haired girl who can't be much older than twenty, but this is going to be her second child. She looks up at you with her head lowered as if you might smack her, and her mouth sulks as she talks. Having noticed even more signs about the sheriff race, I ask what the general feeling is about Sneed and she tells me she's a niece of his, but not close.

'I'm a *poor* Sneed. I was raised by my mama.'

Her apparent lack of loyalty to the Sneed family opens a door and the drinkers charge in to give their opinions. They don't like Sneed at all. He's too strict on drunk driving.

Oh.

I buy everyone a drink and move up closer to the big man, whom I'll call Emerson. Emerson's pear-shaped head reminds me of a medium-sized bag of laundry with some chins added at the bottom. He works up at the La-Z-Boy factory and just came off his shift. It's getting on for midnight, when the bar closes, and the barflies start to drink faster and faster. Emerson and another man order beers in pairs and down them one after the other with barely a pause for breath. I try to keep up but it's not possible.

'How's the moonshine situation down here?' I ask, gasping at the gaseous chill of yet another beer coursing down my throat into my stomach.

'You want some moonshine?' asks Emerson. He has friendless eyes, a character actor in the play of life, Falstaff without a king, but now there's a certain comradeship: I bought him a drink, he bought me a drink.

'Damn straight,' I say, falling easily into the vernacular.

He says he'll get me some tomorrow night. 'I'll have to go up in the hills and get it, but I'll do it.'

'I'll pay,' I tell him.

He waves me aside. 'You jes buy me a drink, we'll talk about that. Be back here around ten o'clock tomorrow night an' I'll take care a ya.'

I stumble back to my room, so drunk and exhausted I can't even be bothered to take a jacuzzi. I go to sleep and then wake up an hour later with a dry mouth and a headache. I lie on my back for half an hour, trying to will myself to sleep, but as usual it doesn't work. I feel apprehensive about something but I don't know what.

I turn the light on. Maybe I'm anxious because the subject of my book, the trial, has faded, subsumed by the more clamorous demands of the movie business. I've brought the trial transcript with me. I take it out of my bag and locate a postcard of the Magnolia House which projects out of the pages about halfway through. When I stopped reading, Judge Raulston had adjourned early on Wednesday afternoon to give both sides time to prepare their arguments on the admissability of Darrow's vitally important expert witnesses.

On Thursday morning, 16th July 1925, the opening prayer was typically biased and threatening. 'We thank Thee for thy blessings upon us all, and for Thy watch, care and protection over us; we pray Thy blessings upon the deliberations of this court, to the end that Thy Word may be vindicated, and that Thy truth may be spread in the earth.'

William Jennings Bryan Jr stood up and made the argument for the prosecution. From all accounts it was a lacklustre performance given in a voice so low (and so in contrast with papa's) that there were frequent requests for more volume. In essence, he argued that expert testimony was not required in this case because the matter was simple. The defence admitted Scopes had taught evolution, which was against the law so what was the purpose of expanding the matter? Furthermore, he claimed, expert testimony in this case was in fact only expert *opinion* which, unlike other testimony, was not subject either to contradiction by fact or to the rules of perjury.

There was a short adjournment and then the Judge came back to give the floor to the defence. Well, to give it to them with a caution. 'We have some lawyers in the case who at times indulge in a lot of wit ... The floor of the courthouse building is so heavily burdened with weight ... and the least vibration might cause something to happen and ap-plause might start trouble.'

In mock humility, Hays responded that he was embarrassed by the Judge's suggestion that his argument would cause 'such thunderous applause that the building might come down.' He then went on to argue that to not allow evidence on evolution was to hear only one half of the case, the prosecution's. Bryan had stated to the press that this was to be a 'duel to the death' between evolution and revealed religion. If that was so, then under simple rules of fairness the defence should be allowed to 'reveal' their side.

Hicks reiterated Bryan Jr's argument and Ben McKenzie followed. McKenzie, who later became a good friend of Darrow's, was an amusing and likeable old Southern gentleman, and opened his argument as follows:

'I want to say this. Since the beginning of this lawsuit and since I began to meet these distinguished gentlemen, I have begun to love them, every one, and it is a very easy task. In fact, it was a case when I met Colonel Darrow, a case of love at first sight. These other gentlemen come right on, but you know they wriggled around so rapidly that I could not get my love turned loose on them until I got a chance ...'

Then he began to defend the Christian version of creation against that of science, stating confidently what the defence witnesses would say if they were allowed to testify. Eventually, Hays asked him how he could possibly know what they'd say without first hearing them? McKenzie responded rather irrelevantly by asking Hays if he believed the story of divine creation.

Hays replied, 'That is none of your business.'

Judge Raulston asked him to apologise to McKenzie for his rudeness.

'Instead of those words, I will say I think it doesn't concern General McKenzie.'

'And I will say to you,' said McKenzie, 'that I have as little concern as to where you emanated from or where you are going to as any man I ever met.'

'Now, may I ask for an apology, your honor?'

'Yes, sir.'

McKenzie apologised. 'I did not mean to give offense. I beg your pardon.'

'It is like old sweethearts made up,' said Hays, mocking the old man's protestations of love earlier in the day.

Court was adjourned until the afternoon.

After lunch, the Judge once again warned of the dangers of applause and the possibility of it bringing down the building.

Now, at last, the Great Commoner was to be heard.

Bryan was so used to talking to the crowd that much of his speech was made with his back to the Judge, who, by rights, he should have been addressing. In his book, Scopes says he made a poor beginning, that the brilliance he had seen when Bryan spoke in Salem was sadly diminished.

His tone was jovial as he derided evolution and Darwin, but to an educated observer he came across as merely ignorant. As Mencken put it, 'Somehow he reminded me pathetically of the old Holy Roller I heard last week – who damned education as a mocking and a corruption. Bryan too is afraid of it, for wherever it spreads, his trade begins to fall off, and wherever it flourishes he is only a poor clown.'

At one point, he read from Hunter's biology textbook, the one Scopes had used, and laughed at the enumeration of species. 'Two thirds of all the species of all the animal world are insects and sometimes in the summertime we feel that we become intimately acquainted with all of them ... Now we are getting up near our kinfolk, 13,000 fishes. Then there are the amphibia. I don't know whether they have not yet decided to come out or have almost decided to go back.'

This got a big laugh.

'And then we have mammals, 3,500, and there is a little circle and man is in the circle. Find him, find man! There is the book they were teaching your children, that man was a mammal and so indistinguishable among the mammals that they leave him there with 3,499 other mammals.'

He waited for the applause to die down and then added:

'Including elephants,' which got a huge laugh.

Next he read from *The Descent Of Man*, in which Darwin describes the way in which man may have developed. It is full of technical terms and Latin names and Bryan's intent was clearly to make it seem nonsensical, an affront to common sense and a poor reason to 'undermine the faith of these little children in a God who stands back of

193

everything and whose promise we have that we shall live with Him forever by and by.'

He spoke of Nathan Leopold and how Darrow had suggested that because Leopold read Nietzsche at university he had become a murderer. This was precisely the danger of taking God out of education and replacing Him with concepts like the survival of the fittest and Nietzsche's morally unaccountable 'superman'.

'The Bible,' Bryan said in closing, 'is not going to be driven out of this court by experts who come hundreds of miles to testify that they can reconcile evolution – with its ancestors in the jungle – with man made by God in His image ... The facts are simple, the case is plain, and if these gentlemen want to enter upon a larger field of educational work on the subject of evolution, let us get through with this case and then convene a mock court, for it will deserve the title of mock court if its purpose is to banish from the hearts of the people the Word of God as revealed.'

He then sat down. The trial record noted there was 'Great applause'.

Once it died down, Dudley Field Malone stood up to argue for the defence. Malone, the lone Catholic on the defence, though divorced and remarried to a suffragette, was exceedingly well dressed and fastidious. He was the only attorney on either side who had never taken his jacket off in spite of the incredible heat, a fact which had been widely noted in the press.

Malone stood in the body of the courtroom, thinking for a moment, and then slowly he removed his jacket. He folded it carefully, and laid it over the back of a chair. The court became quiet.

He started gently, sitting on the edge of the defence table. Having chided Bryan for his anti-education bias, he pointed out that it had been seventy-five years since Darwin's theory was first explained and that much had been learned not only to confirm it but to contradict the Bible. Cities had been discovered showing a high degree of civilisation 14,000 years ago. 'Are we to hold mankind to a literal understanding of the claim that the world is 6,000 years old because of the limited vision of men who believed the world was flat and that the earth was the center of the universe?'

He spoke of how, three centuries earlier, Galileo had been prosecuted by theologians. 'Haven't we learned anything? ... Are we to have

194

our children know nothing about science except what the church says they shall know?' He spoke of the burning of the library at Alexandria and how a plea had been made of Kalif Omar to spare it because it contained all the truth that had been gathered up to that point. 'And the Mohammedan general said, "But the Koran contains all the truth. If the library contains the truth that the Koran contains we do not need the library, and if the library does not contain the truth that the Koran contains then we must destroy the library anyway." '

He defended the young against the old. 'The least our generation can do, your honor, is to give the next generation all the facts, all the available data, all the theories, all the information that learning, that study, that observation has produced – give it to the children in the hope of heaven that they will make a better world than we have been able to.'

To everyone's astonishment, the audience began to cheer for Malone, who now turned toward Bryan. 'My old chief ... I never saw him back away from a great issue before ... We have come in here ready for battle. We have come in here for a duel ... but does the opposition mean by a duel that our defendant shall be strapped to a board and that they alone shall carry the sword? Is our only weapon – the witnesses who shall testify to the accuracy of our theory – is our only weapon to be taken from us so that the duel will be entirely one-sided? That isn't my idea of a duel.'

Now his voice began to rise, getting louder and louder like an old-time preacher. The court was either in absolute silence, transfixed by him, or they were cheering him, and cheering him more loudly than they had Bryan. Scopes, glancing over at the old Commoner found his reaction to Malone's speech startling. In his book, *Center of The Storm*, he wrote, 'I have never seen such a great change hit a human being as fast as it did Bryan. Malone spoke for only twenty minutes. There was only dejection on Bryan's face; the victory that had been his only a few moments before was suddenly, disastrously dissipated.'

'There is never a duel with the truth,' Malone continued. 'The truth always wins and we are not afraid of it. The truth is no coward. The truth does not need the law. The truth does not need the forces of government. The truth does not need Mr Bryan. The truth is imperishable, eternal, and immortal and needs no human agency to support it ... We are ready. We feel we stand with progress. We feel we stand with science. We feel we stand with intelligence. We feel we stand with fundamental freedom in America. We are not afraid. Where is the fear? We meet it. Where is the fear? We defy it. We ask your honor to admit the evidence as a matter of correct law, as a matter of sound procedure, and as a matter of justice to the defense in this case.'

'Profound and continued applause,' states the trial record.

In truth, the audience – who had applauded Bryan less than an hour ago – now went completely wild. The judge banged his gavel and called for order, but could not stop the cheering and yelling and clapping. A policeman was seen banging his nightstick on a table so hard he split it. When another officer came up to help him restore order, the man said, 'I'm not trying to restore order! Hell, I'm cheering!'

Malone had stolen Bryan's day.

Finally, the cheering died down. Stewart tried to repair the damage done by Malone, but nothing could rise to the level of Malone's great speech for reason and fairness.

When court was finally adjourned, the reporters rushed off to file their stories, many of which contained Dudley Malone's speech in its entirety. Scopes stayed behind, sitting next to Malone, and the court-room gradually emptied out.

Soon only he, Malone and William Jennings Bryan remained.

Scopes reports that the 'Peerless Leader,' the 'Great Commoner,' the one time 'Boy Orator of the Platte,' the author of the marvellous 'Cross Of Gold' speech, the most brilliant speaker of his generation, sat in his rocking-chair over by the prosecution table, fanning himself with his palm leaf fan. Every now and then he would let the fan drop and just stare ahead vacantly. Eventually, without turning to look at Malone, he spoke.

'Dudley, that was the greatest speech I ever heard.'

'Thank you, Mr Bryan,' Malone replied softly. 'I am sorry it was I who had to make it.'

Head Symptoms

The next morning when I wake up the light is still on and the trial transcript lies across my sour stomach. I get dressed and, exhausted and hungover, plod across the parking lot to the Frontier Diner, picking up a *Herald-News* on the way in. Hoping to quell a continuing feeling of dread and disorientation, I order eggs and bacon with biscuit and gravy and settle back in the damp, airless greasiness of the place to read.

Another victim has been claimed by the railroad track. A young boy, honour student at the high school, no history of drugs. Inexplicable, the curse of Dayton.

I look across the page.

'Scopes Trial Festival Attracts Crowds.'

Funny, I haven't seen any crowds. The first paragraph of the article says that more than a thousand people 'viewed the play'. What do they mean, 'viewed'? Today is Thursday and tonight is opening night, so how can anyone have *viewed* the play, let alone one thousand of them? I read the headline again. 'Scopes Trial Festival Attracts Crowds.'

'Attracts'. Present tense.

As I read on, however, panic blossoms in the pit of my stomach. The article clearly states that the last performance of the Scopes Trial was on Monday, *last* Monday, three days ago.

I read the article again. Apart from the headline, *everything is in the past tense!*

As documented in the Desmond/Moore biography *Darwin*, Charles Darwin, who was either a hypochondriac or permanently damaged by his trip on the *Beagle*, probably the former, wrote a note to his new doctor in 1865, listing his symptoms:

'For 25 years, extreme spasmodic daily and nightly flatulence, occasional vomiting, on two occasions prolonged during months. Vomiting preceded by shivering, hysterical crying, dying sensations or half-faint, and very copious very pallid urine. Now vomiting and every passage of flatulence preceded by ringing of ears, treading on air, and visions. Focus and black dots, air fatigues, specially risky, brings on the Head symptoms ...'

A *trifle* compared to how I'm feeling.

I pay as fast as I can and rush back to my room. I grab my notebook with the tickets pinned inside, and, with churning stomach, head for the bathroom. I sit there and stare in horror at the tickets.

They were for last weekend.

I'm a week late!

The central event of my book lies irretrievably in the past, I missed it, and it won't happen again *for another 360 days!*

I start walking around the room, banging into the jacuzzi and muttering, 'How did this happen? How did I make this incredible mistake? What the hell am I going to do?' I've told Tom, my publisher, about the idea of spinning the whole book out from the re-enactment – 'the hub from which all the spokes of the book will radiate' and all that bullshit – and he liked it. He liked it a lot, in fact.

'Excellent idea,' he had said. 'It gives it a centre, gives it unity.'

Now there's no centre and no unity and I'm out here floating in a vacuum, incompetent and faint, dots before the eyes, head symptoms, ringing ears. I've even got the copious and pallid urine.

A friend of mine taught parachute jumping in California. In every group there was one arrogant prick who wouldn't listen to instructions, bragged about his fearlessness, and mocked those more cautious than himself. Sometimes when the time came for this character to make his jump, my friend would say, 'Okay, jump!' and then as the man hurled himself from the plane, he'd yell, 'No, *wait!*'

Hopeless though it was, they all tried to get back into the plane, clawing at the air, trying to turn back time. This is how I feel. There must be a way to *go back* – and yet I know there isn't. The *Beagle* has left for the Galapagos, I just tripped out the door without a 'chute, I'm irredeemably ruined. This is a disaster.

I hurry over to the gas station across the way and buy some cigarettes. Light up. Feel sicker. I don't smoke. I can't handle this. I sit down and consider. But what is there to consider? It's a catastrophe, no way to pretend it isn't. I know how this happened. When I booked the tickets I was so obsessed by my script – with making money, with staying afloat, with scrabbling for respect and meaning!!! – that I made a rapid and completely erroneous assumption: the real trial ran over two weekends with a week in the middle and I assumed the weekend of the re-enactment would coincide with the date of the *last weekend*. Instead, just to exacerbate an already severe condition of existential panic, these psychic Baptists chose the *first* weekend, hoping to tip me over the edge.

But even this reasoning does not work. Today is Thursday, 23rd July. The real trial was completely finished by 22nd July, which was a Tuesday. There is no excuse. A balanced person would have checked the tickets for the play and *then* booked the flight. I didn't have time, I just snatched up a phone and …

Time! This is the problem. I don't have time to reflect. I don't have time to reserve airline tickets on the right day. I don't have *time* for anything, not even for my own daughter, not even for this book, not even for my own rage. Maybe my brain is being consumed by its own unfulfilled ire – the corruption of politics by money, the Pope's attitude to contraception, corporate phone systems which prevent you from speaking to a human being, fat little men who sneer at you around their cigars, the barbarity of the death penalty, I could go on – so many peeves large and small locked corrosively inside my brain because I have no time to vent them.

Late? It's astonishing I got down here at all.

I'll have to lie, it's the only solution, it's what I've always done.

Who'll know if I was here on the wrong weekend? Who's going to check? I'll find the woman who directed the play, I'll get the script, I'll talk to Sheriff Sneed and ask him how it went; I'll *imagine* the play.

I call Denise. I want to tell her what has happened and then burst into tears. I know she'll be sympathetic. I don't tell her. We talk for a few minutes and then I begin to feel nauseous and hang up. If I decide to tell the lie, what am I going to do down here for five days? I lie down and then get up – and trip over the jacuzzi again.

If only I believed in God. Here is a moment tailor-made for prayer. I'm on my knees already! My first book, and I've screwed it up before writing a single word of it! God help me!

I get up and *again* trip over the jacuzzi. It's everywhere.

That's the problem: it's none of the above, it's just there's *too much stuff in my life*, too many projects, too much pressure, too much confusion, too many green jacuzzis!

Fine! I'll move rooms. Action of some kind! I'll finish my script! Clear the decks, get ready for the next storm. I move to a pair of rooms on the other side of the motel – there's plenty of rooms because *no one's here*, they were all here *last weekend*, enjoying themselves, making sceptical jokes and having atheist sex (silent orgasms, none of that 'Oh, my God!' nonsense) – all this while I toiled over my wretched script about New Yorkers tearing each others throats out.

I set up my computer and start to work on the script, thinking if I can just concentrate on one thing for an hour, this panic will subside. But I can't and it doesn't. I keep going back to my stupidity, my lack of organisation, the *consequences*.

What if I lie about the play and get found out? Clearly no one in Dayton is going to like the book. Suppose someone reads it and busts me. 'He wasn't even down here for the show! He's an atheist *and* a liar!' I remember reading about a reporter who wrote a touchingly realistic piece about teenage junkies, won a Pulitzer, and then it was discovered there were no teenage junkies. She'd made it all up. She was ruined.

I'm ruined. This is the end.

I lie on the bed and go to sleep. An hour or two later I wake up feeling more optimistic. I've been punching myself in the head since I was five. I've recovered before, I'll recover again: a nasty blow, down but not out.

I decide to go see the editor of the local newspaper. I'll do some research into the boy who just got killed on the tracks. No getting up off the canvas for him.

'Bizarre,' says the editor. 'We are the pedestrians-killed-by-trains capital of America and we don't understand it. Sometimes it's suicide, sometimes it's someone gets stuck on a bridge and tries to outrun the train, and sometimes, like this one, it's a mystery. Everyone says he was a good boy, didn't do drugs, honor student, happy at home, no girl trouble. An accident? There's a *massive* light on the front of these trains and the horn is deafening. How can it happen?'

He shakes his head, confounded. The evening of his death, the boy played with his young niece and then stayed up to watch TV while the rest of the family went to bed. A couple of hours later, a train driver saw a figure walking away from him along the track. He hooted his horn – a teenage boy turned and glanced over his shoulder into the bright light, then turned, raised his arms – and took it. Within five seconds he was dead. He had changed his clothes as if to meet someone. That's all anyone knows.

He gives me the phone number for Gale Johnson, the director of the play and of Joe Wilkie, a science teacher at Dayton High. I think it might be interesting to interview whoever now occupies the Scopes position down here.

I go back to the hotel and call Sheriff Sneed. I remind him of his offer to let me ride with one of his cops. 'Sure,' he says, 'you come on down any ol' time you like.'

I pick Friday night. That should be amusing. Next, I call Kurt Wise. He's taking a group of Bryan College summer students on a Cave Geology Tour on Saturday afternoon and invites me to come along.

Spelunking with Christians – who could ask for anything more? Things are looking up.

Now I call the director of the play, Gale Johnson. Gale agrees to have lunch with me on Friday. She sounds defensive.

That evening, I dine at The Western Sizzler along the highway on the other side of town. I get talking to two high school girls, Christina and Samantha. Both knew the boy killed on the tracks but not well. Samantha's father and uncle died by train, the father a suicide. Christina is a Pentecostal and tells me about speaking in tongues.

'You have to open yourself to the Lord, let him come in you, speak through you. I had a friend took all kinds of drugs, liked them, but she said speaking in tongues was the best high she ever had.'

Samantha, who admits she's been through a 'bad' phase, catches my eye and winks as if to say, 'Yeah, right.'

I go back to the hotel and call Denise. I tell her how I've managed to miss the re-enactment. She is silent for a moment. I can imagine her in our apartment overlooking the East River, but I cannot quite imagine the expression on her face. Is she concerned, as I am, that I am losing my mind?

'This is incredible, Matthew,' she says, and I think I can hear her smiling.

'No, it is, it is ...'

'As we say in Brazil, it looks like you've stepped on the ball here.' This is a soccer metaphor: a player who steps on the ball, trips and falls headlong.

'Yes,' I say. 'That's how it looks, doesn't it?'

'No, it is *incredible*. How did you do this?'

'I don't know.'

She can hold back no longer. I hear her start to laugh on the other end of the phone. I start to laugh too, and fall in love with her again.

When we have finished laughing, she says, 'Well, it's funny. That's good. The book should be funny.'

'I'm not sure it should be this funny,' I say, and she starts to laugh again. She isn't worried, you see. She has faith.

I wait until 11.30 to go to the Best Western bar. Half an hour of speed-drinking is all I can take, never mind the addition of potentially lethal moonshine. The bar is more crowded; several rednecks surround Emerson perched around his bar stool. Right next to him is a stocky grey-bearded man slumped forward on the bar, asleep. His arms are folded in front of him and his face rests on the surface. His mouth, which is squashed out sideways, lies in a small puddle of dribble and emits a steady, restful snore audible above the juke.

Emerson turns toward me with glazed eyes. 'Ah, tharyare,' he says. 'Gotcha moonshine. Me an' my buddy here,' he indicates the sleeper, 'had to go up the mountain.'

'So,' I say, looking at the comatose man, 'good stuff?'

Emerson studies his companion for a moment, considering, then looks back at me with his small, hard eyes.

'It is,' he says. 'Course it's different for me, I'm 300lbs, I can take it.'

He produces a brown paper bag and slips it to me. I look inside. There's a jam-jar in there about a third full of clear fluid.

'Let me pay you for this,' I suggest.

'I had to go up the mountain,' Emerson repeats with a distant expression. 'Missed a night's work, but it's okay, you're a good guy.'

I offer again to pay.

'I wouldn't take your money. Went up the mountain, missed a night's work, but I wouldn't take your money, no sir.'

I buy everyone a drink. One of the rednecks, Mike, the toughest looking of them all, and buzzing with inebriation, asks me what I'm doing in Dayton. I tell him I'm writing a book about the Scopes Trial.

'Shee-it,' he says. 'Drink that moonshine.'

'Here?'

'No, man,' he says irritably, as if I should know the etiquette of moonshine consumption, 'take it to the fucking john.'

I do. I drink. To my surprise, it's excellent. I have friends in New York who'll spend a hundred bucks for a spindly bottle of grappa. This moonshine is better than any grappa I ever drank. It's smooth and interesting with a faint, leady, car-radiator aftertaste. And it's strong. I sit down and take another sip. Even before the liquid touches my lips, the fumes rise up my nose and make my eyes water.

Why am I surprised it's so good? I remember a junky friend of mine responding to an anti-heroin campaign on TV by saying, 'Of course, the one thing they don't tell you is it *feels great*. Why else would so many people do it? If they'd just acknowledge that one fact up front, they might get somewhere. Instead they give you half the truth and leave you to find the rest out for yourself.'

I recap the contraband and go back out into the bar.

The mood is different tonight, a slight hint of violence under the raucous good humour. I keep going off the radar. A man I was talking to a minute ago turns and looks at me in surprise.

'What are you doin' here?'

'I'm just here. This is where I am.'

'Well let me tell you sumpin. If it crawls on its belly, walks or flies, I'll shoot the sumbitch.'

'That so?'

'Yeah. Love to hunt.'

'Okay. Good ...'

Mike launches into a long story about a Rottweiler and a man named Fluff – pronounced Flurrff. Fluff had a beard, though I can't remember why this was relevant, and didn't believe the dog was as tough as everyone said it was. One night in a bar, he bought it a beer and started tormenting it.

203

'He kep lookin' between its legs an' slappin' it in the balls. Shee-it! That dawg, as true as I tell ya, that dawg jes kep lookin' over his shoulder like "Whas this guy doin'?" An' everyone was tellin' Flurff to lay offa that dawg, but he jes kep on with "This ain't no tough dawg" and slappin' its balls 'round, an' all of a sudden, as God is my witness, that dawg turn and done sunk his teeth into Flurff's leg an' we couldn't pull him off. Sumbitch took it over the head with bottles an' God knows what else ... wouldn't let go. Somebody ran out an grab a two by four an' started whackin' it over the head. Sheee-it! Flurff? Eighteen stitches in the leg – the Lord knows I'm tellin' the truth.'

Everyone shakes their heads and laughs. There's a few moments of nostalgic silence, then: 'If there's one thing I'm proud of in my life,' says Emerson, as the laughter dies down, 'it's what I did today. I was pallbearer at a funeral and the grass was so slick I thought we was all gonna go over. I was on the back like a brake.'

Everyone falls silent. Fluff is forgotten. Emerson stares at his beer. 'Federal laws,' he says, sadly. 'You can't bury no one on their motor-cycle no more.'

'He had a bike?' someone asks.

'He did not,' says Emerson.

No one says anything for a while and then another redneck stumbles over and shows me a straight-edge razor he just bought. It's old and rusty but still sharp.

'That's a beautiful straight-edge,' I say, gauging the distance be-tween myself and the door. There's no logic in here. Subjects rise up out of nowhere and disappear halfway through. I never heard so many suicide stories. The best is about a man who shot himself under the chin, blew the top of his head off – and lived.

'Now he's bald on top 'cause they grafted some of his back onto the top thar.'

'That's amazing,' I say.

'What's amazing?' asks Mike, who was telling the story.

'Well, you know, that he blew the top of his head off and lived.'

'I'll tell you what's amazing,' says Mike, eyeing me narrowly. 'That evolution bullshit. That's what's amazin'. You don't believe that evo-lution bullshit do you?'

'Yes, I do, you hillbilly, redneck moron, and furthermore my great-

great-grandfather was Charles Darwin,' is what I feel like saying. Instead I shift from one foot to the other and in a low, cowardly voice say, 'Well, you know …'

'You *do*,' he says, grinning ominously. 'You believe that sheeit!'

'Well, there does seem to be some evidence.'

'Yeah? So how come I ain't never seen no monkeys around here? I ain't seen no monkeys around here, have you?'

'No.'

He moves closer.

'No, I haven't.'

'Okay, then let me ask you sumpin else. If we came from monkeys how come there's hundreds of monkeys in the world an' you don't never see no man come outta one of 'em?'

How to begin to answer?

'Let me buy you a drink,' I suggest.

'Bull-sheeeit! Tha's what evolution is. Bull-*sheeit*,' he insists, grinning at me furiously. 'You believe in that sheeit?'

Am I going to be forced on my knees to admit to a literal interpretation of the Bible? Is Fluff to be called to work his magic on my testes? I realise that I'm profoundly and strangely drunk. I skid my eyes toward the barmaid who, mercifully, claps her hands together and says it's time to close. Everyone deflates. Emerson revives the snoring man. He looks around, bemused. He has a pleasant, flat face with almond eyes that won't focus.

I bid a swift goodnight and hurry along the wall back to my room, clutching my jar of moonshine.

CHAPTER TWENTY

Stumped

Having been ejected from boarding school at the age of fourteen, I moved back home to the mill house. By now my mother's drinking was persistent and depressing. She still cooked well, but it was accompanied by the frequent hiss of uncorking cider. I began to drink with her on occasion.

It took me less than a year to get thrown out of the next school, a small secondary modern in a nearby village. I have few memories of the place. It was ugly, it was school. I don't even remember why I was expelled, but when I asked my father if he could remember, he thought for a moment and then said, 'I think it had something to do with a bus.' And I think he was right. I remember an altercation of some kind and the face of a startled middle-aged woman with permed hair and pointed glasses, but that is all. The vivid memories I do have of that year, as you will probably have come to expect by now, are of a sexual nature.

But I won't go into them in any detail. Suffice to say, the school 'slut', so named for wanting what everyone else wanted and getting it with honesty and enthusiasm, became pregnant after an encounter with me in a haystack. She was the daughter of a lorry driver and not a great beauty above the collar bone.

An abortion was clearly indicated, but I visualised my father's strained but polite face as he looked from me to the girl and back again while I explained my urgent need for money. Nor was it hard to imagine, once the excruciating encounter was over, the scathing comments from my mother, as soon as the necessary libation had been uncorked and consumed.

I sent away for a book, available through *Exchange & Mart*, which listed Merchant ships in need of crew. Ever the hero, I had decided to bolt.

Figuring the girl was pregnant anyway, I had her as often as I could.

I told her I was working on an abortion plan and daily checked the mail for news of ships leaving out of Southampton. Whether my ever more vigorous (desperate) lovemaking brought on an early miscarriage, or if it was a hysterical pregnancy in the first place, I do not know, but one morning I arrived at school to be told that all was well again. I gave up plans for a life in the Merchant Marine and set about destroying the last remnants of an education.

Whatever caused me to get kicked out must have been relatively serious because I was already in the educational gutter. To get washed into the drain took some doing. In my case, the case of a spoiled middle-class boy, the drain came in the form of the Università Per Stranieri, an exotically-named language school operated out of a cubic palazzo, the Palazzo Galenga, in Perugia, Italy.

My parents had given up. In less than a year I could go to work. Here was a place to tread water.

The school was attended largely by young Americans and English either in between school and university or, in the case of some females, as an alternative to the more expensive European finishing schools.

At first I lived with a family, an old couple who had a beautiful 23-year-old daughter. About a month after I was there I discovered a small circular shaft connecting my room and the bathroom next door. It was an empty pipe through which a speaking tube had once passed. On either side of the thin wall, were two metal caps, retained in a bracket by a single twist. There was even a handle on each cap to help you get it off. I removed the one in the bathroom, hid it, and placed some items around the hole to distract attention but not to obstruct my view of the bath. I went to my room and ran a test. With the cap on my side removed, a two-inch diameter cylinder provided an excellent view of the bathroom and in particular, the bath.

It was still light when I heard the daughter go in to take her bath before going out for the evening. I slowly unscrewed my cap, slid it down the wall a few millimetres and, through a wary crescent, watched as she undressed. As the crescent was so small, I assimilated her in sections, but, as I put the pieces together, it seemed she had the body of Italy itself, timeless and classic, the form of a statue in the Uffizi: a long slender neck, sloping shoulders, small breasts, a high waist swelling to broad hips whose sweeping outer line had all the elegance of a swan.

She was so beautiful I began to sweat. I wanted to see more, wanted to see her whole. She stepped into the bath. I lowered the cap and pressed my eye closer.

I felt the cap sliding from my fingers.

I fumbled for it. It scraped against the wall and fell. The daughter's head snapped toward me. Her elbows flew toward each other across her breasts. I had drawn the drapes in my room, but they were thin. If I removed my eye from the hole, light would shine through from my side and make the hole glaringly visible on hers. However, if I kept my eye in place, light from *her* side might be powerful enough to penetrate the tube and illuminate my terrified eyeball at the other end.

She stared at the hole, unmoving, intent. I stared back. The expression on her face could have been one of uncertainty or 'I see you back there, you filthy little *testa di cazzo* and I'm going to stare at you until you take your eye away from that hole and cap it.'

Thirty seconds passed like this. I was afraid to blink. Her stillness, the intensity of her expression, her attitude of outraged modesty was a magnificent rebuke, *if* she could see me; but I still wasn't sure. Finally, out of courtesy to her, if indeed she was seeing me, I looked away to study another part of the bathroom. The movement of my eyeball must have sent a reflection back down the tube because it was at this point that she began to scream.

I capped the hole and went out for the evening.

In the morning, the hole was glued shut and the atmosphere was chilly. The daughter had left for work already. The parents moved about, their heads bowed, their eyes never meeting mine.

That day, before they could write a letter to my parents, I met an Italian student who was looking for someone with whom to share an apartment. I called my parents and conned them into paying my half. The Italian was almost never there, he had a girlfriend he stayed with most nights, so at the age of fifteen I essentially had my own place. It had a large kitchen at the back and two bedrooms at the front divided from each other by a wood partition which stopped a few feet short of the ceiling so that both rooms could benefit from the single fan swaying on its stalk above.

I settled in to enjoy the remaining months of my education.

Perugia was a town perched on a series of hills overlooking the

Umbrian Valley. In one form or another it had been there since at least 300 BC. Once you had climbed up its winding streets you reached a plateau. The main street ran from a cathedral at one end to a small park with views of the valley at the other. In the evening, for an hour or two before dinner, the inhabitants of the city and the many students (there was also an Italian university in the town) promenaded up and down this street, stopping now and then for coffee or a drink at one of several outdoor cafés. It was, for younger people, an extended flirtation conducted by the play of eyes, the torment of feigned indifference and the relief of an over-the-shoulder glance, a one-second flash of teeth, dark eyes fixing on you, and then the hair again. And on she walks, her final message of solace and encouragement sent by the sway of her large hips.

I learned enough Italian to get by and then started to travel the country. It was hard to hitch out of Perugia because the roads that came down off it, like veins from the pupil of an eyeball, had no final intent. Only when you reached the base could you find the road that led to the highways. To walk down off the hill was exhausting so I took to stealing scooters, which I would ride out of town until they ran out of gas. I would then hitch wherever the mood took me. I started with small trips, to Florence and Rome, both of which were only a hundred or so miles away, but eventually I hitched the country from one end to the other, up to Venice in the north and down to Naples and Sicily in the south. Often I went alone, sometimes with friends, once with two English girls. I drank wine until I vomited and hitched until I fell asleep. I saw hills sparkling with fireflies and skies alive with shooting stars. I woke with the smell of Italy in my nostrils, farm land, eucalyptus, wild rosemary, heat.

It was one of the most vivid periods of my life; but it was also hard. I was younger than the other students, fifteen to their eighteen to twenty. The women were old enough to be intimidating, but not experienced or confident enough to want a boy lover.

I only slept with three and three-quarter women.

One was a striking American, one was English, and one was a beautiful French girl. The last was a woman from Australia whom I met in the final week of my stay.

She was pretty, if a little overweight, and I remember thinking as I sat drinking with her in a bar, how kind she seemed. We came back to my place and it was only when I had her on the edge of the bed and pulled up her skirt that I noticed one of her legs was an odd shade of pink and had a hinge in it.

'Is it going to bother you?' she asked, looking at me with a hopeful but slightly ashamed expression, as if she should have told me before we came up the stairs.

'Not at all,' I replied gallantly, partly out of politeness, partly out of genuine compassion, and partly – well, she was willing and I was fifteen and one leg more or less was both literally and figuratively beside the point. She unstrapped the limb and slid it off the stump. It was a plastic limb and made a skittering noise as it hit the wooden floor.

On I jumped and was, I'm sure, as clumsy as usual, with less to cling to, more so. However, she at least was grateful if not satisfied and afterwards we lay for a long time in each other's arms, two incomplete people staring at the ceiling.

I had the fear.

Not fear in the specific – not a moment of explicable fear – but a malaise as physical as mental, a constant unease, fear like that vast fungus which extends for miles underground.

By way of illustration:

Carlo was a student at the regular university, one of those demented Italian intellectuals, intense and fanatical one minute, full of seductive bonhomie the next, Communist one month, anarchist the next. He had a twitchy, defensive charm that went well with his lank dark hair and black beard. People found him odd, but they liked him.

One day, Carlo did not turn up for class. For several days, none of his fellow students saw him. No one knew where he was. Before passeggio, as the evening walk was called, students gathered on the broad steps of the Cathedral. Sometimes there would be a couple of hundred divided into groups, discussing the potential of the oncoming night. One evening, a week after Carlo's disappearance, a friend of his, Guiseppe, came up the steps toward us. He was accompanied by a young man. Both looked sombre. Guiseppe informed us that Carlo was dead. He had been killed by a car while riding his motorcycle home to visit his mother. The young man, a friend of Carlo's from his home town, had brought the news. We were shocked and sad. For all his intensity, there was, thinking of him in retrospect, something frail and vulnerable about Carlo. He had the quality of a neglected child, impudent not out of arrogance but out of necessity.

For the next few days Guiseppe and his friend were often around. The friend was clean-shaven and always wore a beret and dark glasses. When you spoke to him, he smiled and shrugged but rarely said anything. Sometimes when we talked about Carlo, it was with affection, at other times with humour.

After a week or so we stopped talking about him and a few days after that the clean-shaven young man came up the steps of the Cathedral and removed his dark glasses and beret.

It was Carlo.

The whole thing, he told us, had been an 'intellectual exercise'. He wanted to witness the effect of his own death, wanted, as it were, to attend his own funeral. It was amusing, nothing more. I did not believe this. I believed his purpose was to assess his value in the world, to see if he could see himself reflected in the mirror of our grief. He needed his funeral eulogy in advance when it could still do him some good.

I could have used an affirmation of some kind myself, something to repudiate my growing conviction that I was, and always would be, completely insignificant. I looked at the future and saw no place for myself out there. I was middle class but had, by rejecting education, closed the doors which would otherwise have led to opportunity and contact with my own. I had fewer qualifications than the average factory apprentice, but unlike him was denied the fellowship of the working class.

As the time approached for my return to England, to return a man ready for work, my nerve was failing me. I travelled the country alone, often through areas infested with rural Mafia, and, in spite of often blistering reviews, continued my attempts at coital adequacy, but for all this, and all my public display of arrogance and bravado, when I was alone, I could no longer hide from myself this great unease. I was a prisoner who had struggled for ten years to escape. Free at last, I found myself bewildered, an agoraphobic awash in space: how could I know which way to run when there was no wall to bash my head against?

I lay there with my incomplete Antipodean, thinking about these last six months and the ten-year war preceding it. In most respects I'd won.

For someone my age – never mind a descendant of Charles Darwin – I was staggeringly ignorant. I couldn't spell or do long division, and if you asked me if Vladivostock was the capital of Poland or a Russian poet, I'd be completely, well … stumped.

Yes, I'd done okay. Here I was, after all, rewarded for my academic failure by a six-month sojourn in Italy. But, putting aside justifiable pride in my anti-achievement, I had also, though I hated to admit it, been hurt. What charm I'd had as a child was replaced by the alternating cowardice and drunken swagger of the lost. That was the victory of the schools.

Through the open window, I could hear a boisterous group of English and American students making their way up the steep street below. These were young men and women with *prospects* – you could hear it in every self-assured laugh, in every braying shout; these were the good children, captains of teams, winners by reflex, the entitled. And I would never be one of them, never join that community of ease. At least in mind, I'd always be elsewhere, lying in the dark with a cripple in my arms.

CHAPTER TWENTY-ONE

Sediment In The Mouth

Gale Johnson looks like one of those young moms you see in commercials selling washing powder. She's in her thirties and the prettiest woman I've met in Dayton so far, blonde with big eyes set among freckles. She has kept herself in shape.

We are having lunch at the Peking Palace on the highway and I'm secreting charm from every moonshine-and-guilt-polluted pore in the hopes of wresting a script or video from her which will allow me to pretend – if I have to – that I saw the play. But there is a gulf between us. She is nervous and defensive and my charm machine is not operating at full capacity on account of my hangover. I sense – and this will later be confirmed – that Gale has 'lived', and has in consequence developed a certain intuitive suspicion of men like me. I am in my best clothes and I am shaved, but the sinner is still visible to Gale and it reminds her of things she'd rather forget.

Gale and her husband, Carter, are Presbyterians, as William Jennings Bryan was. She was born in Abington, Pennsylvania but when she was eight moved with her family to Fort Lauderdale, where her father owned a TV repair shop. She and Carter have been in Dayton for seven years, having been sent here to 'plant' a church. They don't have a church building of their own yet, renting one instead from the Methodists. When she first came here, she found it dreary. They were outsiders and had a hard time attracting a congregation. Their congregation is now around eighty. It's been eighty for a couple of years now.

One of the elders in the church said maybe they were trying to 'grow corn in a bean field,' meaning Rhea County is a Baptist and Church of God area which makes Presbyterianism a hard sell.

There are two branches of Presbyterianism, she tells me, Presbyterian Church of America and Presbyterian Church, USA. Their branch is the former, referred to as PCA, and is the less liberal of the two. In trying to describe what her branch believes, Gale mentions Calvin and the five points of Calvinism.

'What are the five points of Calvinism?' I ask.

'Well, there's the Tulip. Let me see if I can remember them, 'cause I was raised as a Baptist and came to this late in life ... Total depravity of man ...'

'That's the starting point?'

'That's the T of Tulip, yes.'

We're in trouble here. Total depravity of man?! This is too close to the bone.

'The U is er ... unconditional ... I'm not sure what the U is ... I wish my husband was here, he could tell you.'

'Unconditional something,' I offer.

'Anyway, where we differ from Baptists is in the idea of election – that man left to himself would never choose God because in his unregenerate state he has no desire for God and so God in his grace and mercy reaches out to you ... There's a drawing of the Holy Spirit and you can't resist it.'

'You think that's true?' I ask. 'Seems to me man has a great desire for God.'

'Do I think that's true?'

'Well,' I say, laughing, 'I guess you do, of course.'

Gale says she believes God put a desire for a general kind of *spirituality* in man, but that's very different from wanting Jesus Christ. 'And so they'll search to fill that void and that's where you get some really wacky philosophies and religions, false religions.'

She tells me about her own life, how as a child in Fort Lauderdale, she went to Church, but when she got into high school, she rejected it all.

'Were you a wild kid in high school?' I ask.

'Yeah.'

'Drugs, pre-marital sex, the whole thing?'

She nods affirmatively, but moves quickly on, telling me how she became an actress, did some dinner theatre, and then went to New York. She found New York exciting, 'a lot of incredible beauty and talent, but I couldn't handle the pain that I was seeing, the people sleeping out on the park benches with a newspaper for a blanket.' It got so bad she couldn't ride the subway anymore. She says God intervened and led her to question the meaning of life and of her part in it. She would go to auditions and there would be 5,000 actors trying out for a single part. She imagined herself in twenty years, living in a tenement apartment, having achieved nothing. 'And so I turned my back on theatre and I gave it up, I came back home to North Carolina where my family was living. I spent a long time searching and praying, 'What do you want me to do with my life?'

After a while, she went back to graduate school and got a degree in special education and then went on to work with disturbed and abused children who had been taken away from their homes because they were in such bad shape.

I point out that she left New York to escape pain but ended up in an even more painful environment and that maybe what she couldn't take in New York was not the pain but her inability to do anything about it.

'That's a very good observation,' she congratulates me. But even after she had her job, she was still searching. She went to a seminary so she could learn more about the scriptures, and that's where she met her husband. For the first few years of her marriage, she avoided even going to the theatre. She wanted to put it out of her mind; but, she tells me, if you give something up for God, he'll often give it back to you. When she got to Dayton, the opportunity to be in a community theatre production of Neil Simon's play, *Rumors* came up and she took it.

She met a lot of actors and then the director of *Rumors* asked her to direct *The Crucible*, up at Bryan College. Because she knew the actor who played Darrow, she went to watch 'The Scopes Trial.' She found some of it confusing and asked Bryan College if she could stage a new version the following year.

'How can I see it?' I ask.

'Well, um, I don't have a videotape available and I don't really feel comfortable giving a videotape to anyone, um ...'

'So, there is a videotape?'

'There will be, yes, for the actors.'

I tell her I bought the tickets, I just couldn't make it. I'll pay her for a tape, give money to her favourite charity. She smiles unyieldingly. I tell her about the book, my desire to show what Dayton was like seventy-five years ago as opposed to how it is now. I've done a lot of research, I know things about Rappleyea that could be helpful to her ...

'I don't have him in my play.'

I try to hide my shock. 'No? You should. He's a fascinating guy.'

'Oh, he is, there's a lot of colourful people. H.L. Mencken, I don't have him in either, for other reasons, because sometimes his relatives come and visit and we didn't want anyone to be uncomfortable by portraying him ...'

No Mencken!? I can't believe this. Two of the story's most interesting characters, gone, the men who started it and the man who reported it. It's incredible.

I tell her a lie. I tell her my daughter was sick. The re-enactment was central to my book, but I couldn't leave. I just couldn't make it. This is a disaster for me. Please, won't she give me the tape?

She laughs. 'I don't know how the re-enactment will really help in the book. I mean, are you going to have any of the arguments in there?'

Yes, I am. But I want the tape because the other half of the book is about modern Dayton and the re-enactment seems like a large part of that.

'Well, one of the things about my play,' she begins, as if answering my question, but, in fact, simply changing the subject, 'is we had street scenes, placards ...' She goes on to tell me about a scene between two reporters, one of whom is 'more pro-Bryan and the other one is a cynic.' She tells me about how long she rehearsed, how hard it was to work with amateurs. She tells me Sheriff Sneed is great, totally relaxed, but won't rehearse, just turns up for final dress rehearsal. She tells me they pass out sheets to the audience, telling them to react as the real audience did in 1925. She tells me people came this year from the Mencken Society in Baltimore, people from Nashville, people from Washington. One time, not this year, a group of atheists came up from Atlanta on a bus called 'The Atheist Bus'. This year, she felt there were more pro-Bryan people.

'We didn't see any reaction from the audience that was overtly in favour of Darrow.'

She suggests people for me to visit, old men who were at the real trial when they were five.

She doesn't want to give me the tape. She has no mercy.

I decide to drop the subject and come back to it later. I ask her if she had any complaints. She tells me some people from the Mencken Society were upset because she did not include a part of the trial where Darrow asks Bryan if he believes the six days of creation were 24-hour days or periods. It is perhaps the most important moment in the whole trial, revealing how the Bible can be interpreted differently by different people. 'I wasn't trying to avoid that,' says Gale, innocently, 'it was just it seemed to me it flowed better if I went in this direction ...'

I ask again if I could have something to help me write about the re-enactment, even just the script. 'You've got to help me,' I plead as fetchingly as I can, hoping to appeal to some Christian mercy in the woman, or pity.

'Well, um ...' she says. 'How long will you be in town?'

'I'm supposed to go back Sunday lunchtime but I'd stay if you were going to be nice to me.'

She laughs almost flirtatiously, it's like a burst of light, a flashback. And it gets switched off fast.

'Well, I say ... I'm just trying to think ... I'm going out of town and I'm not going to have ... If you could come back, maybe ... and ... I just wonder though how's the script? ... Is it that it would just shorten things for you because you wouldn't have to ...?'

She's calling me lazy now?!

No, I tell her, I know as much about the trial as she does, probably more. I'm just interested in her angle on the thing. It's all a little strange to me. Had I been there, I would have seen it. I wasn't there – now I can't. Where's the logic? (Where's the logic? There's a question.)

'Okay, why don't we do this?' she suggests efficiently. 'If you can be back like when I'm back from out of town, the video will be available and you and I could watch it together?'

I tell her I'm going to be out of the country until at least September.

'Well, you can just call me when you're in town and we'll watch it together.'

Like I'm just going to be passing through Dayton some time and we'll ... But, I can see I'm not going to get anywhere with this today and start paying the bill.

She asks me if I'd like to come and see her husband preach on Sunday.

She has me by the balls. That's not entirely fair; she does have me by the balls, yes, but the offer is made sweetly and includes lunch afterwards. Anyway, I'm curious. She seems such a poignant character, a pretty, sexy cheerleader wounded by the big city, washed up in Dayton. I wonder what the husband will be like.

However, sympathetic as I am to her, as I drive off to see Joe Wilkie, the John Scopes of the modern high school, I feel angry and resentful. Her refusal to help me is un-Christian. The whole enterprise starts to irritate me. The very word, 're-enactment' is a lie. It isn't a re-enactment – the trial took two weeks, this takes a couple of hours – it's an *interpretation* and there's something sly about the concept, neither fact nor art.

Joe Wilkie is a big man. He has a large face with a beard around it. He's brought his wife along and she's large too and they're both hunched over a table at the Frontier Diner. Their faces are inexpressive, the eyes watchful, as if some other being lurks inside, hidden and suspicious. To try and warm them up, I ask some general questions about Dayton kids. Do most of them want to get out of Dayton when they leave high school? No, he tells me, most of them want to go work at La-Z-Boy. It's pretty good money. About 30% of them go on to college or trade school. He cites as an example of a Rhea County high school success, a man who's now Vice-President of the Sara Lee cake-making company.

Joe, who is a Baptist, went to Rhea County High himself and has now been teaching there for sixteen years. He mainly teaches regular science classes but he has also developed one class called 'Ideas and Issues In Science.' Based on a book he wrote, he had to get special permission from the state of Tennessee to teach it. In the science classroom, he teaches evolution. 'As far as teaching creationism in the science class room, no; but in the class that I've developed, of course that's the whole point of it.'

His wife watches me with mistrust from the side, as if she came here to protect him. I ask him what he himself believes and he tells me he 'chooses' to believe in creationism. He cites a couple of examples of phenomena which would seem to suggest a younger earth. One has to do with how the earth's magnetic field 'can't flip in two thousand, four thousand years,' but a creationist working out west was working in some lava and his 'magnetic compass flipped as he went through the layers.'

Then there's delta filling. Given how much sediment comes out of the mouth of the Mississippi river, the Gulf of Mexico would have filled up by now if the world was much older than ten thousand years old. Hmm ...

When I mention Kurt Wise, Joe is full of admiration.

'I think he committed academic suicide. If you talk to some of the evolutionists, they will tell you – I'm not going to say any names but one of them did tell me this – he said that in his opinion Kurt did do just that.'

Suicide ... It keeps coming up. I mention this to Joe and wonder out loud what kind of despair might have lead to the most recent death on the tracks. He tells me there's been a general rise in teen suicide in the area. Why does he think this is, I ask.

'It's because they don't know Jesus Christ as their Lord and Saviour,' states Joe the Baptist with absolute certainty. 'They don't have anything to look forward to, they don't have inner peace. Living like that, of course you'd look at the world and say, "What's the use?" That's my personal take on it, and I guess you would think I would have that personal take because I am a Christian and I believe that Jesus Christ is ... He is the difference. He *is* the difference.'

I thank him for talking to me and then depart, leaving the two of them at their table, staring after me.

CHAPTER TWENTY-TWO

Where Did Cain Get His Wife?

I came down here to see if anything has changed in seventy-five years and the longer I'm here, the more apparent it becomes that little has. There must be Daytonians who believe in Darwin's theory of evolution, but I've yet to meet one. There must be people here who don't believe in God, but I haven't met one of them either. In fact, it seems to me that the religious and political mood of the town is worse now than it was then. In Dayton in 1925, as well as the unchanging Fluffs and Mikes and preachers and literalists, you also had George Rappleyea and John Scopes, and even those who disagreed with them, did so with a certain regard for good manners and fair play. Scopes went swimming with William Jennings Bryan Jr, one of his prosecutors; Darrow stayed at the house of one of the witnesses against his client, and the whole event was cooked up in an amiable, exploratory fashion. Now such a thing would be unthinkable. There's been a narrowing of views and a widening of the division between them. On afternoon television shows designed to provoke violence, people howl at each other about personal matters as the audience goads them on, but in bars and restaurants, even in homes, it is considered impolite to discuss any matter of importance, and politics and religion are taboo. The colourful habit of friendly debate has been bleached out by the incessant, unifying glare of television, and in consequence people are ill-equipped to deal with dissent.

If something like the Scopes Trial was staged now, people would be afraid for their lives.

Perhaps to describe the trial as taking place under conditions of 'fair play' is overstating it. Judge Raulston ruled against Darrow's expert witnesses. Having come all the way down to Dayton, they would not be allowed to testify before the jury. This was a disaster. If the testimony of Darrow's expert witnesses was not in the trial record, it could not become part of an appeal, which would thus become much narrower and less capable of bringing about change. The defence argued vociferously and finally won the right to read some scientific testimony into the record, but not with the jury present. It was Friday and Darrow asked for the day off so his expert witnesses could prepare their statements. After further argument it was agreed the defence could have until Monday to prepare and court adjourned for the weekend.

Mencken, whose scathing remarks about the 'primitives,' 'yokels,' and 'Neanderthals' as he referred to the locals, had so angered Dayton there was talk of running him out of town, now decided to leave voluntarily. 'All that remains,' he wrote, in his final despatch, 'of the great cause of the State of Tennessee against the infidel Scopes is the final business of bumping off the defendant.'

The next morning, he caught a train back to Baltimore and so missed one of the great dramas of legal history. He had underestimated Darrow.

Although Tom Stewart was claiming a 'glorious victory' for having excluded the defence witnesses from appearing before the jury, Darrow guessed that *personally* William Jennings Bryan did not feel victorious at all. His pride had been hurt by Malone's great speech, and in his sense of failure, in his perceived humiliation, lay the possibility of a comeback for the defence. Bryan wanted an opportunity to redeem himself and Darrow would provide one.

He issued a press statement taunting Bryan for not wanting the jury to hear the defence's expert witnesses. 'Bryan has not dared to test his views in open court under oath ... Bryan, who blew the loud trumpet calling for a "battle to the death," has fled from the field, his forces disorganized and his pretensions exposed.' Bryan shot back with a statement that included the remark that 'jungle ancestry' struck at the root not only of Christianity but of civilisation itself. The stakes were raised back up again, from legal detail to philosophical war.

Other factors were putting pressure on Bryan to make a good showing down here. A few days earlier, he had spoken to friends about founding a Christian college for young men on the hill above Dayton. Now a philanthropist in Florida had come through with a pledge of $10,000. Bryan College might actually become a reality, and if it was to carry his name, he'd surely like that name to be associated in the minds of the locals with grand oratory and rousing victory. He was ripe for what was to follow.

On Monday, Hays was allowed an hour to read excerpts from the scientific and religious scholars into the trial record. He actually read for over two hours in the overwhelming heat of this the hottest day. In their statements, an anthropologist, a psychologist, three zoologists, an agronomist, and two geologists, all eminent in their fields, described in detail how evolution occurred, how it had been proved, and how it was almost universally accepted in the academic world.

Professor Newman, a zoologist from the University of Chicago, tried in his statement to explain not only evolution but the nature and methods of science itself. 'When we admit that the evidences of past evolution are indirect and circumstantial, we should hasten to add that the same is true of all other great scientific generalizations. The evidences upon which the law of gravity are based are no less indirect than those supporting the principle of evolution ... The law of gravity has acquired its validity through its ability to explain, unify and rationalize many observable facts of physical nature. If certain facts entirely out of accord with the law of gravity were to come to light, physicists would be forced either to modify the statement of the law so as to bring it into harmony with the newly discovered facts, or else to substitute a new law capable of meeting the situation.'

In other words, science, unlike religion, is fluid, and in teaching it you can only teach what is best understood at the time.

By midday the heat was intolerable and many of the reporters who had stayed on in Dayton left court and did not come back for the afternoon session, a fact they would regret for the rest of their lives.

After lunch, when court reconvened, the air was so hot and the courtoom so stuffy and overcrowded that Judge Raulston suggested they all move down onto the Courthouse lawn beneath the shade trees. As soon as they were down there, Darrow got into a fight with the court about a sign under which the jury would now sit, saying READ YOUR BIBLE in large letters. It was clearly prejudicial and Darrow wanted it removed.

J.G. McKenzie accused the defence of being 'aligned with the Devil and his satellites,' but Darrow won the battle and the sign was taken down.

And now came the high point of the trial, the moment which has made it famous to this day. As Hays stood up to make a request, Malone leaned in to Scopes and whispered, 'Hell is going to pop now!'

'The defense,' said Hays, 'desires to call Mr Bryan as a witness.'

After the babble of surprised voices died down, Hays explained that if the defence was to be prevented from presenting their experts on science, then they wanted to call Bryan as an expert on the Bible.

Calling a lawyer from the other side to be your own witness was so unusual that all the prosecution lawyers immediately jumped to their feet. All around the world people listening to the trial on their radios moved closer. There were so many people talking in court that the court reporter could not transcribe every word.

According to Scopes, General Stewart was the most vociferous in objecting to Bryan being called, but Ben McKenzie appears more in the record. For a moment it looked as if the Judge might sustain their objections, but Darrow's brilliant assessment of Bryan's state of mind proved entirely correct. The Great Commoner got to his feet. Here was his chance and he wasn't going to let it go. Raising his arms for quiet, he declared himself more than willing to take the stand, so long as he had the right to call Darrow, Hays and Malone as witnesses when his turn came.

'Call anybody you desire,' said Raulston, 'ask them any questions you wish.'

'Then we will call all three of them,' Bryan stated.

'Not at once?' mocked Darrow.

'Where do you want me to sit?' Bryan snapped back.

News that Darrow was putting Bryan on the stand radiated out from the courthouse. 500 people had left the courtroom and taken their chairs down onto the lawn. Within an hour, there was a crowd of 3,000, standing and sitting wherever they could.

Throughout what followed, Tom Stewart constantly raised objections to Bryan testifying, but the more he did so, the more it looked like the great man required protection, and Bryan himself would wave him off with a plucky speech about his courage and how determined he was to face down the infidel, Darrow.

Darrow began by asking questions designed to establish Bryan as an expert on the Bible. Yes, Bryan admitted, he had studied the Bible for over fifty years and written and spoken about it widely.

'Do you claim that everything in the Bible should be literally interpreted?'

'I believe everything in the Bible should be accepted as it is given there. Some of the Bible is given illustratively. For instance, "Ye are the salt of the earth." I would not insist that man was actually salt ...'

'But when you read that the whale swallowed Jonah – how do you literally interpret that?'

'I believe in a God who can make a whale and can make a man and make both do what He pleases ...'

'The Bible says Joshua commanded the sun to stand still for the purpose of lengthening the day, doesn't it, and you believe it?'

'I do.'

'Do you believe that at that time the sun went around the earth?'

'No, I believe that the earth goes around the sun.'

'Have you an opinion as to whether whoever wrote the book – I believe it is Joshua, the Book of Joshua – thought the sun went around the earth or not?'

'I believe he was inspired.'

'Can you answer my question.'

'I believe that the Bible is inspired, an inspired author. Whether one who wrote as he was directed to write understood the things he was writing about, I don't know ... I believe it was inspired by the Almighty, and He may have used language that could be understood at that time instead of using language that could not be understood until Darrow was born.'

He got a good laugh here, and some applause, but Darrow pressed on. If the day was to be lengthened, wouldn't it in fact be necessary for the *earth* to stay still? Bryan used an old chestnut to illustrate his belief in the power of God. If he, William Jennings Bryan, a mere mortal, could pick up a glass of water, thus defying the laws of gravity, imagine what God could do.

'I read that years ago,' said Darrow impatiently. 'Can you answer my question directly? If the day was lengthened by stopping either the earth or the sun it must have been the earth?'

'Well, I should say so,' conceded Bryan.

'Have you ever pondered what would happen to the earth if it stood still?

'No.'

'Don't you know it would have been converted into a molten mass of matter?'

Bryan replied that Darrow could testify to that when he got on the stand.

Darrow began to ask questions about the Flood.

Included in the Bible admitted into evidence, the King James Bible, were the calculations of Bishop Ussher. Using these, Darrow and Bryan fixed the date of the Flood at 2348 BC and that of Creation at 4004 BC.

'You believe that all the living things that were not contained in the Ark were destroyed?' asked Darrow.

'I think the fish may have lived,' replied Bryan.

Again, there was some laughter.

'Have you any idea how old the Egyptian civilization is?' asked Darrow.

'No.'

Had he ever read anything about the origins of other religions?

'Not a great deal.'

Darrow asked him if he knew anything about Buddhism or Confucianism? Did he have any idea of the number of people who lived in Egypt 3,500 years ago, or China 5,000 years ago?

'No.'

'Have you ever tried to find out?'

'No, sir, you are the first man I ever heard of who has been interested in it.'

'Where have you lived all your life?' Darrow asked in amazement.

'Not near you,' said Bryan.

'Nor near anyone of learning ... You have never in all your life made any attempt to find out about the other peoples of the earth – how old their civilizations are – how long they have existed on earth?'

'No, sir, I have been so well satisfied with the Christian religion that I have spent no time trying to find arguments against it.'

This was the essence of his defence against the charge of ignorance and he did as well with it as he could; but, as Darrow's questions increasingly revealed not just Bryan's ignorance, which was forgivable, but his *satisfaction* with his ignorance, which somehow was not, his supporters began to applaud a little less enthusiastically.

'Have you any idea how far back the last glacial age was?'

'No, sir.'

'Do you know whether it was more than 6,000 years ago?'

'I think it was more than 6,000 years ago.'

'Have you any idea how old the earth is?'

'No.'

'The book you have introduced in evidence tells you, doesn't it?'

'I don't think it does, Mr Darrow.'

Darrow pointed out that the Bible which the state of Tennessee claimed evolution was in conflict with, contained Ussher's calculations and, as they had just agreed, these claimed the earth was created 4,004 years before the birth of Christ, thus making it less than 6,000 years old. Darrow hopped around, keeping Bryan off balance, jabbing at him and then circling around to jab again in the same place.

'Do you think the earth was created in six days?'

Bryan hesitated.

'Not six days of twenty-four hours.'

The crowd gasped. Bryan, the 'Fundamentalist Pope' had committed blasphemy. True fundamentalists believed (as most still do, including Kurt Wise) that when the Bible says six days, it means Monday through Saturday, six literal, twenty-four hour days. Darrow pressed on.

'Doesn't it say so?'

'No, sir.'

Stewart, seeing things going badly, tried again to make another objection. What was the purpose of this line of questioning? Before the Judge could answer, Bryan spoke up.

'The purpose is to cast ridicule on everybody who believes in the Bible, and I am perfectly willing that the world shall know that these gentlemen have no other purpose than ridiculing every Christian who believes in the Bible.'

'We have the purpose,' said Darrow, 'of preventing bigots and ignoramuses from controlling the education of the United States and you know it, and that is all.'

There were more objections from Steward and counter-arguments from Darrow and Hays.

'Your honor,' intoned Bryan, trying to get himself back into the proceedings, 'they have not asked a question legally, and the only reason they have asked any question is for the purpose – as the question about Jonah was asked – for a chance to give this agnostic an opportunity to criticize a believer in the word of God; and I answered the question in order to shut his mouth, so that he cannot go out and tell his atheistic friends that I would not answer his question. That is the only reason, no more reason in the world.'

Perhaps wearying of his protestations, or having absorbed his apostasy on the six literal days issue, or maybe even because they liked Darrow and felt Bryan's attack was unfair, the crowd did not cheer.

Malone, the hero of Thursday, stood up. 'Your honor, on this very subject, I would like to say that I would have asked Mr Bryan – and I consider myself as good a Christian as he is – every question that Mr Darrow has asked him for the purpose of bringing out whether or not there is to be taken in the court only a literal interpretation of the Bible … We are here as lawyers with the same right to our views. I have the same right to mine as a Christian as Mr Bryan has to his, and we do not intend to have this case charged by Mr Darrow's agnosticism or Mr Bryan's brand of Christianity.'

Malone's speech was greeted with 'great applause'. Bryan flinched visibly. The audience was applauding a direct attack on *him*, William Jennings Bryan, their 'Peerless Leader'! Coming as it did on the heels of his own courageous bleatings, which had received none, the effect must have been devastating. Caught between wanting to please his Fundamentalist supporters and not wanting to appear entirely idiotic to more educated people, had he made a terrible error in admitting he did not believe in the literal six days of creation?

Raulston told Darrow to continue.

'Mr Bryan, do you believe that the first woman was Eve?'

'Yes.'

'Do you believe she was literally made out of Adam's rib?'

'I do.'

'Did you ever discover where Cain got his wife?'

'No, sir, I leave the agnostics to hunt for her.'

Darrow went back to the six days of creation.

'Does the statement, "The morning and the evening were the first day," and "The morning and the evening were the second day," mean anything to you?'

Again – what else could he do? – Bryan held to his previous statement. 'I do not think it necessarily means a twenty-four hour day ... I think it would be as easy for the kind of God we believe in to make the earth in six days as in six years or in 6,000,000 years or in 600,000,000 years.'

'Do you think the sun was made on the fourth day?' Darrow continued.

'Yes.'

'And they had evening and morning without a sun?'

'I am simply saying it is a period.'

'They had evening and morning for four periods without the sun?'

'I believe in creation as there told, and if I am not able to explain it I will accept it. Then you can explain it to suit yourself.'

'Do you believe the story of the temptation of Eve by the serpent?'

'I do.'

'And you believe that is the reason that God made the serpent to go on his belly after he tempted Eve?'

'I believe the Bible as it is, and I do not permit you to put your language in the place of the language of the Almighty. You read that Bible and ask me questions, and I will answer them. I will not answer your questions in your language.'

'I will read it to you from the Bible: "And the Lord God said unto the serpent, Because you hast done this, thou art cursed above all cattle, and above every beast of the field; upon thy belly shalt thou go and dust shalt thou eat all the days of thy life." Do you think that is why the serpent is compelled to crawl upon its belly?'

'I believe that.'

'Have you any idea how the snake went about before that time?'

'No, sir.'

'Do you know whether he walked on his tail or not?'

The audience laughed.

Darrow had more questions, but as he was in the middle of asking

the next one, Bryan launched off into another of his martyred protestations.

'Your honor, I think I can shorten this testimony. The only purpose
Mr Darrow has is to slur at the Bible, but I will answer his question. I
will answer it all at once, and I have no objection in the world, I want
the world to know that this man, who does not believe in God, is trying
to use a court in Tennessee ...'

'I object,' said Darrow.

'... to slur at it, and while it may require time, I am willing to take
it.'

'I object to your statement,' said Darrow, losing his temper. 'I am
examining you on your fool ideas that no intelligent Christian on earth
believes!'

Suddenly, the two men were on their feet, glaring at each other.

Everyone stared at them in shock. Was Bryan going to hit Darrow or
Darrow Bryan?

Raulston banged his gavel and adjourned court until nine the following morning.

Darrow, the hero of the hour, strode away across the lawn, surrounded by the crowd and by admiring reporters, off to file their stories
around the world.

'For Bryan,' writes Scopes in his account, 'there was only despon-
dency; he was left alone on that green, spacious lawn, a forgotten,
forlorn man.'

Insulated by the adoration of his flock and by his own complacency,
had Bryan never considered any of the questions Darrow raised? Had
he entered this fight against science without once thinking about its
potential for revealing the absurdities of his own faith? If this was so,
and it seems possible, the experience must have been shattering. He had
sought to re-invent himself with this new cause and instead had been
dismantled. He must have known he did not have long to live and this
would be a part, a large part, of his legacy, this humiliation at the hands
of Darrow.

'His career,' wrote Mencken a few days after the trial, 'brought him
into contact with the first men of his time; he preferred the company of
rustic ignoramuses. It was hard to believe, watching him at Dayton, that
he had traveled, that he had been received in civilized societies, that he

had been a high officer of state. He seemed only a poor clod, deluded by a childish theology, full of an almost pathological hatred of all learning, all human dignity, all beauty, all fine and noble things. He was a peasant come home to the dung pile.'

Bryan comforted himself with the thought that he still had two chances left in which to redeem himself. He would put Darrow on the stand and question him and he'd dazzle the world with his closing argument for the prosecution.

CHAPTER TWENTY-THREE

Achtung, Rocky!

It's Friday night in Dayton, exactly seventy-three years – and one irretrievable week – after Darrow humiliated Bryan, and I'm in Sheriff Sneed's office, staring up at Deputy Sheriff Rocky Potter, who is going to take me out on a tour through the Tennessee night.

Rocky wears a tight brown uniform and resembles a 250lb sausage with a tennis ball perched on top. He is six foot-two and his chest and arms are so swathed in muscle that he's forced to adopt the posture of a gunslinger, arms out from the side, elbows slightly bent, hands hanging away from his hips. His shoulders are square and wider than the average doorway. A thigh-sized neck emerges from these shoulders and on top of the neck rests a shaved head, in the middle of which are two small eyes and a Zapata moustache.

As I'm introduced to him by Sneed, the eyes check me out with the cold, almost angry suspicion of the cop. I instinctively shrink back. Rocky does not stand, he *looms*, and looking up at him, I'm reminded of a character in a boy's comic book, the corporal who, at the last possible moment, comes plunging through a wall with a growl of righteous indignation and starts tossing Germans and howitzers around.

'Achtung! It's der Amerikaner, Herr Rocky!'

'Yaaagh!!!'

A power-ifter for the cops, Rocky later admits that although he can bench 460 pounds, he can't run a hundred yards without getting puffed; but God help you, I think to myself, if he gets to you before then.

A writer tends to be impressed by a cop. He's the physical manifestation of the writer's art. While the cowardly scribe sits in the comfort of his lair trying to envision the dramatic extremes of life, the cop is out there plunging around in them. A writer wonders what lies beyond the door – the cop kicks the door down and enters.

Sneed completes the introduction and Rocky smiles at me amiably as he reaches out to shake my hand. I'm ready for it and tense the limb to avoid injury. Rocky turns and beckons me to follow.

'I'll show you the jail, then we'll go serve some warrants,' he says, and we walk out the front of the sheriff's office and around the back to the Soweto-like structure that lies behind.

On one side are a few cells for the trusties. On the same side are a couple of cells for men who need to be protected and the cells for the female prisoners, though I did not see any. On the other side is the meat of the place, two lines of cells known as the Grey Bar Motel. Designed to house no more than fifty men at most, it often contains sixty to seventy. I meet two jailers, an older man with a wooden leg and a strange dent in his head, and a woman, Billie, who takes my arm, grinning and laughing, and leads me back.

Tough but obviously well-liked, she's one of those women of in-domitable good will and optimism. She unlocks a door and pushes her way in. She can't be more than five feet and has to be approaching fifty years old. She carries no weapon.

Country boys, lots of them, stripped to the waist – lean, manipulat-ive, whining – crowd around her as we go down the first row. Here is space. Here is space divided by bars and saturated with nicotine. Here is no space, no privacy, just time, dead time, lots of it. Bunks crammed against walls, dirty mattresses on the floor or rolled aside, eight to ten in cells built for four. Kids playing cards, kids jammed in the corridor, men in despair, lying on the six feet by four feet area to which, I suppose, they have some claim. It's a camp, a sleepover, a bazaar, bizarre. Some are in here for a night, some for years. I wouldn't last a week, not because of violence, not for want of comfort, but for lack of solitude.

'Hey, Billie, can I take a shower?'

'Hey, Billie, what about that sandwich?'

'Hey, Billie, did my bondsman come through yet?'

She bats them aside, affectionate but firm, more den mother than jailer.

They look at me, figuring the deal. Who is he, why is he here, what can I get out of him? One of them, nineteen, long blond hair shaved along the sides, one pupil paper-white (shot out by a BB gun, I'll bet), winks at me and grins. My nervousness gives way to a sense of camaraderie. I've stolen things with kids like these, worked with them in factories, dealt with them on film crews. They're the sad adventurers, exuberant boys of unfixed ambition, losers without sufficient will or intelligence to escape their destiny; boys who, in celebration of careless youth and limited freedom, dodge this way and that for a couple of years before eventually being taken by what they dread far more than this: the inevitable mouth of the long tube of the production line which will suck them in, set them on a march of endless days marked by 32,000 sorry punchings of a clock, and then, once they are exhausted, will blow them out the other end, into retirement and death.

We leave and go along the other row, much the same but for the added frisson of attempted murder – Jimmy McKenzie's assailant lurking deep in the furthest cell, awaiting results of a test of his insanity.

It's still light as Rocky, carrying a large wad of warrants to be served, leads me to his car, talking about eating. He has to eat a lot and frequently because of the lifting.

Rocky was born in Battle Creek, Michigan in 1960, but his mother was a Dayton native and when she split up with her husband in 1979, she decided to move back. Rocky came through a short while later on his way to Houston, Texas, where he was planning to work on the oil rigs. He stayed with his mother a couple of weeks and was impressed how friendly everyone was and how the town was so peaceful. When he got to Houston, he worked a few days hefting barrels, but didn't like it, missed his mother, and decided to try life in Dayton. He worked seventeen years at the La-Z-Boy factory, serving as an auxiliary cop on evenings and weekends.

Now he's full-time, always working the night shift, seven to seven. His wife, his second wife, works at Long Johns, one of the eateries out along the Highway. Between them they have three kids, two hers, one his. He has breakfast with them when he comes home, sees them off to school, then sleeps. In the afternoon, he runs errands, lifts some weights, and when the kids come back, he plays with them or helps with their homework. Around six, he eats one of his many meals in their company, kisses them goodnight, and hits the road.

Our first stop is to check on a runaway girl whose parents have taken out a warrant on her, to try and get the courts to control her. As we're driving up the hill, a pick-up comes down toward us and stops. There are two men in the cab. The driver leans out.

'Hey, Rocky, just saw a pair of shitheads in a red Chevy Camaro, you might wanna keep an eye out for 'em.'

Rocky talks to them for a while (they turn out to be off-duty fellow officers) then thanks them and we continue.

'Is there an exact definition for "shitheads"?' I ask.

'Shitheads,' he explains, 'is the term we use around here for the bad guys. Shitheads. Friday night. Lot of shitheads cruising around.'

We pull up outside a house one step up from a trailer and moments later are joined by the parents of the runaway. She has not come back. They seem defeated almost to the point of indifference. Their daughter's got a new boyfriend. The boyfriend's a drug user ... It's a familiar tale. Rocky explains to them who to see at the Courthouse, what their options are, and they thank him deferentially.

Soon we're back cruising around the county. It's not the best night for serving warrants, not yet at least, because the shitheads are out drinking or doing whatever it is shitheads do of a Friday night in Dayton; but for me it's an opportunity, a guided tour. The warrants lead us to the flickering satellites of crime and misadventure: a preacher whose wife has taken out a restraining order to stop him beating her; a man who keeps throwing rocks at local kids; another who refuses to pay rent. None are in. After each visit, Rocky rechecks his warrants, looking for one that might either end in success or provide some entertainment. There's been a dispute in the Little League Football team. One of the VPs of the team, a woman, needs to be served a warrant to appear in court where the matter will be settled. An ex-beauty queen from some local contest, she has long blonde curly hair and is in consequence known as 'Little Mermaid.' She lives in a nice middle-class home up in the hills. But she's not in either.

We get a call directing us to a neighbourhood across the tracks, Morgantown, a domestic dispute. We cross back over the highway, bounce over the tracks, weave along sunset streets, and soon find ourselves in what can only be described as a rural slum. Decaying one-storey wooden houses with peeling paint behind chain link fences. Dirty children playing among cars rusting in the yards and on the street. Even the trees look dusty and worn out.

The windshield of the car becomes like a camera or a telescope, no longer a frame through which you idly gaze, but something purposive with which you seek. I find myself watching differently, hoping to see something Rocky misses, a figure running off alongside a house, the red Camaro. It's strange how quickly the instinct takes root.

Many people are outside in the heat, lounging around, drinking, playing with the children, but we're still a hundred yards away when I know the house we're going to. A couple in the yard, two children, a tableau of aggrieved shock.

We pull up and Rocky gets out. I follow, slightly behind, face expressionless. A woman in her late twenties, prematurely faded, once attractive, bad teeth. A man in a baseball hat and jeans, ginger hair and beard, shirt off. Both are moderately drunk. Two boys: one a five-year-old, already with dark resentful eyes, the other under two, in diapers and nothing else, no shoes, no shirt. The younger child's filthy skin is covered in red dots, like small bites. On his shoulder is a red mark about the size of an adult hand.

The woman shows Rocky a similar mark on her neck running up toward her ear, through which, she claims, she can no longer hear. Her ex-husband has been down here trying to pick up the smaller of the kids, his son, but he was drunk and hit them both when she disputed custody. Rocky tells her the smacking is a domestic matter and as he didn't see it, she has to swear out a warrant if she wants to prosecute him for assault or get a restraining order. Meanwhile, he'll go in search of Dave (although that's not his name) to get his side of the story.

We turn the car around and drive up a track toward Dave's mother's house. Dave is a regular down at the jail, Rocky tells me, that's how it goes, the same band of petty miscreants circling through. We've been driving around for about an hour since we left the jail, and something's changing in me. At first I was afraid, wary, hoping nothing bad would happen; but now there's a different feeling. I have begun to feel the power.

You drive down a bad street and it's as if you're invisible. No one looks in your direction, yet everyone is acutely aware of you. It's respect, it's fear, it's *fun*. And now, suddenly, I'm hoping there's going to be some trouble, some resistance, no guns, please, but *something*, some minor altercation which will reveal the extent of the power. I'm ready to hit someone if I have to. (Preferably after Rocky's softened them up a little first.)

We're on a dirt road overhung with tall trees clattering with cicadas and now there he is up ahead in the waning light, Dave, pale-skinned, stumbling along, jeans at his hips, shirt off, scrawny as a boy. He has long dirty blond hair hanging out of a baseball hat. He looks back, sees us coming, but does not run. Rocky stops the car and gets out. Dave grins involuntarily up at him. A narrow face, more bad teeth.

'Hey there, Rocky,' he says.

'Hey,' says Rocky, keeping a little distant, unafraid but ready. 'So what's been happening?'

Dave explains he's just come out from five weeks in the slammer. It was not his turn to take the kid, but he figured as he'd missed five weekends, his ex-wife might bend the rules a little.

'Yeah, well maybe she might have but you're drunk and you shouldn't have hit her,' says Rocky. 'I'm going to have to take you in.'

'But I just got out, Rocky …'

'I know it.'

'Oh, man, do I have to go back in again?' he pleads, but clearly without expectation of success.

''Fraid so. You know how it goes. Drunk in public. No way 'round it.'

For a moment Dave seems to be figuring the odds. Make a run for it?

'Tell you what,' offers Rocky, 'take the P.D. and I'll overlook the domestic violence.' (P.D. stands for public drunkenness.)

'Thanks, man,' says Dave.

'Get in the car,' Rocky tells him, opening the back door.

'Ah well, shit happens,' says Dave as he slides into the back seat, uncuffed, compliant, and unaware that the offer Rocky made him has no value. It's the ex-wife who has to press charges on the domestic matter, not Rocky.

Rocky and I get in the front of the car and Rocky turns it around.

'Yeah, shit happens,' Dave repeats from the back.

'Yep,' says Rocky.

'I just got out, now I'm going back in.' He shakes his head. How do these things happen to him?

'Ah well,' says Rocky, giving no lecture.

'How come there's no door handles back here?'

'That's so you don't jump out,' Rocky tells him.

'Makes sense,' laughs Dave.

Rocky initiates a conversation about some relatives of Dave's. It's amiable, the gossip of a small community, but an ever-growing database is refined in Rocky's head, a picture of the town, connections that might prove useful at a later date.

We arrive back at the jail and take Dave in. He sits down in the narrow, congested booking area, and lights a cigarette.

'Not you again,' says the jailer with the wooden leg.

Dave holds to his philosophy. 'Shit happens.'

'Shit happens if you're stupid,' says the jailer.

Dave laughs. 'Guess so.'

We return to the car.

Crrkkk! A radio message: A grandmother has called the station to rat out her grandson who, she believes, just went into the woods to access his dope stash and is currently out delivering in a white Pinto.

Rocky finds some rock music on his regular radio and the chase is on. The kid used to be okay, Rocky tells me, but his father got shot dead in a bar fight and now his son's gone bad, drugs, threatened to kill someone.

Hm, I'm thinking, maybe I don't want to catch this particular shithead after all …

It's dark by now and we are back in Morgantown, looking left and right down side streets, when suddenly a massive form looms up ahead of us: a pure-bred Cherokee woman weighing in at 300lbs., not including her front teeth, which she must have left somewhere else because they certainly aren't in her mouth.

Rocky tells me she's the street mama, a half ton vigilante who watches over the neighborhood and often calls the police.

Rocky asks if she's seen a white Pinto come through.

'No, ain't seen no white cocksucker Pinto. Why?'

Rocky tells her who he's looking for.

'Oh, that pussy-assed little bitch motherfucker. He come around here, I'll call you.'

'Okay,' says Rocky. 'Thank you.'

When I ask if I can take her photograph, she tells me, 'No, you can't take no Indian's picture, you be stealing our spirit.'

We drive on. Sometimes signals from cellular and mobile phones bleed onto the police scanner. It's the ears of the night patrol, shards of existence vacuumed out of the dark atmosphere. To me, even the dullest of conversations seem sacred and revealing when they detonate inside our travelling shell. 'You know how I like ham, well my dawg just stole two slices,' says a voice. Then in quick succession: 'We're just gonna have to pray harder.' 'Hell, I'm having mah baby tomorrow, I don't have time to visit wid you.' Now we hear two men talking. One of them is so wasted we can barely understand him. We look around but there are many houses nearby and one looks no more degenerate than the next.

One evening, Rocky tells me, he was driving along a street when he heard a woman's voice. 'There's a cop going by,' it said. 'He's a good-looking young thing, I wouldn't mind fucking him at all.' Rocky looked around and saw an attractive woman of about forty sitting on her stoop, talking into a mobile phone. 'Oh, he's looking at me,' she said. 'Yeah, I could sure take this boy ...'

As we rise up out of Morgantown, we hear a young woman's voice break in, sexy and inviting. 'You come on by here, you know where I am.'

'What time should I get there?' It's a young man's voice, anxious and excited.

'Well, I'm free now, so why don't you get your ass up here right now?'

We're in a low-rent development and Rocky thinks we might be getting a signal from the town's white hooker, a pretty woman in her late twenties who's reputedly selling pussy to the fifteen-, sixteen-year-old boys for $30-35 a pop.

We drive past a safe house for battered women and then past some young black males who say, but with neither aggression nor fear, 'There's Five-O!' a reference to the old TV police show, 'Hawaii Five-O'.

Now, looking out the front, we see three black teenage girls, standing on the corner. Rocky pulls over.

One of them is without doubt the best-looking person I've seen in

Dayton, dark-skinned with huge eyes and an astonishing smile. I think to myself, no wonder a lot of black men oppose integration. Who in their right mind would want to deflate these lips or flatten these fine buttocks or lighten this blue-black skin or in any other way dilute this phenomenal beauty?

Rocky talks easily to the girls about a friend of theirs who called him a while back to enforce a restraining order on her boyfriend. She swore she'd never see the man again. Now she's pregnant by him and they're living together. If there's any racial tension here it's not apparent. If there's any tension at all, it's that these women are so refreshingly free of the prudishness of the Lord-be-with-you white girls, it takes your breath away. It's all laughter and flashing eyes and thrust. It's amazing in fact, how different they are. The white girls down here who dress provocatively do so with an almost spiteful defensiveness: how dare you look at me!? There's nothing like that here, no hypocrisy and surely no shame: for these girls the body is a source of simple joy and amusement.

Passing by my window is the biggest of them. She has two horse-size, gravity-defying cheeks packed into (and partially out of) a pair of tiny shorts. And she is *flaunting* them. Furthermore, this rump has the ability to *talk*. As it goes by, it bumps up and down and then suddenly it stops in mid-stride – like a double-take – and I hear it say to me, 'So, little white boy, think you could handle this fine black wazoo?' And now, catching my look, the owner of these taunting chubbies laughs raucously, the cheeks shudder back to life, dismiss me with a shrug – 'Uh-*unnn*, I don't think so, mister!' – and pump off around the front to offer the same monumental challenge to Rocky. He waves them off laughing, and we leave.

Rocky needs food. We're almost at the Wendy's when we get a call. An accident out on some country road. Now this I had not thought of and it scares me. I don't want to see a scattering of limbs, gushing blood. I don't want to hear someone yelling at me, 'Put your finger in the hole!' or 'Hold his guts in!'

Rocky switches on the siren and two sets of lights. One of these, the regular one, is on the top of the car. The other is a recently installed set that seems to be *inside* the car at the base of the windscreen. They're like strobe lights and they're so techno-bright and harsh and silvery they more or less blind you. It's like driving a disco at seventy miles an hour. Rocky narrows his eyes and soon we're doing ninety.

Rocky doesn't like road accidents either, he tells me, and recalls one where a child got run down in front of his father. The boy was decapitated and the father picked up the head and tried to put it back on the body, talking to it all the while, saying, 'You're gonna be okay, you're gonna be all right.'

We swoop off the highway. The narrow road ahead now becomes a swallowing intestinal tube of darkness down which we plunge at speed, the flying disco, and I'm feeling sick. Soon we see more flashing lights. Rocky pulls in behind an ambulance and several other cop cars. We're not the first on the scene and the scene is not so terrible. A massive biker sits on the grass verge at the end of a 350-foot skid mark. The bike lies another thirty feet ahead like a full stop at the end of a long winding sentence. Beyond the verge is a ditch and a hedge.

The biker is bloodied, grazed, but not gushing. His right shoulder is completely skinned and clearly hurts as he hefts himself up onto his knees and starts muttering about a ring he's lost. He looks like a flayed hippo down there on all fours. The medics tell him not to move so he settles back onto his haunches, dazed. People start to emerge from unseen houses along the road. The atmosphere is almost festive. One of the locals is a tall, shirtless old man, thin but for a bulging white stomach. Sheriff Sneed arrives with his wife. He gets out and comes to stand beside me as the biker is lifted onto a gurney.

'This guy,' he nods at the old man, who's moved up next to us, 'he's always out here with his shirt off and a basketball in his tummy.'

'Yeah,' grins the old man, 'I'm always hanging around without my shirt, it's true. Just wish I could find some young people to molest.'

Everyone laughs uneasily, including Sneed, who soon gets back into his car and drives off. Now, out of the darkness runs a stocky young man in shorts and nothing else, no shoes, no shirt. It turns out he's the brother of the man who crashed. Having ascertained he's still alive, the guy picks up the bike, which is mangled and covered in gasoline, and switches it on. To everyone's amazement, it starts. The man rams it in gear with his big toe, and rides it away. Rocky and I hunt around for the ring for a while, and then give up. We return to town to see if Little Mermaid is home yet.

She is, and she is indeed very pretty, with glittering vivacious eyes full of flirtation and the knowledge of her beauty. Her husband hovers in the doorway behind her, possessive and protective, as Rocky talks to her about the fired coach. Except for drunks everyone is polite and helpful if you're a cop, *attentive*. There Rocky stands with his nine millimetre Ruger at his hip, and there they stand on the lip of their home, so glad he's out there culling shitheads for them. And how happy they are when he leaves, taking the faint aura of threat with him – everyone has secrets, a little pot in the bedside table, a taste of moonshine, a memory – and how good it feels to bolt the door and return to dinner, unbusted, confirmed: good citizens deserving of protection.

Back in the car, Rocky shuffles his warrants. 'Ah, here's one that might be fun,' he says, smiling. 'Better do it before it gets too late.' It's a bad cheques warrant to be served on a woman named Sue (not her real name). 'She's a treat, last time I arrested her – it was a P.D. thing – she says to me, "Rocky, you wanna know what I think of you?" and then she lifts up her dress and pees all over my car.'

We drive up a hill and approach a trailer park, a desolate gently sloping field. It's filled with tilting, dented oblongs up on breeze blocks, some in rows, a few scattered around as an afterthought among the litter of slumped cars and pick-ups. Sue's a crafty one, Rocky tells me. If he drives directly up to her trailer, which is one of the first, she'll hide inside, not answer the door, and he won't be able to serve her; but she's into everyone else's business, so if he drives *past* her trailer, as if going somewhere else, she'll come out to see who's in trouble, and then he'll turn around and nab her.

We drive slowly by her trailer. There's only a dim light inside.

'I don't think she's in,' I say.

'She's in,' says Rocky, grinning. 'Watch.'

We reach the end of the trailer park, turn down the far side and out of sight, and do a U-turn. By the time we come back around the corner, Sue's on the steps of her trailer, watching.

I was imagining a crone – that's the type I see pissing on cars, an old misanthropic eccentric – but no, this woman is young, not even thirty, long-limbed and country pretty. And furthermore, she's smart and capable (or maybe I should say she seems capable of being smart and capable), reactions brisk, actions efficient, an air of outspoken confidence, almost arrogance.

When Rocky braces her with the warrant and she realises her mistake, she impatiently exclaims 'Gee-hah!' as if not just this, but her entire life is something she has accidentally fallen into, something beneath her from which, much to her irritation, she cannot extract herself. Had she been given different opportunities, one senses she could easily have become an efficient executive in some commercial enterprise.

'Wait there,' she tells Rocky imperiously and goes back inside. A moment later she returns with a child (a clean, neat child) on one hip and a bunch of papers in her free hand which, according to her, prove someone stole her cheque book and forged her signature.

'Well, I still gotta take you in, Sue,' Rocky tells her, 'but you'll get a bail bond, it's no big deal.'

Her boyfriend arrives on foot, a reasonable, likeable guy who pushes his lips down over his bad teeth when he smiles, but for some reason he can't drive and the truck is running hot and what about the kid?

Patiently, taking each problem one at a time, Rocky suggests ways to get the business dealt with. The boyfriend can put some water in the truck, Sue can drive it down to the station, the boyfriend comes along with the kid, it won't take long to process, if the truck needs more water, there's a hose outside the jail, and they can all be back in an hour or two.

Sue organises a few things for the child to play with while mommy does her jail thing and puts them in a bag. The child is strapped safely in the back and Sue jumps into the truck and makes a capable turn toward the exit, her boyfriend at her side.

No brake lights.

Rocky shakes his head. Sue, he tells me, used to be a good girl, excellent student, cheerleader (I think), and then got into drugs and one thing led to another: this, the trailer park, the child, the departed husband, debts, the overheating truck without brake lights, warrants, court dates, fines, each alone tolerable, but combined a great pressing weight which only the most energetic or larcenous could throw off.

Drugs are always blamed. To me, however, they seem merely a symptom of an aspiration, a desire for profound connection and transcendent meaning in a world which fails to provide either. 'The War

On Drugs,' is a misnomer, as if drugs had character, a will of their own; as if drugs could fight back. If it's a war at all, it's not a war on drugs, but on people, or on reality, a war of denial, a show put up to distract us from some awful truth. (God is dead?)

Back at the jail, Sue efficiently fills in a bureaucratic form with a swift, clean hand. There must be some way, I think, apart from the transitory high of drugs, to provide this woman with a philosophy or practice which inspires her, some engine for this drifting life which does not require the abandonment of reason. There must be something other than Christianity, with its cryptic myths, outdated morality, and distant miracles – something other than modern religions like Scientology, the nitwit invention of a third-rate sci-fi writer with its silly intergalactic myths and crude lie-detector tests – there must be something other than this to imbue her life with, for want of a better word, 'spiritual significance.'

Nor is this snobbery, that she is poorer and less educated and therefore more in need of solace. No, it's clearer, that's all, with someone like Sue or Dave because they are denied even the Western *illusion* of meaning, monetary success, transformation through acquisition, an expensive car, new tits or a nose job, an apartment on the Upper East Side ... I may be more deluded by apparent success, I may be rowing harder and moving faster, I may have cast myself adrift from God a little more consciously, but in the large scheme of things, the difference between us is infinitesimal.

Christianity, so long as it is shackled to the Bible, is completely inadequate for the needs of complex modern life. Its symbolism, though often beautiful as art, has become spiritually worn out and provides neither authentic inspiration, nor comfort, nor the provocation of intelligent conscience. And when it makes a statement that might cause discomfort, such as 'It is as hard for a rich man to get into heaven as for a camel to pass through the eye of a needle,' it is conveniently overlooked or tortuously reinterpreted.

On winter nights in New York, I pass by the churches along Park Avenue and Fifth and marvel at the sight of homeless people freezing to death on the steps. The doors of these, the richest churches in America, are locked. The heat is on inside, so in the morning wives of investment bankers and stockbrokers can come and pray in comfort without the stench of poverty reaching their depilated nostrils. God is dead and it's the church who killed Him.

The church and the aeroplane. When you fly to the jungle and encounter two tribes each with different beliefs, do you say to yourself: 'I wonder who's got it right here, the cannibals who believe they're ingesting the spirit of their enemies when they eat them, or the guys who fuck mud because they believe it fertilises the earth?' No, interesting, quaint even, but each belief is clearly as absurd as the other.

How much longer can our fearfulness and bigotry protect us from seeing how *comprehensively* preposterous all religious beliefs are? As Kurt Wise, creationist professor at Bryan College, said in a different context, 'Let's not be chauvinistic.'

There is the argument that there must be *some* kind of spiritual being because all cultures, independent of each other, have *some* form of God. Every culture also has *some* kind of tool for eating. What does that prove? Only that everyone shares the same *desire* for clean rice.

All early religions started with numerous gods, clearly defined and frequently visible. The God of War, of Love, of Alcohol, of Harvest; gods in the form of dogs or horses, mountains or trees. With Judaism and Christianity it came down to an indivisible (and almost invariably invisible) God with a few sidekicks. The Muslims, coming after both Judaism and Christianity, are even more emphatic on the point. 'There is but one God and Allah is his name …'

It doesn't take a mathematical genius to see where we're heading. After one comes zero. At which point, religion will be relinquished to history, 'the fairy tales of conscience.'

The whole thing is plainly laughable, and yet it's not. To argue about whether God exists or in what form seems as sophomoric and redundant as to argue about how many angels can dance on the head of a pin, but once you get past that, once you recognise God as an invention and start thinking about what *caused* His or Her invention, then suddenly the subject becomes serious again, and poignant.

I remember hearing C. Everett Koop, a paediatrician and ex-Surgeon General, say 'There are no atheists at the bedside of a dying child,' which, unintentionally, is both the best argument *for* God and the best *against*.

If my daughter was dying and asked me, 'Is this the end?' would I lie to her? A million times yes. Anything – the more fantastic the better – a wiser, kinder father on the other side, an extraordinary new world, continuation, reunion, reincarnation, *anything* rather than have her face the horror of oblivion. And if *I'd* do that, rationalist that I am, parents who lived X thousand years ago would certainly do the same. This is how and why God was invented. We know from the earliest writings of the Sumerians – who established a civilisation 4,000 years before the birth of Christ – that mortality has always been terrifying.

Once the various myths of an afterlife were invented they had to be perpetuated and developed for the surviving brothers and sisters, and gradually the stories would pass down, developing and changing. God has a beard or a turban, He (or She or They) live in heaven, in the bodies of animals, in the mountains. He wants you to cut your hair this way, wear a hat on Saturday, eat fish on Friday, whatever. As any good liar will tell you, the way to make a lie believable is to *elaborate the details*, as the more you have, the more credible the anecdote becomes. 'How could he have invented that? It must be true.'

Then came another thought: if the carrot of eternal life keeps everyone happy and docile when dangled at one end, what might we achieve if we jammed a carrot of terror up the other end?

'If you kids misbehave, God'll toss you in the other place.'

'Other place? What other place?'

'Well, it's a … it's a … lake of fah!'

Full circle in a historical minute: a party game, a whisper passed from ear to ear, distorted by the political and social ambitions of the speaker and then further distorted by the spiritual needs of the listener. Unlike the party game, however, fantastic claims require fanatical defence. As faith lies outside the realm of rational debate, the infidel must eventually be evangelised on the rack.

History has taught us this repeatedly. Perhaps it's time to accept and recognise this need for gods and *consciously* invent new gods before the old ones drag us down. A new religion unique in its recognition of its own inventedness and as fluid and honest as science. Perhaps it's time for a female God. You see the urge for this with the New Agers, a sudden reverence for Mother Earth, brought on, no doubt, by the realisation that, through male-dominated technology, we could now destroy her.

Yes, enough of that masculine shit, what we need is a Goddess! Sue would be inspired, Dave appropriately chastised.

All this, I'm thinking – not for the first time, it's true, but with new sympathy and an increased sense of urgency – as I watch Sue wearily finish her form. A fat bail bondsman lumbers in malevolently and Rocky taps me on the shoulder, bringing me back from my pantheon into the reality of Dayton after dark. We exit past the boyfriend with the child (Rocky hasn't added to Sue's problems with a charge on the brake lights, just a warning to get them fixed), and off we go, to Wendy's, finally, two Chicken Burgers and a pair of Cokes which we take back to the empty Sheriff's office.

Sneed, a Republican, is fighting for his life against Paul Smith, a Democrat who was Sheriff a few years back. Smith, according to almost everyone was tough and played dirty. He and his deputies owned various bars around the county. There was trouble. Now, according to his own campaign statements, he's 'reformed'. Smith has various ads running in the *Mountain Morning News*. One of them is titled, 'Out Of The Mouth Of Babes,' and purports to be letters written by teenagers and children in support of Smith. All are anonymous. One accuses a Sneed deputy of repeatedly asking the writer, a teenage girl, for a date in return for not charging her with something. Another says, 'I've seen my brother beat with sticks for no reason at all when he was fourteen years old … If that's a good job I'd like to know what a bad one would be … Leon has older people fooled. He's not what he seems on the outside. It matters inside. For the sake of our children,' (shouldn't that be '*us* children?') 'and the protection of Rhea County, vote Paul Smith.'

The last letter is the peach. 'We are afraid to come forward because we know how he works. Please give your vote to Paul Smith. We know he has done a lot of things in his life time but people can change and we know that Mr Smith has but Mr Sneed stays the same. But we believe the Devil has him right in under his wing.'

I like Leon, Republican or not, and I'm amazed by the vicious tone of these attacks. Rocky shrugs. Southern politics is rough, that's how it is.

Once we've finished eating, we go in search of inebriated shitheads. Out on the highway to Chattanooga, just beyond the county line, is a bar called The Pleasure Zone. It's a low building with a backyard strung with coloured lights where people dance. We lurk our side of the county line, drunk-hunters in our blind, waiting for the first unsteady flight of blind-drunk prey. The irony of this does not escape me, particularly as Rocky now confides that in his entire life he's only ever drunk two beers and never smoked a single cigarette.

We wait a while but the highway is shithead-free and as I'm due out spelunking with the Christians tomorrow morning, I tell Rocky I have to get some sleep. He drives me back to the station. I thank him and wish him well. As I drive to the motel, I notice I'm thinking like a victim again. Instead of seeking villains out the front, I'm watching out for cops in the rear.

Back in my room, I take a sip of moonshine to slow me down for sleep. Lying in bed, running the night through my head – glimpses of lives only previously imagined – I wonder what the admirable Rocky is doing. It's two in the morning. He has another five hours of prowling the county in practice of his dark, lonely trade. What do you think about while Mermaid sleeps beside her lucky husband and Sue, dreaming her marijuana dreams, moves closer to her boyfriend as the trailer chills? What do you think about when in all the darkness a single yellow window glows?

Not work for the unstable or depraved, I think, and fall asleep.

CHAPTER TWENTY-FOUR

Barefoot In The Glass

Two days after my encounter with the one-legged woman in Italy, I flew back to England. In the next ten years I had over thirty jobs, most of them menial, some of them bizarre.

Among other things, I was a bricklayer, a packer at a picture-framing company, and an unpacker in the china department at Harrods. I was a spotlight boy in a nightclub, an assistant film editor, and even, for a while, a rent-by-the-hour cleaning maid. At eighteen I was an unpaid researcher for a documentary company which specialised in making films on tragedy and deformity, and at twenty-two a poorly-paid sex writer for magazines. At various times I was a salesman of posters, second-hand cars, candles, bags and belts from Morocco, and finally owned a company which sold leather goods on behalf of stoned artisans in basements. When it went bust, I drew the curtains, unhooked the phone until all my creditors got bored, and wrote an unpublishable novel. I was a sheet-metal worker, hired hand in a freezing factory, welder, van driver and semi-pimp. For a while my closest friend was a con man. Toward the end of this period, a thief and I almost bought a minicab company together.

I lived with two nightclub hostesses, the first of whom, an older woman − she was twenty-eight − finally taught me to make love adequately. Both gave me money to one extent or another. I lived with the first for a year when I was eighteen. The second lasted longer because she got out of the game, the game being her selling sex for money while I waited home for the poignant sound of her douching on her way to bed. I was stabbed in the leg with a fork by a six-foot-tall, half-African, half-Irish nightclub singer with whom I had a brief affair, and the next night had a hole jabbed in my side by hostess number one wielding a broomstick with a nail driven through it. When she took to punching me in the face while I slept (again because of the singer), I decided to leave and move in with hostess number two. Number one then came around and attacked my new flat with a barrage of milk bottles at dawn. When I went out to remonstrate, she dragged me out onto the street to fight barefoot in the glass.

But before all this began – before all this fucking, forking, nailing, punching, and milk-bottling – in the gap between coming home from Italy and leaving home for London – I was sent to a Freudian analyst, a black woman from Mississippi named Marie Singer.

Marie's mother was a ruffler, a woman who put ruffles on curtains and sheets. Her father was a cotton picker and civil rights activist. The family was poor, but Marie and her brothers and sisters were always smartly turned out, the hems of their dresses, their sleeves and collars, sometimes even the cuffs of their pants, elaborately ruffled.

By force of will, Marie dragged herself out of a rural life into a Southern university, and then, I don't quite know how, on to Cambridge, England, accompanied by an alcoholic poet, Mr Singer, who died, leaving her, a beached exotic, in grey East Anglia. Marie was in her fifties by the time I met her, and looked like everyone's ideal black mama. She was brilliant, honest, inspiring, and kind. She was more than a shrink to me, she was my saviour and muse and I loved her.

There was a day before I went to see her which I forgot. That is to say, I was about sixteen years old and found myself somewhere, deep in thought and it was evening; but I could not, no matter how hard I tried, remember the rest of the day, the events that brought me to where I was. This was shocking – an alcoholic blackout without the alcohol. I went to bed and stayed there for a week with the heat turned up, hoping it would make me sleep.

Life was not easy at home and perhaps I'd simply decided to withdraw. My mother now drank almost every day. Capable of charm and warmth, she still performed the role of mother with every appearance of love – until she drank and then her eyes would close and gloom would alternate with scathing cruelty, most often directed at my father. Most of the time, we walked around her – and around her problem – as if nothing was amiss. Some days were worse than others. Some days were good. Sometimes the whole family would sit down to dinner and talk and laugh and be happy. When we went to our small cottage in

Norfolk, my mother was at her best. But even on these windswept days, the bottle lay at the end like a dreaded exclamation mark.

My brother, Francis, who was around ten or eleven at this time, was at the local grammar school. He was an amiable child of many hobbies, a sweet and funny boy growing up with a rueful smile in the unhealthy shadow of his mother's alcoholism. Ludovic, my youngest brother, aged six or so, already displayed the thuggish tendencies which would characterise his teenage years. I adored them both. My sister, however, was another matter. Eighteen months older than me, she was now on the verge of college. Soon she was taking driving lessons. Trapped by my instability and lack of education, I wept when I saw her drive down the lane after passing her driving test, independent at last, free to leave.

I worked for my father, welding refrigeration coils. I wrote poetry, though not much of it. I thought of becoming a hobo or joining the Merchant Marine. Most days I drank or smoked pot. Sometimes when I was high, I would imagine myself a writer. Perhaps because of my childhood eczema, I always found it hard to sleep. Now it became almost impossible.

When I was committed to Marie's care, I was suicidal. By the time I left I was a writer. Like bookends propping up the shabby literature of my education, stand these two magnificent women. Mrs Marshall taught me the pleasure of creation, and taught it so well that the sadistic prep-school conformists who tried to beat it out of me, pissing on the flames and stomping on it with their stinking brogues, could not quite succeed, leaving alive an ember for Marie to blow back to life.

Marie lived in a tall, narrow house in Little St Mary's Lane, an old street leading down to the River Cam. When I first went to see her, I was too young to drive a car. With the wages from my father, I bought a motorcyle, an AJS 350, and drove into town on that. The room where she saw patients was at the very top of the house, three flights up. At first, I lay on the couch to talk, but as lying on my back was at that time synonymous with masturbation, I would get an erection, which distracted me, and perhaps even her, from the analysis. I moved to a chair, turned at an angle away from her.

I looked out of the window at the roof of St Mary's Church, the church where my mother came to worship when she was in college, where I was baptised, and where later Sarah and I were brought for our few years of churchgoing. A row of rounded crosses, like clover leaves, ran along the ridge. Sometimes I would imagine myself firing a rifle at them one by one.

I got in the habit of remembering dreams, sometimes three or four a night. These I would bring to Marie like gifts the following evening. I went five times a week for about two years and slowly began to see that I was not a random scrap of disordered matter, but an odd mixture of my mother and my father. In spite of my lack of mathematical ability, I shared with him a rationalist's view of the world. As time passed and I was able to forget school, I became curious again, as he always was, and soon after that, began to feel a capacity for hard work. Meanwhile, the strange beauty of my dreams convinced me that if I could find a way to reach inside my head while I was awake, I'd find a rich, poetic imagination such as I believed my mother had. I was, like her, melancholic and romantic. Perhaps, I began to hope, I might be able to combine all these inherited characteristics and create something from them called Matthew.

Marie encouraged me to start writing short stories. They were rarely more than two or three pages long and tended to be observations of intense moments. One described the moment when a young man decides to ride his motorcycle down a long hill and across a busy road without stopping. Another was about an older man and his life of sad but delicious solitude. The only thing on earth he loves is a rare flower he has grown, which is now dying.

Marie knew a woman in Cambridge who was a published short-story writer and sent me to see her. I can't remember her name, but she took me seriously and said I had talent. This was a woman who produced work. What she said had value.

I began to read enthusiastically. I read all the novels of Fitzgerald, Hemingway, Steinbeck, D.H. Lawrence, Thomas Hardy, Zola, and Raymond Chandler, along with plays, newspapers, history books, magazines, and poetry, any scrap of paper with words on it found anywhere at any time.

When I turned seventeen Peter, Francis's father, gave me a car, an old Morris Minor. Soon afterwards, I decided to leave home and go work in London. I had friends who were getting a flat. I left Marie and didn't see her again until shortly before her death twenty years later. We went out and drank too much and she was sad and scurrilous.

On the day I left home, it was still summer. I could hear thunder shifting in the sky above. I hugged and kissed my mother goodbye – I always loved her, no matter what she did, and always felt we understood each other – and started to drive. When I got to the motorway about twenty miles away, the storm broke and rain began to batter the car. I turned on the windscreen wipers but they did not work. I thought about turning back. Instead, I pushed my seat forward, and reaching through the side window, wiped the rain from the windscreen with my hand. I kept on doing this until, an hour later, I arrived in the city.

In London, I went to another psychiatrist for a few months. There was something Germanic about her – she was, in fact, German – and though she was well-meaning, it was a rough transition from my beautiful black mama. The only appointment she could give me was at eight in the morning. As I was soon working in a nightclub, shining a spotlight on two cabaret shows a night, the first of which ended at midnight, the second at two, and simultaneously holding down a full-time job researching documentaries, I would simply fall onto the couch and go to sleep.

The documentary company, taking advantage of my lack of education, didn't pay me. I researched a couple of documentaries for them, both about diseases. Now they asked me to research one on the effects of disaster.

I had gone almost nine months on three to four hours sleep a night, often less. On Sunday mornings, when I could have gone to bed by three a.m. and not woken up until deep into the afternoon, I waited up for my working friend and then drank heavily with her, so that what benefits might have accrued from a long night of sleep were dissipated by chronic hangovers. I was comprehensively exhausted.

'What kind of disaster?' I asked, an ominous feeling rising inside.

'All disaster. How does it affect a village when the mine collapses and kills all the men? What happens to a man after he's had his legs amputated? Marital disaster, death of children, fatal diseases, bankruptcies, murder, suicide, aeroplane crashes. Communities and individuals. Psychologically and socially, how do we survive disaster?'

How am I going to survive this disaster? was the question in my mind. Long-term sleep deprivation makes you paranoid. Why had they chosen me to destroy with this gruesome work? I was getting stabbed and assaulted in my personal life. Now this? I was horrified. Days, weeks, months of grief and mutilation stretched ahead.

I began work. I saw some terrible sights and learned two interesting things. Several of the men I interviewed became compulsively sexual after their disasters. It was as if, having felt the wings of death brush against them, they now had to compensate by plunging in among the arms and legs of life. The second thing I learned was that if a community has a disaster which receives little media attention, it unites and remains united for years, whereas a community which suffers both disaster and heavy press attention fractures into a hierarchy of grief and contention.

It was all so painful and I was so exhausted that within a couple of weeks, I began to develop a nervous tic. To be more precise, I began to develop a nervous *sneer*. I'd be interviewing some poor sap whose wife had left him two days after he got hit by a lorry and was paralysed for life, and I'd feel my upper lip curl up on one side.

'So,' I'd sneer at him, 'did your wife come to the hospital to visit you, or did she just straight away take the kids and move up to Manchester with your best friend?'

As he replied, I would wipe at the lip with my fingers and it would straighten out. Moments later, however, up it would curl again, a ghastly involuntary tilde of contempt.

There were complaints and I was fired.

I retreated to the mill house, slept for a few weeks, and then got up and wrote a play. When I was fully recovered, I returned to London determined to be a playwright. I went to visit a friend of my parents, an unusual man, brilliant but unrealised, who was staging plays in a church hall in Holborn. He encouraged me and eventually staged a reading of my first play.

He also let slip the secret of my mother's affair and the real paternity of my brother, Francis. When I next returned to the mill house for the weekend, I looked at my parents differently. My father seemed almost heroic for having stayed all these years to provide stability for his four children. I never consciously blamed my mother for what she had done and never told her I knew her secret. Her suffering became more comprehensible in one way at least, because I now shared an element of it. It is said that keeping secrets drives men mad and in later years when I interviewed old CIA men for a script I was writing, it was remarkable how many of them were semi-deranged alcoholics. It was hard to know this crucial fact about my brother and keep it to myself. How it must have been for my mother I can only imagine.

I say I did not consciously blame her. This is true. However, it was around this time that I began a habit which financed my writing for several years. I'd take a menial job and after a month or so would call in and say my mother was dying of some painful disease. Few employers would fire you outright and while they continued to pay, I'd write frantically, creating imagined life while being sustained by her imagined death. Sometimes you could buy a full month this way. One employer eventually called up and said, 'Listen, mate, how long's it going to take for your fucking mother to die because this is getting expensive.' Usually, a secretary called and, with tight-lipped regret, would inform me that my employment was terminated.

After a while I stopped writing plays. I didn't like the milieu; perfume and fur at one end, humourless Marxist at the other. During this period, I had became an assistant film editor. After two years, when my apprenticeship was over and I knew how shots connected, I wrote a small movie based on a nightmare I had about a revolution in England and the effect it has on a soft, middle-class young man like myself. I gave it the title *Violent Summer*, and decided to direct it.

I was in one of those phases where no courage is required to do something dangerous. A decade of largely menial work had stretched my patience to the limit. I could not stand another ten years being told by people I did not respect to do something I did not find interesting. I reached back into my not-so-distant nightclub past and acquired half the money I needed to make the film. The rest I got from a theatrical producer I met. I managed to pull a cast and crew together and then, having actually never seen a professional film camera before, started to direct. The lead in the film was Bruce Robinson, who became my lifelong friend. The film was sold to one of the independent TV stations in Britain. It was well reviewed.

It had taken me ten years to get to this point – ten years of weird employment, much of it humiliating – but here I was at twenty-five, a screenwriter and director. Had I gone to college, would I have been able to pull this off so quickly? Perhaps. Would I have met so many interesting people along the way, worked in so many strange places, or felt so directly what it was to be one of the dispossessed? Doubtful. Driven by desperation, not caring if I was jailed, I had jumped many of the apparently logical steps and forced myself into a position I seemed not to deserve. But in fact higher education, seeking as it does to winnow out the fools, is the worst place for a writer to get an education and where I had got mine was the best. What would the works of Shakespeare or Dickens be, for example, without the idiots and reprobates?

If, as someone said, the measure of an educated man is that you can drop him down the chimney of any house and he'll be able to talk to whoever he finds in the living room, I was at twenty-five an educated man. I was also, unfortunately, a drinking man, and partly because of this, didn't make another film for three years.

Spelunking With The Christians

Kurt Wise is in a frenzy of activity. Several white vans, replete with Christian youth, are parked outside the front entrance of Bryan College, waiting to depart on the creationist cave tour and Kurt is dashing from one to the other making sure every young believer has a flashlight. I don't have a flashlight and I'm late – and there doesn't seem to be a place for me in any of the vans. I go from one to another, past rows of uninviting faces. Finally, I find a van with an empty seat right at the very back. I clamber past a group of clean-cut types of both sexes and settle in for the ride.

Apart from me there are eight people here and they all ignore me. The girls are in their late teens, early twenties. A handsome young blond man sits in the passenger seat at the front, navigating.

As we leave Dayton and head out into the country, they start to discuss a talent show they had last night. In one of the skits a man was supposed to dress up as a woman, but some of his fellow students ruled against it because of a verse in Deuteronomy forbidding men to put on women's clothing.

They debate this earnestly. (I say 'debate' not to suggest there's anything deep about it, but because during the entire day I never witness anything which even verged on 'argument'; all are unfailingly polite to each other.) Some think it was right to cancel the skit because after all, it's in the Bible – no cross-dressing, end of story – but the handsome boy up front and the driver, a dark haired older kid, suggest the verse existed to stop men dressing as women to *avoid going to war* and so has no relevance in this context.

A girl in front of me, with short dark hair, bright eyes, a beautiful complexion, but ineffably prissy and wholesome, starts to speak about music. Her dogmatic proclamations are made in a sing-song tone so upwardly inflected they sound like questions. (I later notice that many of them speak like this.)

'I'm like coming to terms with the fact I don't want to listen to secular music? I mean, my parents don't like it? And I'm supposed to do what they say? Plus, you know, it's the Devil's music?'

They've all been listening to a song by Nine Inch Nails called 'God Is Dead.'

I ask them why they've been listening to this and they tell me about the course they're taking. Run by The Summit Ministry, it's a two-week summer camp where they study 'World Views.' They compare Christian music to secular music, creationism to evolution. Tonight they're going to watch a movie, *Contact*, in which a preacher is portrayed unflatteringly. (I thought everyone was portrayed unflatteringly – to put it kindly – but the preacher certainly had the worst haircut.) It's a course in defensive strategy designed to help young Christians, particularly those going on to a secular University, to withstand attacks on their faith.

'I hear like intellectuals, a lot of them commit suicide?' squeaks a zit-encrusted teenage boy, apropos of nothing. ''Cause they believe what they're taught, evolution an' all, so they got nothing to live for?' And now he fixes me with a mordant look, like maybe I'm one of them.

'That's true, statistically true,' says another young man. 'They don't have God in their lives, they don't have Jesus as their personal saviour.'

'Amen,' says one of the girls.

It's almost as if I'm the centre of a joke and don't know it. Can they really be talking like this? Do they know who I am? Have they been instructed to behave this way? 'Give him a good strong rush of the Word, kids, but make it look natural, like you're just chatting among yourselves.'

But I don't think so. This is how it is, a constant reiteration of their agreement with each other. Younger, less adept in the art of atheist-detection, they haven't yet caught on to my awful condition. They don't know who I am, they just don't like the look of me, an oddly-dressed, unwelcome old fart hunched at the back of the van, scribbling in a notebook. The girls are wary, with the confused intuition of virgins, the boys are politely indifferent. We've been driving half an hour before

257

they ask me why I'm here and when they do I keep it simple: a book on The Scopes Trial.

To some degree this puts them at ease and interests them, so when sandwiches are produced and they see I have none, they kindly offer spares. I decline. It's too hot to eat, the air conditioning fails just short of me. If I extend my foot, I can feel the last wisps of cool air evaporate around my ankle.

Most of the people in the van are from rural states, South and North Carolina, West Virginia, Pennsylvania, Utah, and Minnesota. Many have been home schooled, most are pleasant but uninteresting, the weird similarity of their views making it hard to distinguish one from another. The boy who looked at me when talking about the suicide of intellectuals, has a resentful, suspicious quality. The handsome young man is handsome – and aware of it. Chrissie is prissy. And then there's Erica.

Erica is an obstreperous, bright, energetic, outspoken, fresh-faced, no-nonsense type – what you see is what you get – except that beneath the surface, lies something both provocative and vaguely sullen. You have the feeling that were she not a Christian she'd be commenting on guys' asses and using the word 'studly'. As a Christian, however, she is forbidden from expressing herself this way and so this bold, rambunctious quality finds outlet in outrageous statements of another kind.

'I have no friends, nobody likes me, but I don't care,' she cheerfully declares at one point, 'I have no soul mates, so what?'

Older than the others, perhaps slightly embarrassed at being here, she seems more worldly. She's popular, but only as 'a character'. She's too careless and self-absorbed for intimacy, too unpredictable and uncensored to be trusted, and anyway she'd rather be the centre of attention than deal with the complexities of friendship. Blonde, with long fine features and a well-toned body, she's brought along a bike helmet. 'I'm just bound to smash my head against something,' she states matter of factly, 'that's the way I am.'

After about an hour, we arrive at Grassy Cove, a pastoral valley between faint blue mountains, and turn off the main road onto a dirt track. As we bump along, we pass three rugged country boys walking in the same direction. One has a bandana around his head, but to me they appear utterly harmless. The people in the van, however, particularly the females, sit up alert, and with slowly rotating heads study them with suspicion and hope out loud that they don't come into the cave with them. They want to avoid infidel intrusion and the possibility of mockery.

The vans park not far from a farm at the base of a hill and everyone gets out. After a short but vehement set of instructions from the farmer, ('Don't stray off the path, don't set off my dawgs') the group starts up a long, steep, winding path through the wooded hillside. There must be at least fifty of us and we all tramp along contentedly in the heat, talking about poison ivy and sumach.

All but one. Half a mile up the trail, Erica has an asthma attack. Down she sits on a root in the path and out comes an inhaler. A small crowd, myself among them (grateful for the opportunity to rest), gather around her in concern. She takes a couple of puffs and then – what a trooper, what a gal! – up she gets and marches on.

As we approach the main body of students gathered in a small grove above us, the heavy, humid air is licked with strands of coolness. The temperature, around eighty-five degrees, drops fifteen as I penetrate the group and stare in horror at the source of this ominous and unnatural chill.

I expected a big yawning mouth with a souvenir shop to one side. I thought we'd plod dutifully within, along well-defined paths until it was almost dark – and then turn around and exit, going, 'Boy, was that something or what?' But clearly this is to be an experience of an altogether different order and magnitude.

It's a slit!

The entrance to the cave is a ragged horizontal slit, like a mouth clumsily hacked into a pumpkin at Halloween. Even more alarming, it's at ground level. Doughty Christians insert themselves into it with difficulty, slither down in steep descent – and disappear. This is not for tourists. This nasty, malevolent gash which at its highest is no more than three feet, can only be an invitation to something worse. There's no souvenir shop and not a single reassuring sign saying, 'Mind Your Head,' or 'Don't Touch The Stalactites.' It's a real cave, one of those narrow, lethal warrens into which children fall and emerge alive only when the TV movie lies about it a year later. It's a perfect cave for adrenalin-deficient professional spelunkers with miners' helmets, ropes and pitons. It's not a cave for a gang of infantile Christians and a middle-aged atheist with a panic attack.

I move closer. Another Christian crams himself through the orifice. Before he disappears from view, I see him clutching and scrabbling as he skids down and away, and, peering in more deeply, I see that once you're in it's instantly as black as the inside of a vagina, although in all other aspects it's the welcoming vagina's absolute antithesis: a chilly, jagged, dangerous, claustrophobic place, a nightmarish geological maze full of ancient fissures and loose prehistoric detritus, a place of horror and death.

I look around to see if perhaps there's a gang of fellow cowards girding for an act of humiliating resistance – and see Erica raise her arms to put on her bike helmet. My God, she has a tattoo on her lower back! Half obscured by the waistline of her jeans it instantly disappears as, with the helmet now buckled, she lowers her arms. My curiosity is aroused and fear subsides. At last a friend perhaps, a fellow sinner, albeit a reformed one.

I hurry over and murmur in her ear.

'Saw the tattoo, what's it of?'

She gives me a falsely weary look, turns her back, leans slightly forward, and raises the back of her sweater. My hopes are dashed. It's an Ikthus, that hollow fish you see on the back of cars, and while it suggests a potentially intriguing frustration – she wants to be tattooed like every other kid, and why did she put it near her arse? – the choice of symbol is a resolute denial of the motives which put it there. There's no fantastic story to be told, no past degeneracy with which I can identify.

Which leaves only the cave and its malicious grin.

Flashlight-less, intensely dubious, I squeeze through the hole along with Erica, the handsome boy, and several others. The downward skid is actually quite short. I find myself inside the cave, muddy but uninjured.

Blackness. Without a flashlight, I don't stand a chance. While everyone else is panning their beams around the ceiling of the cave and making exclamations of joy, I am a blind man. Kurt, who invited me on this trip but did not tell me to bring a flashlight, is long gone, scurrying off into the cave, eager but anxious. Perhaps it was a deliberate symbolic omission, a way of showing me how utterly unenlightened I am.

'I don't have a flashlight,' I admit, in a weak voice. Several beams of light swing away from the ceiling toward my pallid face. 'No one told me,' I whine, blinking in the light and smirking with embarrassment.

'Here, have mine,' says the handsome boy, 'I can share with Marie.'

I protest with obvious insincerity and snatch the flashlight from his hand.

I point it now at a young woman who has, with *her* flashlight, managed to locate some fresh graffiti and a couple of empty beer bottles just inside the cave. 'I bet it was *them*,' she says, meaning the rednecks, the obvious inference being that only infidels would do such a thing.

Because of the large number of people who wanted to come on this trip (idiots!), Kurt has divided us into small groups, each one departing five or ten minutes after the one before. As Kurt cannot be at every 'point of interest', he has stationed older students at each, all of whom have a piece of paper on which is typed what Kurt *would* have said had he been there.

'The Flood Did It.'

That's the basic message. What 99% of geologists believe took millions of years, Kurt and his fellow creationists believe was done a few thousand years ago in a matter of months when Noah was forced to sea with all the animals on earth, including his family but excluding the fishes, as Bryan so helpfully pointed out. Quite a load, but that's another subject – the physics of wooden ships, load-potential of – on which the creationists have produced numerous unintentionally comic papers.

We're asked by the first of Kurt's surrogates, a young woman, to observe a well-preserved fossilised brachiopod in limestone. A brachiopod is a kind of shellfish. We are 1000 feet above current sea level and you can find fossils like this all across America at similar elevations. If brachiopods decay or if they get moved any distance, the muscle that holds the shells together fails, and the shells separate. Modern brachiopods, if they're found whole at all, we're told, are usually found with the shell open and the opening facing upward. This fossilised brachiopod appears to be complete, has its shell closed, *and* it's on the tilt. To

Kurt, this suggests that 'the critter,' as he playfully calls it, was still alive when it was deposited, which suggests it was buried rapidly, which suggests, as Kurt puts it, 'a global diluvial catastrophe.' When I later read one of his typed sheets, he then adds: 'Does this sound familiar?'

To this crowd, indubitably so.

The student, reading Kurt's words, goes on to talk about the large stalagmites near the entrance. Kurt argues that as these stalagmites, though large, occupy less than 1% of the available space in the cave, they may not be as old as other geologists think; if they were, they would have filled the place up and we wouldn't be here.

We now leave this 'room' through a three-foot diameter hole and enter a subterranean canyon with occasional offshoots. Its floor is muddy and the ceiling craggy and uneven, but the walls are tall and smooth. More of a skinny passage than a canyon, it's so narrow two people can only cross at certain points. It wiggles and zigzags left and right. Ahead of me Erica wiggles and zigzags too, unerringly locating every available outcropping of rock against which to smack her helmeted head.

To me the canyon seems like a vertical crack sheared open by some inexplicably potent geological shift, a deep crevice which might, because of some *other* geological shift, snap shut at any moment. Kurt tells us, however – through another designated student – that this canyon was made either by water dripping through cracks and joints and slowly dissolving the rock over millions of years, *or* by a massive flood. In the latter case, which is the one Kurt prefers, water would come crashing in, carrying with it rocks and pebbles and then, when the water drained, crash out again, thus creating these canyons in a few months instead of aeons.

The cave is so grotesquely dramatic, so *tortured*, that Kurt's theory – suggesting an upheaval as violent as one's own alarm – does have emotional resonance. Certainly I can imagine a roiling wall of grey mud and rock roaring and cascading into the cave and carving out this infernal canyon. I can imagine it because I *am* imagining it – such things and worse – and when each cataclysmic vision jolts into my brain, there's always a little figure on the receiving end of it who looks a lot like me.

Perhaps it's redundant to say, but I am not enjoying myself. However, even in my state of barely controlled panic, it does occur to me that Kurt seems to want to have his cave and eat it too: a deluge so fantastically fierce it burrowed this vast warren out of solid rock in under a year, yet not so fierce as to pulverise the delicate, twin-shelled brachiopod.

Next stop is the ooids and oolites. Pronounced oh-ids and oh-lights, these are found in the next cave along, a low-ceilinged, dripping cavity. Ooids are formed by grains of sand rolling around collecting calcium carbonate deposits. When enough of these ooids are found in a rock, the rock is called an oolite. I don't really understand how all these ooids and oolites, which are found only in oceans and caves, suggest once again the old in-and-out-in-a-year theory, but needless to say they do. As the pleasant girl who is reading Kurt's notes concludes, 'Anyway that's what Doctor Wise says, which I think it makes sense, although I am an accounting major, so I haven't really studied the subject much.'

'What would the evolutionists say?' I ask.

'They would say it took millions and millions of years,' says the girl.

'That's the only words you need to know if you're an evolutionist – "millions of years, millions and millions of years," ' chimes in a second female in a tone of weary but tolerant exasperation: when will those credulous evolutionists get with it?

Kurt's surrogate now draws everyone's attention to a stalactite descending from the low roof. A steady trickle of water forms a succession of drops which dangle for half a second on its tip and then fall with a plop onto the receptive tip of a stubby but erect stalagmite growing up towards it from the floor.

Erica, who has asked a couple of irrelevant questions in a careless tone ('If the water was flowing this quickly, wouldn't Noah's boat get turned over?') which would suggest rebellion if it did not more suggest attention-seeking, and who, in spite of her own dumb questions, narrowed her eyes when I asked mine, now plays a trump card to regain centre stage.

'Can we lick it?' she asks, approaching the stalactite.

Nervous laughter betrays group prurience, but disapproval can only be voiced by admitting it, so Erica extends her tongue and gives the stalactite's scrawny glans a thirsty lick.

Before I can slam on the brakes, I hear my voice echoing into the cave: 'My God, *will you look at the size of that tongue!*'

It is indeed a whopper. In fact, it's the longest tongue I've ever seen and, as now becomes evident, it is a famous tongue.

'Show him what you can do with it!'

'Do that thing, Erica! Go on.'

'Show him! Do the wave!'

Once again, Erica rolls her eyes, emits a sigh in the gratifying glare of a dozen flashlights, and looking me in the eye with an expression that's both provocative and yet completely devoid of sexuality, opens her mouth so I can peer inside.

The tongue is undulating.

The undulation starts at the back and moves forward like a gently sloped but fast moving wave. It's a more or less straight line, this approaching ripple, and as it reaches the tip and narrows, another wave starts at the back and begins its undulation toward the front, and then another and another. I'm enraptured. I've never seen anything like it in all my life, these sets of soft pink breakers, and I'm in the process of imagining what it would feel like if ... when the mouth shuts and Erica struts off amidst applause.

Next stop, the Rough Room. If only. But no, it's merely a room with rough walls, a contrast not only to Erica's tongue but to the smooth walls elsewhere, proving, so Kurt theorises, that erosion here was caused by long term chemical reaction from water getting stuck in here after the Flood. And now, the theorist himself appears, Doctor Kurt, scampering out of the darkness, his big glasses muddied, the eyeballs behind them anxious and intent, hands filthy, clothes in disarray – and then he's gone! – without a word, scurrying onward to who knows what disaster, and soon we are scrabbling and slipping and squeezing along to *our* next destination, Hanging Falls, another awful passage, and at the end of it a circular room where, at last, we stop.

Inside the room lurks our new guide, a smiling, sanctimonious young man. When we are all gathered inside the room, he tells us to sit down and switch off our flashlights. Then, out of the absolute blackness, comes his pious young voice:

'Why don't you lead off, Brittany?'

'*My God is an awesome God!*' sings Brittany in a sweet, high voice, and then the rest join in, '*Be praised!*' and then they all sing together: '*My God is an awesome God! Be praised!*' The room sounds like a small cathedral, more bass, less echo, but it is, I have to admit, pretty awesome, particularly in the darkness.

As the hymn (which turns out to be awesomely repetitive), continues, I start to think about the Flood theory, which I like – the drama of it, the simplicity – but then, all of a sudden I hit a problem, something I'd never thought of before.

Where did all the water come from?

One day the earth is dry except for rivers and oceans. Then it starts to rain and there are 'fountains' which spring up from below. A few weeks later, the water level over the entire globe has risen so high it covers even Mount Everest. That's a lot of extra water to appear out of nowhere.

The song ends and in the reverent silence which follows, the young man says 'How about that?' in a soft, unctuous voice.

How about *this*, think I, and pose my question.

All the flashlights snap on and point my way again, but even before I'm blinded by their glare, an answer comes out of the darkness.

'The canopy theory?' says one of the girls, the question mark at the end a gentle chiding reminder, as if I've forgotten something I must surely know somewhere back there in my fuzzy old head.

I shrug. No idea – ready to learn. Enlighten me.

'Well, it's the theory that the earth was surrounded by a vapour canopy before the flood, and it didn't rain, it was like a greenhouse effect, and that would explain why they found greenery in the Poles and like frozen mammoths in the North Pole and they had like green leaves and stuff in their stomachs and the theory is that it was like a tropical forest the whole way around it, like a greenhouse with the canopy all around it, and God caused the canopy to fall and that's what would create all that water.'

A boy speaks up, better informed than her, closer to Wise's wisdom.

'Doctor Wise says that the canopy theory can't on its own explain the Flood because if there was more than five feet of water in the canopy, the canopy would have to be so thick the vapour would be all the way down to about five feet off the ground, all the way up and all the way down to five feet.'

'All the way up to where?' the girl asks defensively.

'The atmosphere.'

'What if the atmosphere was different then?'

'You never know,' the boy says, dismissing her politely from the conversation, and goes on to explain an additional theory having to do with water trapped underground and a 'mantle' at the bottom of the sea moving and pushing up the water.

'And all this took how long?' I ask.

'Sixty days,' says the boy.

'Sixty days,' repeat several other voices with absolute authority. (When I check later, the Bible seems to say forty days, but maths was never my strong suit so maybe I missed something.) Anyway, I'm impressed. They've thought about the question and come up with an answer to conform to their Bible; but I can't help thinking there's something about the whole exercise that's painful and contorted, and almost tragically self-defeating. After all, if you believe in a God who can create *the entire universe* in six days, why entangle yourself in science to explain how he got the H_2O for a mere flood? Unable to resist the lure of science, creationists have been seduced into a rationalistic trap. Their attempts to explain miracles through science can only end in sorrow: a miracle explained is a miracle destroyed.

But I don't say any of this because everyone is now wandering off toward the final and most horrific room of all.

Imagine a vast, meandering, asymmetrical cavern, whose furthest reaches cannot be seen by even the most powerful flashlight. Imagine that the floor and ceiling are smooth and flat, and eerily in parallel with each other. Now imagine that some force has lowered the ceiling so it's only two to three feet from the floor and, making matters worse, the whole thing appears to be supported only by occasional rough columns formed by stalactites and stalagmites fusing together, each column tapering in the middle like some weirdly guttered candle. Then imagine that on top of this massive slab there's a billion tons of mountain. And now imagine some loony creationist asking you to crawl into this awful, ill-supported geological death-gap, which, if it collapsed, would spread you a hundred yards in all directions and leave you flatter than a dime, all so he can expound, through delegates, some nutty theory which every reasonable man on earth knows is utter hogwash. Only a fool would enter.

In I crawl. Like most people I'd rather die than look ridiculous. As we scrabble along on our bellies, the new guide informs us that if you tap the floor you'll discover it's hollow. Within seconds, all the kids are hitting at it with their fists and hammering at it with their boots, making an ominous drumlike sound.

The cretins are going to bring the roof down! My fondness for the Flood theory (or any other for that matter) diminishes with every second. I simply want to leave, to be above ground, *anything* rather than this pressing sense of entombment.

We reach some central point, a column of particular interest (to them, not me), and slump down to listen to a lecture. I remember none of it. Erica is just ahead of me on her belly. The Ikthus is visible in the gap between her pants and sweater. I concentrate on the fish and manage to quell my urge to blunder out backward and rush howling through the tunnels in search of light.

Finally, *finally*, we're backing out, twisting and turning to the sound of Erica's helmet cracking and scratching against the ceiling, and soon we escape the jaws of the parallel slabs and are on our way. The mood lightens immediately, suggesting that perhaps I was not alone in my claustrophobic terror. The girls become chatty. One of them teases another for having a crush on the guy who washes the windows at Bryan College.

'Oh, great,' says the girl, 'thank you for telling all my secrets, why don't you just give me a paper-cut and have done with it?' Another pair discuss a movie they like. A third confides that several romances have been born in the last week or two.

I ask what the rules are. Most of them are obvious, no drugs, no cigarettes, no alcohol. A girl fills me in on the dress code. 'No tank tops, no tube tops, no halter tops, no spaghetti straps, no short shorts, and you have to have a one-piece bathing suit.'

'Anyone breaking the rules?' I ask. 'Anyone taking drugs, smoking?'

'Of course not,' says Mordant-Boy, 'there's no pot two rooms down from me. Which I can't smell most nights.'

Kurt shoots out of a hole in the wall, and stares at us, as if counting. He looks fractionally calmer than last time.

'Did you lose anyone yet?' I ask, jovially.

'No, I don't think so,' he says, blinking and smiling in the light, and then he darts off again, scrambling away along the canyon. At a more leisurely pace, we follow. Seeming younger than their age to begin with, the prospect of getting out makes the students seem almost childlike.

Erica starts to sing:

> *Who's the king of the jungle?*
> *Hoo, hoo, hoo!*
> *Who's the king of the sea?*
> *Bubble, bubble, bubble!*
> *Who's the king of the Universe?*
> *And who's the king of me?*
> *His name is*
> *J − E − S − U − S! Yes!*
> *He's the king of the jungle,*
> *He's the king of the sea,*
> *He's the king of the Universe*
> *And he's the king of me!*

As we leave the stomach of the cave and wind our way up through the oesophagus toward the promise of daylight, the girls become almost evanescent. One of them asks me if I'm a believer. I guess they've rumbled me.

'Maybe,' I say, smiling.

'Mebbe,' Erica repeats, imitating my accent.

'You're not, are you?' the first girl suggests in a sly, almost flirtatious tone of voice.

'Well ...' I say, and say no more.

'You should come and sit in on some of our classes,' she says. 'It would be really helpful.'

We're in one of those rare areas of the cave wide enough for two people to walk side by side, and Erica now pulls alongside and gives me a sincere squint from under her bike helmet.

'Do you know what, Matthew, I have the most incredibly sceptic mind, but there's no way I can refute creation and biblical Christianity because there are no contradictions within the Bible.'

'Okay,' I say, 'so let me ask you a question. "Thou Shalt Not Kill." There's absolutely no qualification in that, is there?'

'Not in that part of the Bible, but in other parts of the Bible there are.'

'So then there *are* contradictions because "Thou Shalt Not Kill," is an absolute statement.'

For once, there is a moment of silence.

' "Thou Shalt Not Kill" is a *commandment*,' says Erica, as if it made a difference.

'It's a commandment direct from God, right?'

'Yes.'

'So "Thou Shalt Not Kill," must be what He means.'

'But in other places in the Bible ...' says the girl who started the conversation, and then flounders to a halt.

'In other places in the Bible there are *clarifications* of that,' states Erica, with a slight edge in her voice.

'But what needs clarifying?' I ask. "Thou Shalt Not Kill" – it's pretty definitive, isn't it? Besides, it seems like a good commandment to me. What's the problem?'

'Well, what about capital punishment? What if somebody bad kills someone?'

' "Thou Shalt Not Kill," ' I say, and shrug apologetically. 'That's what it says.'

'But everyone deserves to die ...'

'Yeah, we *all* deserve to die,' chimes in another female voice.

'But do we deserve to die by each other's hand, or by God's?' I ask.

'By God's hand.'

'Well, there you go then.'

'But sometimes God works through man.'

'Yeah? And how do you know when God's working through a man and when the man is just *saying* God's working through him?'

'Well ...' Erica says, as we round a bend and enter the cave's throat.

I turn and look at her in the light of the approaching mouth, waiting for some further disputation. But there is none. She moves from my side and walks ahead. I glance around at the other students. The girl who asked me if I was a believer offers a tight smile, the rest don't meet my eye.

As you exit a matinee and are surprised to find it's still day outside, so we at last crawl up out of our hole and emerge blinking into the heat and light of the afternoon.

Erica has decided to find a place in another van, but I continue to talk about religion with the remaining kids as we drive back toward Bryan College. The atmosphere is friendlier than it was on the way here. They know who I am, they've absorbed it, and are willing to talk freely about themselves and their beliefs. Their religion, they tell me, is the only true religion, unique because Jesus Christ, the son of God, set foot on earth. No other religion can make that claim. The girls state categorically that they would not marry a non-believer. In fact, they wouldn't even marry a Catholic unless he was born-again because it would be hard to live with someone who you knew was going to hell.

Of all their beliefs, I tell them, this born-again-or-go-to-hell thing is the one I find hardest to take. If God is so perfect, why would he care whether you believed in him or not? It seems so petty.

By mutual consent – accurate or not I do not know – we agree that one quarter of the world is Christian and of that quarter, half are born-again Christians who'll go to heaven. This means, I point out, that seven-eighths of the population of the world is damned to eternal hell.

They nod. Yes, this is true.

'What about a child, in rural China say, who's had no opportunity to hear your message. He doesn't even know what "born again" means – and he dies. And God throws him into a lake of fire? I mean, what kind of a God is that?'

There's a silence. The girls appear not to have considered this. They have nothing to say. A faint shadow of anxiety is visible, of doubt even.

'It's not like God chooses some people to die,' says a boy up front, meaning 'die' in the sense of being condemned to eternal hell. 'All people are basically bad and we cannot hope to get into heaven by ourselves. Jesus was the only one who was pure enough to take on our sins and erase them, and the question is not really, "Will some people go to hell?" the question is "Why were we chosen to go to heaven?" '

I cannot help but think of Hitler's *Mein Kampf* and a phrase which I

270

found so chilling I still remember it twenty years after I read it. It describes the first time Adolf saw an Orthodox Jew. 'My first thought was: Is that a Jew? But the longer I stared at that strange countenance, the more the question in a different form turned in my brain: Is that a German?'

I'm not saying these kids are Nazis – I like them, in fact – *but* ... believing in a literal hell, a burning lake, an inferno of unimaginable suffering, they accept with equanimity that seven-eighths of the world, including me, will end up in it.

Forever.

Either they don't really believe this or in fact there *is* something Nazi-like about them: their Final Solution is one of extraordinary scope and brutality; a holocaust of souls which makes the Führer's merely physical extermination of the Jews seem positively amateur. 'Our Father' is far more ambitious: he's going for the eternal destruction of not just Jews, but Hindus, Homos, Muslims, Buddhists, Catholics, atheists, agnostics and presumably Scientologists and others on the lunatic fringe. Seven-eighths of the people He creates, He then destroys. The only place you get worse odds is in the abattoir.

The girl I'm looking at as I'm thinking this is an accounting major. How on earth can she become an accountant? Then what? A mother? Little League? A nice home? One of those vans with a sliding door down the side? Knowing what she knows, how can she even *contemplate* this? How could you enjoy the comforts of a suburban life knowing that your God is going to flambé just about everyone you meet? But there she sits, as optimistic and contented as any teenager I ever met.

I remember watching an interview with a Holocaust survivor in which the interviewer asked if, while in the camp, she knew about the extermination? 'We couldn't believe it,' she replied. 'But wasn't there evidence all around?' the interviewer asked. 'No, no, you don't understand,' the woman objected. 'We *couldn't* believe it.' Meaning they as a matter of survival, they could not *allow* the horrific truth to penetrate. And perhaps that's how these Christians handle it too. In a different way I do the same. When I sign the credit card slip at an overpriced restaurant and groan at the pains of overindulgence, my white face is

271

turned from the Southern Hemisphere where a black mother buries a black infant in a bag which wouldn't fit a Big Mac.

I let the subject drop and am glad to arrive back at the college to be offered hotdogs off a barbecue grill.

(The flames! The flames!)

I take my food over to a patch of grass and sit down next to a couple of fellow cave-survivors in a loose circle of other students. One of them, who I have not seen before, a young woman with short blonde hair and a ring in her nose, asks me what I'm doing down here. I speak about the book and then, exhausted and vaguely depressed, I go find Kurt, thank him, and leave.

Consenting Adults

I drive back to the motel, looping up behind the town to cross the railroad track at 11th Street. I park and get out. A wreath on a stick marks the spot where Gary met his end. It's as colourful as a child's birthday cake, a white dove surrounded by clashing flowers, but out here beside the tracks there's something especially sad and hopeless about it and I drive away dispirited, thinking of heaven and hell and dead friends and relatives who I'm sure are in neither.

Back in my room, I locate the Gideon Bible and search for the phrase in Deuteronomy about women's clothing. Deuteronomy is known as the Second Law, the Ten Commandments in Exodus being the first. This more recent set of instructions was, like the first, given to Moses directly by God. By this time, however, Moses had been wandering in the wilderness for forty years, which may explain why some of it seems a little off. One wonders if the old man didn't put his own demented spin on things before passing it on to his flock.

It takes me a while to locate the exact passage about cross-dressing and along the way the surrealism of the 'laws' begins to cheer me up. At times, I laugh out loud.

In chapter 21, verses 10 to 14, you are told that if after a battle you see a female captive whom you find attractive, you should take her home, shave her head, let her mourn her mother and father for a month, and then go in and have her. If you don't like the experience you can kick her out, but, in a concession to feminism I suppose, you are not allowed to sell her.

Chapter 21, verses 18 to 21 suggests the following remedial treatment for your delinquent son: take the boy to 'the elders of his city and say unto them, "This our son is stubborn and rebellious, he will not obey our voice; he is a glutton and a drunkard." And all the men of his city shall stone him with stones that he die.'

If you 'find no favour' in your wife, we are told in chapter 24, or discover some 'uncleanness in her,' all you have to do is write her a 'bill of divorcement,' and show her the door. The woman can then get another husband but if he doesn't like her either and divorces her, you can't take her back because 'after that she is defiled; for that is an abomination before the Lord.'

Chapter 25, verse 11 warns that if a woman sees her husband fighting with another man and interferes 'then thou shalt cut off her hand, thine eye shall not pity her.'

Finally, I find the verse I'm looking for: 22:5. 'The woman shall not wear that which pertaineth unto man, neither shall a man put on a woman's garment: for all that do so are abomination unto the Lord.'

How ironic it is, I think, that the Bible, which has enabled Christianity to survive so long, will eventually be its downfall. I saw a debate on television recently on homosexuality. There was a gay man, a lesbian, Jerry Falwell, and some other smooth-faced Baptist minister. Falwell was spouting 'Love the sinner not the sin,' and quoting from one part of the Bible that condemns homosexuality and the other preacher was quoting from some other part.

And the gays were quoting biblical stuff right back!

Insanity! Don't kiss the stick that's beating you, don't examine it and say, 'Well, there's no nails at *this* end.' Of course not, that's the *handle!* Reject it absolutely, the entire billy club, the cudgel from end to end. Would you listen to medical advice from the same era? Does one argue about the composition of Mars with an astrologer?

My uncle has lived with the same man now for forty-five years and they were an integral part of my childhood. They were elegant, kind, and witty and – further endearing themselves to me as a teenager – had a bachelor pad in Mayfair where I would sometimes stay. They were interested in and amused by each other, they were solicitous and respectful, and never bickered like the heterosexual couples. In terms of how two people should live together they were, and remain, by far the best role models available. For much of their life together, their homosexuality was a crime punishable by imprisonment.

And where does all this prejudice and violence come from, or where at least does it acquire what little dignity it has? *Directly* from the Bible.

Recently the Pope reiterated the church's position. 'Homosexual acts,' he stated without equivocation, 'go against natural law.'

I lie back on the bed and think about the kids in the van. A phrase from Deuteronomy stopped them from dressing up as women. But what about the rest of it? If 22.5, the cross-dressing rule is a rule to live by, then why not 25.5, which allows you to rape your widowed sister-in-law? Or 25.11, which lets you chop your wife's hand off in the highly unlikely event she feels inclined to interfere when someone beats you up?

According to these Christians, the laws were proclaimed by God. As far as I know, no one has heard him repeal them. How, then, can you argue that one is sacred and to be obeyed but not the others? Do these young Christians therefore believe in stoning rebellious boys to death and raping and mutilating women? It seems unlikely, but then how can they not see the inconsistency, not to mention the absurdity, of it all?

I start typing out my notes.

When I've finished, it's getting late, but I feel guilty about the screenplay, so I start working on it. I work for an hour or so on a big action scene at the end. It's preposterous, involving a giant balloon escaping from the Thanksgiving Day Parade in Manhattan with my hero and villainess on top of it. I enjoy this kind of thing, but it isn't exactly what I set out to do when I started writing, and I remember how I felt during my first year in Hollywood when I learned there were people who did what I now do: men in their forties earning hundreds of thousands of dollars to write scripts like this. How sad they seemed, these rich men up in the hills, writers of real talent having it leached out of them as they sat wrinkling in their hot tubs or dining at Dan Tana's or Chasens or The Palm. They made me sad, but they also enraged me. If they had given up, why couldn't they make way for me, constantly broke and full of artistic conviction? What I now realise is they were even sadder than I thought. The way they swaggered around, the latest European actress on their arm, their uneasy charm, their talk of dinner parties with Jack Nicholson, all this was nothing but a veil for their embarrassment. They had fallen into the golden trap and knew it, but they had *not* given up. They still believed that with a little luck they could turn it all to their advantage.

Yet again.

When I moved to Hollywood, I was thirty-one. After directing *Violent Summer* at the age of twenty-five, I did not make another film until *Hussy* when I was twenty-eight. In between, I wrote a script for David Puttnam with my friend, Bruce Robinson, who a few years later wrote and directed the classic, *Withnail and I*. We rented an office on Denmark Street and drank a lot. Then I wrote other scripts, some for myself, one or two for other directors, but none of them worked out.

Hussy, which starred Helen Mirren, was a glamorised version of my eighteenth year, when I worked as a spotlight boy in Churchill's, a cabaret nightclub on New Bond Street, and had an affair with one of the 'hostesses'. Had I told the real story, which does not reflect well on me and did not have a happy ending, it would have been more interesting.

By this time, 1978, I was living with an English actress, Victoria Tennant. She had been in one film when she was seventeen or eighteen, but then married and abandoned her career for almost ten years. When I met her in New York, where her husband owned and ran one of the leading discos, she was ready to go back to work. I was in America doing research for an updated version of the 1731 novel, *Manon Lescaut*. In the book, Manon is exiled to New Orleans. I had substituted Las Vegas and was on my way there with my producer, an appetitive Englishman known as The Body, to check it out. I was drunk most of the time as was he. He knew Victoria and we all went out to dinner.

It was like having dinner with a beautiful robot. There was no sense of true participation or excitement, no flirtation, no humour. She'd been through so many nights like this, she could deal her conversational cards as effortlessly as a croupier. Her mother, Irina Baronova, had been one of the great ballerinas of her generation, a Russian. Her father, an Englishman and member of that now extinct breed, the gentleman agent, had handled, among others, Laurence Olivier. She was educated, intelligent, and cultured. She saw all the movies and plays as they came out and had read all the books you should have by twenty-seven and could talk about them smartly; but she was muted and withdrawn. She drank two glasses of wine and ate very little and that wisely. She was slender to the point of frailty.

As the night progressed and I drank a bottle of wine to each of her glasses, I became determined to provoke a reaction. If she dealt me a card, I'd chew it up and spit it back. She asked me if I'd seen Baryshnikov dance in ... I asked her how her father died – it was in fact the key to her character though I didn't know it then. She'd tell me about it politely and then ask me what my favourite film was. And so it went.

Toward the end of the evening, it seemed to me that one or two of my bizarre remarks fell into her large brown eyes and made them shimmer with unease. Next thing I knew we were in the back of a limo driving somewhere else. I glanced at her without her seeing me and she looked so sad I said, 'I love you and I want you to come to England and live with me,' or words to that effect, and oddly enough I meant it.

Even more oddly, a month later she arrived. Having endured a long and fruitless marriage, playing her role with stoic grace until the very last moment, she found herself looking into the surprised face of her husband as she said goodbye. And then with surgical speed, she removed herself to England.

We were together for almost five years. She could organise a complex set of flights or a large dinner party with equal ease. She knew wine and resorts and restaurants and famous people. When we went out, she got dressed in a matter of minutes, no matter what the occasion, asking no opinions and always looking good. She was a woman of lists and phone numbers. She was, intentionally or not, a professional wife. She was also loyal and supportive and intelligent and I was heartbroken when, having again performed her wifely duties to the very last minute, she left me with the same surgical élan as she had left the man before.

I should not have been surprised because, though intellectually alike, we were constitutionally incompatible. She was placid and calm, I manic and anxious. She was controlled, I was uncontrollable. She was steadily and efficiently ambitious while I was so driven and resentful I committed professional hari kiri at every opportunity. She was, to sum it up, in far better shape to succeed than me – except for one thing: she wanted to stay emotionally pristine, and drama, as any fool can tell you, is all about shit.

'How did I get into this shit?' 'Not *more* shit!?' 'How do I get out of this shit?' This is what it's all about and being able to understand and convey the exquisite and agonizing subtleties of all the varieties of shitty emotions and experiences is the methane fuel of good acting. Victoria disdained shit and kept it at bay at all costs.

She had to. It was how she survived. When she was in her teens, her father crashed his car almost at the gates of their house in some farflung suburb of London, killing himself and profoundly injuring her brother and sister who were with him. When her mother went into a prolonged collapse, Victoria had to take control, and to take control of the situation, she had first to take control of herself. If she, the last one standing, allowed herself to crack, chaos would engulf them all. She became more than an adult; she became mother to her mother, and lost her youth. I never saw her drunk. I never saw her angry. Three non-professional tears escaped her in three years. They were tears of sympathy for me.

One day she was offered a supporting role in an American mini-series about the Second World War, an overblown melodrama dressed in the skirts of sincerity, ('Fifteen Hours of Gut-Wrenching History!') She took the job. When the thing was ready to be dumped on the public, she was invited to Los Angeles to do publicity and I went with her. By luck, one of the producers was moving out of her apartment and so we moved in, thinking to stay for a few months.

Now the machinery of Hollywood set to work on its latest European acquisition. Everyone was 'very excited'. The agency was excited, the producers were excited, and pretty soon there was a publicist on the payroll and he was *incredibly* excited.

When cults do this, it's called 'love-bombing'. They get you in a room and love you for hours on end while simultaneously depriving you of sleep, and forty-eight hours later you're a Moony or a Scientologist or some other equally asinine thing. Well, that's what happens in this situation, only it takes slightly longer. 'You're really talented.' 'You're so beautiful.' 'You're going to be a big star.' 'You *are* a star.'

We'd walk into one of the many gruesome occasions set up to promote this histrionic extravaganza and there'd be a ring of suit-backs. When one of the suits saw her coming, the hoop would breach and a dozen lips would draw back and teeth would emerge, hundreds of them.

'Honey, you were great in the show, just *great*, come over here and meet the head of TV for ... Oh, and, er ...?'

'Matthew.'

'Yeah, Matthew, go fetch yourself a drink.'

Off I'd go to fetch the first of many drinks. When I looked back, I'd see the petals of this toxic flower closing around her, she in the centre, a fragile but glowing pistil. And to my horror, I saw she was quivering with pleasure.

A year later, we did a film together, *Strangers Kiss*, which I co-wrote in two weeks during eight weeks of pre-production, fuelled on little but hope. I then directed it in nineteen days. Only when it was over did my co-writer and I realise that the day we started writing we had been only eleven weeks away from wrapping the picture. At the time it was the largest deferment film ever made. We had $150,000 cash from Michael White, the English producer, and managed to persuade our cast, crew, and services to contribute their services against a share in the profits to the extent of a further million and a half dollars. We got so into the habit of pitching the concept of deferment – 'It's a way for you to invest in a movie without having to have money. All you need do is contribute your energy' – that one night when out to dinner at a Japanese restaurant, we pitched the owner, who agreed to cater the production on this basis. Every day, the restaurant would deliver fifty excellent Japanese meals to the set.

Victoria and I, and our two partners, Blaine Novak, whose original idea this was, and Doug Dilg, who was the physical producer, owned the company which made the film and it was one of those incandescent productions about which you are nostalgic for the rest of your career. Without pay, everyone worked tirelessly and well to produce something of which they could be proud. Several careers were founded on *Strangers Kiss* and years after the film came out, Doug would send out cheques at Christmas time according to our profits and everyone's investment. Some people received cheques for five dollars, some for five thousand. We were scrupulously honest.

In the film, Victoria played the emotionally muted girlfriend of a Fifties gangster who finances a movie for her to act in, hoping it will bring her to life. But when it does, when she starts to enjoy the process, he becomes jealous and starts to intrude, holding back money and questioning her sadistically when she comes home. He sends someone down to the set to watch her, and finds she is having an affair with the lead actor. To everyone's surprise, not least hers, the gangster forgives her and offers marriage. She takes pity on him and allows herself to be drawn back into the suffocating relationship. The role was tailor-made and she did a good job.

Amusingly (though only in retrospect) she went on to play the part in real life, forcing me to play the sorry cuckold. She was offered a role in a comedy with Steve Martin. The movie was called *All of Me*, and there was a lot of rushing around with jars of cremated ashes, funny walks, and things like that.

A few weeks into shooting, she came to me in the back room of our apartment where I was labouring on something no one would ever make and said, 'I've fallen in love and I'm leaving you.'

'Fallen in love with *who?*' I asked, stunned. We had made love the day before and she had said, 'That was so good.'

'It doesn't matter,' she replied and smiled involuntarily, as if embarrassed.

'It matters to me,' I insisted, and after a while she told me.

'It's Steve.'

'Steve who?'

'Steve Martin.'

'You're fucking kidding me,' I said. But she wasn't.

She packed quickly and left to go stay with friends.

That night I went to a wedding party. There were balloons. I wrote a note and tied it to one of them and let it go. The note said, 'Help!' and beneath it was my phone number.

No one called. I couldn't believe what had happened and the irony of it did not escape me. I kept wandering around saying, 'I can't believe this,' and 'My God, in this town, all the clichés *do* come true.' Now when I drove around town, I wore shades no matter how dark it was so if she saw me she wouldn't see the pain in my eyes. I did not behave well. Like most abandoned lovers, I could not allow myself to see the logic (logic!) of her choice. How could she leave *me* for Steve Martin?! A joke's a joke, et cetera. Looking back on it, of course *I* was the joke, albeit a rather sad joke. How could she *not* leave a drunken, abusive failure for a charming, clever, genuinely talented multi-millionaire comedian? I had worn her out. She had stuck it as long as she could, trouper that she was, and then, with the same decisive swiftness with which she had left her previous husband, she left me. I have rarely seen her since.

She and Steve got married. He wrote a role for her in his next movie. She played a 'quirky English girl' and wore hats. It was more irritating than funny and no more roles were forthcoming from that source.

Unless an actor writes his own movies (as Steve does), he or she isn't working until someone offers them a job. As today's new talent steps off the plane at LAX, yesterday's 'new talent' is suddenly and brutally ignored. The light of admiration dims, praise ceases to rain down. Unseen, the flower wilts.

For writers, it's different. Writers can always work. The organism blooms in the dark. *Strangers Kiss* took me to numerous film festivals where I exploited my recent heartbreaking bachelorhood to the full, and then I started writing again. I wrote constantly, stopping only to drink, screw around, and exercise. There were car crashes, weird sexual encounters and even weirder love affairs, miscarriages, cocaine binges, fights, and many blackouts.

After a year of this I was offered a movie to write and direct for Showtime, the cable company. *Slow Burn* was a novel based on a true story about a kidnapping in Palm Springs. The producer was Joel Schumacher, who is now a big director. I spent two months in Palm Springs and could never find the beach. I was convinced there had to be one because why else would anyone endure that heat, but in the end I was persuaded there was no beach, just a bunch of senile golfers in search of the next hole. The movie starred Beverly D'Angelo, Eric Roberts, and a very young Johnny Depp. It was okay and did well. The writer of the book on which it was based hated what I had done so much that in his next book, he wrote in an English scriptwriter with short hair called Matthew. Matthew got killed in a manner so excruciating it made even the unsuperstitious me wince as I read it.

Next I wrote and directed *Heart Of Midnight*, an independent movie for an eccentric Hungarian/Australian producer named Andrew Gaty. Andrew had distributed *Strangers Kiss* in Australia, where he had made a lot of money. Now he was in America to make a dangerous career switch. He was a stocky, powerfully-built man with thinning hair, crazy eyes, and a broad smile. He was staying at the Beverly Hills Hotel in possession of a terrible script which he flapped at me as we sat beside the pool in a cabana, I feeling rather self-conscious. After I'd read it and rejected it, he told me I could do what I liked with it so long as the location and the basic premise remained the same. I didn't really want to do it, but Andrew was irresistible. The more I said no, the more insistent he became. His visions of our future together, founded on this single film, became increasingly optimistic and outlandish, as did his charm and humour. Rejection was the stone he honed himself on, and pretty soon, sharp as a razor now, he cut me loose from my good taste and reason. Aside from Andrew's relentless and persuasive charm, Denise was pregnant with Anna Bella and I needed the money. I started to rewrite the script as we entered pre-production.

Eventually, I cast Jennifer Jason Leigh as the lead and she was everything I'd hoped for. I also had a production designer named Gene Rudolf who was exceptional. But I had written the script too fast and it walked an uncomfortable line between art and exploitation. Andrew was so optimistic and determined he listened to no one and so miscalculated the budget that we were in the red before we began pre-production.

We built the main set (a defunct sex club) in an abandoned town hall in Charleston, South Carolina. I went down a couple of weeks ahead of Andrew, who flew back and forth between New York, where he owned an apartment on Park Avenue, and LA, where he was now engaged in all kinds of complex financial negotiations to do with foreign sales and distribution pick-ups, none of which I understood when he'd call me in the evenings. A couple of days before he was to join us permanently in the South, the line producer, the man who actually deals with the nuts and bolts of production, took me aside and said, 'We're several hundred thousand dollars over-budget, but if you speak to Andrew, don't tell him. I don't want to undermine his confidence while he's out there in LA trying to sell this thing.'

I had so much to think about myself, I merely shrugged. This couldn't be true. How could a movie that was supposed to cost less than a million be 'several hundred thousand' over budget? Half an hour after Andrew arrived, I came out of my office and found him leaning against a wall, face buried in his arms, sobbing.

'For God's sake, Andrew,' I said, 'pull yourself together, people are watching.'

'I'm ruined,' he told me. And he was.

We managed to complete the movie, but, even beyond the fact that it was flawed, it was cursed. Companies went bankrupt around it. What little money it made, never reached Andrew and he was forced to sell his Park Avenue apartment in New York and rent a smaller one in Los Angeles, where he remains.

Never use the word 'heart' in a movie title. It is a word begging for affection. Never use the word 'midnight' either because it begs to be found exotic when in fact it's merely tired and sleazy. The combination of the two words was the kiss of death. I'm not saying this was our only problem, but I'm convinced it compounded all the others that *Heart Of Midnight* had. I wanted to call it simply *X*, which would have been much better. The film, which dealt with sexual perversity and violence, was gang-raped by the critics. As the father of the movie, I suffered more than I acknowledged at the time, partly because I knew they were right, it was not a good film. However, just because you have an ugly kid and *know it*, doesn't make it any easier to hear about it thirty times in a single week.

By the time the film came out, Anna Bella had been born and I wanted to stay home and watch her grow, at least for the first year. I decided to write a mainstream Hollywood movie and make some money.

I went out and pitched *Consenting Adults*.

Pitching is when you go out and tell a story to anyone who'll listen and has money – studios, producers, actors with their own companies – and hope they're sufficiently interested to pay you to write it. All writers do it differently. I'm told there are writers who go in and say, 'A man and a woman! She's got claustrophobia, he's afraid of open space! They have to get from LA to Chicago!' And get the deal. I've never been able to do this. My pitches last at least thirty minutes and are really an outline for a script.

I used not to be very good at this. One morning soon after I arrived in LA, I found myself in one of those typically deceptive Hollywood offices – pine tables, fat white sofas and armchairs – pitching to a producer and his D-girl (the person who administers the development of material). I was about halfway through and explaining a particularly interesting point in the story when I saw the producer's head start tilting toward the back of the sofa. He rested it there a moment and then his eyes began to glaze over and he fell asleep. I turned toward the D-girl and continued pitching. No deal.

With *Consenting Adults*, it looked as if no one would go for it, so I went home and started writing. Then a bright and aggressive man named Chip Diggins, who had heard the pitch, pushed it through at Hollywood Pictures (a now defunct division of Disney) and I got paid to finish it. I was lucky – at first. Everyone connected with the development of the script was smart and creative and we had fun which, of course, is often the key to good work.

The film got made with Kevin Kline and Kevin Spacey. The director was Alan Pakula, who was notorious for torturing writers, but I was happy to be tortured; the thing was getting made.

I liked Alan. He was a tall, grey-haired man, deliberately professorial and fundamentally a gentleman. I hoped, secretly, that he would become my mentor, something I had never had. This didn't happen for various reasons, but I learned a few things from him none the less. 'Everything is possible if you don't panic,' he would say, shutting the door on his line producer only days before shooting, 'and nothing is possible if you do,' he'd add, sitting down with me to start going over the ending for the fiftieth time.

He had started as a producer, producing among other things, *To Kill A Mocking Bird*. As a director he had made such films as *All The President's Men*, *Klute*, and *Sophie's Choice*. He was married to a handsome society woman and author of popular historical books. The two of them knew everyone in New York from Arthur Miller to the Mayor. He could charm anyone into just about anything. He was a good craftsman and, usually, a great actors' director. He was urbane and capable.

There was one thing he was lousy at, and it drove him insane: he could not write. Whenever he tried, it ended in disaster, and I think this is what caused him constantly to chew over scripts – including scripts by such writers as William Goldman – until he'd chewed out much of what was good in them.

In the case of this movie, the process unquestionably made the script worse, and it got worse still when he finally laid hands on it himself. Something that was witty and clever became slow and turgid.

Consenting Adults is the story of a man, Kevin Kline, who gets tempted into a bizarre wife-swap by his persuasive neighbour, Kevin Spacey. Each will cross the street in the night and have sex with the other's wife while she is sleeping. At first, Kline resists. It's a ludicrous proposal, they'll wake up, they'll know it's not their husband, it's disgusting, it's *wrong*. But Spacey is relentless and knows how to manipulate his friend. You do these things precisely because they *are* wrong. You do them because the risk *brings you to life*. Kline is a coward, he's pussy-whipped, he's lost his edge, no wonder he's depressed. All of which is true.

And underneath it all is Kline's passion for the other man's wife and for fresh sex in the suffocating time of AIDS. Meanwhile, Spacey's wife almost seems to be colluding in the plan, tempting him with glances and subtle messages of the body. Finally, he does it, creeps in there in the dark, slides into bed, wordlessly has sex with her, and then goes home. In the morning when he wakes up, guilty in his own bed, he hears the sound of sirens. The woman has been bashed to death with a baseball bat. It's a set-up. DNA proves Kevin Kline had sex with her, Spacey has an alibi out of town ...

It gets more complicated, and in the end, in my version, it turns out it was a life insurance scam set up by Kline's own wife in collusion with Spacey. Who better than a wife to understand her husband's weaknesses and how to manipulate them? For reasons I could not understand, Alan hated the idea of the wife being the villain and eventually tacked on a much more conventional happy ending. It wasn't until long after the movie came out that I realised that in his previous film, the wife had been the villain. He didn't want to be seen to repeat himself, which was understandable but had nothing to do with what was right for my story.

Still, it was a big Hollywood movie. When Kevin Kline agreed to play the part, I called my parents. My mother was too drunk to come to the phone, so I spoke to my father. I heard him shouting to her in the next room. 'It's Matthew on the phone, he says a man called Calvin Klein has just agreed to be in a film he's written.'

This was too much. Even he had to know who Kevin Kline was, but his 'mistake' made the point. Had I searched the world for a profession which would impress them less, I could have done no better than what now, with a little success, became 'show business'.

Consenting Adults made a profit, not a large one, but enough not to be an embarrassment, and a lot of people had read the script before Pakula changed it. I was in demand. Studios offered me work. My fee went up. The next movie I wrote (actually rewrote, although not a word of the original script survived) was *Color Of Night* in which Bruce Willis starred.

The director, Richard Rush, had directed one interesting movie some time ago, *The Stunt Man*, but things had not gone so well for him in recent years. I knew this when I went up to his house and, looking down into his murky pool, saw a garden-table-plus-attached-sunshade rotting at the bottom.

Richard was always polite to me and I liked him well enough, but he too had a fatal flaw. He possessed all the external attributes, all the musculature, of a great director. He was relentlessly stubborn and full of conviction. He was as good a technical craftsman as Alan was, perhaps better. Unfortunately, he wasn't as bright as he thought he was, and that of which he was stubbornly convinced was frequently wrong. When I spoke to Dino de Laurentis about him, he said, 'He fink too much. He fink too much.' In a way, he was right. Had Richard simply listened to the people around him, not just me, but Bruce Willis, David Matalon, the producer; practically anyone, he would have saved himself a lot of energy and made a better movie.

At a certain point, my frustration became obvious and I was not invited to watch any of the shooting. When I entered the screening room to view the first cut I was already dubious. The first scene of the film showed Bruce Willis, playing a psychiatrist, having what is euphemistically known in the psychiatric profession as 'a treatment failure.' He is lying on the couch almost asleep with boredom when his whining patient suddenly tosses herself out the window.

We now realise Bruce's office is at the top of a skyscraper. The wide shot that tells us this shows the woman diving out through the glass. This is followed by a shot from inside a lower window as the patient goes wailing by. There's a high angle of her falling away, and a low angle of her falling closer. Then there's another wide shot of her falling down the side of the building (she still has a long way to go), and then another from below and another from on top, and then one through an even *lower* window as she whistles past even quicker and ...

This went on for what seemed close to a minute and was so unintentionally funny that I was unable to suppress my laughter. I knew at once that we were in serious trouble. It was a little thriller and should have cost ten million at the most. It ended up costing forty million and was overblown and melodramatic to a truly fantastic degree.

When they asked me what I thought, I told them the only solution was to see Bruce fall asleep at the start of the film, have the woman jump out the window, and then let the picture run as it was until the end when you cut back to Bruce waking up to find the woman still in the room, whining. It's an old device, of course, but still ... a *psychiatrist's* nightmare! That's funny. Done like this, the picture would work brilliantly. What a wheeze. You could have put back all the stuff which had to be cut out as too laughably excessive, including the protracted treatment failure.

But no one would go for the idea, least of all the director. They were taking it seriously. I was so angry at what Richard had done that I bought a poster from a science magazine, 'Penises Of The Animal Kingdom,' which consisted of anatomically correct illustrations of animal cocks in order of size, starting with man, then dog (yes, dog), hyena, pig and so on until it reached elephant, and then last but certainly not least, whale. Next to the whale penis, I wrote, 'But you're the biggest dick of all' and was about to send it when he had a heart attack – which he survived – so I didn't.

When the film was about to open, I called my mother and told her under no circumstances to go and see the film or to read any reviews – there was probably little danger of her doing either anyway by this time – and then I flew to Brazil and stayed there for three weeks. Many movie critics secretly, and even not so secretly, want to be screenwriters and will often flatter the director, a potential employer, at the expense of the writer, a potential competitor. Thus if a movie is good, the director gets all the credit while if it's bad, the writer often takes most of the blame.

I was vilified, the movie flopped, but I survived and one job followed another for the next seven years, up to now, each one bringing an increase in pay and none, up to now, getting made. It may sound comic to say this, but I am a good screenwriter and worth every cent. The best Hollywood writers, and I consider myself to be among these, are often better than their more critically admired playwright colleagues. The trouble is, their best scripts don't get made. I know several writers like myself who have work tucked away which is far superior to everything they've had produced. As Kubrick once said, 'Just because a script has been turned down by every studio in town doesn't mean it's a work of genius, but it is a good start.'

When Joe McCarthy decided to go after some artists in his anti-Communist campaign of the early Fifties, he didn't chase down the painters and the poets. You could say rock and roll has had more influence than cinema in the latter half of the century, but in terms of *potential*, movies have it all. They are capable of conveying extremely complicated ideas – as complex as the novel if you so wanted – but with far more emotional force. And yet they don't.

Even with McCarthy long gone, 95% of Hollywood movies are at best sentimental and at worst violent *and* sentimental. In the most technologically advanced nation in the world, an extraordinary number of them are also as tritely superstitious as tarot cards. There are hard-bitten, unsentimental film *noir* imitators, but their cynicism is superficial, apolitical, an exercise in style which challenges nothing. A miniscule percentage of films deal with complex subjects, but almost always reach acceptably sentimental and politically correct conclusions. And then you have films which are genuinely contentious and daring. Maybe there's one of these every other year.

If you run around pitching long enough, you notice certain themes abort immediately. Suggest there might be something twisted or brutal in this capitalist haven, and no matter how dramatic and compelling the story is, you can hear the toilet flushing before you even say goodbye, and the most important thing you learn is that a HAPPY ENDING is almost mandatory. The bolder you are in probing the uglier corners of American life, the more important it is to have a HAPPY ENDING or at the bare minimum – excuse me while I puke – a 'Life Affirming' one. Tragedy, a form of drama which has worked well for the last two thousand years, is absolutely taboo, and you can't help wondering why? Why is the richest and most powerful country in the world so insecure that anything even remotely critical of the status quo is as welcome as someone coughing up blood in a cigarette commercial?

And in that question lies the answer.

Movies have *become* commercials. The word 'art' has become an expression of contempt. If you send someone a script and they say 'It's an art movie,' it's tantamount to having someone spit in your eye.

When the studios began, they were owned by a group of ex-vaude-villians from the East. These were not men of culture but they were men of complex ambition and they were *individuals*, and part of what drove them was a desire for a kind of respectability which money alone couldn't buy. Consequently, they felt compelled to make a few good movies every year, some of which were somewhat radical. These days the studios are largely owned by corporations whose only interest is profit and the protection of their image. Consciously or not, every executive is aware of this. The oyster effortlessly finds the grit, but what is then produced is not, unfortunately, a pearl.

If the very rich in America refuse to make the connection between crime and economic inequality, we the film makers, refuse to find a link between the lies we tell and the way our audience behaves. We are too ashamed to ask ourselves what effect it has on society when the artists, the supposed advocates of truth, become mere propagandists for corporate fantasy. How does my impoverished redneck feel, for example, when he takes his jumbo-sized Coke and his tin of Skoal back to his cabin, turns on the TV, and finds nothing there which reflects, let alone sympathises with, the gravity of his condition; where, in fact, he sees only success and happiness and victory? Add to this neglect, the inescapable message in every movie he likes (action movies) that in the end the true hero solves his problems with a gun, and you have all the ingredients (including, you can be sure, the gun) required to send our twisted hillbilly out in search of a cathartic shoot-out.

And if this line of reasoning appears naïve, then one must ask oneself an even more depressing question: if movies can have no influence for bad, how can they possibly have any influence for good?

The phone rings in my room at the Best Western, startling me. I've been staring, eyes out of focus, at the screen of my computer. My villainess and hero drift above New York. She has just attempted to spray the crowd with some awful chemical, but my hero and I have thwarted her. Because I intend to kill her in about ten seconds, I've got her hanging at the end of a dangling rope.

I pick up the phone.

'Hello?'

Perky, religious little Amy up at the front desk tells me some students have come to visit me from Bryan College. They're in the lobby. I switch off the computer. My villainess will have to hang on a little longer – there's Christians to be met.

CHAPTER TWENTY-SEVEN

Stumbling In The Wilderness

Big moths blunder against the lights as I walk along the humid gangway to the lobby. Two Bryan College students await me. One is the young woman with the ring through her nose, Laurie; the other is her friend, Matt. The boyish Laurie explains she heard me speaking about my book on the lawn at Bryan College. Could she and some of her friends take me out to lunch tomorrow and talk some more? I tell her I don't know what I'm doing – tomorrow is Sunday and I'm still hoping to extract a tape from Gale Johnson – but why don't she and Matt come back to my room, I'll take their number, and we can chat a while? There's a moment of hesitation – a process of calculation, a rapid measurement against a code? – and then they come with me down the walkway. We enter my room – the one where I work – and sit down. They ask me how I enjoyed the caving and then we talk about Kurt Wise.

They seem far more authentic and accessible than the other students. They exist outside of their faith. I tell Laurie this, saying I found some of her co-religionists too good to be true. She doesn't understand and gives me the old 'everyone's a sinner,' line, but it's done with a certain reserve. Matt thinks what I've experienced is the social awkwardness of kids who have been raised by Christian parents, home-schooled by Christian parents, and had a social life centred solely around the church. Knowing nothing but this society, they're made uneasy by the secular world and become self-protective.

Ten to fifteen minutes pass in pleasant conversation, then there's a knock at the door and three more students stand outside, a boy and two girls who, it now turns out, Laurie left in her car, expecting to be back soon.

'We're just chatting,' I say as I invite them in.

'Yeah, well we wanna chat too,' says one of the girls, laughing.

'We were supposed to just ask you for lunch,' Laurie tells me.

'I'm sorry,' I say to the new group, 'I didn't know you were out there.'

'That's okay,' says one of the new girls, 'our friends don't know manners, they're from the United States.'

'Where are you from?' I ask.

'I'm from Dayton, but that's different, I come from a little town and we know how to be proper.'

Everyone laughs. The new kids have the same qualities as Laurie and Matt. They're funny, responsive, at ease, smart. They tease each other and make fun of themselves. There's nothing prissy about them, they're forthright and not defensive.

'So, are you allowed to be out this late?' I ask.

They all laugh. 'Occasionally we stay up past eleven,' says a girl.

'Eleven? I'm shocked!' I say. They laugh again.

They ask what the book is about, how I got the job, where I came from originally. I don't tell them I'm a descendant of Darwin, but recount some of my school life, ending with, 'I was a bad kid, but *then* ... I reformed.'

I give them a look which they can take any way they want. They laugh again, particularly the girls. 'What made you reform?' asks Laurie. '*If* you have reformed.'

I explain how I got interested in writing, about the psychiatrist who gave me hope. They listen attentively, ask intelligent questions, and make interesting comments. They're good company. It's a real pleasure to have them here.

The phone rings. It's Denise. Without telling her why, I ask if I can call back in half an hour and hang up.

'My wife,' I explain, 'I couldn't tell her I was in a roomful of Christians.'

This gets a huge laugh. Emboldened, I ask:

'So, did you all come down here to convert me?'

'No!'

'I hate that word!'

'We're not that way. There are some people,' Laurie says, 'who'll do that, get in your face, "If you don't do this, don't do that ..." We believe in living Christian lives, if people see that maybe it'll have an effect. That's all.'

But they are more interested in finding out what I'm doing than they are in talking about their faith, which I alternately tease them about and probe them on until eventually Laurie gets irritated.

'You seem to have more of a problem with us being Christian than we do,' she says, and makes a gesture almost of frustration: Look, here we are in your motel room, curious about you, interested in what you do, we're not just Christians, we're *people*.

And she's right. I feel mawkish and ashamed and change the subject.

Erica's name comes up. One of the boys says that within a day or two of being in camp, she had memorised the names of *all* the other students and the camp counsellors. It was something she'd learned from a book.

I ask about misbehaviour at the college.

'So, you want to dwell on *that* now?' asks Laurie, smiling.

'We all behave impeccably,' states another, laughing.

'We all have our struggles with the rules,' says the third girl, 'Which ones to follow, which ones not to follow ...'

On the dress code, they point out that it's partly a cultural thing. Americans in general are more 'modest' than Europeans.

'That's true,' I say, 'in Europe there are nude beaches all over the place. I don't suppose you get much nudity down at the boat dock here ...'

One of the girls says she and some friends do occasionally go skinny-dipping up in the mountains at night. I'm surprised they'd venture into the mountains when it was dark. Aren't they afraid? But they're not. They love the countryside and talk about it enthusiastically. They go hiking through it, play in it, sleep in it. We talk about the Pocket Wilderness, a nature reserve which used to be part of the Dayton Coal and Iron mining operation. One of the girls, Christie, tells me if you know where to look you can still see the mine's ventilation shafts. When they leave a few minutes later, she offers to show them to me if I'm around tomorrow. I accept.

I go to bed and have a strange dream about sweet-natured Christian girls spelunking on their hands and knees.

Sunday is as intolerably damp and hot as every other day, but in the small church where Gale Johnson's husband preaches, it's almost cool.

I'm in my Sunday best (jeans and a shirt) and have the place of honour beside the pastor's wife. Two boys stir restlessly on the other side of her as their father, Carter Johnson, preaches. He is not a bad preacher, seemingly reasonable and not at all excitable. Maybe this is the problem, the house is less than a quarter full.

The sermon, a lengthy musing on some biblical verse, seems to be about the 'motivation for being holy.' Should it come out of fear, the desire for reward, or for the love of God? It's a pretty simple question, but it takes half an hour to ask it and another half to answer it. He talks about a 'holy lifestyle,' and a 'God-pleasing life.' In spite of some lingo borrowed from the self-help movement, it's the same old fire and brimstone when he finally gets down to it, so I tune out and start to think about my new religion.

This would definitely be part of it, this sitting here.

When I lived in LA, a year would sometimes go by without my noticing. Even in New York, where there are at least distinct seasons to hew mnemonic notches on the short stick of life, still I'm always running: to the gym or to be depressed, only ten hours left for work, find time for the wife, the daughter, friends, but someone's trying to get me to switch phone services and there's too much mail, much of it from total strangers wanting things I do not have, a pile of it, not enough time, not enough time, so I automatically rip up all the envelopes with charity requests without even looking inside and ...

What? Not even look inside? I know, it's terrible, but I'm just so busy, and with so much misery on offer, how do you select? Is a child with cancer more deserving than a lonely geriatric with Alzheimer's? Should you look for bargains? Fifty bucks, for example, funds a brace of Manhattan AIDS sufferers for a day, while the same outlay feeds a six-pack of African heteros with the same disease for a month – *but* the Africans are probably going to die anyway, and to choose one is to deny another and it's overwhelming how much suffering God showers us with and it's all so horrific and I'm depressed already, and anyway I've got to keep shifting things *aside*, have to cut a path, a little leeway, please! because there's more coming down tomorrow, *more* work, *more* telemarketing pricks, switch or buy, *more* words to write, *more* life to organise and suddenly – in a New York *minute* – even with the seasons, *years* have gone by without a moment of reflection.

294

What life?

And that's what church should be: a segment of time to interrupt, to *terminate* this frenzy of mindless activity. At worst, like now, the inaction is merely boring and the brain gets a chance to wander philo-sophically. At best, if one organised it right, the experience would jolt you awake and remind you of your place in the order of things, that you *have* a place in the order, that actions have consequences, that life is beautiful, ugly, serious, funny, very short *but still magnificent*.

It strikes me what a strange building I'm in. You don't park in it, or eat in it, or work, sleep, or shop in it; it serves no material function and produces no material benefit (except to the pastor) and yet it's one of the biggest buildings in town.

It's ripe for takeover. Remove the imbecilities of conventional relig-ion – including God – and what remains is no less incredible: a cavernous room purpose-built to provoke reflection! Incredible. Maybe one could even let God in now and then, like on the third Sunday of every alternate month. God – you never know ... (The place would also remain available for AA meetings, these being the last example of faith at work still to be found in church. Twelve steps like twelve disciples, submission to a higher power, and the real chance of recovery through communion with fellow sufferers.)

How I wish I had more time to study all the religions, to pick and choose the elements I'd use in mine. A touch of Buddhist humility here, a pinch of Muslim asceticism there, the better hymns of Christianity, something Hindu (is that bare feet?), something New Agey, massage or whatever, and of course a large dose of Tantric sex to keep the congre-gation frisky.

'Mrs Wilkins, why don't you show us what you learned last week? Any volunteers? *Hold it! Just one!* Okay, Jimmy, it's your turn. Hmm, leg over that way, arm over there ... Interesting. Hold still, Jimmy, here she comes! Oh, Mrs Wilkins, how *fine* you are ...'

Suddenly, everyone around me is standing. Lost in Mrs Wilkins' exertions, I failed to notice Pastor Johnson's sermon coming to an end. There's some singing to be done, so I stand up and listen.

Gale sings prettily, with a simple, unaffected voice. I look around to check the other songbirds. To my surprise, I see my little flock of visitors from last night. They're across the aisle, chirping sweetly.

295

After the service, I go talk with them. They offer to take me up to the Pocket Wilderness right after the service if I'm free. There's a swimming hole at the top of the creek. Along the way they could show me the ventilation shafts from the old mine and then we could all swim. I tell them I'm having lunch with the Johnsons but could meet them at the motel around two. Gale has to give a Sunday School class, which she doesn't think will interest me, so I'm to be at her and Carter's house in an hour and a half.

I drive up into the hills to a small white church I saw when cruising with Rocky. I enter and sit down. It's a poorer, fatter crowd than Carter's, but they seem to have more fun. There's some Mexicans across the aisle and behind me an amiable hillbilly retard. The pastor is a good looking man who cannot be much more than thirty, if that. His dark hair is well cut and in his Calvin Klein glasses, snappy plaid shirt and khakis, he could be a grad student or a preppie gay waiter, but his accent is almost incomprehensibly country. He never stops grinning, but *never*, and bounces from one foot to the other, as if the music's in him, or the Holy Spirit, or cocaine.

'I appreciate the Lord today, yes I do,' he says every ten sentences or so.

The place is democratic in form, but conservative in content. A member of the congregation, a man around fifty, asks to be heard.

'I don't never seen a time in my life like this one. Young people using bad language in the schools and the teachers just turn away. As hard as it is for me to say this, we need to be responsible for our children.'

'I hear ya.'

'If they need the rod, they need to git it. That's the way it is, no matter what the Government says, it don't make no difference. It's not abuse, it's love and correction. The Bible tells us if we don't correct them, we don't love them.'

'Tha's right, brother.'

Now a pudgy little fellow in his early forties gets to his feet and starts to 'witness'. He talks about being saved, 'I am saved, yes I am!' Oh, the great happiness of it! 'Oh, I love the Lord!' And now, as he gets into it, he jumps up and down in place like a fat, beaming child. It seems completely ludicrous to me, but everyone else claps and says 'Amen' with great admiration and much beatific grinning and he sits down well satisfied.

A mother comes to the front with her four-year-old child and they sit at an upright piano. She slams her fingers into the keys and the two of them start to sing old-style gospel music, and it doesn't hesitate or hold back a thing. Everyone gets to their feet and joins in, swaying and slapping their hands together, myself among them. I'd have this in my religion too, this music, and this would be the way to go: upbeat, wailing. 'Oh, yes, Mrs Wilkins, you can dance if you want to.'

When the song is done, I see it's time to go, and manage to escape before the collection box gets to me.

Half an hour later I'm inside the Johnson house, a comfortable but modest middle class home on the suburban side of the highway. Gale goes off to cook, the kids are kept at bay, and Carter and I talk in the den. Carter comes from a medical family. His father was a doctor as is his brother. His grandmother and sister were nurses. He was in pre-med himself when he changed his mind and decided to go into the ministry. He loves to teach and to watch the beneficial transformation which takes place in people's lives if they commit themselves to God. I had thought, from his sermon, that there was something forgiving about him, something gentle, and this seems to confirm it; but as we start to talk about heaven and hell, his face, which had been suffused with pleasant enthusiasm, now becomes increasingly stern. His mouth turns down and becomes resolute and his eyes become hard. He is convinced there's only one God (his), one heaven (where I presume he's going), a hell (where me and the other seven eighths are headed), and so on. It's in the Bible and the Bible is the word of God and has no errors. I ask him about TULIP, the five points of Calvinism.

He tells me the T is for *T*otal Depravity of man. No man is pure, all are sinful, and every act is tinged with sin.

The U is for *U*nconditional Election. God has already chosen, or elected, who will go to heaven and who will not and there's nothing we can do about it. (So perhaps I was wrong and I'm going to heaven and he's not.) Man is so fundamentally bad that left to his own devices, he would never choose God. God, however, will *interfere* in some people's lives to bring them into the fold. These are the elected. When I ask Carter why he would choose *not* to save so many of his own creations, he admits 'that's the $10,000 question, and the ultimate answer is – nobody knows.' In Romans, chapter 9, Paul responds to the question by saying: 'Does not the potter have the right to make out of the same lump of clay some pottery for noble purposes and some for common use? What if God, choosing to show His wrath and make His power known, bore with great patience the object of His wrath prepared for destruction? What if He did this to make the riches of His glory known to the objects of His mercy?' In other words, if you beat one of your children the others will be impressed by your mercy in *not* beating them.

The L is for *L*imited Atonement. Christ died on the cross not for all men, but only for the unconditionally elected. 'His death was sufficient to pay for the sins of everybody, but it was *effective* only for the elect,' Carter informs me. 'All will *not* be saved. We don't believe in Universalism.'

The I is for *I*rresistible Grace. Ultimately the chosen will not resist their salvation.

The P is for *P*erseverence of the Saints, which means that those who are chosen will stay chosen – whether they like it or not.

The concept of TULIP, particularly that of Unconditional Election, seems almost surreal. It's as if the purpose of religion itself has been squeezed out by some perverse theological contortion. Under this system, there are no rewards for good behaviour. It doesn't matter how hard you try, if you're pre-selected for hell, hell is where you'll go. Imagine how Mother Theresa must be feeling if she drew the wrong straw.

When I talk to him about the reality of hell, and how depressing it must be to walk among so many condemned people, he admits – as do so many Christians – to a sense of unease.

'I think, Matthew,' he says, hesitantly, 'that the reality or the truth of hell has not gripped me like it ought.'

Gale enters and tells us it's time for lunch. In we go to a slightly austere dining room, and grace is duly said. To my disappointment, the boys aren't going to eat with us. I can usually ignite a spark of rebellion in even the most dour of children and had looked forward to sparking up these two juniors. Instead I sit alone with Gale and Carter, he at one end of the table, the master, she at the other, his wife. They are cordial and I appreciate their hospitality, but something grim permeates the house – a miasma of things forbidden, the bleak outline of puritanical displeasure – and something else too, an awkwardness, a distracted quality in both my hosts, as if they want to blurt something out but cannot yet bring themselves to do so.

When lunch is over and small talk exhausted, I check my watch and tell them I have to go meet my young Christian friends. No sooner do I stand than they pounce on me. Carter grasps my left hand.

'Do you mind if we pray for you?'

Before I can answer, Gale has my other hand. I've just eaten their food, I still want the tape, and anyway there's something about a preacher – the last remnants of some atavistic superstitious regard? – which can render even the staunchest atheist bewilderingly passive. Instead of objecting vociferously, I comply with a shrug.

So there we stand in a line in the dining room, three adults holding hands, heads bowed, me with my eyes defiantly open, flushing with embarrassment and shame. I've given few clues to my non-belief but they've got me pegged. Rev. Johnson prays for my salvation in a grave but hopeless tone such as one might apply when praying for a man who, dying of lung cancer, continues to smoke. It lasts about a minute and finally I'm out in my car, tapeless, but free.

I'm relatively fit. I swim and run, but these young Christians are a different species. They neither smoke nor drink and probably never have; they're in their prime and they're leading me up the side of a creek toward the waterhole at an unbelievable pace.

It's killing me.

They came for me in Laurie's car, a large old station wagon. Matt and a pleasant, handsome young man sat in the back. I sat next to Laurie, who drove the big vehicle with relaxed competence along the narrow lanes, her left leg drawn up onto the seat and resting against the door, a single hand working the steering wheel. When we got to the Pocket Wilderness, a craggy, wooded area with a boulder-strewn creek, Christie was already there in her car.

Twenty minutes later, I'm exhausted. We plunge on along a path above the creek. My friends spring over fallen trees and hop adroitly aside when a snake is seen lying across the path. I plod behind, trying to wheeze quietly.

Christie shows me a rough opening in the side of the hill, a jagged but deliberate aperture. It's one of the ventilation shafts from the mine. Along here there used to be a railway delivering coal and iron back to the foundry; now there's not a trace of it. When you see photographs of the valley eighty years ago, there are thousands of acres of industrial buildings, smoke stacks, railway lines, mine heads, winches – a valley crammed with vigorous commercial enterprise – and it's all gone, nothing, not a sign except this: some holes in the side of a hill, the clogged breathing tubes of an extinct subterrranean creature.

Having shown me another shaft, Christie turns back. That was it: she came along only to show me this and now, having some other obligation, she's headed home without even the refreshment of the swimming hole.

The path descends into the creek. Now our route ascends in a series of jumbled and irregular steps, some in the form of boulders, steep and hard to climb, others in the form of long, shallow rises dotted with ankle-twisting stones. The kids leap from boulder to boulder, clamber friskily up narrow gullies, commit themselves to landings on slick, moss covered plates of rock, land, slip, regain themselves (laughing), and gallop on. My legs are shaking and my shirt is damp with sweat and clings to my torso like a disease.

I have a morbid horror of breaking my wrists. Unable to type, I'd be at zero in a month and lose my apartment in six. I'm gasping and my head throbs. I want to remove my shirt, but what lies beneath is too disgusting. I'm white, oleaginous, saturated in foie gras and booze, no longer glamorously dissolute, merely pathetic in consequence.

Finally, a mile or so later, we arrive at the swimming hole, that quintessential emblem of idyllic rural America. Nor is it disappointing. It's a waterfall amid a scatter of majestic boulders and tall trees, a clear and icy pool, a jutting rock from which to plunge.

Laurie removes her shirt to reveal a one-piece swimsuit descending into her shorts. She dives into the water with the shorts still on. The boys follow. I'm wearing long, baggy denim shorts and underneath them a red swimsuit which didn't used to be as tight or brief as it now is but was always on the skimpy side even in secular company. I don't want to remove my shorts but figure if I don't I'm going to have to walk all the way back with an extra five pounds of dampness clinging onto my faltering buttocks and chafing at my sad old balls.

I drop the pants and dive in. The water is astoundingly cold. I swim under the heavy curtain of the waterfall and recline behind it and then swim out again. Matt and Laurie climb up the side of the fall and reach the jutting rock. It's a twenty-foot drop. Holding their noses, they jump. Now the other boy does it, then Laurie and Matt go again. What about me? Aren't I going to do it?

The coward grunts his declination and swims sportily below, showing off his marvellous stroke. Matt and Laurie climb up a third time and wrestle with each other on the edge. Matt pushes her. She falls and lands feet first, unharmed, then paddles to the side, smiling, not angry in any way. She lies back on a rock and watches Matt jump, twisting in the air. He swims to her and sits nearby. Although they do not touch, I suspect they're going out together.

We talk in the heat, cooling ourselves occasionally with a dip. Most of the time they are engaging and engaged, and then they seem to inexplicably pull back as if collecting themselves. I don't know if it's because I swear without noticing and offend them, or if it's just an awkwardness brought on by the difference in our ages. Then again, perhaps they have a plan – like the Johnsons – a sudden forced baptism, say?

Laurie tells me she and Matt hitchhiked to California together and had a great time. Now Matt is leaving in a few weeks to spend a semester at a college in Egypt. They discuss other academic programmes abroad. There's an international network of Christian schools and colleges which they can attend, and after that missions, hospitals, and relief organisations where they can work. If you compare them to kids from similar economic backgrounds but in regular schools, their potential for an absorbing life seems greater. True, they probably won't take as many drugs or go to as many clubs or have as many sexual encounters as their secular counterparts, but they can and probably will travel, study and work all over the world via these church organisations.

Laurie has already had a more interesting life than most. Born in Atlanta, Georgia, she lived in the south-east until she was thirteen when her parents moved to Peshawar, Pakistan, to work for SERVE (Serving Emergency Relief and Vocational Enterprises), a Christian relief organization. Originally sent to care for the four million Afghan refugees who fled the Soviet invasion of 1979, SERVE remained when the occupation ended ten years later to help rebuild Afghanistan's infrastructure. During this time, Laurie travelled in China, India, the United Arab Emirates, England, Switzerland, Germany, and France. Conventionally schooled in the early years in America, her parents later decided to try home-schooling, 'or self-guided education' as it is sometimes called. This kind of schooling, she believes, while sometimes lonely, makes a child independent and self-disciplined. Encouraged by her father, she read widely, but still feels she has educational gaps.

In a letter she writes me some months later, she describes Afghanistan and her own work there. 'Afghanistan is pretty screwed up – a discouraging place to work. It has the highest amputee rate in the world (thanks to extensive landmining by the Soviets), the highest infant mortality rate in the world, and one of the highest illiteracy rates. There are no reliable phone systems, water systems, sewage systems, or electricity supplies. And the civil war goes on, fraught with human rights abuses, age-old hatred and tangled ethical dilemmas. I worked for SERVE in Mazar-I-Sharif, Afghanistan for the summer between my sophomore and junior years here at Bryan College. I flew in from Peshawar on a tiny Red Cross plane (the only way in and out of the city) right after a battle. The place was a sandbagged, shot-up disaster. War is an odd thing. It can seem normal when you're in it. Life goes on, and human beings become accustomed to catastrophe.'

You could also make a case that the intellectual lives of Laurie and her friends are richer than those of most non-Christian kids of their class. They have thought seriously about the nature of existence, albeit from a position which tends to be fixed at the outset, and make a better case for their own interpretation of it than would the average student. Most whom I spoke to had studied other religions and philosophies, which, again, an ordinary kid might not have. Some whom I met during the cave trip will be narrowed by their unrelenting consciousness of their faith and the lack of it in others; but looking at my hiking pals – now plunging into the water again as I lie prostrate on a boulder – I don't believe this will be true for them. These three could fit in anywhere.

And then there's their 'spiritual' life. At least one of these splashing kids will likely end up working in a refugee camp or somewhere similar, doing genuine good, their religion irrelevant to the grateful recipients of their charity.

It is this idea of spiritual peace through service, for which I most envy them.

I remember the period in my childhood when I wanted to be a missionary of some kind, a worker among the dispossessed. I remember the imagined sensation of waking up each morning sure that where I was was where I should be and what I was doing was unquestionably right. The serene clarity of such an existence, dreamed of at seven but never tried, is, I realise, something I still long for. Perhaps the void I've tried to fill with sex and love, with alcohol and drugs, with illicit romance and relentless work, perhaps this lifelong gasping vacuum is actually just hunger for this state of grace.

I close my eyes and stretch out further on the rock, arms thrown wide like Jesus on the cross, and think about my new religion.

It will be taught that there are three circles of responsibility, each of which must be satisfied if you are to live a full and happy life.

The first is responsibility to yourself. This is not selfishness, but a simple, practical matter. Buddhists say that a person should measure his or her wealth by what can be done without. But to understand what you can do without you must understand what you cannot do without. You must be accurately aware of what you need to maintain mental equilibrium. I myself require four things beyond the obvious necessities of food, sleep, and shelter. I require exercise, work, books, and perhaps most important of all, solitude. I can do without people and without love or sex – at least the kind requiring another person – for fairly extensive periods, although I'd much rather not. If I lack any of the other four, however, I rapidly sink into depression and anxiety and start to go mad. This, of course, benefits no one.

The second circle is the responsibility you have to those who you know, starting with your immediate family and friends, but expanding out to people you deal with at work, in shops, on the phone. If you use your energy and imagination to bring happiness or relief to people, then pleasure and relief will be your reward. If you constantly make any-one's life even marginally worse, or if you fail those who need you, you will be, whether you are aware of it or not, contaminated by shame and despair. All this is obvious if not necessarily easy.

Last, and most important, is the third circle. This is your responsibility to the world beyond your own direct experience. Here the result of action or inaction is seemingly invisible. Why should you care about a faceless African starving to death in a village you never heard of, and what possible effect could it have on you if you ignore his plight? Materially, none. And it is precisely this – that there is no reason to care for him – which makes it vital that you do. To neglect this distant stick-figure who shares nothing with you except his humanity, is to deny the possibility of epic humanity. To care for him, to take action for him, is, on the other hand, to confirm humanity in its grandest sense.

Before I can think more about this, I feel water dripping on me. Laurie and her friends are out. 'You wanna go back?' asks Laurie, as I remain supine on the hot, flat boulder.

'Sure,' I say, looking at her differently.

Here is a woman half my age, who, for all her theological faults, is, any way you cut it, far closer to fulfilling the obligations of her three circles than I am. In comparison to hers, my life seems ill-considered and without purpose.

The return journey is even more anxiety inducing than the one which brought me here. Climbing *up* a rock is one thing, climbing *down* another. When you go down, your head is at the wrong end. You can't see what your feet are doing and if you try, if you poke your head out, you overbalance and fall. It is a testament to my professionalism that as we walk and scramble at breakwrist speed down the rocky gully, I continue to dig and probe. I ask Laurie if she and Matt are boyfriend and girlfriend.

'No,' she says, 'just friends.'

And the cock crowed thrice ...

Finally, they return my damp, floundering body to the motel. I thank them effusively, particularly Laurie. They nod, and in that way of theirs, fade away in polite retraction. I rush inside and light a cigarette. Oh, blessed relief – survival.

I'm running out of clothes and my sneakers are filled with mud and water. I wash them in the sink and then put them out in the humid air before finding the laundry room. I dump everything into one of the machines except for a pair of shorts and a T-shirt which I'm wearing. The motel is situated between the upper points of a U-shaped road, each end of which connects to the highway. Looking out through the laundry door, I see Laurie's car turn off and slide down the road alongside the motel on the opposite side from my room. She is alone and doesn't see me. I head back toward my room, expecting her to have made the curve of the U and be arriving. She had said she would deliver a paper we had spoken of. Instead, I see her take a small offshoot from the U and pass behind another part of the motel, a new extension. I wait for her car to emerge. It does not. I wait. I can see the rear fender of her car. It's parked behind the building.

My curiosity grows. Is she concerned that to visit me alone might appear sinful and so has hidden the car and now awaits a deserted forecourt to make her dash toward me? Or is she in some kind of spiritual crisis? After a while I get in my car and drive around as if going someplace. She sits in the front seat, alone. I draw up alongside. All the windows are open.

'Hello, Laurie, what are you doing?' I ask.

And then I see another figure in the car, Matt, lying on his back on the wide front seat, his head resting on her lap. Blushing, but continuing to stoke his hair affectionately, Laurie says, 'Oh, just talking.' Matt does not sit up. I apologise and drive away.

Well, well, well. Tut tut. And so on. Not boyfriend and girlfriend, eh? I like them all the more for this. They are more filled with humanity and romance than with theology and dogma.

A short while later, Matt brings me the paper I wanted and I apologise again. He does not seem as embarrassed as Laurie did and shrugs. It's not a problem. He tells me he'll be passing through Manhattan on his way to Egypt. I won't be in town at that time, unfortunately, but I promise to get him the names of some cheap hotels and the numbers of two YMCAs. He gives me a fleeting smile and walks away.

CHAPTER TWENTY-EIGHT

A Ticket Home

The next morning when I wake up, even the air conditioning can't fight the humidity which now resembles the creationists' water canopy, except unlike that dense fog, this stuff doesn't stop five feet from the ground, it goes all the way down. Rather than go out, I decide to stay in my room and finish reading the transcript of the trial which brought me here.

Tuesday 21st July, was the eighth and last day of the trial. After the prayer, Judge Raulston said he didn't think Darrow's interrogation of Bryan had any value in determining the case and would not help a higher court decide the issue on appeal. This case was not about how God created man but about whether Scopes taught something prohibited by the state. The court was therefore expunging Bryan's testimony from the record.

Darrow stood up. 'Of course, I am not at all sure that Mr Bryan's testimony would aid the Supreme Court, or any other human being, but he testified by the hour there and I haven't got through with him yet.'

But he had. The court would not permit him to continue.

In that case, Darrow said, as he was not permitted to bring on any other witnesses and could offer no further arguments against this narrow definition of the crime, the court might as well bring in the jury and instruct it to find Scopes guilty. The defence, while still pleading not guilty, would offer no objections. Clearly the case could only be settled on appeal.

Bryan was appalled. He had been robbed! There would now be no opportunity to cross-examine Darrow, nor to make his closing arguments, which he had been working on for weeks! He stood up and complained that he had been deprived of the chance 'to answer the charges made by the counsel for the defense as to my ignorance and bigotry.'

As he was clearly about to make a speech, Darrow asked the Judge, 'Why can't he go outside on the lawn?' But the Judge permitted the old man to continue. Bryan begged the press to publish his closing arguments and also the questions he would have asked Darrow had he been given the opportunity. Darrow stood up and said loudly that he'd happily answer the questions in front of the press. In fact, why not stage a debate?

Bryan did not agree to this and rambled on, bemoaning his fate. 'I simply want to make that statement and say that I shall have to avail myself of the press without having the dignity of it being presented in the court, but I think it is hardly fair for them to bring into the limelight my views on religion and stand behind a dark lantern that throws light on other people but conceals themselves.'

Malone said that *all* of the defence lawyers would be happy to answer any questions Bryan might have in any forum he desired; but again Bryan did not take up the challenge and eventually sat down.

The jury was called in and, having received its instructions from the judge, was told by Darrow that under the circumstances it had little choice but to find a verdict of guilty and that he had no problem with this. The jury was out nine minutes and then came back with a guilty verdict at 11.23 a.m. The fine had to fall somewhere between $100 and $500. The judge decided on the minimum and set bail at $500. Both these sums were paid by the Baltimore *Evening Sun*. Scopes made a short statement saying the statute was unjust and he would continue to fight for academic freedom and it was all over but for a few polite and conciliatory speeches.

Darrow went back to Chicago. Bryan stayed on in Dayton, giving speeches and sermons, looking for a location for Bryan College, and, most importantly reworking his 15,000 word 'closing argument.'

It would indeed be his closing argument. Five days after the trial ended, he ate one of his customarily large lunches and died in the ensuing post-prandial snooze. Few newspapers published his closing speech in its entirety, it was far too long, and most didn't publish it at all.

On hearing of Bryan's death, Mencken wrote 'God aimed at Darrow, missed, and hit Bryan instead.'

The Scopes case eventually came up on appeal before the Tennessee

Supreme Court. The verdict was overturned on a technicality: the jury not the judge should have set the fine. A retrial was considered but Scopes was no longer employed by the state. Stewart, the prosecutor, let the matter drop, thus denying Darrow the chance to take the case to the Supreme Court. And that was it. The law was not repealed until 1967.

George Rappleyea, the man who brought the trial to Dayton, left town soon after it was over. He went to Canada, then to Mobile, Alabama, then New Orleans, and finally ended up in Miami. Along the way, he invented a new kind of road surface which was used on runways, and a device which improved aerial mapping cameras. During the Second World War, he was involved in a boat-building enterprise. After the war he was secretary and treasurer of a company called Marsarlis Construction. In 1947, along with Marsarlis and four other men, he was arrested for attempting to smuggle arms to British Honduras in violation of the National Firearms Act.

Rappleyea and Marsarlis served a year and a day in prison. George died in Miami in 1966 but was buried in Arlington National Cemetery where, coincidentally, the author of 'The Prince Of Peace', William Jennings Bryan, had insisted on being buried. What Rappleyea did to earn a place in this exclusive boneyard of patriots remains a mystery.

Scopes moved to Chicago, where he occasionally had dinner with Darrow and his wife. He took a postgraduate course in geology. He was still considering a return to teaching, though at the college level, when an application for a much-needed fellowship was turned down by the president of a university who wrote, 'Your name has been removed from consideration for the fellowship. As far as I'm concerned you can take your atheistic marbles and play elsewhere.' Realising his notoriety would follow him wherever he went in academic life, Scopes left college and took a job as a geologist with Gulf Oil of South America. He spent several years in Venezuela and Mexico and remained in the commercial sector until he died.

Darrow tried a couple more cases and then retired. He died in 1938.

Arthur Garfield Hays went back to his law practice in New York. He continued to take civil rights cases until his death in 1954.

Dudley Field Malone got divorced again and remarried again. For some reason, his practice began to fail and he moved west. He spent the last ten years of his life in Hollywood, where he became a character actor in the movies. He died in 1950, the same year as I was born.

I decide it's time to go home. I call Chattanooga airport and find there's only one plane I can catch today which will make the connection to New York out of Atlanta.

I have two hours to get there. I pack, check out, and start driving.

I'm going past the walking track just beyond the Chamber of Commerce – and there's Gloria! Of course! Because I'm a week late for the re-enactment, *she's* down here for her friends' wedding. At this precise revelatory moment there's a crack of thunder, the canopy bursts, huge drops of rain begin to fall, and Gloria's determined march turns into an ungainly canter away from the highway. I realise I don't have time to give chase and still make my plane.

A minute later, the rain is so heavy I'm blind if my speed exceeds twenty-five miles an hour. A minute after that, I don't need whatever shoddy American car I've rented, I need an ark. I'm crawling along at ten miles an hour, the windows are misted up, and I'm low on gas. This continues for an hour.

When I finally arrive at the outskirts of Chattanooga, I get lost. I go on one highway and then another. I get off and get back on again. The rain, which has remained dense for the last forty miles, suddenly dwindles to a mere storm. Looking around in growing panic for a sign directing me to the airport, I see a huge jointed truck start to skid. The long trailer behind it swings sideways, lunges into the cab and launches it over a cliff. A half second later the rear of the trailer tilts up at the back, and the whole rig plunges over and disappears from sight.

As if in shock, all traffic instantly stops.

To be utterly cold about it, there is no need to stop. There is no obstruction, the truck is *gone*; but still everyone has to slow down and gawk in horror at the ripped barrier. One or two people park on the hard shoulder, venture out into the rain, and look down at whatever lies below as if they might actually do something.

I now have twenty minutes to get to the airport, give back the car, be issued a ticket, find the gate, and hurtle down the tube into the plane. And yet I cannot hurry because if anything happens, if I crash or get caught speeding, I'm out of Sneed and Rocky's jurisdiction and could easily face jail time. I lean out my window into the rain and yell at someone. 'Which way's the airport?' and they tell me it's the next exit. 'How far?' 'About one mile!'

Terrific, except the traffic is moving at one mile an hour, and even with my poor mathematical ability, I can figure out that if nothing changes ... well, it's going to take me a while to reach the exit.

Suddenly, my desire to be home becomes intense.

I want to sleep in my own bed, have a choice of books to hand, and feel the plaque-removing supersonic buzz of my own supersonic toothbrush. I want to put on my Issey Miyake suit and drive my big black Japanese Sport Utility Vehicle downtown to eat sushi at Nobu and drink sake. I want to stand despised among the wives of stockbrokers, waiting for my beloved daughter to emerge from her overpriced school in her little green uniform. I want to watch foreign films and eat fresh vegetables not cooked in batter. Then there is the matter of my wife, with her conviction and her wide smile and her round Brazilian buttocks.

I do have a life, you see, this is what I realise – flawed, perhaps, but interesting and profoundly colourful in its way. What I do not have is gas. The warning light has been on for thirty minutes and the needle is way below zero. I get on the hard shoulder and speed toward the exit, grimacing inarticulate excuses, and suddenly everything speeds up.

I'm on an empty road, park in an empty lot, throw my keys into a waiting slot, pick up a ticket from a grinning uniform, dart through the airport, arrive at a gaping gate, check in, fly down the tube, sit steaming on an empty plane, find myself in Atlanta leaning against a stucco column talking to a buffed-out, Miami-based female coach and physical therapist (her lips forever compressed by exertion) whose father is in the CIA, (a cold individual, she tells me) and soon am sitting on the New York plane beside a man in a grey suit, and I'm tired and don't want to talk to anyone, but when he speaks to the stewardess he's English, so I look at his boarding pass, which is on the armrest between us, and see his name is Chapman and think, okay, one more conversation before going back into my little room to type for a year.

Chapman lives in New York and owns a factory near Atlanta which recycles human skeletons. He tells me the skeletons are boiled and washed before being turned into screws which are then used to repair broken bones. The screws, unlike metal pins, fuse with the bones and the healing process is more complete.

So I flew south with a woman who grows flowers in Mexico and fly home with a Chapman who mills bones in Georgia. Had I been on time for the re-enactment I would never have met either.

CHAPTER TWENTY-NINE

92760

When Bryan died, everyone said it was Darrow who killed him. 'He died of a broken heart,' someone said.

'Broken heart nothing,' Darrow responded, 'he died of a busted belly.'

But I think it's possible Malone and Darrow did in fact kill him. The line holds, and then it holds no longer. A happy man gets hit by a car and lives. A sad man stubs his toe, it gets infected, and he's gone. If Bryan's faith had been holding him together all this time, shoring up the line, and suddenly his faith was shaken, faith not only in himself, in his sense of who he was, but also in the book he had relied on all his life, who knows what that might do?

I've always thought it would be fun to write a scene where someone is receiving a massage and dies. The masseur doesn't notice and keeps on massaging the corpse until it's time to get paid. Whenever I have a massage I always ask the masseur or masseuse if this has ever happened to them. One time I got a qualified yes. The masseur had been called by someone whose lover had AIDS and was dying. The man wanted to die, the pain was so intense, but he couldn't let go. Would the masseur go there and massage him so he'd relax and die?

He did and he did.

I remember my mother. One week she was alive, sitting up on the hospital bed, commenting humorously on the other patients in the ward. A week later, she was dead.

After she found out my father was in love with someone else, she no doubt longed to kick him out; but she could not. It was too late. She was too sick and she needed him. She insisted, however, that she didn't care: if Cecil wanted to see his lover, fine, what was it to her?

My father took her at her word, but after a while her pain became so visible and so profound, he could not endure it and ended the relation-

312

ship. Perhaps more humiliated by this than by the affair itself, she lashed out and wrote an anonymous letter to the woman's husband. The pain was amplified. My father settled back into his life with my mother. Although he had chosen to remain with her she could not let the matter rest. Often when he was thinking of nothing in particular, she would say, in her typically schoolgirl fashion, 'You're pining for the love of your life, aren't you?' and no assurances to the contrary would pacify her.

Soon it was discovered she had cancer. Cecil was stoic, cheerful, decent. She became quieter. They still had things in common, the children, their intelligence, the *Times* crossword puzzle, a few old friends, and their shared contempt – part snobbery, mostly conviction – for Margaret Thatcher and her gang of arrivistes and bullies. At times I believe they were even happy in a curious way, it was hard to tell. One day, Hugh, her closest brother, came to visit her. By now his wife, Jean, had died. In the course of discussing their lives, Hugh said, 'Well, it's just most unfortunate that you married the wrong man.'

My sister, Sarah, found Clare crying many hours later. How could he say such a thing?

When everyone but my father realised she was going to die before too long, she came to visit me in America. A friend of mine lent me his house in New Hampshire and we drove around the countryside, she, my father, my wife, and my daughter. For some reason, he arrived later than she, so we were alone with her for a day or so. When she spoke to my father on the phone, they bickered, but on the night he was due to arrive she was concerned that everything be the way he liked it, the bed, the reading light, his pillow. For all the pain they had caused each other, a grudging admiration existed between them, a wry, enduring affection.

Alcohol and cigarettes attacked one part of her body after another and limbs and organs began to concede defeat – or victory? Finally an artery in her leg put up a barricade, a clot, and said, no more blood shall pass through here. Nothing would dissolve this insultingly small challenge and giving the entire leg its independence was the only alternative. Clare knew the empire of her flesh was not long for the map and told my brother, Francis, there would be no secession. In the end, her opinion was irrelevant. The doctors were sure she wouldn't survive the operation.

They injected her with something to combat the pain. When given the choice of being washed by a nurse or my father, she chose my father. He diligently sponged her down and tucked her in. They injected her again. She asked him to hold her hand.

He said to her, 'You know I do love you.'

She turned and looked at him and said, 'I know.'

A few minutes later she slipped into unconsciousness. My father sat beside her, unable to let go of her hand athough he knew she could no longer feel his steady grip. After about five hours, she died.

And he *did* love her. We all loved her. No amount of abuse, no decades of anger or frustration – nothing she could do – and she did and said some terrible things to all of us – could stop us loving her. Maybe it was because the melancholy ten-year-old child was always so visible, peeking out, afraid, through the despairing alcoholic eyes of the sixty-year-old woman. The yo-yo she brought with her the day she met my father was not an affectation but symbol of a desire not to grow up. And, in the most unsatisfactory way, she never did; she never controlled her own life and never used her brilliant mind. It was tragic, this fear, this resolute and fatal reserve, this misplaced pride: gulping down her counterproductive medicines of gin and cider, she stumbled alone, an obstinate child, through the desert of her mental illness. Anything was preferable to the humiliation of admitting weakness to a stranger.

My relationship with her had worsened over the years. I adored her because she was funny and morbid and a rogue, but in the last decade no real relationship was possible because everything was distorted either by alcohol or by its absence, by viciously expressed alcoholic despair, or by guilt and craving. I knew too much of what it was to be a drunk and nothing of what it was to be her. I watched her sink into inebriated gloom, eyes closed, moaning in excessive sorrow at the state of the world or at the awfulness of some acquaintance. I knew from my own researches that alcohol was a depressant. If only she would stop it, even for a month, I thought, maybe she could muster sufficient optimism to ask for help, and then perhaps, at last, she could retrieve some final remnants of happiness. I lived in America. All things were possible. I could not stand by and watch her misery and not intrude.

So I broke the code of silence. I'd call her on the phone and say, 'Why don't you go to AA? Don't you realise how much happier you would be if you'd just get this out of your system?' I wrote long impassioned letters, evangelical and blunt. I thought I could save her life and in the effort lost her affection. Once the most loved son (or so I thought), I now became 'The Hollywood Mauler,' a clumsy, insensitive scold.

One day my father called me. He couldn't say for sure, but it seemed to him she might not last much longer. I should consider coming over to England. *Consenting Adults* was being edited. I had work and was being offered still more. For the first time in forty years, I was the good schoolboy, good reports, almost a prefect. I was terrified that if I was absent even for a few days, I'd get found out, the momentum would be lost, and I'd flounder backward into obscurity and debt.

Denise told me to pack and leave. My relationship with my mother was so powerful and confused, I could not allow myself to miss this last opportunity.

I flew out the next day.

As a would-be doctor and a Socialist Clare had an absolute commitment to the National Health system. When it worked, as it had when we were children, it was a system that benefited all and neglected none. By the time my mother needed it, it had been starved and beaten by a succession of callous Conservative governments, elitist scum who then threw up their hands and cried, 'It's just not working!' and anyone with money was barging to the front of the line, elbowing back the less fortunate to snag a place on the beleaguered operating table. But not my mother. Die first.

Which she did. She was in a large public ward. Though I've seen far worse under the privatised American system, it was a dismal place none the less. I went out and bought her an expensive miniature TV to distract her from her death. For some reason it wouldn't function in the hospital and anyway it embarrassed her. When I came the following day, it was hidden away.

I stayed for three days. Whenever I could, I went and sat with her. Sometimes my sister was there, now living and working in Cambridge, or one of my brothers. Most often I was alone with her or with my father. There were many things I wanted to talk to her about but I could not bring myself to do so. I wanted to thank her. I wanted to tell her I knew about Francis and who his real father was. I wanted to tell her that

315

no matter what pain she had caused me it was outweighed by love and that in surviving both I had become who I was, good and bad, and that that was okay. I wanted to tell her I forgave her. I wanted to hear her say she loved me and that she was not angry about my letters. Perhaps I would have liked her to apologise or explain. But her pride forbade any show of sentimentality or defeat and no revelations were forthcoming. If I extended so much as a toe into the unacceptable territory of maudlin reflection, she sniffed and looked away. There would be no deathbed confessions here, no conversions, no apologies. Death tiptoed through the ward with long exaggerated steps, sometimes for amusement pouncing forward, only to freeze and step back, laughing at the shocked face upon the pillow. Acutely aware of this fatal pantomime – aware of little else, in fact – I could not acknowledge it. My mother and I pretended to chat without concern while in the background the orchestra tuned up for a Requiem Mass.

Soon, I had to return to Los Angeles, to my own struggle for survival. When I went to say goodbye, I hid my suitcase behind a counter – let her not see the reality of my departure – and then walked over to her, half sitting on her mechanical bed, a Plexiglas oxygen mask pressed to her face. Even harder to bear than the thought of her physical pain, was the fear I could see in her eyes above the mask, an anxiety which at any moment seemed as if it might become a look of horror. I had seen this same expression when she was trying not to drink. She did not share with anyone what it was she was afraid of then, nor would she confide in anyone now. Did she know this was the last time she would ever see her eldest son? She, who had accompanied me, blubbering with fear, to the doctor for inoculations or to the dentist for fillings, now faced the terror of death without me. I was needed by my own life, the life she gave me.

I sat on one side of the bed, my father on the other. They talked inconsequentially, my father with his ever-practical cheerfulness. Her large breasts, the same ones that fed me forty years before, were visible through a gap in her pyjamas.

Eventually, I said determinedly, with my own mendacious brand of cheeriness, 'Look, I have to go. Get better and then it's back to Barrington and I'll come and visit you there very soon.'

I kissed her and slunk off to retrieve my bag. Unfortunately, I had

316

miscalculated the angle and she could see me from her vantage point in the large ward; but she showed scant interest.

I waved. I clenched my fist. And left.

Next time I saw her she was in a small container the size of a milk carton and I was driving her home.

On my return to Los Angeles, I wrote her a letter, thanking her for all she'd given me, for her love, and hoping she would soon go home (to die was the implication). It was an unusually explicit letter for our family, almost American you might say. A day or two later, my father called again. The clot in her leg was going to kill her very soon.

That afternoon in Los Angeles, the jury came back in the trial of a group of white cops who had beaten a black suspect, Rodney King, insensible and were caught on video. The cops were found not guilty and LA was suddenly torn by riots. I waited a day, experiencing the feeling of a city under siege, then figured I could sneak out unnoticed. I flew to England the following night with Denise and Anna Bella, the three of us looking down at the city to marvel at the idiocy of blacks burning their own neighbourhoods to protest white violence.

My youngest brother, Ludovic, met us at Heathrow Airport the following morning. He sidled up in the pervasive chill of sour tobacco smoke and murmured, 'She's dead.'

'Oh,' I said, 'thank God.'

During the last years of her life I had often wished for this. Her pain was so palpable, the despair and bitterness, the sound of her voice when I would call too late in the day. What was the point in living if living was so utterly devoid of pleasure? And then there was the tension: always waiting for the call – she's fallen downstairs, she's broken her neck … The family was in orbit around her sorrow.

We got in the car and started along the drab motorway home. I became almost feverish in my relief. I'd been expecting her death since I was a child. Not that I didn't love her. I loved her. I loved my mumma, my mamae as they say in Brazil, my short, sad Shrubby Seablight. I loved her deeply, but with such overwhelming pain. Her depression was an affront to love, shrapnel from the womb, a long, bending test of love, and now the test was over.

By the time we got home, my father was in a frenzy of organisation, as if his talent for this would enable him to dodge the complex emotional consequences of her life and death. In the afternoon, Denise and I were sent into Cambridge to buy envelopes for the invitations to the funeral. My sister, Sarah, gave me specific instructions. A number and a letter designating the size. We parked the car and walked to a stationery shop called Rymans; but when I saw the size of the envelopes they seemed too large. I asked the woman who worked there if I could use a phone to check.

'I'm afraid that's not company policy.'

I explained I was trying to organise my mother's funeral. It was a local call. It would only take a few seconds. I would happily pay. The face pinched into itself like a fist. A sympathetic look but a firm no. If the envelopes were the wrong size I could bring them back. I told the woman I had arrived from Los Angeles that morning. I was very tired. My mother died only last night. If the envelopes were wrong, I'd have to drive out to the village and then come back. It would take an hour. 'Please ...'

'I'm sorry.'

There was the phone, I could see it on the wall. I was insistent. The woman, at first only wilfully obedient and correct, now looked up at me with obstinate trepidation. I insisted on seeing the manager. A balding man with a wretched swipe of hair pasted across his oily dome came hurrying up the stairs. Mr Filz.

Mr Filz seemed angry. 'It's not company policy to allow customers to use the phone.'

I began what was to be a series of questions.

'What harm could it do?'

'That's not the point. It's company policy not to let people use the phone and I'm the manager.'

'I understand that but ...'

Before I could develop a logical argument (did he think the man who came up with this policy was thinking of this particular case?) Denise self-detonated. Her face red with fury, she started screaming at him. How dare he behave like this? What kind of a man was he anyway? Didn't he have a heart? Is this what it meant to be English?!

I studied her, thinking her next move would probably be to start throwing things. Instead, she threatened to walk out. Checking that

318

nothing impeded a swift retreat back into the basement, Filz gestured encouragingly toward the front door. I have no appetite for physical violence. I went to pay for the envelopes.

When we got back, the village vicar was at the table, the greedy priest scrabbling at the atheists in their grief. All we wanted was to use the church, the only building large enough in the village to accommodate all those who wanted to bid the reprobate goodbye.

He was a limp little man with damp, protruding eyes and a weak chin. 'Are tears being shed?' he asked solicitously, as if dealing with cretins.

When, just to bait him, I brought up some larger issue of faith, I think it was to do with the obvious inefficacy of prayer – the poor and miserable seem to do it most and get least – he hesitated and then looked up at me.

'Discuss? But not now?' he smiled, rubbing his hands together.

Trying to comfort us in advance for the gruesome peculiarities of the crematorium (or 'The Crem' as he referred to it affectionately) he said, 'The coffin will be to one side. The curtains will come around, but you must realise, she's not there.'

'Where is she then?' I asked, genuinely surprised, thinking, Why burn an empty coffin? and only when it was explained did I realise he was talking about her 'spirit'.

Unfailingly polite, but probably somewhat condescending, we began to argue every detail of the service in a desperate attempt to keep religion to a minimum. We wanted my brother Francis' father-in-law, also a vicar but one who knew and liked my mother, to take charge of the whole thing; but the grasping and insensitive local would not relinquish power.

'Of course I'm delighted that Reverend Shiress will be involved, but this is my service.' On the subject of additional prayers (and there were we attempting *subtraction*), he said, 'I like to personalise, so instead of saying, "Dearly beloved who has gone beyond", I like to say, "Dearly beloved *Clare* who has gone beyond." '

Soon it became apparent he was on a fishing expedition, in search of a character to feed into his personalising machine.

'Who was this woman?'

We should have said, 'Fuck off,' instead we merely shrugged. Who knew?

'Was she a happy woman?'

'No, she wasn't.'

'A good woman?'

A laugh and then, 'Well, yes and no.'

We really couldn't help him – she was a mystery to us, irreducible by cliché – nor were we inclined to yield to his authority as consoler. There were details to be organised, that was all. We wanted one thing, he another, and even in our sorrow we would not quite give in and, in spite of our sorrow, nor would he.

There was an argument over who should play the organ. K, my parents' oldest friend, the woman who had introduced them, had a son-in-law who was a professional pianist and organist. Along with two of her children, he was to play a piece of classical music. We suggested he should stay on the organ and play the music which would accompany us out of the church. No, he wouldn't have that. One piece of music from outsiders, fine, but the official (the official!) organist should have the honour of the finale.

My father, now thoroughly irritated, decided he would try and get 'The Red Flag' as the last piece of music in honour of my mother's left-leaning politics. In its original form it's called 'Tannenbaum' and is a traditional German song about fir trees. Referring to it as such, he slid it past the ignorant churchman, and finally we won the battle for the second half of the service.

'The Church has swallowed whole nations and the question of indigestion has never arisen,' says Mephistopheles in *Faust*. This was more like a ferret nibbling at a wounded rabbit cornered in a dark hole; this was the petty exercise of power by a small man, but underneath it lay the blind, resolute lust of the Church: here were atheists in mourning, here was an opportunity. To hell with common decency or compassion, make the sale, bend the will. It was as tough a negotiation as I've ever seen in Hollywood.

Atheist though I was, I would occasionally imagine my mother looking down on me. One time I went out to the garage. There was her tiny Mini Minor, versions of which she had driven since I was a child. To my amazement, I found myself patting the roof affectionately and speaking to her, 'Oh, mumma, I do miss you,' then I stepped back, embarrassed at what the old cynic would think of me if indeed she was above.

Sometimes after a night of drinking, my mother would shuffle off to bed, leaving her children behind, stunned by the cruelty of her despair. Often we would then discuss the conundrum of her alcoholism, and get ferociously drunk.

Now she had shuffled off into death and the tradition continued.

My father went and got some old photographs. In every one of them my mother wore the same look of melancholy alienation. So sad did she look in one or two, you might think she was in mourning or deranged. A group photograph taken in St Cast, the French town where we often spent our summer vacations, showed everyone sitting on the steps of the house, Clare on the top, separate from Cecil, right in the corner of the frame looking out as if meditating on some loss. What was she thinking? Was she thinking of her dead brother? Or of a lover?

After a few hours of this, during which many amusing memories were spoken of – occasions when her mordant wit, her eccentricity, her gift for laying into pomposity and affectation were at their most extreme or endearing – we started to discuss the disposal of the ashes. By this time, everyone had drunk a lot. Ludovic, who now owned his own computer-training company in Cambridge, and Sarah, employed in a semi-diplomatic position with the Franco-British Council, were eerily reasonable and diplomatic. My father moderated cheerfully, but you could tell his mind was elsewhere. Francis, meanwhile, my mother's son by Peter, now a photographer with two children, was making bizarre faces and speaking in an odd voice. I understood his pain, his more than anyone's, but I didn't want to talk about my mother's ashes with a drunk. I suggested we wait a year and bury them then. The idea was eagerly embraced by all, I suspect for the same reason, and then abandoned a short time later for reasons I cannot now remember.

I thought my mother's death would bring us closer. I thought, in a way, she was an impediment. Now, sitting in her house, I began to see how central she was to the whole scheme. She may have been an imploding sun, but she was the centre of our small universe. Our concern for her was the means by which we expressed our love for each other. Without her, there was no gravity.

I went to bed depressed.

The next day we burned her in a dismal crematorium. You would think that even if you set out to build the most hideous building on earth, somehow, by some accident, one brick, one tile, a *doorknob* ... *something*, would retain some element of beauty. But no. Next to a motorway, the squat, degenerate building hugged the ground, governmental, sullen, resolute in its ugliness.

The village vicar had the nerve to produce ... an egg. He held it up between his unworked hands.

'This is an egg, but it is not an egg. It looks like an egg, but in fact it is an egg shell. It's hollow. So it is with Clare. Her body lies over there behind the curtains, but Clare, the Clare whom we all knew' (liar, he never knew her) 'has gone to heaven ...'

Oh, you *fucker!* How dare you! Shut up before I strangle you! But no ... on he went, the petty egomaniac pissing a torrent of banal clichés on the individuality of my mother, a one-size-fits-all, generic, unisex eulogy ... on and on, taking up the rag of who she never was and twisting it until the last drips of meaning had been wrung from it and nothing was left but the municipal stink of false sanctity.

The efficient whirr of machinery, and she was ashes.

Another day passed, a Sunday. The family was together, all the children, a rare thing this, and an almost festive air prevailed.

On Monday morning, it was my job to go into town and collect the ashes and have them back before the memorial service at the church. She was not to be buried there, but up in an abandoned graveyard that lay on our land, and still we had not decided when to dig her in; best therefore to have her handy. Off I drove, through the countryside, past St Anne's Prep School, and up to a gaunt, dark-reddish funeral home in a grim section of the town: run by the Co-op, some quasi-Socialist outfit, I believe, and appropriately utilitarian. I parked outside, went in. A gloomy, unprepossessing lobby indistinguishable from any other administrative gape, except for an overwhelming smell of shit ... A Mr Theobold, more flustered than funereal, produced the container, a cardboard box large enough to contain a bottle of port; but, when I took hold of it, heavier than port. On the box, a label:

Name of Deceased, Ruth, Clare Chapman; No. of Cremation 92760. Date of Cremation 8\5\92. Remarks: Cambs – Co-op.

Poetic.

I needed to pee so badly I decided I had to brave the toilet even though it must, I figured, have recently exploded. Theobold ushered me through a flap in the counter and directed me toward the rear. Entering the toilet, I was surprised to note that it was not the source of the smell. In fact, it smelt better in here than anywhere else. Where then did this overwhelming stench come from? I would soon find out. When I came back into the lobby, I could see Mr Theobold off to one side, furiously at work with an air-freshener, laying down a sickly scent on some previously unseen coffins, and only then did I realise that what I had smelt was the smell of death.

It was Monday, first thing in the morning. A couple of dead 'uns had been lying up here over the weekend and the smell of their decaying flesh had, I supposed, been augmented by some last-meal leakage. Rotting fried eggs and baked beans on toast ...

'Would you like a cup of tea now, dear? Hello? I said would you like a ...?'

Carrying the carton, I walked out to the car and headed for the boot. But no! I could not put my mother in there. So I took her with me into the car. I thought of laying her on the floor in the back, but that too seemed somehow disrespectful, so I let her sit next to me, upright, all strapped in and safe in the passenger seat. How many times had she rescued me from prep school and driven me home, as helpless as this, to lie at home in bed, pretending to be sick, listening to the buzz of flies circling the room and the distant hum of a vacuum cleaner?

I was relieved to get her out of the funeral parlour, felt, in fact, almost heroic: I was rescuing her from the bureaucratic aspects of death, the hospital, the crematorium, the funeral home, and was returning her to a place where, in spite of herself, she was loved. Every now and then I would reach across and pat the carton with my hand and say, 'Okay, mumma, okay ... I'm taking you back to Barrington. That's where you belong. You're going home.'

Back at the house, I took her upstairs to the spare bedroom. In the final year of her life she had moved in here, for medical and emotional reasons, and this was where I was now staying. Ludovic stormed in to get dressed for the memorial service. He looked around at the room and said, 'This is kind of spooky, isn't it?'

'Spookier than you think,' I said, and nodded at the carton reclining on the bed.

The family walked up the lane together, hungover in the bright day, toward the village church. Many, many cars. A woman walking out the churchyard gate in tears, waved at us that she could not go in. Her husband, Alf, a friend of mine whom I'd worked with in my father's factory (he taught me the song, 'Balls to your Auntie, arse against the wall!' which we would sing loudly together when things got dull) had died only a few weeks ago and the memory of his funeral was too recent. Alf too?! I didn't know.

We walked in and I could recognise no one. It turned out that almost everyone from my father's factory had come, and most whom I had known when I worked there, were either dead or had moved away. We sat at the front, myself, Denise and Anna Bella, and Francis and his wife Gilly, daughter of the imported vicar. My father was nearby, completely in control and dignified. I thought I'd be able to handle myself with equal aplomb and I did for about three minutes, until the first hymn, 'All Things Bright And Beautiful'.

I read the words but could not sing. Tears stung my sinuses as I was thrown by memory, a sudden surge of nostalgia for my lost past, for Christmases at Mrs Marshall's school at Kingston village, the Harvest Festival in autumn, my young mother, elegant and alive in her bright summer frocks. Next to me, Gilly sang with wonderful pure certainty, provoking further recollections of lost and squandered innocence.

My uncle's boyfriend of over forty years, as much an uncle to me as any other, gave his speech. My daughter began to wriggle and complain, death no damper to the incessant itch of childish energy, begging for cheese brought by Gilly, kicking her feet against the pew. I kept whispering in her ear, 'I'm begging you, please, please, please be good. My mother has died and I'm very sad. Please, please be good.' Who cared? Not her and rightly so: it was life that mattered – action, kicking, cheese.

The trio played Bach's poignant Double Violin Concerto in D Minor. More tears, more nose-blowing into a handkerchief stolen from my father.

The local vicar performed (at least, no eggs this time) and our vicar followed, the latter so sure of the idea of renewal (life is like a dry seed, heaven is the flower) that it was almost comforting. The petty vicar smiled enviously. At last we were all singing 'Jerusalem' and only a blessing remained before we filed out to the subtle strains of 'The Red Flag'.

Outside, there were many people to speak to. An old employee of my father's who built the garden wall and got so drunk one Christmas party that he could not ride his bike home. An architect who used to come for drinks on Sunday morning until such parties became impossible.

Now, as we started home along the village green, I looked ahead and saw my father walking beside Peter, his ex-business partner, my mother's great love, father to my brother. Two distinguished, handsome men, my father, head held high, alert, polite, the other still with the upright, sprightly bearing of a runner.

By the time we got home there were already fifty to sixty people in the house, half of whom I didn't know, some whom I knew quite well, and a good ten or so I hadn't seen for twenty years, including Mrs Marshall, my primary school teacher, the only good teacher I ever had, aged almost eighty now, but as bright as ever. I wanted to sit beside her and recall my childhood, but somehow when I tried to talk to her, my attention skidded away and all that remained was a sense of unease.

Whatever this occasion was, it didn't have the vigour of a wake or the flamboyance of even more primitive ceremonies where there is wailing and tears. No songs, no drama, no ceremony. I was emotionally exhausted, unsatisfied. My mourning lay out in the future, waiting for me, waiting until we could all be alone together: me, my memories of her, and the infinite sadness of her final absence. My brothers drank heavily. Ludovic put on a hat and dark glasses so he looked like a gangster and shouted across the room. Once, as I crossed in front of him, he grabbed my chest and pinched me. 'Don't be so boring! Have a drink!'

I had a drink. I remained boring. I had another. Nothing happened. No matter how much I drank, I remained sober. Or rather, as I drank, and drank a lot, I sidestepped the glow of intoxication and simply became hungover.

Slowly the thing wound down. Anna Bella met a boy named Max

and they sat on a wall, talking, then went over into the barn to play. Suddenly, there was a scream and Max came rushing across the yard:

'Anna Bella! She's dying! She's dying!'

From behind the barn I could hear her screaming. I imagined some accident involving the sewage disposal system or a fall from the thatched roof which I often used to climb up as a child. Soon, however, it became apparent she had simply fallen into some stinging nettles. We took her, howling, into the sitting room and covered her with calamine lotion. We spent most of the rest of the day in here, I feeding the fire, my wife caring for the kids, both of us avoiding the hilarity in the back of the house.

When I was my daughter's age or younger I discovered a place further down the river where girls went to swim in the summer. Climbing a tree, I hid myself on one of the branches and waited. When they finally came, I watched them change. Little pink bodies against the green grass and the slow brown river. Unfortunately, as one floated on her back, she saw me and they all came out of the water. I jumped out of the tree and started to run, but they brought me down like a pack of beagles. It was a hot day and I was wearing only shorts. Two of them held me while a third used a towel to pick some nettles. They then beat me with them.

The itch – and I was used to itches – was comprehensive and extreme. I was *encased* in itch. I ran back to the house, shrieking with pain, and my mother plunged me into a calamine bath. She was at her best at times like this, crises rousing her from despair and giving her a sense of purpose. She despised illness, but dealt with it efficiently and, at least in my case, kindly. Hours passed before my body recovered and the blisters subsided. She sat by the bath and talked to me. The house was very quiet.

Of all the ceremonies, the burying of the ashes was the one I cared about most. No vicars, no religion – her ashes, our land. I had thought of it (and, to be fair, not told anyone) as being just me, my father and my brothers and sister. I wanted one thing where those of us who had had to tolerate her for thirty to fifty years (and love her) were alone with her, simply. We five knew her so much better than anyone else, gave so much more to her, took so much more from her, were hurt by her, formed and deformed by her ... and yet, in the end, it was not to be. In drunken bonhomie, ex-wives, children, old friends, new friends, all were invited as if to the launching of a boat.

I went upstairs to the large bathroom where my mother had sat next to me as I recovered from my nettle-beating. I lay on the floor and put my fingers in my ears and tried to remember that quiet summer afternoon. Soon, however, it was time to bury her, and down I trudged to find everyone gathered outside the front door, ready to go. By now ex-wives were sloppily embracing new wives. Boredom and indifference had been subsumed by love. Promises were being made of eternal friendship. The meek had become bold and the bold maudlin.

The alcoholic mother who died of lung cancer was to be buried by her drunk children between cigarettes. Evolution, bullshit. We all stumbled up to the abandoned graveyard, one with the carton, another with a trowel.

In spite of everything leading up to this moment, there was something so sad about the little pile of ashes – my mother! – being poured out of the plastic inner container into the ground – that's all that's left of her!? – that when Francis started to cry, so did I. In went the ashes, into the little hole, and then a small plant – more plastic here around the roots – was put on top and the earth was tamped down. My uncle's boyfriend, the most gentle and considerate of men, gave me a melancholy look and hugged me. I hugged my wife and Francis – and it was over. I cannot remember if Ludovic, who, as the youngest, had suffered most from her alcoholism, or Sarah, who was closest to her at the end, cried or not. My father did not cry, I remember that. He cannot cry, he says. It's something to do with school or the war or being English at a certain time.

All funeral-related wounds healed and my sister and my brothers and I speak to each other frequently and with affection. For all my faults, they are my allies in all matters and I am theirs. We live different lives in different parts of the world but share an identically sardonic sense of humour. In part this is inherited from our mother who despised hypocrisy and affectation and found the desire for respectability hilarious. And if there is something sad in our assumption that people don't lead the lives they pretend to, it is also true that we tend to be more tolerant and forgiving than those who have suffered less.

After a while, the plant above my mother's ashes, a lilac tree, withered and died. A new plant was put in and she's still down there, her ashes filtered ever deeper by rain – not her, you understand, the shell not the egg. No, she's gone, not here, departed. And seven years after her death, I still miss her. Extraordinarily so. I thought I'd get over this, but no. I miss her letters, written at such cost in her deceptively clear and optimistic hand. I miss watching her demolish pomposity with a single lazy flick of her barbed tongue. I miss her anecdotes, and – always humour – I miss the comedy which can only be fully appreciated by someone who has known you since birth.

'This boy is allergic to life.'

We all failed her completely. She was a woman with a disease and none of us could force her to a doctor. Intolerably stubborn and self-destructive as she was, at least once a week, I think, 'I wish she was here so I could tell her about …'

Then, in spite of my beliefs or lack of them, I say, 'Still thinking of you, mama, and all is forgiven.' Because all *is* forgiven. After all, if I can't forgive her, how can my child forgive me for whatever my sins are?

CHAPTER THIRTY

'Saint Matthew's Epilogue'

When I got back to New York, I called Carter Johnson, the pastor, to ask him some further questions about Calvinism.

'No, let me ask *you* a question,' he interrupted in a suspicious tone. 'Who are you? Meaning: there is no Matthew Chapman in New York.'

I said, 'I beg your pardon?'

He said, 'Matthew, I've looked you up on the internet, can't get an e-mail address, can't get a Matthew Chapman in the phone book. Are you actually Matthew Chapman?'

'Yes. Why do you ask?'

'Well, the reason I ask is that I tried to look you up – you can look up almost anybody via the internet – and I couldn't find a Matthew Chapman in New York at all. I had the address, did a search. Nothing. *Nothing.*'

Here was an odd twist: a man who believed in God, but not in Matthew Chapman.

When I first went down to Dayton, I was stretched to the limit. When I missed the re-enactment a month later, something snapped. Contrary to what Pastor Johnson believed, I still existed, but my journey, begun almost as a lark, had changed me. The Matthew Chapman who went south in June was not the same Matthew Chapman who returned in July.

I came to understand, not just intellectually but emotionally, that faith is often all that holds a person together. When I think about my mother, I must conclude that had she been a believer, had she been in the habit of faith rather than cynicism, she might easily have stopped drinking and lived a happier life. Considering faith's poignant causes rather than the often irritating details of its consequences, I began to see just how cruel my attack on Denise's faith had been.

There was a period in our marriage when we almost broke up

because of our philosophical differences. Tennessee made me look at her faith with kinder eyes and at my lack of it with more suspicion. Was it an accident, I began to ask myself, that I, a sceptic and an atheist, married Denise, a woman of a thousand faiths? Could it be that I unconsciously hope that even though I have no faith, I can benefit from hers? A friend of mine says, as a comment on our different characters, that if you flush the toilet at one end of our house it flushes clockwise, while if you flush it at the other, it flushes counter-clockwise. I'm not so sure. Sometimes I think Denise has so much more certainty than I do that while her toilet flushes clockwise, mine just splashes around and doesn't flush at all.

After thirteen years, our religious views remain in conflict, but our experience of life begins to merge. As individuals we are the same; as a couple we have become something else, an unlikely amalgam, the best product of which is Anna Bella, our daughter, half Brazilian, half English, and totally American – half Denise, half me, and wholly herself. Denise and I have survived poverty, wealth, success, failure, a near plane crash in Brazil, the murder of her sister, riots, earthquakes, the last years and death of my mother, and perhaps most remarkably, our violent arguments. As I seem to need her in my life to apply the plunger of her conviction to the turbulence of my uncertainty, I am learning how to keep my mouth shut.

Looking at my life objectively, I can see there is some nobility in it. I work hard to provide my daughter with everything she might need to fight her way into an interesting and relevant life; against the odds, I have written some beautiful scripts, two or three of which might yet get made; and I do my best to be kind and fair to everyone I meet. If you put who I am and what I do on a scale, the good would far outweigh the bad.

But still something is missing.

'That life is worth living,' wrote the philosopher, George Santayana, 'is the most necessary of assumptions, and, were it not assumed, the most impossible of conclusions.' For twenty-five years I have worked for myself. During this time no one has told me when to wake up or when to go to bed, nor how many hours to work in between. I have invented a set of rituals by which I trick myself into a state of calm productivity. But I have not learned how to trick myself into a state of philosophical calm. In a letter Laurie writes me after I have returned to Manhattan, she describes how faith gives her 'peace of mind not dependent on external circumstances,' and 'a quiet, deep certainty.'

I came back from Dayton with even less certainty than I had when I went. As much as I was touched and inspired by Laurie, the preachers, whose faith seemed fanatical in its conviction, cruel in its form, and useless in its effect, ultimately disgusted me. If I went down an atheist, I came back an agnostic, refusing to share with these men the arrogance of any conviction in a matter so clearly unproveable either way.

In his autobiography, Darwin, who also called himself an agnostic, wrote that the magnificence of the universe almost forces one to conclude that God exists. However, he continued, 'can the mind of man, which has, as I fully believe, been developed from a mind as low as that possessed by the lowest animal, be trusted when it draws such grand conclusions?' He goes on to say that the problem is further compounded by 'the probability that the constant inculcation in a belief in God on the minds of children has produced so strong and perhaps inherited effect on their brains, that it may now be as difficult for them to throw off their belief in God, as for a monkey to throw off its instinctive fear and hatred of a snake.'

For this monkey at least, he's right. There is a saying in Brazil, 'I do not believe in witches – but that they exist is beyond question.' With this in mind, I often find myself talking to my dead mother, sometimes out loud, and imagining her in a place where she has at last found happiness. The comforting, childlike belief in the existence of an afterlife obviously suggests a similar belief in the existence of God. Intellectually, however, as an adult, I have no faith in either.

I am made happy, even ecstatic at times, by my wife and daughter, by love in all its forms, by the beauty of nature, by a witty remark, or by art, but I have no unifying theory to relieve a persistent, though not chronic, philosophical pessimism. That anything exists for any eternal purpose seems to me unlikely. I do not walk around all day brooding about this, but when I am facing a crisis, I see that believers have access to a cosmic tranquilliser that I can not use.

I am aware that it would be more pleasant to have faith, but what can I do? Should I force myself – for therapeutic reasons – to believe in something which at best seems charming but unlikely, and at worst seems dangerous and absurd?

To quote Santayana again, 'Scepticism is the chastity of the intellect, and it's shameful to surrender it too soon.' I am too proud to abandon my agnosticism for organised religion or – almost worse – disorganised religion, that laughable stew of whimsical superstitions that constitutes the so-called New Age. I have a craving for a larger meaning, but refuse to satisfy this spiritual hunger with theological junk.

But I've been wondering of late if my intellectual chastity must *ipso facto* deny me the peace that everyone else obtains through surrendering their reason? Must the sceptical virgin starve out in the cold while the whores gorge themselves at the fires of belief? Is it possible for rationality to somehow provide the comforts of faith? All that is missing (all!) is something neither ridiculous nor vicious, which, like an awe-inspiring bridge, starts before birth and ends after death. What is missing, I suppose, is the *sensation* of God.

When I was an aspiring saint I worshipped a God who, though infinitely vast and powerful, was capable of the most intimate compassion. I was part of a family – God, the father, Mary, the virgin mother, and brother Jesus with his cousin-like disciples – and the fantastic rituals celebrating these relatives inspired a feeling of profound inclusion in divinity.

What an art Christianity is! The music, the paintings, the poetry. On Christmas Eve, my mother would turn on the radio as a carol service was broadcast live from King's College Chapel, Cambridge. I was usually too busy running around in a hysteria of materialistic anticipation to savour anything as elevated as this, but on one occasion during my religious phase, I lay down next to her on the sofa as she listened, glass in hand, to 'Silent Night' sung by a solitary boy whose voice had not yet broken. I closed my eyes and saw feathered angels gathered around a God resembling Da Vinci, who smiled down at my mother and I from the dark sky above.

I have never felt so magnificently safe since then, nor so happy, and I probably never will; but I do not intend to give up trying. Sometime soon I'm going to see what happens if I satisfy the demands of my third circle of responsibility: a trip to Africa when I can find the time.

On the morning when the doctor informed my mother and I that I was 'allergic to life', we emerged from his office in shock. She held my scabby little hand in hers but said nothing as we walked away down a long corridor in the hospital where she would later die. After a while, I turned and looked up at her. She moved her head irritably.

'Ridiculous,' she said. 'Allergic to life. Abso-luuutely ridiculous.'

She started walking faster so I was forced to trot at her side. When I next raised my head to study her, she was smiling.

'Allergic to life!' she exclaimed dismissively. 'You're no more allergic to life than I am,' and we pushed through the big doors and walked out into a cold bright day, laughing.

The End

Bibliography

The *Herald-News*, Dayton. Various issues, 1998/9

Barlow, Nora (ed) *The Autobiography of Charles Darwin* (W.W. Norton & Company, 1958)

Bowlby, John *Charles Darwin: A New Biography* (Hutchinson, 1990)

Broyles, Bettye J. (comp.) *History Of Rhea County, Tennessee* (Rhea County Historical and Genealogical Society, 1991)

Cherny, Robert W. *A Righteous Cause, The Life of William Jennings Bryan* (Little, Brown 1985)

Cornelius, R.M. (ed) *Selected Orations of William Jennings Bryan – The Cross of Gold Centennial Edition* (Bryan College, 1996)

Darrow, Clarence *The Story of My Life* (Da Capo Press, 1932)

Desmond, Adrian and Moore, James *Darwin* (Penguin, 1991)

Larson, Edward J. *Summer For The Gods* (Basic Books, 1997)

Levine, Laurence W. *Defender Of The Faith* (Oxford University Press) (The Last Decade – 1915-1925)

Marshall, Sybil *An Experiment In Education* (Cambridge University Press, 1963)

Mencken, H.L. *Heathen Days* (Vol. 3 of autobiography)

Mencken, H.L. (ed) *A Mencken Chrestomathy* (Vintage Books, 1982)

Rhea Historical Society *The World's Most Famous Court Trial*. Transcript of the trial, first published 1925. (Bryan College, 1990)

Rogers, Elizabeth (ed) *The Impossible H.L. Mencken – A Selection of His Best Newspaper Stories* (Anchor Books, 1991)

Scopes, John T. and Presley, James *Center Of The Storm* (Holt, Rinehart, and Winston, 1967)

Stone, Irving *Clarence Darrow For The Defense* (Doubleday, 1941)

Weinberg, Arthur (ed) *Attorney for the Damned – Clarence Darrow in the Courtroom* (University of Chicago Press, 1957)

Zenfell, Martha Ellen (ed) *The Old South* (APA Publications (HK) Ltd, 1996)

Acknowledgements

I would like to thank the inhabitants of Dayton who, though they often disagreed with me, were usually kind and welcoming. In particular, thanks to Gloria, Kurt, Laurie, Matt, Sheriff Sneed, and Rocky. Thank you to Diogo, my stepson, for use of his poem, 'The Bridge' and his loyalty. I would also like to thank Tom Hedley for encouraging me to write this book, and Sarah Such, for encouraging me to cut bits out of it. Thanks are also due to my father, who told me things he didn't have to, corrected things I couldn't know, and endured the sometimes surprising consequences of their exposure. To K Brunt and James Cornford many thanks for, respectively, information on my mother when she was a student and background on the Cornford/Darwin side of the family. Most of all, I would like to thank my wife, Denise, my daughter, Anna Bella, my sister, Sarah, and my brothers, Francis and Ludovic, for supporting me in this effort to tell an often painful story.